PSYCHOLOGY OF
ADOLESCENCE

PSYCHOLOGY OF ADOLESCENCE

by
LUELLA COLE, Ph.D.

FARRAR & RINEHART
Incorporated
PUBLISHERS   NEW YORK

First printing, February, 1936
Second printing, January, 1937
Third printing, July, 1937
Fourth printing, July, 1938
Fifth printing, July, 1939
Sixth printing, January, 1940

COPYRIGHT, 1936, BY FARRAR & RINEHART, INC.
PRINTED IN THE UNITED STATES OF AMERICA
BY QUINN & BODEN COMPANY, INC., RAHWAY, N. J.
ALL RIGHTS RESERVED

To

FLORENCE GERTRUDE JENNEY

*a Teacher and Friend
of My Own Adolescent Years*

PREFACE

IN preparing and writing this book I have kept in mind three major aims. First, to include only objectively proven facts. This limitation automatically ruled out certain topics that are of interest but about which too little is known, and it restricted consideration of other topics to a relatively brief compass. Only studies based upon pragmatically determined results have been included; those dealing with subjective observation have been omitted because the points reported, while possibly true, cannot be regarded as established facts.

Second, to present a relatively comprehensive picture of the adolescent years. To this end, a determined search of the literature for all kinds of relevant information was made. Presumably because measurement along social and ethical lines is of comparatively recent development, many previous books on adolescence have dealt primarily with physical and mental growth and have more or less disregarded other types of development.

Third, to make the book as useful as possible. The facts have therefore been interpreted to show both their general importance and their practical usefulness. Therefore, the book's main value will lie in its frequent applications to specific problems. Many previous studies, although excellent in other respects, have tended to present the teacher with facts—and then leave her to make her own applications. It is hoped that these illustrative materials will enable teachers to transfer the principles of adolescent psychology to their everyday procedures in the classroom.

L. C.

Berkeley, California
February, 1936

TABLE OF CONTENTS

PREFACE   vii

PART I: INTRODUCTION

Chapter I: CHANGES IN THE HIGH SCHOOL POPULATION   3

PART II: NORMAL ADOLESCENCE

Chapter II: PHYSICAL DEVELOPMENTS OF NORMAL ADOLESCENCE   17
    Skeletal and Muscular Growth: Outstanding Facts—Causes of Increases Shown—Specific Growth Rates—Bodily Proportions—The End of Growth
    Physiological Growth: Circulatory System—Respiratory System—Digestive System—Nervous System—Glandular Systems—Relative Growth of the Bodily Organs
    Hygiene for Adolescents
    Illustrative Case Studies

Chapter III: EMOTIONAL DEVELOPMENTS OF NORMAL ADOLESCENCE   53
    Characteristics of an Emotional Experience
    The Life History of Three Major Emotions: Anger—Fear—Love—Objective Measures of Emotional Development
    Emotions and the School: Avoidance of Emotional Disturbances—Provisions for Outlets of the Emotions—Recognition of Emotional Disturbance—Instruction concerning the Emotions
    Illustrative Case Studies

Chapter IV: SOCIAL DEVELOPMENTS OF NORMAL ADOLESCENCE   101
    Spontaneous Social Life during Adolescence: Friendships—The "Crowd"—Leadership

CONTENTS

Organized Social Activities: Types of Extracurricular Activities—Distribution of Extracurricular Activities
Illustrative Case Studies

Chapter V: MORAL AND RELIGIOUS DEVELOPMENTS OF NORMAL ADOLESCENCE   143

Attitudes on Sociological Matters: Attitudes on Social Problems—Racial Prejudice—Student Snobbishness—Superstitions
Attitudes on Moral and Ethical Problems: Development of Honesty—Cribbing—Insight into Criminal Behavior
Attitudes on Religious Matters: Traditional Attitudes—A Psychology of Religion—Emotional Crises
Significance of Adolescent Moral and Religious Development for the Teacher
Illustrative Case Studies

Chapter VI: INTELLECTUAL DEVELOPMENTS OF NORMAL ADOLESCENCE   186

Measurement of Adolescent Intelligence: Difficulties of Test Construction—Influence of Elimination on Norms—Limits of Mental Growth
The High School Population: Distribution of Abilities—Changes in Distribution—Failures and Eliminations
Development of Individual Mental Capacities: Memory—Concentration—Imagination—Organizing Ability—Reasoning, Thinking, Judging, Generalizing—Special Abilities—Summary
Spontaneous Intellectual Interests
Practical Significance for the Teacher
Illustrative Case Studies

PART III: TYPES OF ADOLESCENTS

INTRODUCTION   239

Chapter VII: THE NORMAL ADOLESCENT   241

The Range of Normality: Physical—Emotional—Social—Moral—Intellectual
Illustrative Case Studies

Chapter VIII: THE DELINQUENT ADOLESCENT   258

Characteristics of Delinquent Adolescents: Level of Intelligence—Physical Condition—Educational Record—Social Competency—Emotional Maladjustment
Characteristics of a "Delinquent" Environment: The De-

CONTENTS

linquent Home—The Delinquent Neighborhood—The Delinquent School—Summary
The Prevention of Delinquency: Foretelling Delinquent Behavior—Treatment of Predelinquents
The High School and the Problem of Delinquency
Illustrative Case Studies

Chapter IX: THE EMOTIONAL DEVIATE   284
Neurasthenia: Illustrative Case Studies
Hysteria: Illustrative Case Studies
The Fanatic Adolescent: Illustrative Case Studies
The Adolescent with Feelings of Inferiority: Illustrative Case Studies
The Psychopathic Personality: Illustrative Case Studies
The Prevention of Abnormal Personalities: Permanence of Traits—Recognition of Unusual Behavior

Chapter X: THE INTELLECTUAL DEVIATE   328
The Brilliant Adolescent: Characteristics—Training—Personal Adjustments of Brilliant Pupils—Illustrative Case Studies
The Adolescent with Inferior Mental Capacity: Characteristics—Training—Personal Problems of Dull Adolescents—Illustrative Case Studies

Chapter XI: THE VOCATIONAL MISFIT   357
Examples of Vocational Maladjustment
Vocational Guidance in the High School: Information in Regard to Occupations—Information concerning Personal Traits—The Vocational Counselor
Illustrative Case Studies

PART IV: THE ADOLESCENT'S ENVIRONMENT

Chapter XII: THE ADOLESCENT AND HIS HOME   387
Desirable Characteristics of Homes for Adolescents: Emancipation from Home Control—Parental Adjustment to Society—Pride in the Home—Security in the Home—Prevention of Maladjustment.
Typical Behavior of Unemancipated Adolescents
Illustrative Case Studies

Chapter XIII: THE ADOLESCENT AND HIS SCHOOL   414
The High School Curriculum: Values in High School Training—Required Work—Elective Courses—Vocational Courses—Integration of Required, Elective, and Vocational Work

Adjustments to Individual Differences: Homogeneous Grouping—Special Classes—Individualized Instruction
Teaching Methods
Illustrative Case Studies

Chapter XIV: THE ADOLESCENT AND THE COMMUNITY — 459
Lack of Protection
Educational Influences: Research concerning Motion Pictures
Illustrative Case Studies

PART V: CONCLUSION

Chapter XV: THE END OF ADOLESCENCE — 485
Adult Development: Physical—Emotional—Social—Moral—Intellectual
Prevention of Adult Maladjustment: Dangers of Arrested Development—Contribution of the High School to Adult Happiness

APPENDIX — 491

INDEX — 499

LIST OF TABLES

TABLE		
I.	PER CENT OF ADOLESCENTS WHO WERE WORKING IN 1930	8
II.	PER CENT OF ADOLESCENTS IN 1930 WHO WERE MARRIED	9
III.	RELATIONSHIP BETWEEN HONESTY AND (A) LEVEL OF INTELLIGENCE, (B) TYPE OF HOME, AND (C) DEGREE OF SUGGESTIBILITY	158
IV.	EXPRESSED ATTITUDES OF CRIBBERS AND NON-CRIBBERS	162
V.	NORMS FROM TESTS OF INTELLIGENCE	189
VI.	A TYPICAL FRESHMAN CLASS	196
VII.	MEDIAN INTELLECTUAL LEVEL IN ONE SCHOOL, 1921–30	198
VIII.	HIGH SCHOOL CAREERS OF 6,141 FRESHMEN	201
IX.	COMPARATIVE ELIMINATION OF NONGRADUATES WHO FAIL OR DO NOT FAIL	202
X.	GROWTH IN ABILITY TO FIND MAIN POINTS IN READING MATTER	212
XI.	DEVELOPMENT OF VARIOUS SKILLS AND APPRECIATIONS	218
XII.	COMPOSITION PREFERENCES OF 7,309 BOYS AND 7,232 GIRLS	221
XIII.	THE FIVE MOST POPULAR PLAY ACTIVITIES AT AGES FIVE, TEN, FIFTEEN, TWENTY	222
XIV.	PER CENT OF SUBJECTS PASSING EACH ITEM	229

LIST OF TABLES

TABLE

XV. PER CENTS OF ONE HUNDRED COLLEGE WOMEN REPORTING PROBLEMS — 243

XVI. HISTORY OF ONE THOUSAND JUVENILE OFFENDERS — 269

XVII. SCORES OF PROBLEM AND NONPROBLEM CHILDREN — 274

XVIII. RANGE OF I.Q.'S IN THE FIRST GRADE OF ELEMENTARY SCHOOL AND FIRST YEAR OF HIGH SCHOOL — 329

XIX. COMPARATIVE DEVELOPMENT OF REGULAR AND CONTINUATION SCHOOL PUPILS — 348

XX. MENTAL AGE AND GRADE PLACEMENT — 348

LIST OF CHARTS

CHART

I. PERCENTAGE OF INCREASE IN HIGH SCHOOL ENROLLMENT BETWEEN 1880 AND 1930   5

II. PERCENTAGE OF INCREASE IN COLLEGE ENROLLMENT BETWEEN 1880 AND 1930   7

III. AVERAGE HEIGHT OF BOYS AND GIRLS FROM BIRTH TO MATURITY   19

IV. AVERAGE WEIGHT OF BOYS AND GIRLS FROM BIRTH TO MATURITY   19

V. RELATION OF BOYS' TO GIRLS' AVERAGES IN STRENGTH, FROM MEASUREMENTS IN 1835 AND 1923   23

VI. CHARACTERISTIC PROFILES AT SIX AND SEVENTEEN YEARS OF AGE   25

VII. PROPORTIONS OF THE HUMAN BODY AT VARIOUS STAGES OF DEVELOPMENT, SHOWN SCHEMATICALLY   27

VIII. LUNG CAPACITY OF TWO BOYS AND TWO GIRLS FROM SEVEN TO SEVENTEEN YEARS OF AGE   30

IX. ONSET OF PUBERTY FOR 8,752 BOYS AND 9,201 GIRLS   36

X. GROWTH CURVES FOR VARIOUS BODILY ORGANS   42

XI. GROWTH CURVES FOR EMOTIONAL MATURITY   72

XII. PLAN OF A NEIGHBORHOOD   109

XIII. VOLUNTARY GROUPINGS OF 153 BOYS IN SECONDARY SCHOOL   113

LIST OF CHARTS

CHART

XIV. SOCIAL CONTACTS OF A POPULAR AND AN UNPOPULAR BOY — 116

XV. INFLUENCE OF A NATURAL LEADER IN MOLDING PUBLIC OPINION — 117

XVI. DEGREE OF VOLUNTARY PARTICIPATION IN EXTRACURRICULAR ACTIVITIES — 130

XVII. DEVELOPMENT OF RACIAL PREJUDICE — 152

XVIII. RELATION BETWEEN RELIGIOUS TRAINING AND CONCEPT OF GOD — 170

XIX. STANDARD GROWTH CURVE OF INTELLIGENCE — 194

XX. PER CENT OF FRESHMEN, 1921–30, WITH MENTAL AGES OF THIRTEEN AND ONE-HALF OR BELOW — 199

XXI. EDUCATIONAL PREPARATION OF SIXTY-SIX DULL PUPILS IN HIGH SCHOOL — 200

XXII. GROWTH IN MEMORY — 206

XXIII. GROWTH IN CONCENTRATION — 207

XXIV. GROWTH IN ABILITY TO UNDERSTAND THE SAYINGS OF JESUS — 216

XXV. GROWTH IN ABILITY TO INTERPRET CARTOONS — 217

XXVI. GROWTH IN MECHANICAL APTITUDE — 219

XXVII. DISTRIBUTION OF ABILITIES IN ONE HIGH SCHOOL CLASS — 230

XXVIII. PROFILE GRAPH OF ONE PUPIL'S STANDING — 437

XXIX. EFFECTS OF HOMOGENEOUS GROUPING FOR DIFFERENT TYPES OF PUPILS — 440

XXX. EFFECT OF MOTION PICTURES ON RACIAL ATTITUDES — 469

PART I
INTRODUCTION

CHAPTER I

CHANGES IN THE HIGH SCHOOL POPULATION

ADOLESCENCE as a universal phenomenon among the young of all social classes is a product of modern civilization. It is something new under the sun. In primitive societies there is no such stage of development. There is only a short period of puberty, or time of sexual maturity, and then the boy or girl is admitted to adult society and responsibilities. A primitive girl who was last year both socially and physically a child is this year a married woman. The boy who last year was playing childish games in the village streets may have passed through a nerve-racking initiation ceremony and may now be out hunting in deadly earnest for food for himself and his wife. There is no time in primitive economy for ten years of adolescence. Nor has there ever been time, except for children of the leisure class, until the last two or three generations. The great-grandparents of present-day adolescents were usually married and maintaining themselves economically by the time they were eighteen. They finished their schooling by the age of twelve or thirteen, went to work shortly after, married any time after sixteen. There was little more time for adolescence than in more primitive periods. It is only recently that education has been extended and marriage delayed until a true period of adolescence has become an almost universal phenomenon in American life.

To be sure, "gilded youth" has always enjoyed a short period similar in character to modern adolescence, but only one child in a thousand belonged to this class. And if this one child were a girl, she had little chance of postponing marriage for long after she was physiologically mature. Although one finds an adolescent boy here and there on the pages of history, the adolescent girl is a brand-new product of modern times. She did not exist in sufficient numbers to be of importance educationally before a century ago at the earliest. The period since then has been so short, and experimentation in the matter so meager, that no one yet knows much about educating the average adolescent girl.

The reasons for the emergence of a universal adolescence among modern young people are not far to seek. The basic explanation is economic. There is so much wealth in the world and it is so easy, with machines, to create more wealth that the labor of boys and girls is no longer needed. The same "machine age" that dispenses with the crude labor of children in their teens has so altered human existence that in all lines of work above that of the day laborer special training is needed. Machine civilization is highly specialized. The years of adolescence, which have been wrested from the period of adult labor, must be used to prepare boys and girls for the modern world.

These are economic causes; there are others that are largely idealistic. Even before the development of the economic changes above described, there had emerged a political and legal ideal—backed up by religious and moral attitudes—of equality for all. To this end, public education was devised. The great difficulty in applying the ideal to practical life was the almost universal need for children and adolescents to work, in order that the world might be fed, clothed, and housed. With the release of youthful labor that came with machinery, educators were for the first time able to keep all children in school long enough and regularly enough to permit them to profit, in so far as their innate abilities would permit, by a reasonably good education. In working toward an educated and enlightened public—the basis on which any democratic government must rest—educators have seized upon the adolescent years and have made every effort to extend schooling of some kind as long as possible. With economic pressures working from without and the ideals of democracy working from within, there has emerged the first universal, compulsory period of adolescence the world has ever known.

The development of the situation may be shown definitely

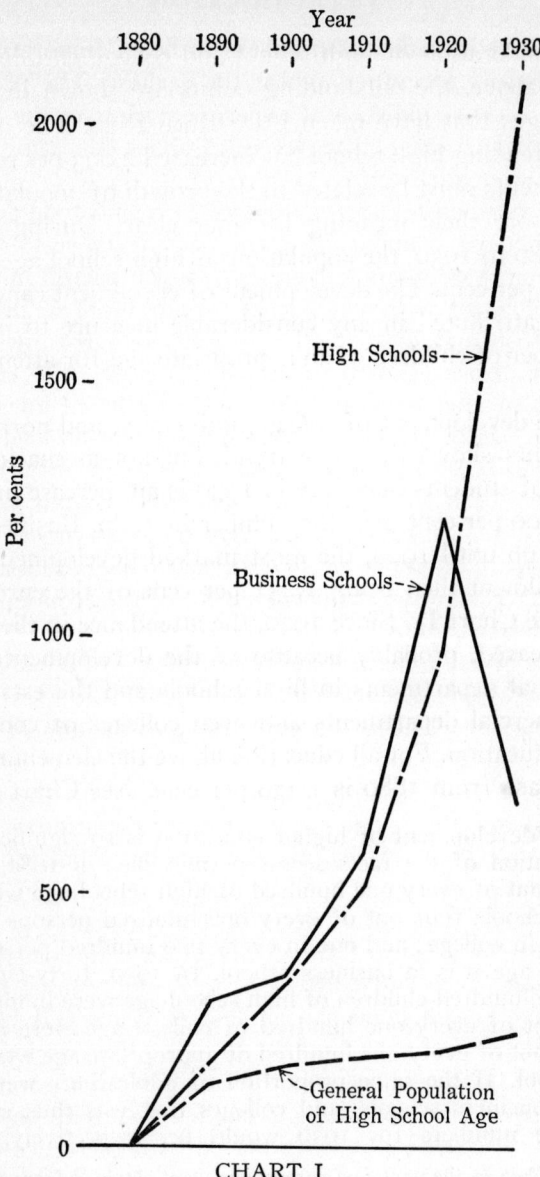

CHART I

PERCENTAGE OF INCREASE IN HIGH SCHOOL ENROLLMENT BETWEEN 1880 AND 1930

by a consideration of high school and college enrollments.* In Chart I above, the outstanding points are shown in regard to the changes that have taken place since 1880. The number of pupils attending high school has increased 2,093 per cent. These developments must be related to the growth of population, however, before their meaning becomes clear. During the years from 1880 to 1930, the population of high school age increased only 236 per cent. The development of enrollment cannot, therefore, be attributed in any considerable measure to increase in the number of children of an appropriate age for attending high school.

The development of college, university, and normal school enrollments shows the same trend, but not as markedly. The number of students in college in 1930 is an increase of approximately 700 per cent over the number in 1880. Business schools showed, up until 1920, the most marked development of all, † the enrollment then being 1,231 per cent of the enrollment in 1880 (see Chart I). Since 1920, the attendance in these schools has decreased, probably because of the development of better commercial departments in high schools and the establishment of commercial departments and even colleges of commerce in higher education. For all education above the elementary school, the increase from 1880 is 1,438 per cent (see Chart II).

The development of higher education is so significant that a recapitulation of the facts seems permissible. In 1880, only five children out of every one hundred of high school age were in secondary school; four out of every one hundred persons of college age were in college; and one in every two hundred persons of appropriate age was in business school. In 1930, forty-eight out of every one hundred children of high school age were in high school; twelve out of every one hundred of college age were in college; and two out of every one hundred of appropriate age were in business school. If the same proportion of adolescents were in high schools, business schools, and colleges that was thus enrolled in 1880, the numbers for 1930 would be, respectively, 466,061;

* All data in the next few paragraphs were obtained from the Biennial Report of the Department of Education, Vol. II, 1930.
† In proportional growth, not in actual size.

54,160; and 361,069—with a total of 881,290. Instead, the actual enrollments are, respectively, 4,514,008; 179,756; and 1,132,419—with a total of 5,826,183. In other words, the increase in popula-

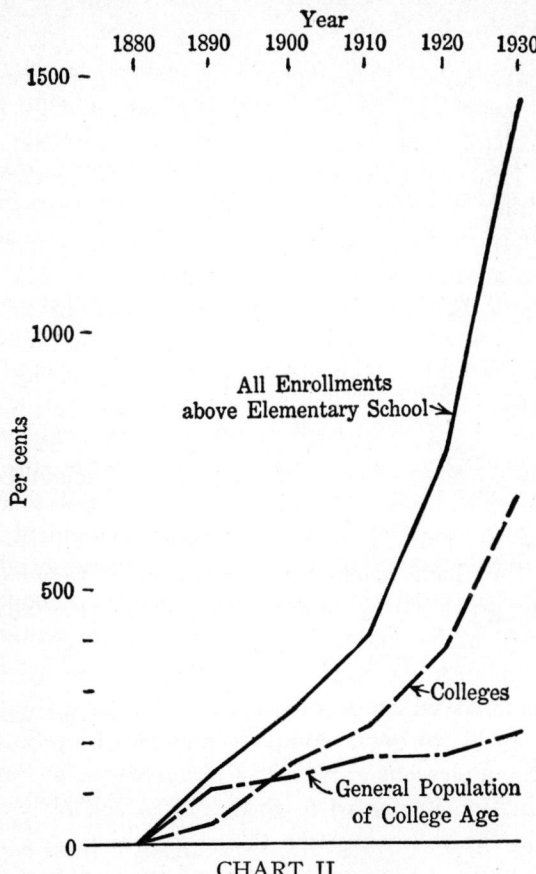

CHART II

PERCENTAGE OF INCREASE IN COLLEGE ENROLLMENT BETWEEN 1880 AND 1930

tion cannot possibly account for the enormous increase in adolescent attendance in institutions of learning.

The main impetus in the increased enrollments above described has come since 1910. Because of its recency, no one can say with any certainty what form of education is best for this army of adolescents, what curricula should be offered, or what standards of achievement are possible. Far too little is known about the potentialities of these thousands of additional students for anyone to become dogmatic on these points. Two conclusions may, however, be deduced: (1) That the educational program appropriate for the 215,616 pupils in high school in 1880 is probably not desirable for the 4,514,008 students in 1930. (2) That an adolescent life in which only five out of one hundred children are in school while ninety-four are working or married must be very different for the adolescents themselves from a life in which approximately every other child is in high school. Education above elementary school did not condition the lives of many children in each generation before 1910; now the high school bids fair to be one of the dominating influences in the development of ideals and modes of thought.

The adolescents who are in some sort of school constitute by no means the entire population whose ages are between thirteen and twenty-one. Many boys and girls drop out of school as soon as they have reached the age at which they can legally do so. Some go to work, some marry, some—especially girls—simply live at home, and some go into such special schools as those dealing with art, music, dramatics, dancing, or athletics —enrollments of which seem not to be included in the above figures. In order to get a complete picture of the nature and needs of the adolescent group, it is necessary to include everyone. Information in regard to those not in school is therefore presented in the following two tables in which data for 1930

TABLE I

PER CENT OF ADOLESCENTS * WHO WERE WORKING IN 1930

	\multicolumn{6}{c}{Ages}					
	10-13	14	15	16	17	18-19
Boys	3.3	9.2	16.3	32.7	49.9	70.7
Girls	1.5	4.0	7.6	17.0	27.5	40.5

* Figures for Tables I and II were taken from the 1930 census, Vol. 2 and Vol. 5.

only are used. For boys, the per cent who are out of school and working * increases from 3.3 per cent for the years between ten and thirteen to 70.7 per cent at eighteen. For girls, the similar figures are from 1.5 per cent to 40.5 per cent. The proportion

TABLE II
PER CENT OF ADOLESCENTS * IN 1930 WHO WERE MARRIED

	10-14	15	16	17	Ages 18	19	20	21
Boys			.1	.2	.6	2.2	5.8	11.6	19.7
Girls	.2	1.3	4.3	9.9	19.2	28.6	37.8	45.2

* Figures for Tables I and II were taken from the 1930 census, Vol. 2 and Vol. 5.

of boys who marry during these years is small, but 19.2 per cent of the girls were married by the end of their eighteenth year.

The situation as regards both work and marriage has significance for the schooling of adolescents. It is clear that vocational training or guidance of vocational choice—especially for boys—must be given by the age of fifteen at the latest. Any teaching that deals with matters of making a home, any education in sex, any teaching about the bringing up of children must also be given early. Probably the last year of required schooling could be devoted to such topics, with much better results for society than are likely to be otbained by further doses of a more conventional curriculum. The public school is the only institution to which facts of universal value can safely be relegated. No one can force a private school to give this subject or that. If vocational guidance and sex education are to be given anywhere, it must be in public school and before the children are old enough to absent themselves if they want to. This matter will be returned to in a later chapter.

The data presented above were obtained in 1930. It is probable that the situation there outlined has changed somewhat. Since 1930 the country has been in the throes of a serious depression, and there is every indication that when the world returns again to a

* Some of these are presumably attending such special schools as those listed above.

settled condition there will be fewer jobs than before. There are, at the moment of writing, some 4,000,000 men out of work—without counting the enormous reserve of married women who would gladly work if anyone would hire them. No sane person can believe that there will be for a long, long time 4,000,000 more jobs. Machinery has never ceased from the day of its invention to throw men and women out of work; far from slowing down, the process has been accelerated of late years. The world can now not merely get along without the labor of adolescents; it actively does not want their labor. In some states the compulsory school age has been raised two years, purposely to keep adolescents from working and thus competing with adults. The result of the depression has been, then, further to lengthen the period of adolescence, thus postponing marriage and the time of economic independence.

Other items from the general census indicate a change in the proportion of adolescents and adults in the total population. With the decrease in the size of families and the restriction of immigration, the preponderance of adults in the population is getting greater with every decade. This change means that the modern world is an adult world to which children and adolescents must learn to conform. In the earliest census the average age of the population was only sixteen; the country was young; adolescence was the average age of the population. Now the average age has risen, putting increasingly greater burdens of adjustment upon adolescents. In the next census the effect of the depression upon the birth rate will undoubtedly cause another rise in average age level.

Because a long adolescence is so new for any boys except the sons of wealthy families and for practically all girls, far too little is known about the period. Up until some twenty-five years ago there were no investigations or experiments. There were anecdotes of great men during their youthful days. There were diaries written by boys or girls; there was an occasional chapter in a biography. Such records, while valuable, are of little use in obtaining a picture of the average adolescent, who writes no diaries and about whom no anecdotes are preserved. Even yet, such studies as are made of the later years of adolescence—eighteen to twenty, for instance—concern themselves mainly with college students, a highly selected group. Above the compulsory school age it is very hard to get a balanced picture. To date, experiments and investigations, while suggestive and valuable as far as they go, come far short of furnishing an adequate knowledge of what boys and girls are really like from the ages of thirteen or fourteen until twenty or twenty-one. Some facts are known, of course, but not enough; many investigators have sought to analyze the adolescent, but no writer of textbooks has ever succeeded in synthesizing the pieces and emerging with a reliable picture of the average boy or girl.

In the absence of adequate data in regard to the adolescent period, it is obviously impossible to draw profound conclusions in regard to the curriculum. It is fairly obvious, however, that a curriculum inherited from previous centuries, intended for the special training of a scholar, and dependent on an I.Q. of at least 120, will never do for the average adolescent, who is neither highly intelligent nor scholarly. But, beyond agreement that the classical curriculum is utterly inappropriate, there seems no consensus of opinion. Some high schools have gone in for vocational training; some have provided only the time-honored subjects but in homeopathic doses; some have essentially abandoned the curriculum and have concentrated on character building through sports and extracurricular activities. The curriculum of the elementary school has been examined with scrupulous care, but only here and there have there been constructive efforts to fit the curriculum of the high school to the needs of its pupils. The essential explanation of this situation is the lack of adequate information about adolescents. No one can fit an environment to the needs of an organism when the organism's characteristics are still unknown.

Curiously enough, much is known about the social objectives to be reached by the end of the adolescent period, if adult life is to proceed normally. The chief sources of such information are the clinic, the insane hospital, and the juvenile court. The clinical psychologist in any of these three places has constantly before him the human wreckage that comes from a failure to develop out of adolescent attitudes into adult points of view. The school, as perhaps the most important agent during this period, must so conduct its affairs that its boys and girls will be encouraged to outgrow their immature ideas and attitudes by the end of adolescence. This matter of objectives will be returned to in detail in a later chapter.

Adolescence, in its social and educational significance, is then a relatively new phenomenon, although physical adolescence—or puberty—has been recognized for untold centuries as a period of importance. Until recently, the educated adolescents were persons who came from the upper and wealthier classes of society; they were educated to be either professional men or gentlemen of wealth; they were, in overwhelming proportions, boys; they were intellectually capable of a classical education; they were the few survivors of an elementary curriculum that was not far from twice as hard as that taught today. Because of these special circumstances, information derived from the group attending high school and college before about 1910 is not relevant to the problems of modern secondary and higher education. Not much is known about the army of young people that has recently marched into institutions of learning in ever-increasing numbers. Even less is known concerning the desirable content of the curriculum. However, there is a small body of determined facts, and these it is worth while to present in an organized fashion.

The remaining chapters of this book will deal with such data as are available and with such inferences as seem obviously implied by the data. There will be, first, a section in which the average adolescent is described—physically, emotionally, socially, intellectually, and morally. Descriptions inevitably dissect the organism under consideration. And it is a fault with many textbooks that analyses are not followed by syntheses. In order to put the adolescent back together again, after the detailed examination in the first part of the book, there will be a section devoted to various types of adolescent—the "normal," the delinquent, the mentally inferior, the mentally superior, the neurotic, and the vocationally maladjusted. Ample case studies of typical individuals will be furnished. A third section will discuss the adolescent's adjustment to his world—his family, his school, his church, his friends, his job, and his community. Finally, there will be a brief chapter presenting the criteria by which one can know when adolescence is at an end and adulthood has begun. At all times, the discussion will stick to known facts and to specific cases. It is hoped that by means of this organization the reader may acquire a sympathetic understanding of the many-sided problems of boys and girls and may develop an interest in bringing about a better adaptation of secondary and higher education to adolescent needs.

PART II
NORMAL ADOLESCENCE

CHAPTER II

PHYSICAL DEVELOPMENTS OF NORMAL ADOLESCENCE

ADOLESCENCE is a period of rapid growth and change. The skeleton grows, the glands develop, the internal organs grow, the brain becomes more complex; in fact, there is hardly a structure in the body that is not in some way altered between the beginning of adolescence and the end. Nor does growth proceed at an even rate in all parts of the body. Every structure has its own growth rate and goes ahead with its particular mode of development, without much attention to the growth rate of any other structure. The resulting lack of balance among bones, muscles, glands, heart, lungs, brain, and viscera is the basis for much of the misery usually accompanying growth throughout this period.

So far as the psychologist and teacher are concerned, the facts about growth are mainly important, not in themselves but in their influence on the adolescent boy or girl. Growth and health are primarily the business of the physician. However, the body, the mind, the emotions, and the total personality are so interdependent that any consideration of one away from the others is dangerous. The teacher's main job is to bring about learning and adjustment to life. But the learner is a living, growing, developing organism. If the teacher does not have at least a rudimentary knowledge of the organisms she is trying to teach, she is likely to regard as traits of personality or intelligence those characteristics that are due primarily to mere growth. For instance, if a teacher does not know that much adolescent restlessness and inattention are due to the muscle cramps, the ravenous appetite, and the glandular developments of the period, she is likely to waste her energy in useless efforts at discipline. The awkward, inattentive daydreamer of sixteen cannot be cured of his characteristics by either extra assignments or sarcasm, but in the course of time, he will "grow out" of these annoying manifestations.

It is therefore necessary that teachers should know the main facts in regard to adolescent growth. They need to understand the physical basis for the clumsiness, malco-ordination, emotional outbursts, restlessness, and irritability that characterize the boys and girls in their classes. With an understanding of the physical changes and developments going forward in the adolescent, the teacher is less likely to penalize her pupils for situations that are natural concomitants of adolescent development.

Growth furnishes the physical basis for emotional, social, and economic maturity. If a child did not increase in stature and weight, if his muscles did not become strong, if his sex organs did not grow, if his brain did not mature, if his internal organs did not increase in size and efficiency to meet the requirements of an enlarged body, the child would never become a man. He would never be able to achieve adult ideas and attitudes, he could never support himself economically, he could never take his place in adult society. Because of these all-pervasive effects of physical growth it seems desirable to discuss the matter in sufficient detail to present clearly the picture of adolescent development. For this purpose, growth in every system of the body must be considered: skeletal, muscular, glandular, digestive, circulatory, respiratory.

SKELETAL AND MUSCULAR GROWTH

Outstanding facts.—The most observable results of growth in the bones and muscles are the changes in height and weight. The charts below present the course of development in both these respects, for both girls and boys. The facts of adolescent growth should be related to developments during childhood and especially during preadolescence—roughly the two or three years just preceding the period of puberty. The charts are therefore

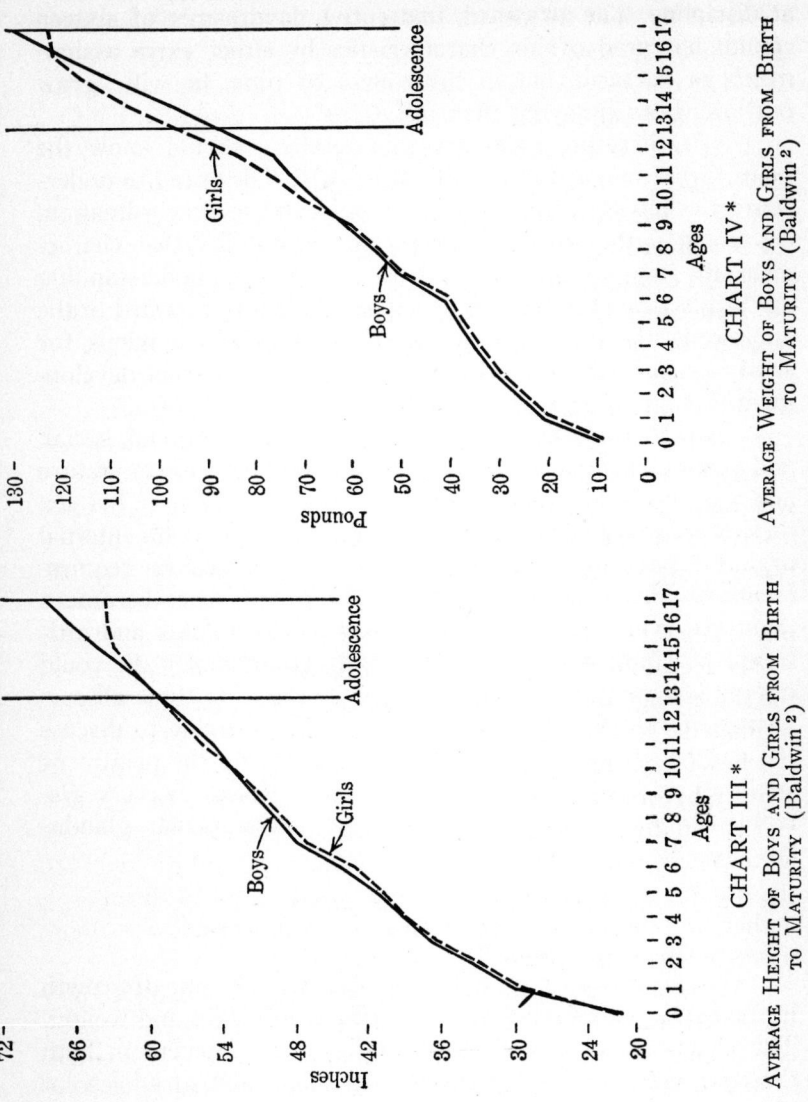

CHART III*
AVERAGE HEIGHT OF BOYS AND GIRLS FROM BIRTH TO MATURITY (Baldwin[2])

CHART IV*
AVERAGE WEIGHT OF BOYS AND GIRLS FROM BIRTH TO MATURITY (Baldwin[2])

* This material is used by permission of the University of Iowa Press.

arranged to show growth from birth to maturity. The adolescent period is marked off.

The curves bring out, especially, two points that are of importance in conditioning the attitudes of adolescents. In the first place, it is clear that growth is rapid during the early years of adolescence. The average boy's increase in weight between his twelfth and seventeenth birthdays is equal to the increases in the ten preceding years. The average height does not show as marked a change, although in individual cases changes in height are sometimes extreme. Height does, however, increase somewhat more rapidly than in earlier years. Some children gain as much as six inches and twenty-five pounds in a single year. Such a child starts the year at, say, 112 pounds and ends it at 137; he has progressed in twelve months out of the flyweights, through the bantam- and featherweights, and into the lightweights. The adolescent increase in size—even if it took place at an even rate all over the body—would be bewildering enough, especially as it follows a period of relatively slow development. The preadolescent child is a fairly stabilized person physically. He knows what he can and cannot do with his body. He is accustomed to his size and proportions and has been at the same stage of development long enough to become well coordinated. Now, suddenly, he knocks over things when he reaches for them because his lengthened legs get him towards objects before he expects to arrive. Who has not been nearly run down by an adolescent who was merely trying to walk across the room to shake hands? It requires some little time for the boy or girl to get used to being, what seems to them, altogether too large—not even Alice-in-Wonderland was more upset by changes in size.

A second point brought out by the charts is the differences in growth rates of the two sexes. In the early years of adolescence, girls are an inch or so taller than boys; then, in a couple of years, boys suddenly shoot up and achieve a greater average height. These differences are not large and, at the average, are not important. The situation has, in fact, received more comment than it merits, so far as the person of average height is concerned. Its position of prominence seems due chiefly to the utter amazement of male investigators that girls should *ever* be taller or heavier than boys. What is important, however, is the situation at the extremes. The tallest of the girls have in magnified form the troubles of co-ordination and the distress over being much too big. These girls are usually taller than the tallest boys of their age. The shortest boys are in equal difficulties; they are usually shorter than the shortest girl.

The matter is brought to a head, for instance, at any dance. The writer has known many girls who either would not go to dances at all or else were miserable if they did go, merely because they were always taller than any boy they danced with. And the short boys are equally depressed, not knowing that in a few years they will be considerably taller. The short girl and the tall boy do not have these troubles; the former is usually regarded as "cute" and the latter as "manly." Adolescents often make quite violent social reactions to what they regard as an undesirable size. For instance, a large girl may go in for athletics and masculine clothes, because she cannot be a "cute, cuddly, little" girl. Or a small-sized boy may become a "grind" largely because he cannot compete on equal terms physically with other boys—and may, if he attempts games, even be beaten by girls. Anyone who doubts the importance of variations in either height or weight from the average should listen to adolescent nicknames: "Shrimp," "Fat-Pants," "Skeeter," "Bug," "Spider," "Cow," "Fatty," "Big Boy," "Whale," "Swede," "Big Bertha," and many others.

Causes of increases shown.—The increase in height during adolescence is due almost exclusively to growth in the bones of the leg.[7] * The arms similarly grow in length. In later adolescence the trunk grows,[4] giving the body its final adult proportions. The increase in weight is due to growth in both the bones and the muscles. The latter form only 27 per cent of the total weight in childhood but increase to 44 per cent by the age of sixteen.[23]

The increase in muscle size and strength is observable in both boys and girls, though more especially in boys—probably because they use their muscles more and are greatly concerned

* Superior numbers refer to the bibliography at the end of each chapter.

over achieving adequate muscular development. Girls are kept from the more violent forms of physical exercise and strain at all times and most of them are prohibited during their menstrual periods from anything more strenuous than merely getting about to their classes or daily work. As a result, the initial muscular growth in girls is often not "consolidated" by exercise, and the muscles, though longer and heavier than in childhood, do not develop further. That the difference in musculature between the sexes is not mainly innate is shown by the development of many girl athletes, by the lack of large muscles in the average professional man, by the excellent musculature of many women in primitive communities, and even by actual measurements.

It happened that in 1835 an enterprising gentleman made a study of strength in the back muscles of boys and girls.[20] In more modern times similar measurements have been made.[2] A comparison of these measures is revealing, as shown in the graph below. The curves above have been derived from two such different sets of data that no direct comparison between them is possible; both have therefore been reduced to per cents. The scores made by the girls have, in both cases, been reckoned as the base, and the scores made by the boys of the same age expressed as the percentage in terms of the girls' scores. Thus for the measurement in 1835 the seven-year-old boys made scores that were 135 per cent of those made by the seven-year-old girls. This ratio gradually increased until twelve; thereafter the rise was rapid. By seventeen, the boys made scores that averaged 180 per cent of the girls' scores. The second curve shows similar facts for measurements made in 1923. Here the boys start with scores that are 109 per cent of the girls' and gradually increase until the early years of adolescence. At this time the boys' superiority becomes more noticeable, but only in the last year shown on the chart does the difference become great; even then, it is 10 per cent less than it was at the earlier period. The girl of today thus shows a marked gain in comparative muscular development over her feminine ancestors, probably because she is more active. The third curve of the chart, constructed after the same principle, shows the relative strength in the arms for measurements in 1923. The modern girl is, in comparison to boys, stronger in her arms than in her back. Girls' games—tennis, hockey, basketball—develop the arms and legs but have less effect on the back muscles. Nor does the average girl's

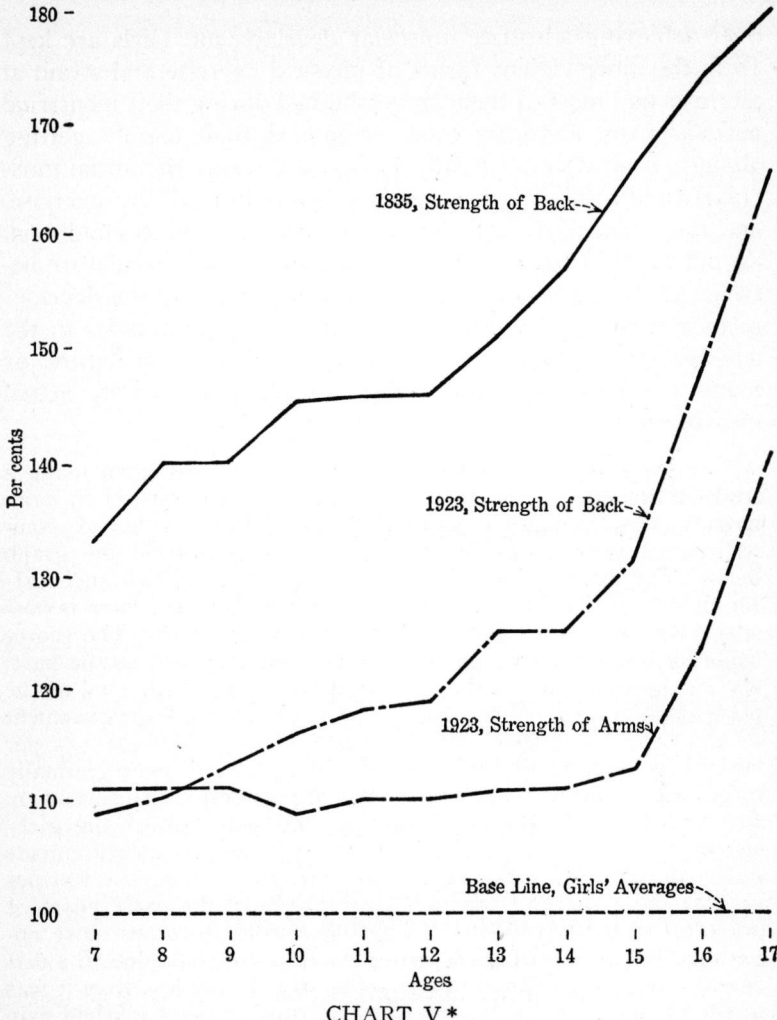

CHART V*

RELATION OF BOYS' TO GIRLS' AVERAGES IN STRENGTH, FROM MEASUREMENTS IN 1835 (Quetelet [20]) AND 1923 (Baldwin [2])

* This material is used by permission of G. Fischer (Jena) and the University of Iowa Press.

work require much lifting or other pulling of the back; but the arms are constantly used in typical "women's work."

On the basis of such data it seems reasonable to suppose that, while there may be some innate difference in muscular development between the sexes, any such native variation is overshadowed by additional differences resulting from environmental and social pressure. It may, of course, be desirable for one reason or another that women should not become solid lumps of muscle, but as far as innate differences are concerned, they could become as sturdy as boys if they did the same things.

Specific growth rates.—It has already been mentioned that the parts of the body grow at different rates and reach their maximal development at different times. The head, for instance, does most of its growing before birth and the rest soon after. By the time a child is six years old his head is 93 per cent as large as it will ever be, and by the age of twelve it is 98 per cent of its final size.[23] On the other hand, the "long" bones in the arms and legs are extremely short at birth, remain short during childhood, and then lengthen quickly during adolescence. The trunk is very long at birth, grows rapidly at first but little during the remaining years of childhood and early adolescence, and then finally lengthens after seventeen years of age. These variations in growth rate give the baby, the child, the adolescent, and the adult their characteristic proportions.[4]

The bones of the face also seem to "take turns" in growing. Usually the teeth become adult size before any other part of the face has lost its childish contours—and the youngster's parents begin to fear their offspring is disfigured for life. At the very beginning of adolescence the nose often begins to grow and soon becomes quite out of proportion. From being all teeth, the poor child seems to have become all nose. Especially does the bridge of the nose widen, causing the eyes to become farther apart. After leaving the child to suffer with his changed appearance for a few months, or perhaps longer, the jawbone comes to the rescue and builds a chin and jaw line that nicely balance the nose and destroy forever the last childish curve. At some

PHYSICAL DEVELOPMENTS

time during this development the face becomes longer and assumes the usual adult oval shape. In actual figures, the face adds nearly twice as much to its length between the ages of thirteen and eighteen as it added in the previous seven years—from five to twelve.[6]

The differences in proportion are well shown in the profiles given below. The first shows a child at the age of four—little stub

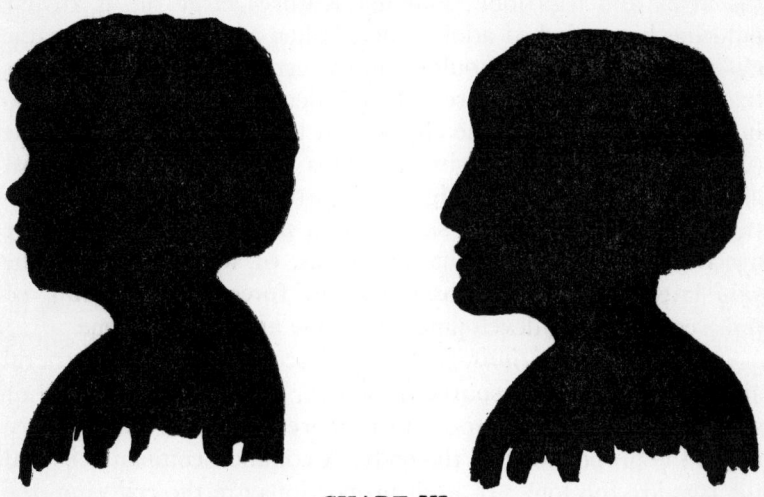

CHART VI
CHARACTERISTIC PROFILES AT SIX AND SEVENTEEN YEARS OF AGE

nose, deep depression above it, bulging forehead, flat lips, delicate chin, and short distance from bridge of the nose to the chin. The second shows the same child at seventeen. Everything—except head size—is different. The forehead is flat, the depression above the nose has been replaced by a real bridge, the stubby nose has assumed an almost Roman shape, the lips are full, the chin is sturdy, and the length of the face is appreciably greater.

While these changes are in progress, adolescent boys and girls are likely to become greatly concerned about their appearance. Their faces are undeniably out of proportion, but there is no reason why they should assume this condition to be permanent. The thought of existing for a lifetime behind such an unbalanced face as many adolescents have is enough to make anyone despondent. They should be told that the situation is only temporary and that the face will recover its symmetry in the course of time.

Changes in the bones and muscles of the body are among the clearest indications of oncoming adolescence. When a boy's shoulders grow broad, his chest deep, his hands and feet big, his arms and legs long, and his features large, he is clearly entering his period of adolescence. When a girl shows the same changes, though the shoulder and chest developments are less marked, and in addition reveals a widening of the hips, she too is adolescent. In fact, the changes in thickness, size, and angle of the pelvic bone—causing the hips to enlarge—is the most clearly indicative, single sign of approaching feminine adolescence. In addition to the skeletal and muscular changes, there are the differential sex characteristics, of which more will be said later; but trained observers can forecast the coming of pubescence by the development of bone and muscle alone.

Bodily proportions.—The adolescent's face and general size are not the only source of worry, however; even if he or she is not too tall or too short, there may be great concern about the proportions of the body. A common complaint is that the legs are too long; if adult proportions are the criterion, the youth who makes this complaint is quite right. The following chart summarizes the situation. To be sure, the baby is much more out of proportion than any adolescent, but he does not care if he is. If adolescents could be taught to regard their thinness, their gangling arms and legs, their fragile wrists and ankles, that contrast so violently with big hands and feet, and their awkwardnesses as incidents of growth that will soon be past, they would be spared a great deal of misery.

Nor are these many changes of bone and muscle effected without discomfort. The growth is so uneven that the bones are sometimes too long for the muscles adhering to them, and the youth experiences the familiar "growing pains." For the same reason, muscles cramp far too easily when he swims or runs. If his muscles lengthen faster than the bones do, he becomes extraordinarily clumsy; his muscles are big enough to operate easily a bigger skeleton than the one to which they are attached. Any of these situations is physically uncomfortable in itself, and it usually leads to social situations that render the adolescent acutely miserable. More than one sixteen-year-old boy has swum at top speed past a

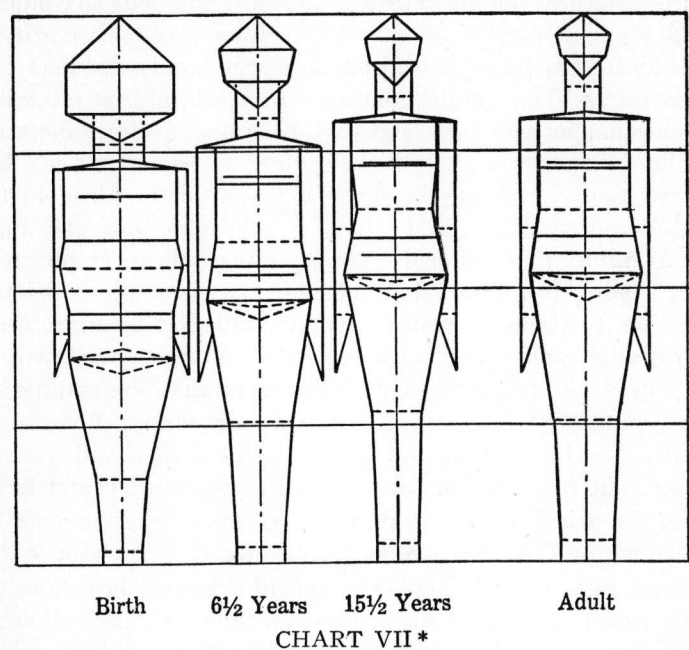

Birth   6½ Years   15½ Years   Adult

CHART VII *

PROPORTIONS OF THE HUMAN BODY AT VARIOUS STAGES OF DEVELOPMENT, SHOWN SCHEMATICALLY (Bean [4])

girl he wanted to impress, only to develop a leg cramp and be forced to let the girl—who had emerged a year or two earlier from his present period of growth—tow him ashore. Such a cramp is punishment enough, but it fades into insignificance when compared to the remarks his peers will doubtless address to him.

The end of growth.—That skeletal growth has practically stopped by the end of adolescence is shown by careful measurements made on college students at the beginning and end of their college career.[16] During the four-year college period the

* This material is presented by permission of the *Anatomical Record*.

bones increased in size only 1 per cent; the increase in size of the muscles and vital organs averaged 4.5 per cent, while the gain in total weight was 7 per cent. In strength, however, these college men increased approximately 25 per cent in the four years, showing that growth in efficiency was still continuing. These figures indicate a real slowing down and stabilization. The skeleton and internal organs are very nearly through with development. The weight continues to increase, partly because of muscular development and partly because of fatty deposits.

PHYSIOLOGICAL GROWTH

While all these changes in bone and muscle are in progress, other developments are taking place in the body. In circulatory, digestive, respiratory, neural, and glandular systems there are typical adolescent changes. Many of these are of vital importance in conditioning the life of the individual boy and girl.

Circulatory system.—The most conspicuous fact in regard to development in this system is the disparity in growth between the heart and its arteries.[23] In childhood, the ratio between the width of the heart and the width of its arteries is 5 : 4. That is, the heart pumps blood into openings very nearly as large as its own width. During adolescence, however, the heart grows faster than the arteries and the ratio becomes 5 : 1. The heart must now pump the blood into an opening only a fifth as wide as itself. This is hard work and puts a strain on the heart for a year or two until growth in the arteries has established an adult ratio. The extra labor of the heart is reflected in an increased blood pressure which rises from an average of 109 at eleven to 124 at fifteen and then sinks back to 112 at eighteen.[8]

During adolescence there is further strain on the heart because of the increase in the total amount of blood which must be driven into the aorta each second.[23] At birth the amount is only 20 grams; at the age of three it has gone up to 63 grams, from which the amount increases gradually until at the age of fourteen 141 grams, or over 200 per cent of the amount in early childhood, must be driven into the aorta each second. The heart itself, however, is only 30 per cent larger and the opening into which it must be driven is barely 10 per cent larger.[23] The heart must, therefore, work considerably harder than it did during the years of childhood.

During this period of adolescent growth practically all boys and girls experience faintness, dizziness, palpitations, headaches, and restlessness. These symptoms are entirely normal, unless they occur in too severe a form. When boys or girls experience them, they should be allowed to rest for a while and should then be examined by a doctor. If their hearts are fundamentally sound, they should merely be warned to keep within the limits of their own vitality. They should not be babied into thinking they are invalids.

It goes without saying that the adolescent heart suffers chronically from the overstrain of athletics. The high school boy is especially likely to develop an enlarged heart. Most girls of high school age have passed through the most dangerous stage. Competitive athletics is, for their hearts, far less dangerous than in the case of their masculine classmates. It is a curious commentary on the general ignorance in regard to physiological growth that the tall, rangy, rapidly growing boy, who can usually stand less strain than any girl in the school, should be the very one on whom social pressure is most exerted to become a star in football, basketball, or track events. Not all the academic inefficiency so often shown by high school athletes is due to either stupidity or lack of application. These children are usually strained beyond their capacity. The high school that will insist upon competitive games can expect a state of lethargy from the participants. The dividends paid by high school athletics are all too often exhaustion and abnormal hearts.

The same results may be obtained just as completely from too much participation in social activities. Dancing, late hours, smoking, drinking, indigestible food at midnight, and emotional excitement burn up energy faster than a reduced amount of rest can replace it. Too heavy a load of any kind is equally serious. The student who is earning his living and attending school at the same time is usually overworked—and quite unnecessarily, since the school can always regulate any student's academic schedule. And there are always a few pupils who study late into the night and worry continually about their work; eventually, they become exhausted.

Adolescents usually feel so vigorous and well that they think their supply of energy is inexhaustible. If teachers want to promote learning and to develop healthy personalities in their pupils, they can make no better start than to keep the athletics, social events, and scholastic load of the high school proportionate to the physical capacities of the pupils.

Respiratory system.—During adolescence the lungs grow, keeping pace with the increased width and depth of the chest. This development is best shown by the lung capacity.[2] Below are presented four individual curves of growth in lung capacity from childhood through adolescence. The consolidated curve

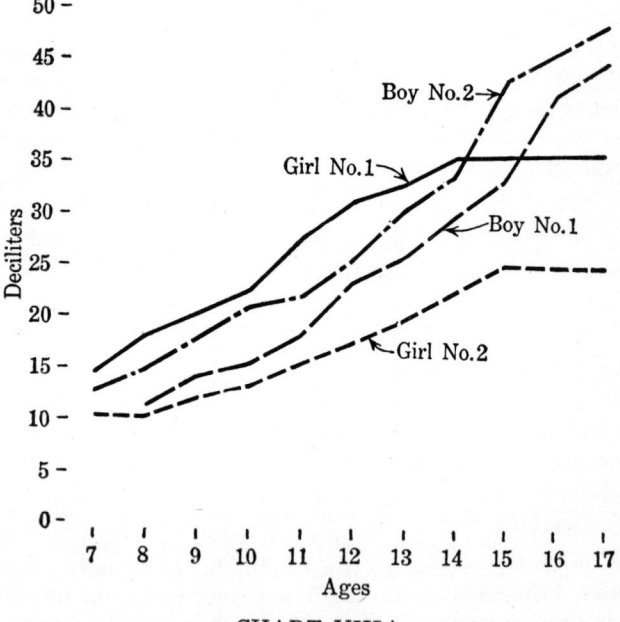

CHART VIII*

LUNG CAPACITY OF TWO BOYS AND TWO GIRLS FROM SEVEN TO SEVENTEEN YEARS OF AGE (Baldwin [2])

* This material is presented by permission of the University of Iowa Press.

PHYSICAL DEVELOPMENTS 31

for all boys is very similar in shape to that for the higher of the two boys' curves shown, while the average for the girls is approximately that of the other boy, with slightly less increase in the last two years. Throughout childhood the average boy is slightly superior to the average girl. During adolescence the rise is many times greater for boys than for the girls, whose curve reaches a permanent level at about sixteen. Some of this difference is doubtless due to the failure of most girls to participate in strenuous games after puberty. The individual curves show many characteristics of the averages but, in addition, indicate the extent of individual variation: thus, during childhood, one of the girls is superior to either boy, while the other girl is at all ages distinctly inferior. With the coming of adolescence, both girls stop developing, while both boys show a marked increase, one of them almost doubling his lung capacity.

In general, adolescent lungs are quite capable of handling any burden that is likely to be put upon them. Although they have not yet reached adult volume, they will develop in proportion to the demands of the organism. Except for actual disease (mainly tuberculosis), they are not likely to become abnormal, as is the case with the heart when strain is put upon it.

Digestive system.—During adolescence, the organs of digestion undergo a marked amount of growth. These changes are usually reflected in the digestive disturbances and changed appetites shown by adolescent boys and girls. The stomach becomes longer and increases in capacity.[23] Because of the rapid growth rate in the size of the body, the adolescent needs considerably more nourishment than formerly, and because of the enlarged capacity of the stomach, he craves more food. The net result is usually a tremendous appetite for three or four years. In some adolescents this condition is so marked that it seems practically impossible for them ever to get enough to eat, although they consume more food in twenty-four hours than most adults need in twice that time. These youngsters are described—in New England, at least—as having a "hollow leg," where presumably all the food they eat is cached. Other changes in the digestive system give rise to vague discomforts whose source the adolescent cannot locate, but to which he often reacts by developing peculiar ideas about his food. Thus, some girls decide they can digest nothing but tomato soup or chicken salad, while boys may decide that only steak and onions can be tolerated.

The digestive difficulties characteristic of the period are doubtless due partly to mere overloading of the system and partly to the difference in growth rate between stomach, liver, intestines, and other digestive organs. Furthermore, the boy or girl usually begins to eat meals away from home during this period. Adolescents can be trusted to add to their natural difficulties by making a lunch of hot dogs, chile con carne, and hamburgers, washed down with ice-cream sodas or milk shakes and followed by banana splits. The ubiquitous bakery cart contributes its share of digestive discomfort. The writer has seen more than one high school pupil make an entire lunch out of two doughnuts, a sweet roll, and as many cream puffs as he had money for. The digestive troubles of most boys and girls could be explained on the basis of diet alone. It requires the entire period of adolescence for most people to learn to eat a reasonably balanced meal on their own initiative—if they ever do learn.

As secondary results of the gradual changes from a childish to an adult digestive system, there appear the bilious attacks, the outbreaks of appendicitis, and the numerous skin infections of adolescence. These secondary effects are usually of great concern, especially a muddy complexion and the numerous skin eruptions. Pimples are the bane of the adolescent's life. Whenever a girl wants to be particularly attractive for some social event she is almost certain to have an outbreak of pimples. Any teacher who expects undivided attention from a girl with a cold sore on her lip or a boy with a small boil on his nose is doomed to disappointment. Adolescents will fuss interminably about these facial blemishes, making themselves and everyone else perfectly miserable; they are the most gullible users of any and all ointments or other treatments; in fact, they will do anything except remedy their faulty diet. The tactful handling of an adolescent with a momentarily disfiguring pimple on the eve of the junior prom taxes

PHYSICAL DEVELOPMENTS 33

the resources of the most profound psychologist. In the course of time, however, adolescents do outgrow their digestive troubles, and their skin becomes clear and normal.

Nervous system.—The number of different fibers in the nervous system is practically complete at birth, but not all the fibers are functioning at that time.[23] So far as gross size is concerned, the nervous system develops very little during adolescence. There is almost no increase in the length, width, capacity, or weight of the brain during these years, because the brain has achieved its adult size during childhood.[23] What growth there is, then, is confined to further development of the fibers, in both length and thickness,[23] and to further contacts among them. Evidence seems to show that the complexity of the brain —that is, the total number of contacts between fibers—is enormously increased during the early years of adolescence. The fibers also become thicker and longer, so that many fibers not in contact during childhood now touch each other. Any more detailed statement in regard to neural growth would become too technical for the scope of this volume.

The facts in regard to neural growth are, in any case, not as important to the teacher as the effects. The increased ability to think and, in particular, to generalize are probably the most obvious results of this increased complexity in the brain. To be sure, part of the ability to think and reason comes from the individual experiences each person has as he grows older. It is, moreover, not true that children are completely without ability to reason; their capacities are doubtless underestimated because they reach so many erroneous results through their lack of knowledge. The increase in ability to do abstract thinking is therefore due in part to increased experience. However, the further development of the brain is important because it furnishes the physiological basis for the more complex forms of thinking in which the adolescent indulges. Indeed, an outstanding characteristic of adolescent boys and girls is their spontaneous joy in mental activity—even if the topics thought about are not always those presented in the curriculum. This point will be further discussed in a later chapter.

Glandular systems.—Besides the glands of digestion the human body contains lymphatic and endocrine glands. The former include the thymus, a gland of rather doubtful functions, although the lymph tissues as a whole apparently influence some activities. The endocrine glands are another matter and merit discussion because of their effects upon the emotional life. The main glands of this type for consideration here are the thyroid, the adrenals, the pituitary, and the sex glands.* Each of these has its own rhythm of growth. In general, the first three have a fairly regular growth from birth to maturity. In contrast, the sex glands remain almost constant in size during childhood and then develop quickly in early adolescence. This sudden growth is caused by the development of the reproductive tissues, the endocrine portion remaining relatively constant throughout life.

Thyroid abnormalities of all kinds make their appearance in adolescence, especially in girls. The combination of excessive thyroid secretion and painful menstrual periods is all too common. Sluggishness, sleepiness, overweight, and leathery skins may all be symptoms of inadequate thyroid secretion, a condition that is prevalent throughout the Middle West. There is usually real improvement after correct treatment. Irritability, excitability, hysteria, fainting, fast pulse, and protuberant eyes may all be danger signals, brought about by overactivity of the thyroid gland. Such conditions require immediate attention if a dangerously serious situation is to be avoided. In their dealings with the unstable adolescent it is recommended that teachers use less discipline, less sarcasm, and more judgment.

The adrenal glands influence the sympathetic centers of the nervous system, and their rate of secretion is, in turn, influenced by emotional states. During the unstable period of adolescence these endocrine organs are a major cause of the disturbances that result from fear, anger, or embarrassment. The sympathetic nerves control to a large extent the pulse rate, the blood vessels of the skin which cause blushing or paling, and the sweat glands. There is evidence that the thymus also affects the amount of perspiration discharged per day.[23] The increase from childhood is marked, and the amount of perspira-

---

* The pineal gland, the parathyroids, and the pancreas have been omitted as having little significance in the present discussion.

tion is often excessive. The results are distressing to the average adolescent. The boy is upset because his shirt sticks to him at the slightest provocation and he is acutely embarrassed when the perspiration of his hands stains the dress of the girl he has danced with. The girl carries on a constant fight against perspiration, with the aid of salves and all manner of deodorants. Neither sex is very successful because the sweat glands are so active and so sensitive. Not only warmth and exercise produce undesired amounts of perspiration; any emotional disturbance is equally fatal. When a teacher sees a luckless student begin to perspire, she would do well to release him temporarily from whatever academic effort he is involved in. If his attention is being divided between the telltale moisture on his forehead and the intricacies of an imperfect subjunctive, he might as well sit down. The veritable bath of perspiration experienced by many adolescents is not to be laughed at. However, with the involution of the thymus (page 43) and the steadying of the emotions, the excessive activity of the sweat glands eventually subsides.

The pituitary regulates growth of the body, the development of sex, and other functions. The size of the skeleton, the accumulation of fat, and the maturity of the sex glands are among its most important effects. The maturing of the sex glands is the most important single development of the adolescent years. Indeed, puberty consists essentially in this maturation, although the evidence indicates that the ability to produce offspring follows puberty by one to two years. This physical capacity is, however, not merely as significant at the moment as the added depths and nuances of emotional life that develop along with puberty. These emotional developments will be discussed at length in a later chapter.

The first of the physiological changes for consideration is the age at which puberty takes place. For girls the age can be determined with fair accuracy as being the time of the first menstrual period. With boys the determination is more difficult and must usually be estimated from the appearance of secondary sex characteristics. The maturity age varies in different regions. The data below are based on results from American children.

The main facts are presented in the next chart. This chart shows two points that merit special consideration by teachers.

The first is the wide variation in the age of maturity. For girls this variation is from nine to eighteen years of age; for boys

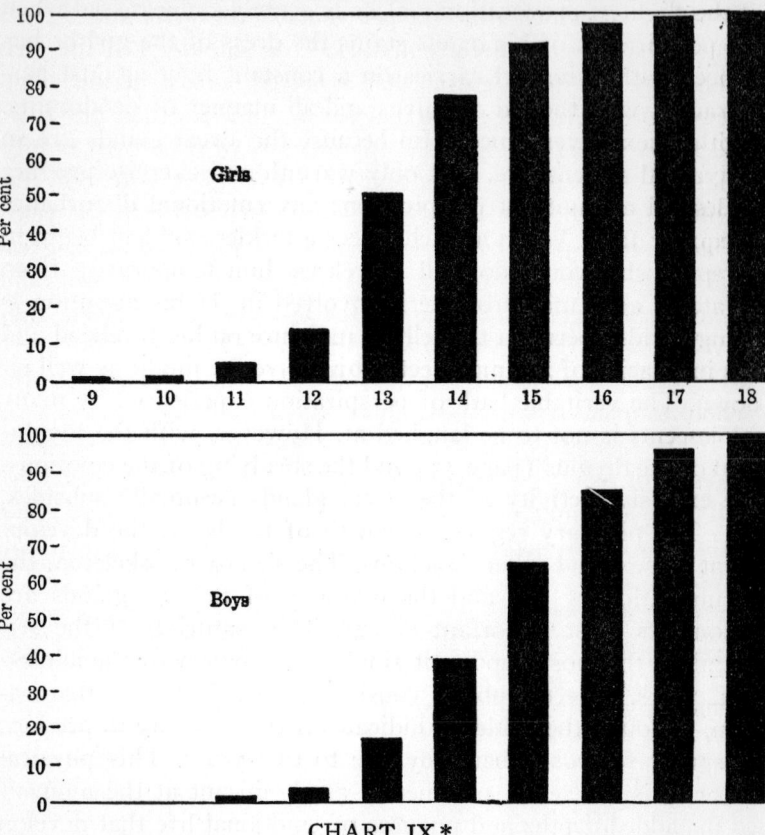

CHART IX*

ONSET OF PUBERTY FOR 8,752 BOYS (Crampton[9] and Baldwin[2]) AND 9,201 GIRLS (Boas,[6] Baldwin,[2,3] and Atkinson[1])

it is considerably less, being only from twelve to eighteen. Because of this wide variation any instruction to be given girls should be presented to them, at the latest, by ten years of age and similar instruction to boys before twelve. The great dif-

*This material is presented by permission of the *American Physical Education Review,* the University of Iowa Press, the National Society for the Study of Education, and the U. S. Bureau of Education.

ficulty with most instruction in such matters is that it comes far too late. If given at all it is usually between fifteen and seventeen, at which time 92 per cent of the girls and 84 per cent of the boys are already mature. Over one-third of the girls studied by one investigator [4] had received no instruction whatever before their first menstrual period and less than one-third had received instruction from any member of their own family. The need for such information as a part of the school curriculum is all too obvious. By waiting until well into the years of adolescence for instruction, the situation is made a great deal harder than it would have been had the teaching been done at an earlier age. By the time boys and girls are sixteen, they have become too self-conscious and have received too much information, erroneous or otherwise, from their friends for the school to make real progress in giving sex instruction.

The second point of interest is the difference between the sexes. Not many girls have matured before the youngest boy; still there are enough mature girls at any age above ten to make girls as a group better informed and more sex-conscious than boys.

Thus, in a hypothetical schoolroom containing one hundred thirteen-year-old children, of whom one-half were boys and one-half girls, there would be the following situation: twenty-five girls would be physically mature and twenty-five immature, while fifteen boys would be mature and thirty-five immature. Because of the paramount importance of sexual maturity to adolescents, this class would show differences in emotional attitude and interest that would make it difficult to teach. The actual school situation is even more complex than the example just given because in any one class the range of chronological ages is about five years, with the children in each age group showing varying degrees of maturity. Thus in a class of English literature in the early years of high school, the majority of the girls will be physiologically mature and interested in love stories generally. Few of the boys will be mature and fewer still of them will have any romantic interests; as a group they will still be interested primarily in stories of adventure. This fact of the variability between the sexes is not of mere academic interest to the teacher. Because of it, for the early years of adolescence at least, she needs to furnish a much greater choice in reading materials than at any other time. In fact, in any class until the last year of high school, this matter of the varying degrees of maturity is sure to create problems of interest and discipline.

The achievement of sexual maturity is of momentous importance to the boy or girl. It is also the source of infinite embarrassment. The boy's organs not only grow rapidly in size until he fears they will show through his clothing, but they seem to react without his volition. There are any number of boys who are afraid to go to a dance for fear their local stimulation may offend some girl. The feminine mind rarely seems able to understand that such reactions are purely reflex and are not intentional insults. At night the boy is often distressed by dreams that seem to him highly indecent. In all probability he masturbates more or less; even if he does not, his nocturnal emissions embarrass and frighten him. If he does not have frequent discharges he becomes acutely uncomfortable from tension. It often seems to him as if he were two people at once —one grossly physical and one reasonably decent.

The average boy has a more violent emotional reaction to his maturity than the average girl because he is more acutely and constantly aware of it. His organs are external. They are subject to the incidental pressure of such external objects as wearing apparel or bedclothes. He is forced to touch himself several times a day when he urinates. To himself, his sexual development seems all too obvious and uncontrollable. If he consults his friends about his difficulties, he receives chiefly smutty stories and misinformation; if he asks his father, he is often met with embarrassment and evasiveness; if he consults an older man, he is lucky if he does not get sent to prostitutes; if, in desperation, he visits some quack, he gets frightened out of his wits. He cannot consult most of his teachers because they are unmarried women. Even his mother can help him very little; she was never a boy and now she has reached a conservative, feminine middle age that is more likely to be horrified than helpful.

Nor are the secondary sex changes at all comforting— quite the reverse. The growth of pubic hair is sure to arouse remarks in the common dressing room of the gymnasium. The hair on arms and legs often makes boys think themselves hideous. The appearance of hair on the face and the resulting introduction into shaving, while generating a feeling of manly development, is uncomfortable. Especially to be pitied is the boy who has needed for some time to start shaving but is not allowed to by his parents. And, as a final drain on the lad's patience, his voice can no longer be trusted; it alternately squeals and bellows. The adolescent boy often will not recite in class, will not sing, will not talk to girls, because he is so afraid of the embarrassing noises he will probably make. Many boys leave school altogether, essentially because women teachers have no comprehension of their difficulties and consequently force them into one uncomfortable situation after another. All in all, it is remarkable that so many boys get through their adolescence without permanent emotional scars.

The girl has less reason for distress, but even so she sometimes manages to work herself up into a state of excitement. She may experience a considerable emotional shock from her first menstruation, whether or not she has been warned of its arrival. There is something understandably terrifying in any hemorrhage that cannot be stopped; bleeding is so associated with unpleasantness that many girls can never dissociate this emotional tone from their menstrual periods. Even after the periods are established girls may experience what boys never do—actual pain from sexual functioning. The relatively few girls who have abnormal organs, who are anemic, or who have a condition of hyperthyroidism have undoubted pain. For the others, the great majority, the pain is slight if it exists at all. For the most part, normal, healthy girls are frightened into thinking they ought to have a pain. In addition, there is the temptation for a girl to enlarge as much as possible upon any faint discomfort from her periods, because her mother will always let her miss a day or two of school and will allow her the luxuries of a comfortable invalidism at home. When most girls have anything they really want to do, they usually get up and do it, whether they are menstruating or not. Hence one may be allowed a degree of skepticism as to the severity of the pain.

The adolescent girl is almost sure to be embarrassed about her menstrual periods. Many situations give rise to such distress. The chances are she will be forced to stand on the side lines during competitive games or to stay on shore when the gang is going swimming. Some of the boys are sure to ask her why—and then everyone is miserable. Her peace of mind is not helped any by such widespread misinformation as the supposition that any boy can tell when she is menstruating by the color of her eyes. She often will not stand up to recite in class because she is afraid there is a stain on her dress. Throughout her monthly period a girl's mind is likely to be divided between her ostensible occupation and this concern about possible stains. This last worry is probably unavoidable, but many sources of distress can be eliminated. This business of standing conspicuously on the side lines of any game or other diversion involving a little exercise is mostly foolishness. By now there have been any number of girls who never paid the slightest attention to their menstrual periods, who swam and played vigorous games just as usual, who never had a cramp in their lives, and who grew up to be healthy mothers of normal children. It seems as if the myth about the delicate and precarious condition of a menstruating girl should be about exploded. If girls were told to take part in any activities they felt were within their vitality—just as at any other time—many sources of embarrassment would be avoided.

The chief secondary sex changes are the development of the breasts, the widening of the hips, the appearance of pubic hair and hair in the armpits, the growth of a light down on the forearms and upper lip, and a moderate lowering of the voice. Girls are usually somewhat concerned about their breasts, especially if they are heavy. In any case, many a girl is deterred from games in which she would love to participate because her breasts move so obviously when she runs or jumps. Some girls are so sensitive they will not even walk across a room if they think anyone is watching them. With all the women teachers there are in any high school there would seem no good reason why girls should not be told how to support their breasts so they will not be conspicuous or uncomfortable. The widening

PHYSICAL DEVELOPMENTS   41

of the hips is likely to precipitate an attack of rigid dieting, on the assumption that fat, not bone, is the cause. Most adolescents are much too hungry to continue the dieting very long, but an occasional strong-minded damsel needs a sane explanation of the change which has suddenly precipitated her from a size fourteen to a size eighteen dress. Most modern girls are annoyed but not unduly alarmed by the appearance of hair on the arms or face; the ubiquitous beauty parlor will tend to the matter. But there are a few girls who are made miserable by facial hair and do not know what to do about it. Of all the secondary changes, however, only the breasts give rise to real concern. Like the boys' sex organs, they are external, they move, and they show through the clothing.

Both primary and secondary sex changes are so profound and so important in affecting schoolwork that no teacher can safely forget about them. And there are no changes in the adolescent period whose effects the school can so well control. To be sure, most schools make little direct effort to do so; suggestions for a more desirable program will be presented in the next section.

Relative growth of the bodily organs.—As a summary of the growth rates shown by the various organs of the body, the chart presented below has been constructed.[23, 4] In this chart the growth rate from birth to maturity is shown for several typical organs. The purpose of this chart is not so much to present facts as to show graphically the variability in growth that results in a body somewhat out of balance during the adolescence years.

The first point on each curve indicates the per cent of the adult weight that each organ is at birth. Thus the brain at birth weighs about 29 per cent of its final weight. By the first year it has increased to over 60 per cent; by the fourth, to 90 per cent; by the sixth year, to 94 per cent; and by the twelfth year to over 99 per cent of its total weight. The heart is at birth only 7 per cent of its final weight. It grows slowly to the age of eight, when it has reached 32 per cent, a little more rapidly until twelve, when it has nearly reached 50 per cent, then very quickly for the next four or five years. It should be noted, however, that even at

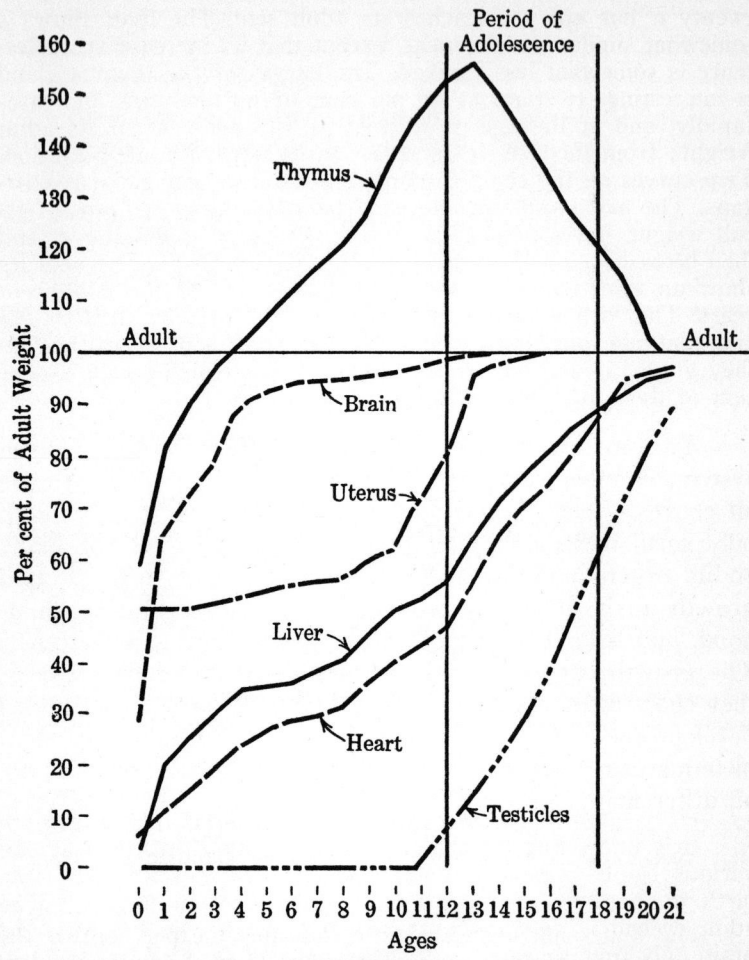

CHART X*

GROWTH CURVES FOR VARIOUS BODILY ORGANS (Vierordt [23] and Bean [4])

*This material is presented by permission of G. Fischer (Jena) and the *Anatomical Record*.

PHYSICAL DEVELOPMENTS

twenty it has not yet reached its adult size. The liver shows a somewhat similar development, except that its increase at adolescence is somewhat less marked. The curve for the thymus gland is interesting. It starts at 58 per cent of its final size, increases rapidly, and at the age of thirteen is 158 per cent of its adult weight; from then on, it decreases to its normal adult condition. Two curves on the chart demonstrate the development of sex organs. The first is for the uterus. At birth it is 50 per cent of its full weight, develops slightly during the years of childhood, and then between ten and fourteen reaches its adult size. The testicles show an even more marked development during the adolescent years. They are at birth less than 1 per cent of their final weight and continue unchanged until eleven years of age. From then on they grow rapidly, but even at twenty have reached only 85 per cent of their final weight.

To some extent, the curves for the organs within a given system resemble each other. The curves for neural growth are all convex—that is, the rapid growth takes place early, with only small increments later on. The growth curves for many bodily organs and for both height and weight show a rapid growth in the first year or two, a slow growth during childhood, and second period of rapid growth during adolescence. The growth curves for the sex organs are concave—that is, they show little or no growth in childhood and then a sudden development in the course of a few years to practically complete maturity. The curves for glandular growth, however, are all different.

It is interesting, in summary, to note the differences among various bodily organs in the extent of their development from birth to maturity as measured by differences in weight.[23] The adult eyeball is only twice as heavy as the newborn baby's, the brain only four times as heavy, and most of the glands from two to ten times as heavy. The heart and digestive organs increase from twelve to twenty times their initial weight. The skeleton increases its weight twenty-sevenfold and the muscles thirty-sevenfold, while the masculine sex glands increase sixty-one times their original weight. These facts are of no immediate practical value to the teacher, perhaps, but they may serve to illustrate the complexity of growth and to impress upon the mind the inevitable disbalancement that must sometimes prevail among the organs of the body.

HYGIENE FOR ADOLESCENTS

It should be clear from what has preceded that the hygiene of the average adolescent is far from perfect. Education for healthy living is badly needed. Because of his increase in size, and especially in the size and strength of his muscles, he is likely to feel he has an unlimited vitality; it is true that during these years vitality is higher than at any other time, but there is still a limit. As a result of these circumstances, the adolescent is likely to become overtired. He still needs nine and one-half to nine hours' sleep,[27] which he seldom gets. He needs to have as much strain as possible, both emotional and physical, removed from his heart and circulatory system. Instead, he usually exercises to the full extent of his capacity and precipitates emotional strain as well. Because of the change that is going on in his digestive system he needs a balanced diet which, without training, he will rarely select for himself. The average number of calories he needs per day is higher between fifteen and eighteen than either before or after.[17] If left to himself he will usually eat too many condiments and too much sweet or starchy food, but will still fail to obtain the necessary number of calories. The restlessness in his digestive organs may lead him into all sorts of peculiar appetites and food preferences. Although these cannot be entirely avoided, the period during which they are active can be considerably shortened by education. The adolescent's increasing number of interests, his emotional experiences, and his reckless burning up of physical vitality all require good hygienic habits of food and sleep.

As already intimated, boys and girls need a hygiene of sex. They need, first, instruction as to the nature and function of the organs of both sexes. Any attempt to conceal such information is utterly senseless, because the facts will be found out sooner or later, anyway; adolescents cannot be prevented from making investigations of their own. Moreover, during their childhood they have already discovered many of the essential facts. The truth about sexual relations should also be given, with a sane emphasis upon the desirability of postponement of such expe-

PHYSICAL DEVELOPMENTS

riences till the adult years and the dangers of casual contacts. A frank, clear, honest presentation will do more to prevent adolescent tragedies than any amount of secrecy. In addition to this basic information, all current superstitions and fears in regard to sex functions should be taken up. It is sheer cruelty to let girls agonize over betraying their menstrual periods by the color of their eyes or to let boys become terrified by normal phenomena. Such discussions do not cause adolescents to think more about sex; their thoughts are to some extent preoccupied with such matters, with or without instruction, but the hours of fruitless discussion can be cut down if the facts are so well known that there is nothing to discuss.

The second positive contribution of the school to the problem is the provision for adequate opportunity for amusements, games, social contacts, hobbies, and so on. Most modern high schools do very well as far as the number of such diversions is concerned. They are not quite so successful, however, in getting all the pupils in the school busy with something, nor are they always able to prevent pupils from undue fatigue. Competitive athletics furnish more than enough diversion but they often do so at the cost of physical exhaustion. The editor-in-chief of the senior yearbook usually has little time for deviltry, but he pays for his preoccupation with fatigue. What is needed is more lines of diversion that are interesting, slightly competitive, social, nonfatiguing, and so simple that anyone can achieve reasonable success. In athletics, for instance, there is needed less emphasis on organized and highly exhausting games and much more equipment for such simple and diverting pastimes as ping-pong, deck tennis, badminton, volleyball and indoor baseball. These are only mildly fatiguing, but they are interesting without being exhausting.

The school should take a most active part in guiding adolescent hygiene. In most schools the routine "hygiene" course has come into such ill repute that the pupils will not take it seriously. What is needed is a course with a new name, taught by people who have the complete respect of the adolescents and are not, themselves, afraid of facts. Such a course should cover matters of diet, sleep, fatigue, over- and underweight, heart strain, skin infections, perspiration, smoking, drinking, and sex manifestations.[19] With a more sensible program for sublimation than most schools offer, such a course should appreciably raise the generally low standard of adolescent hygiene. As a result, the level of academic work would be definitely increased, emotional complexes considerably lessened in frequency, and more normal personalities developed.

ILLUSTRATIVE CASE STUDIES

Experience with individuals is never quite what one might expect from the reading of a general description in a textbook. For this reason, a few case studies will be presented from time to time, so that the teacher may see how such conditions as have just been discussed in general actually come to her attention in the schoolroom. Because it seems desirable to present several studies and because too much such material becomes monotonous, the cases described will be given with a minimum of detail. All adolescents thus described were either in high school or the freshman year of college; all of them were personally known to the writer over a considerable period of time. Details that might be interesting but which do not bear immediately upon the matter under discussion have been omitted in the interests of clarity and brevity. The really interesting thing about all these cases is that the symptoms were social and emotional while the fundamental causes were physical. Except in the case of actual disease, and sometimes then, the bodily condition is usually quite out of sight, except to the trained eye. The pupil's emotional and social maladjustments have become pyramided upon an underlying physical cause. Because of the predominant place of growth and change in adolescent life, every teacher should suspect any deviation from normal as having a possible physical foundation until examination has proved such a cause to be lacking.

PHYSICAL DEVELOPMENTS 47

James was a colored boy who had grown more and more retiring in class, often refusing to recite, staying by himself a good deal, and slipping in and out of the classroom ahead of other pupils or else behind them. In class he had developed a mannerism of keeping his handkerchief over his face much of the time. Feeling that a talk with him was needed, his English teacher arranged a private interview, during which he finally told her he was so ashamed of his muddy and pimply skin that he simply could not have anyone looking at him—hence the attempt at disguise behind the handkerchief. He complained also of hard intestinal cramps and said he sometimes could not recite because the pain was so intense he could hardly stand. Finding that the boy was afraid of doctors, the teacher thought she would make a preliminary investigation of her own, beginning with diet. So she had him list what he had eaten for the previous two days. The list revealed nothing but fried ham, fried potatoes, fried corn mush, fried corn pone, fried white bread, fried onions, condiments of various sorts, and coffee with four spoonfuls of sugar and lots of rich cream. Further questioning brought out the fact that this diet had been going on for years. A trip to the weighing scales proved him to be nearly twenty pounds underweight. With this information in hand the teacher conferred with the school doctor and obtained a list of foods, together with instructions for their preparation. The boy agreed to see the school nurse, who talked with him further about his diet. Neither the boy nor his mother had the slightest objection to carrying out the suggested menu. In two weeks' time the boy's complexion began to clear; in a month he was scarcely recognizable as the same lad. He now stood up straight, looked people in the eye, talked freely in class, went about with people of his own race, made the school basketball team, and became a perfectly normal member of society.

Aleen was a rather large, slow-motioned, stolid girl whose main academic offense was going to sleep in class. When not actually asleep she seemed to be in a daze. Her teachers at first supposed her to be merely stupid and paid little attention to her. However, during an interview with her algebra teacher she conveyed an impression of having much more ability than anyone had supposed. Actually, her work was well above passing, even though she slept through part of almost every class hour. When interviewed, she broke down and wept because the teachers were so sarcastic about her naps and the other pupils plagued her so much; she insisted she made every effort to stay awake, but simply could not do so. Her teacher sent her to the school physician, who had little trouble in diagnosing a hypothyroid condition. Her vital processes proceeded so slowly that she was actually in a state bordering on coma much of the time. In particular, her digestion was so slow and the resulting constipation so severe that she was constantly poisoned by food residues which should have been eliminated days earlier. It argued well for her native ability that, with this handicap, she was passing her work at all. A treatment with thyroid was begun. In a month's time she had stopped going to sleep in the daytime, her mouth no longer hung open, her heart rate had increased from a subnormal 52 to a normal 72, her bowels moved regularly, she had lost some weight, and her whole manner was alert and normal. Now that she could really pay attention in class and could study without dropping off to sleep, her schoolwork improved noticeably. Even more improvement was shown in her social relations. By the end of the year she had achieved a fair popularity—at least, she was no longer the butt of all the jokes.

Frank was a really critical and extreme case of adolescent fear and bewilderment. Between the ages of thirteen and fifteen he had changed from a pleasant-mannered boy who did good, though not brilliant, schoolwork to a disagreeable adolescent with a secretive manner, a fund of smutty stories, and a habit of becoming completely intoxicated about once a month. He was regarded in school as a menace, was not allowed in the homes of most other pupils, and was forced to associate with boys and girls of far less native ability than himself. Once he had been caught stealing money and on two other occasions he had been suspected of theft. On one occasion a teacher had found him sitting in the boys' dressing room after school hours crying bitterly, but when she tried to talk to him he had simply cursed her and left. It was evident enough he was unhappy and it was even clearer he would soon "flunk out." Things came to a head one evening when he stole an auto, drove it out into the country, connected a pipe from the exhaust into the car, closed the windows, and started the engine. A state policeman happened by, started to tag him for parking on the roadway, and then went into immediate action to save the boy's life. His parents became so thoroughly scared that an investigation was demanded. It finally appeared that Frank was in a panic because he had been masturbating and had been told (1) he would die of tuberculosis; (2) he would go insane; (3) he would never be able to marry; (4) he would become infected; (5) he might die in convulsions at any moment. His constant pandering of smutty talk was merely an effort on his part to pick up information. His thefts were for the purpose of obtaining money with which to pay a quack doctor to whom he had gone. His secrecy and avoidance of his old associates were to keep others from knowing how low he had fallen. His occasional wild debauch was a typical adolescent effort to forget his troubles and find momentary peace. A few talks with the school doctor were the first step. He was told that while his sexual habits were unwise they were relatively harmless and would never have any of the results he feared. He was next started on a regime of healthy exercise, proper diet, and regular schedule for his time. With this plan of life he was busy all day and tired enough by night to go to sleep almost instantly. He was helped to re-establish himself with his earlier associates; his schedule of classes was completely changed so that he started all over with new teachers and new classmates. As a final step, his parents were re-educated also so that they could prevent Frank from slipping back into his earlier attitudes. As a result of all this, the boy passed the remaining three years of high school work and was never again delinquent.

Fred entered college with high hopes of athletic fame. He had come from a high school where he had starred in football, basketball, and track; he particularly excelled in the one-hundred-yard dash. Both his junior and senior years he had played through the state basketball tournament, in which his school had each year reached the finals. In order to reach this envied position the team had played two or three games a day over one week end, in a sectional tournament, then repeated this schedule in a regional tournament, and had then done it a third time in the state tournament. He had run the one-hundred-yard dash within a second or less of the national record in eight different meets in his senior year of high school. When Fred entered college he was at once pledged to a fraternity, the football coach welcomed him, and he set out on a happy college career. The first check came from the physician who gave Fred's heart the routine examination. It was only with misgivings and warnings about being cautious that he let Fred out for football practice. On the third day of practice Fred sprinted down the field under a punt—and collapsed with a heart attack. At this point the doctor put his foot down and Fred had to turn in his uniform. The boy was never able to indulge in a single sport during his entire career in college because of his enlarged and overstrained heart. He is now a young bookkeeper with no particular liking for his job, but he cannot do anything active because of his heart. Aside from the crushing disillusion of his college course, during which he could never become the hero he might easily have been, he will be forced throughout his life into types of work that are uncongenial. His high school won two state basketball tournaments and one national track meet chiefly through his efforts, but in return for this brief glory Fred will always be deprived of normal activity. He has already developed a moody disposition and, at twenty-eight, is a discouraged old man in his outlook on life. His life plans—to become successively a college athlete, professional athlete, a college or high school coach—were completely smashed by an unscrupulous burning-out of his vitality, and he has never found any acceptable substitute.

Helen was a large, tousled-looking overweight girl with a muddy skin and the greasy look that fat people get unless they take excellent care of themselves. Her clothes were wrinkled and sloppy, she smelled of perspiration, and she burst into tears on the slightest provocation. In addition to the physical discomforts of being fat, Helen was emotionally starved and socially unhappy. She knew the other pupils did not like her, she had to suffer their gibes and nicknames, she had no boy friends at all. She had never been to a dance and rarely even to a party. The only way she could get a girl to go to a movie with her was to pay the girl's way—and go with another as unpopular as herself, at that. In addition, she was bothered by daydreams of boys—mostly harmless enough—in which she saw herself as the admired beauty and the receiver of affection instead of contumely. The attention of her teachers was called to her because she sometimes became so absorbed in a daydream that her answers to questions were totally irrelevant. Eventually her art teacher became interested in her because the girl seemed to have real talent in spite of her unprepossessing appearance. To this teacher Helen confided that her excess weight was due chiefly to her habit of eating ice-cream sodas to drown her sorrows! Questioning showed she sometimes consumed eight or nine a day, besides munching on candy and cookies between classes. Feeling that the girl's fundamental problem was physical, the art teacher persuaded her to put herself under the care of a physician. When a more reasonable diet had removed about 15 pounds the teacher went shopping with her pupil and helped her get attractive clothes; she also instructed the girl in keeping herself cleaner. Helen's improved appearance caused favorable comment, and the girls began to like her. This encouraged the girl to take off a total of 49 pounds in the course of a year. By the end of the year she had the usual quota of friends, both boys and girls, and was doing better schoolwork than she had ever supposed possible.

PHYSICAL DEVELOPMENTS

BIBLIOGRAPHY *

1. Atkinson, R. K., "A Study of Athletic Ability in High School Girls," *American Physical Education Review,* 1925, 30: 389-399.
2. Baldwin, B. T., "The Physical Growth of Children from Birth to Maturity," *University of Iowa Studies in Child Welfare,* Vol. I, No. 1, 1923, 411 pp.
3. Baldwin, B. T., "A Measuring Scale for Physical Growth and Physiological Age," *Fifteenth Yearbook of the National Society for the Study of Education,* Part I, 1916, pp. 11-22.
4. Bean, R. B., "The Pulse of Growth in Man," *Anatomical Record,* 1924, 26: 43-61.
5. Blanchard, P., and Manasses, G., *New Girls for Old,* Macaulay Company, 1930, 281 pp.
6. Boas, F., "Statistics of Growth," *United States Bureau of Education Report,* 1904, Chap. ii, 132 pp.
7. Brush Foundation and Western Reserve, "Proceedings of the Conference on Adolescence," Cleveland, 1930, 152 pp.
8. Burlage, S. R., "The Blood Pressure and Heart Rate in Girls During Adolescence," *American Journal of Physiology,* 1923, 64: 252-284.
9. Crampton, C. W., "Physiological Growth," *American Physical Education Review,* 1908, 13: 144-54, 214-27, 268-83, 345-58.
10. Fleming, R. M., "A Study of Growth and Development," *Medical Research Council, Special Report Service,* 1933, No. 190, 85 pp.
11. Friesenhahn, H., "Untersuchungen über die Appetitsrichtungen und den Speiseabscheu bei Schulkindern," *Zeitschrift für Kinderforschung,* 1932, 40: 1-54.
12. Godin, P., "Les Proportions du Corps pendant la Croissance," *Bulletin et Memoir de la Société d'Anthropologie de Paris,* 1911, 1: 268-297.
13. Groves, E. R., and Groves, G. H., *Sex in Childhood,* Macaulay Company, 1933, 247 pp.
14. Hall, W. S., "Changes in the Proportions of the Human Body," *Journal of the Anthropological Institute of Great Britain,* 1896, 25: 21-45.
15. Hattendorf, K., "Parents' Answers to Children's Sex Questions," *Child Welfare Pamphlets of the State University of Iowa,* 1933, No. 710, 15 pp.
16. Hitchcock, E., "Physical Growth of Amherst Students,"

* See also the references in the Appendix.

Pamphlets on Physical Education, Vol. II, No. 4, 1892, 37 pp.
17. Holt, L. E., *Food, Health, and Growth,* The Macmillan Company, 1922, 273 pp.
18. Mudge, E. L., *Varieties of Adolescent Experiences,* D. Appleton-Century Company, 1926, 134 pp.
19. Oberteufer, D., "Personal Hygiene for College Students," *Teachers College Contributions to Education,* No. 407, Bureau of Publications, Columbia University, 1930, 121 pp.
20. Quetelet, L. A. J., *Physique Sociale,* Vol. II, 1869.
21. Richmond, W. V., *An Introduction to Sex Education,* Farrar & Rinehart, Inc., 1934, 312 pp.
22. Terman, L. M., and Almack, J. C., *Hygiene of the School Child* (Revised Edition), Houghton Mifflin Company, 1929, 505 pp.
23. Vierordt, K. H., *Anatomische, Physiologische, und Physikalische Daten und Tabellen,* G. Fischer, Jena, 1906, 622 pp.
24. Wile, I. S., "Sex Problems of Youth," *Journal of Social Hygiene,* 1930, 16: 416-427.

CHAPTER III

EMOTIONAL DEVELOPMENTS OF NORMAL ADOLESCENCE

THERE is an enormous amount of information in regard to emotional development both normal and abnormal, during all the periods from infancy to old age. Obviously not all of this material is of equal value to the secondary schoolteacher. It is the author's intention to summarize in the present chapter those items which are immediately relevant to everyday association with adolescent boys and girls. With this object in view, theoretical discussion may be almost entirely omitted. The present chapter will contain: (1) a brief description of what an emotion is; (2) a section describing the development of three major emotions; and finally (3) a section on the part of the school in controlling emotional developments. For the present chapter pathological manifestations will be omitted, since there is to be a section later on dealing with this topic. This chapter will, then, be confined to the normal development of emotions in normal adolescents.

CHARACTERISTICS OF AN EMOTIONAL EXPERIENCE

An emotion has been described in a nontechnical but sufficiently accurate manner as "a stirred-up state of the entire organism." One does not experience an emotion in any single part of the body but throughout one's entire being. A true emotion is a highly arousing experience whose nature needs to be understood before one proceeds to the more specific topic of the role of emotion in adolescent experiences. The participation of the entire body in an emotional episode will therefore be briefly described.

When one becomes angry, for instance, a number of changes within the body immediately take place. Perhaps the first change is the stopping of the ordinary processes of digestion. The peristalsis of the stomach and intestines, in extreme anger, completely ceases. During an emotion only about 15 per cent of the normal amount of gastric juice is secreted by the stomach.[3] It is because of these changes that emotions are often accompanied by nausea and digestive disturbances. In some cases, after the emotion has continued for a period of time, there is a pronounced stimulation of the lower portion of the digestive tract; the individual then experiences severe diarrhea. In the case of more prolonged but less severe emotional difficulties there may be stubborn constipation, probably because the peristalsis is chronically slow and weak.

An almost immediate effect of the onset of a strong emotion is the secretion of adrenalin by the adrenal glands,[3] which are located above the kidneys. This adrenalin acts upon the entire body as a powerful drug; it is, in fact, one of the most powerful drugs in existence. The adrenalin is discharged by the glands into the blood stream, by which it is carried over the entire body within a few seconds. Its action upon different bodily structures is varied. It acts upon the stomach and still further retards its normal digestive processes. It acts upon the liver, causing this organ to discharge into the blood stream the blood sugar that is normally stored in this organ. This sugar is carried by the blood stream to the muscles. It is the "food" which the muscles require for their contractions. The adrenalin further acts upon the small muscles controlling the amount of air that can be taken into the lungs. These muscles become relaxed so that the person who is angry breathes in more oxygen and discharges more carbon dioxide than is normally the case.[3] The breathing of the person becomes more rapid and deeper, as well as somewhat irregular. The adrenalin also acts upon the blood vessels which supply the abdominal organs, driving the blood from the abdomen into the muscles, nervous system, and lungs.[3] The adrenalin acts directly upon the heart muscles and causes the heart to beat more rapidly and

EMOTIONAL DEVELOPMENTS

with more power. As a result of this change, the blood pressure rises for the duration of the emotion. It is the driving of the blood from the viscera into the muscles and to the surface of the body generally that produces the redness of the angry person's face and the general feeling of warmth that he experiences. The adrenalin also causes the sweat glands in the skin to function, thus producing the dampness in the palms of the hands and on the face of the individual. The muscles which control the skeleton, because they are supplied with extra allowances of blood sugar, often contract until they quiver from sheer tenseness. During an emotion the individual has actually a greater strength and a greater endurance than during his usual state of calmness, but he does not have the control over his muscles that he has when he is not emotionally disturbed. Thus, in an actual fight between two people of normally equal muscular development, one of whom is extremely angry and the other of whom is quite calm, the angry fighter has the greatest strength and is likely to damage the other seriously if he ever succeeds in landing a blow, but his muscular control is often so poor that he cannot hit his opponent at all, while the unemotional opponent continues to land much lighter blows whenever he wishes to do so.

It should be obvious enough that an emotion is a serious experience. The changes just described are fundamental to the life processes of the organism. If a person is thoroughly angry, this completely stirred condition of his body persists for a considerable length of time, sometimes as long as forty-eight hours. During this period he is putting a marked strain upon his heart and lungs; he is burning up his reserves of energy and he is temporarily ruining his digestion. When the period of intense emotion is finally over, the individual is left in an exhausted state. A violent emotion rarely lasts more than a few hours, but milder emotional states may last for weeks or even months until the person experiencing them becomes actually exhausted. Neurotics who complain of fatigue are not drawing on their imaginations. They have an actual fatigue so profound that a normal person cannot realize its seriousness.

It appears to make little difference in the internal changes what emotion is being experienced. The bodily posture, the facial expression, and the paling or redness of the body's surface vary from one emotion to another, but these changes are superficial. The deep changes within the body are exactly the same for all emotions and vary only with the intensity of the emotional disturbance.[3]

It has already been pointed out that the adolescent's body is in process of change. There are alterations going on in the bone structure, the digestive organs, the glandular system, and the circulatory system. The body is already in a state of disequilibrium, even during unemotional periods. It is, therefore, in a condition to be easily and thoroughly disorganized by relatively slight emotional stimuli. For many adolescents life consists of one emotional episode after another.

An example may make the situation clearer. Perhaps even before breakfast a boy has begun to worry about his schoolwork and has already lost his temper a couple of times because his favorite necktie is torn and his mother has washed his corduroys, which he infinitely prefers to wear in a condition that violates all ordinary standards of hygiene. During breakfast he may get angry because one kind of food rather than another has been prepared. Perhaps he immediately rushes out of the house in a fine glow of enthusiasm with an expectation of meeting the particular girl with whom he fancies himself in love at the moment, only to find her walking to school with somebody else. He may then experience a half hour of profound jealousy, compounded of his love for the girl and his hatred for the boy. By the time he has calmed down from this emotional spasm, he finds the hour for geometry coming upon him and begins to dread the class because he is afraid of the teacher. When he finally gets to class he may become so congealed with dread of ridicule that he cannot recite when called on. His fear makes him angry, and when another student who knows no more but has greater self-confidence answers the questions originally directed at him, he may become distinctly depressed and experience for a few minutes a second episode of profound hatred. And so it goes through his entire day with one emotion treading on the heels of a previous one, until by night he is exhausted, irritable, and almost impossible to live with.

EMOTIONAL DEVELOPMENTS

The preponderant role of emotions in adolescent life is due partly to the ease with which unevenly developed bodily functions may be thrown into a state of agitation and partly to the adolescent's increased sensibility to social situations. This latter point will be returned to in a later chapter.

THE LIFE HISTORY OF THREE MAJOR EMOTIONS

An emotional experience may obviously be divided, like all Gaul, into three parts. First, there is the stimulus which causes the emotion. Second, there is the internal adjustment already described. And, third, there is the response made. The second of these parts, the internal adjustment, appears to be particularly invariable from birth to death. When a newborn baby becomes angry, the changes taking place within his body seem no different from those developing under appropriate stimulus within the body of an octogenarian. These changes have to be studied by the physiologist and do not constitute a psychological problem. The teacher should understand their nature, but there is nothing she or anybody else can do about them. There are, however, great changes from birth to old age in the stimuli which bring about anger and in the responses that are made. The biography of an emotion must, then, concern itself with the causes and effects of the emotional upheaval. Moreover, the school can do something about the matter by removing unnecessary stimuli and by directing the expression of emotions into channels of social acceptability.

A "life history" of each possible emotion would result in far too long a discussion, even if there were adequate data for such a treatment. Moreover, there is no accepted list of emotions. Some psychologists favor the existence of a single "stirred-up" state that gradually becomes differentiated in response to various stimuli; others list three, four, or five emotions; still others admit about a dozen, and there are a few who list as many as twenty. It seems undesirable to introduce moot problems into this text; in any case, the exact number of emotions need not be determined, so far as the forthcoming treatment is concerned. The writer would be inclined to list fear, anger, love, and jealousy as the most fundamental emotions, with worry, dread, regret, sorrow, and embarrassment as less violent—but often more prolonged—emotional states. Only three—love, anger, and fear—have been sufficiently investigated to furnish data for the type of treatment planned. The discussion will, therefore, be limited to these three, even though this number does not exhaust the possibilities. The treatment below could be extended to other emotions, provided sufficient evidence were assembled. The main thing for teachers to realize is that emotional behavior has typical stages of development that can be traced just as surely as the stages of intellectual growth. Illustrative material from three emotions should make this point sufficiently clear.

Anger.—The first of the emotions to be considered is anger. There have been a number of studies into the causes of anger and the reactions made by angry people. The studies selected for consideration here report the stimuli and reactions for children of preschool age,[17] for individuals in the middle years of adolescence,[8, 12] and for adults.[16] For these groups the causes of emotional outbursts will first be considered.

In the largest number of instances, the children studied became angry because someone tried to take a plaything away from them. The next most important category is concerned with conflicts arising over dressing and going to the toilet. In fact, these two types of situations contribute approximately three-fourths of all the stimuli causing outbursts of anger in the preschool children. Most of the remaining situations consisted of some interruption of the child's activities by others. For the adolescents, 64 per cent of the situations arousing anger among the girls had to do with the behavior of other individuals. This type of stimulus aroused anger among boys in only 36 per cent of the cases. In this category are included such stimuli as the following, which are listed in the adolescents' own words:

EMOTIONAL DEVELOPMENTS

"A professor's daughter acted like she owned the place." (B)*
"I was bawled out for talking in the library." (B)
"A kid in an old Ford cut in in front of me." (B)
"I was trying to study and three students came in and hung around and wouldn't let me." (B)
"The hostess of our sorority gave me the poorest cut of meat." (G)
"Somebody told me the boys were circulating an ugly snapshot of me." (G)
"A friend of mine turned back my alarm clock, making me late; she thought this was a joke." (G)
"The professor explained everyone else's paper but left out mine." (G)
"I was to meet two friends at the theater and they kept me waiting nearly an hour." (B)
"I went to a meeting that was supposed to last only half an hour and it lasted three, and I was sitting in a front seat and couldn't get out." (B)†

These causes of anger are obviously different from those which stimulate the preschool child. They are to be found in the social relationships among people.

In the cases of the girl adolescents, only 26 per cent of the situations causing anger had to do with material objects, while the failure of material objects to function properly caused anger in 47 per cent of the instances recorded by boys. Such instances from both sexes are described by the students as follows:

"I washed my hair after a permanent and it wouldn't set right." (G)
"I spilled a bottle of ink on a paper and had to copy it over." (G)
"The oil from my car leaked out on my new clothes." (B)
"I smeared ink on a drawing on which I had already spent several hours." (B)
"I broke a shoestring." (B)
"I stumbled and fell down in the mud." (G)

* B = boy; G = girl.
† This material is used by permission of the *Journal of Social Psychology*.

These causes of anger are to some extent also social, although they primarily involve objects. The remaining causes of anger as listed by the adolescents were of an impersonal nature, such as anger at the weather, at being hungry and not having time to eat, at having a headache on the day of an important examination, and so on.

Adult causes of anger have also been investigated.[16] There is some continuance of childish irritation at objects that refuse to function immediately and of typical adolescent reactions to social slights—real or imagined. The most common type of stimuli, however, are such as those listed below: *

> "I felt as if I were so inefficient. I said to myself, 'If I had a man working for me and he should do work in that manner, I would discharge him.'"
>
> "I felt he implied, 'You will never know as much about the subject under discussion as Y [a third person].'"
>
> "My anger became rather intense because a businessman told me an untruth and caused me difficulty."
>
> "I get angry at ministers who preach what they do not believe and manufacturers who send out goods of inferior quality."
>
> "The school authorities wouldn't let my boy go to W—— school,† even when I showed them how much he wanted the courses."
>
> "I did all the work on that report, but R stole the credit by talking all the time as if it were all his work."
>
> "I was sore. If this silly remark of his had come to the boss's ears, I'd have lost my job."
>
> "I was all set to go fishing last Saturday, when my wife got sick and I had to do some typing she'd promised to finish before night."
>
> "Every time I think of those filthy tenements, my blood boils."

The three levels of development here shown may be summarized as follows: In infancy and early childhood, anger comes from conflicts over playthings or from situations arising during the process of getting dressed. There are also occasional outbursts of anger because an interesting activity has been in-

---

* This material is used by permission of Warwick & York.
† The last five are from an unpublished investigation of the writer's.

terrupted or because the desire to do some interesting thing has been thwarted. In adolescence, the causes of anger are primarily social. The individual gets into a situation in which he feels himself embarrassed, ridiculous, offended, or annoyed, and forthwith becomes emotional about it. The adult becomes angry if his work or leisure is interfered with; he also is inclined to feel concerned over abtract justice or impersonal social conditions. His reasons for anger are much more practical than those of the adolescent. It is no wonder that the small child, the adolescent, and the adult fail to understand one another's motivation.

The reactions made when one is angry also show a development. The small baby becomes quite rigid; he screams and beats the air with his arms and legs.[20] This is his only reaction, probably because his mental and muscular development is so slight that other reactions are not possible. The preschool child also cries and screams and becomes stiff and kicks and strikes, bites, scratches, stamps his feet, jumps up and down, throws himself on the floor.[17] To a much slighter extent he scolds and talks back. By adolescence the response of talking has become by far the most important.[8, 12] Actual violence is reported in very few instances, although there is frequent mention of such substitute reactions as pacing the room, being generally restless, going out for a walk, or indulging in some violent exercise as a means of working off the emotions. Some slight degree of subtlety is shown by those who refuse to speak to the people who have made them angry. Finally there is a persistence of infantile behavior in the form of stamping the feet or kicking things, on the part of the boys, and by crying, on the part of the girls. Among the adults the verbal responses have almost completely taken the place of all other forms, although women still cry and men still kick things.[16] However, violent responses are less than in either adolescent or child. One may say, then, that the development of emotional responses in anger consists primarily in substituting verbalism for overt behavior.

The duration of the anger also varies, to some extent, with

the age of the individual. In the case of preschool children, the anger lasted less than five minutes in 90 per cent of the cases.[17] For college students the average period was fifteen minutes and the total range from one minute to forty-eight hours.[12] The actual number of anger experiences per week are approximately the same for all groups; the differences are to be found in the situations causing the anger, in the responses made, and in the duration of the responses.

Fear.—The second of the three most powerful emotions is fear. Not as much is known about normal fear as about normal anger, although there is much information concerning abnormal fears. It therefore becomes necessary to base the life story of this emotion partly upon general observation, partly upon clinical histories, and partly upon test and questionnaire results.

The newborn baby is apparently afraid of two things: if he feels himself falling or if he feels the bedclothes jerked out from under him, he shows the clinical signs of fear.[20] A little later he shows unmistakable fear at loud noises. The responses set up by loud and unexpected noises often continue throughout life, although the duration of the emotion is usually only a few seconds among adults. Most of the literature available concerning different kinds of fears would indicate that the typical reaction may become attached to practically any stimulus and is not necessarily attached to more than a few. Most of the things a human being fears he has learned to be afraid of.

Clinical histories show people of all ages to be afraid of all kinds of material objects and social relationships. One may fear sharp knives, snakes, elevators, water, mad dogs, fountain pens, or practically anything else. One may fear people who are big, clever, sarcastic, cruel, overbearing, humorous, sly, and so on. One may be afraid to meet people, to be alone, to be in a crowd, to give a speech, to recite in class, to write an examination, to go to a dance. The number of social situations causing fear seems almost infinite. One may also have relatively remote or general fears—fear of poverty, of death, of disease, of drowning, of becoming blind, of failure, of being separated from one's family, of losing one's job.

EMOTIONAL DEVELOPMENTS

Fears are both learned and "unlearned." There is probably no other emotion that education *could* control so effectively. Most fears disappear in the face of concrete evidence. Fear of lightning may be alleviated by informing people how lightning travels and under what circumstances they cannot be struck. Fear of failure may be lessened by getting people into lines of work in which their performances are demonstrably superior to those of others. Fears growing out of normal sexual functions can be eliminated by adequate instruction. Fear of disease can be considerably lessened by information, plus various inoculations. Fear of subways and tunnels can be brought under control by a study of statistics showing the chances of injury in such places—usually amounting to about one chance in five million. The writer has personally taught many people who were hysterically afraid of the water to swim—and the fear has disappeared. To be sure, it takes time and patience to teach a person how a given fear may be eliminated, but "unlearning" *can* be brought about. A correct system of education would eliminate fears, not cause them. As will be shown subsequently, many emotional upsets grow out of the school situation itself.

In the last few years various efforts have been made, through the use of questionnaires and tests, to obtain information as to the fears and other emotional attitudes of normal children, adolescents, and adults. One of these efforts [14] has yielded information of interest in tracing the development of typical fears. Below is presented a list of the fears, out of a possible ninety, marked by 75 per cent or more of sixth-grade children; these items are arranged in descending order of frequency.

murder	robbers	jail	knives	choking
holdups	accidents	burglars	dying	operation
poison	suffering	wrecks	injury	gun
fire	thieves	enemies	sickness	floods
death	danger	crimes	fights	suffocating

The items marked least frequently (25 per cent or less) by the sixth-graders were:

ability	secrets
appearance	trembling
family	clothes
cats	work

By the tenth grade, the most frequent causes for fear or worry had changed somewhat, as indicated by the list below, which contains items marked by 30 per cent or more of the children. No item was marked by more than 52 per cent and only four by more than 50 per cent.

fire	helplessness	disease	cheating
examinations	collision	operation	appearance
murder	tuberculosis	germs	lightning
accidents	money	crimes	burglars
poison	sins	injury	work
holdups		suffocating	

The list is a curious combination of the outstanding fears of children and those characteristic of late adolescence. These latter are given below. Seniors in college marked very few items; only nine were marked by 25 per cent or more and only four by 50 per cent or more. The nine items are as follows:

money	cash	self-consciousness
ability	examinations	work
appearance	clothes	family

Of the twenty-five outstanding fears of childhood, one—accidents—persists, with over 20 per cent of college seniors marking it: approximately 10 per cent marked "suffering." All the other childish items, however, had almost disappeared, being marked by 5 per cent or less of the seniors. Conversely, five of the nine items marked least by children appear in the list of those marked most frequently by the college seniors.

This test has been given to a relatively small number of adults, but the results show clearly enough that only three fears are important, with a fourth appearing occasionally—money, work, family, and ability. Thus, the numerous fears of childhood have been replaced by a restricted assortment of adult fears. The actual number of items marked on the test used decreased steadily from over fifty for the average sixth-grade child to only five for college seniors. This diminution is obviously the result of education and experience. If an average of forty-five worries can be eliminated between the sixth grade and the last year of college, there is no reason why other fears cannot be obviated, if the world really wants to get rid of them. Thus, for instance, some countries attempt to eliminate fear of poverty, of destitute old age, or of loss of work by a reorganization of society. Fears are made by the physical and social world as it exists. Man is well on his way to conquering the physical forces in the world; it remains to be seen whether or not he can control the social forces. If he can, he will eliminate the majority of fears. Advances in science, in social organization, and in education can unite to cut down the human ravages caused by this most destructive of emotions.

From the above data it is possible to make a few generalizations. Children appear to be afraid of violence of all kinds, whether from persons, natural phenomena, or accidents. Adolescents are afraid primarily of social situations in which they will appear to a disadvantage; they fear also disease and accidental violence. Adults are afraid primarily of such situations as may cause them to lose their jobs or their health, or may bring about injury to their family or friends. The child's fears are relatively simple; the adolescent's fears are social; the adult's fears are extremely practical.

The reactions to fear are not varied. The main behavior is a rigidity and immobility of the entire body. The whole world simply stops in its tracks. The running-away behavior is usually secondary to this complete congealing. The reactions shown by persons of all ages are variations, more or less subtle, on these two central patterns. As children grow older and their intellectual abilities mature, they learn to do their running away before the stimulus appears; that is, they learn to avoid situations that may cause fear. Thus, the pupil who is afraid to address the class in his oral English work develops a spurious toothache on the day he expects his turn to come. He is running away just as actually as if he had fled from the classroom, only in a less conspicuous manner.

The chief development from early childhood to adulthood is, in fact, along lines of subtlety. The small child, when frightened, becomes rigid, whimpers a bit, and then runs screaming to his mother. As he becomes older, this overt behavior meets with ridicule, so he substitutes a rapid swagger for the run, chatters busily to keep from screaming, and seeks the company of his peers instead of his mother. As he develops further, he becomes adept at avoidance and rationalizing. Thus, he announces loudly he is not afraid of snakes—hoping he is too emphatic to be challenged. If this does not work, he announces it is bad luck to touch a snake; something dreadful always happens within a few hours. If this rationalization does not work, he tries something else. If he cannot avoid the object of his fear, he tries to be as nonchalant as possible and hopes no one will notice his hands are shaking, his skin is wet with perspiration, and his face is gray and drawn. The adult who is afraid has usually better control than the adolescent, but a protracted strain will break him down to the childish levels of rigidity, crying, and running away. Many a man collapses completely from fear while his young wife is enduring a twenty-four-hour labor at the birth of their first child. One finds the prospectice father wandering about the corridors, dazed with fear, sitting rigidly for hours, crying actual tears, rushing out of the hospital to escape from unbearable sounds and smells, or practically assaulting the doctors and nurses in his panic. Fear reactions are rarely converted into secondary forms, as anger responses are. They are controlled better as the individual grows older and they are avoided whenever possible; but they are always lurking close behind the individual's defenses.

Fear is destructive because its modes of expression are never useful in learning or in adjustment of any kind. Anger sometimes stimulates people to overcome handicaps. Fear never does anything but disorganize the person who experiences it. Teachers should therefore avoid all situations that may stimulate fear. This point will be brought out again later.

Love.—The third of the fundamental emotions is love. As in the case of both fear and anger, there is a definite development from infancy to adulthood in the stimuli which cause this emotion. It is probable that the bodily background also changes with age, since children are undeveloped sexually and since individuals beyond middle age have lost, more or less, their sexual vigor. Because of the physiological changes at puberty, the bodily turmoil into which love precipitates the adolescent is both profound and unexpected. He has already experienced the emotion which in childhood passes for love, but he has not had the same internal adjustment as now becomes possible. Whereas a small child is just as angry as an adolescent, he is not normally just as much in love.

In psychological literature the person or thing that inspires the emotion of love has been termed the "love-object." The love-objects that are most powerful in arousing the emotion vary with age, just as the situations arousing either fear or anger also vary. The first love-object for babies of either sex is undoubtedly their mother, or the person who looks after them. The mother remains the exclusive love-object during the first years of life, or until she is displaced by the father. She is not usually thus displaced in the affection of her sons, although she is quite often superseded by the father in the affection of her daughters. The reason for this situation appears to be partly that many women are actually more attached to their sons than to their daughters and partly that the average man is unwilling to display his own affection toward his son for fear the boy will become a sissy. By the time his son is perhaps two years old the average man is unwilling to fondle him or kiss him or otherwise display a love which may be quite as deep as that he feels toward his daughter. However, there are no social inhibitions operating against his caressing his little girl all he wants. Consequently, girls in the second or third years of life often transfer their deepest love to their fathers, whereas boys are less likely to do so. In any case, throughout the child's early years of life the parents, or older persons functioning as parents, remain the chief objects able to bring about the emotion of love. As soon as the child goes to school, a particular teacher may displace one or both of the parents, but the teacher comes in the same category as the parents and is therefore not a new type of love-object—though she may arouse the jealousy and antagonism of the parents.

A person of approximately the same age as one's parents is an infantile type of love-object. Some children, however, are allowed, or even encouraged, to continue fixations on parents, older friends, or teachers. If this situation persists into the years of adolescence, the child is far too dependent upon older people for his emotional satisfaction, and he is usually abnormally attached to his own home. If the situation goes on into adult life, it becomes truly serious, because the individual falls in love with people much too old. A young man of twenty-five is rarely happy for long with a woman of forty-five; nor is a young woman likely to remain in love with a man many years her senior. Middle age and youth are appropriately adjusted as parent and child or as teacher and pupil, but not as husband and wife. Dependency for emotional satisfaction upon older generations is a symptom of persistent infantilism.

This fixation upon adults, often adults of the opposite sex, continues normally until the middle years of childhood—that is, till about the eighth or ninth year. From this time on, for a few years, children are usually more deeply attached to some other child of their own sex than they are to anyone else. Parents often resent this situation and sometimes prevent such attachments from arising by keeping their child away from other children. A continued exclusive devotion to the parents, beyond the early years of childhood, is not entirely normal. Older people are a childish love-object, just as stubbing one's toe is a childish stimulus to anger. The second period of development, in which this love-object is another person of the same sex and approximately the same age (sometimes a little older), has often been referred to as the "homosexual" stage of development. This name is somewhat unfortunate because it implies an abnormality where there is none. These attachments seem perfectly normal and are a necessary step in the gradual emancipation of a child from the emotional ties which bind him to his home. This period continues, usually becoming more intense, up to the years of adolescence. It is often so intense that boys and girls eleven or twelve years of age will have nothing more to do with each other than is absolutely necessary.

This type of love-object is obviously not desirable as a permanent stimulus. In some instances, however, an individual remains in this stage of development and becomes permanently attached to other members of his or her own sex. If the public would stop regarding childish attachments as "abnormal" and would look upon them rather as a sign of mere immaturity, an enormous amount of despair would be eliminated.

A third stage is seen when the love-object is another individual of approximately the same age but of the opposite sex. For the majority of individuals this adult and socially approved type of love-object completely takes the place of the two previous types as far as the deepest emotions are concerned. Naturally, girls still love their mothers and fathers and they still love their girl friends, but their deepest emotions are centered upon boys as love-objects rather than upon either parents or friends. Usually the transfer from friends of one's own sex to members of the opposite sex is easy and natural. All that seems needed is the presence in the environment of a large number of possible love-objects. If a girl goes to a high school in which five hundred boys are enrolled, she is presented with five hundred potential love-objects among which she will discover at least a dozen suited to her particular personality. All she needs is enough boys to choose from. Similarly, all a boy needs to distract his emotion from friends of his own sex is a sufficient assortment of girls.

Two good samples of the emotional condition of young girls in the midst of the final shift to an adult love-object are given in the excerpts below, taken from the writings of the girls themselves.[13]

"I was not sincere in my affections. My attention was shifted from one boy to another. I easily "fell in love" with anyone and would sit and dream by the hour of my future happiness with Tom, Dick, or Harry, whoever it chanced to be. I refused to read anything that did not offer a thrilling love plot.

"Accompanying this love for sentimental reading, and running parallel with it, was my intense admiration for older men. I cared nothing at all for any boy of my own age or very near my own age, but certain older men whom I admired were my heroes, and

I worshiped them at a distance. Not for worlds would I tell anyone about this except my dearest girl chum. I felt free to tell her because she too was afflicted in the same way. We used to write letters to them. Of course we wouldn't send them, but it afforded us a great deal of satisfaction. Then we would even write poems about them. I smile to myself now, when I think of it, and yet at the time it was a serious thing to me." *

"My attitude toward boys was the same as a child's. I had always liked boys, and still did. They were good friends. Until I was fifteen I had few girl friends, living in a neighborhood where there happened to be none of my age, and so I always played with boys and continued on this basis of frank comradeship all through high school. At one time all the members of a girls' club of which I was a member had "cases"; that is, each girl had some particular hero, some boy in high school, whom she adored. He was her ideal. She was "in love" with him. Perhaps she knew him to speak to, but this was not essential, just merely to admire from afar, to follow his record in athletics or other high school activities, was sufficient acquaintance. This attitude of theirs was incomprehensible to me. I could not understand their intense and jealous interest in these individuals. As football players or debating orators I admired them all but could see no reason for great individual preference. Finally, however, I pretended, merely for the sake of being like the others, that I too was in love. I centered my attention on one high school hero, and thereafter, in the eyes of our crowd, at least, he was mine. I was to be congratulated on his successes and sympathized with when he failed. But I was not sincere; I was merely trying to be like the others." *

The relatively few people who do not succeed in becoming attached to the adult type of love-object are those who are prevented either by environment or their own nature from making the necessary social contacts. Thus, if a girl attends a girls' boarding school during the year, a girls' camp in the summer, and later goes to a girls' college where the rules are strict, she is to some degree isolated by her environment from contact with boys, especially if she has no brothers who may bring their friends to her home. Since a girl during the six or eight years of boarding school and college is undoubtedly going to become

* This material is published by permission of the D. Appleton-Century Company.

EMOTIONAL DEVELOPMENTS

attached to somebody, and since the only people constantly in her environment are other girls and women teachers, she may become so attached to members of her own sex that substitution of a more adult love-object becomes unlikely. The isolation of a boy in a boys' school and boys' camp during these same years may have equally unfortunate results. There are also a few people whose development is interfered with because of some personal characteristic. They may be too shy or too easily embarrassed to make the necessary social contacts with members of the opposite sex. They may have an actual deformity, or something they regard as a deformity, and so feel themselves unattractive and are unwilling to make any effort at heterosexual adjustment. Usually, however, the adult type of love-object makes its appearance in the early years of adolescence.

The development shown by stimuli giving rise to the emotion of love may be summarized as follows: The first love-objects are adults of the same or opposite sex; the second love-objects are normally persons of about the same age and the same sex; the third love-objects are persons of about the same age and the opposite sex. During the years of infancy and early childhood when the child's chief need is for care and security, he loves most those who give him these elements. When he begins to strike out for himself, he loves most those people who best recognize him as an individual—his friends, who incidentally serve to break the early bonds with his home. Finally he reacts to a type of love-object which, sooner or later, will lead to marriage and will permanently end his infantile attachments to his home.

Objective measures of emotional development.—Within the past five years two different investigators [7, 14] have worked out tests for measuring emotional maturity. The results are expressed in terms of "emotional age," a concept exactly paralleling that of "mental age." Thus, a fifteen-year-old girl with an emotional age of twelve shows the emotional reactions expected of twelve-year-olds; she has a retardation of three years and an "emotional quotient" of 80. Below are presented curves of development from these two tests. One test is so arranged that the average score decreases with age; for the other, it increases. This is a mere detail of test construction. The point to consider is the consistent growth shown in both instances.

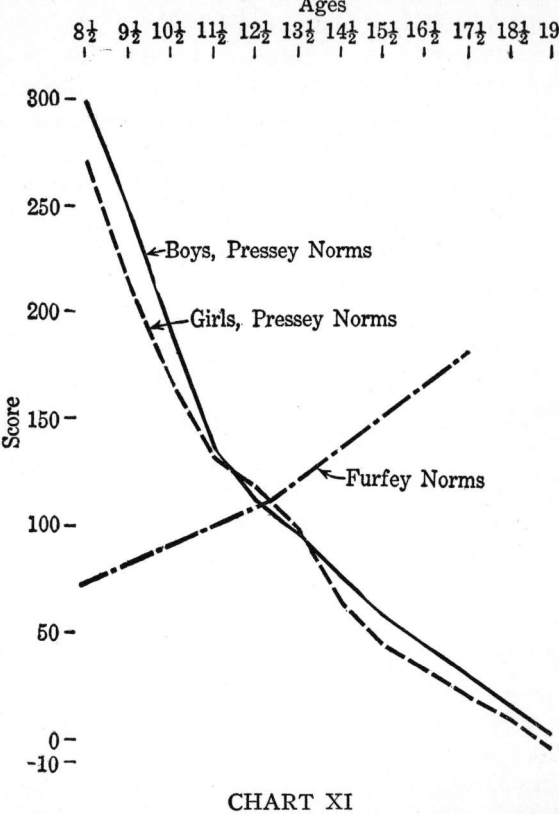

CHART XI

GROWTH CURVES FOR EMOTIONAL MATURITY (Pressey [14] and Furfey [6])

These curves of emotional development show a relation between maturity and emotional responses quite as great as that between maturity and intellectual responses. This type of measure is likely to become as widely used as tests of intelligence as soon as its value is appreciated.

EMOTIONS AND THE SCHOOL

It should go without saying that an emotion is too trying an experience to be indulged in any oftener than necessary. Emotions, if prolonged or frequent, ruin the digestion, cause chronic constipation or diarrhea, effect a marked loss of appetite with resulting loss of weight, burn up the reserves of physical vitality, overtax the heart, and result in a state of exhaustion. They keep the person experiencing them on edge. They disorganize the individual, thus preventing learning and adjustment to social situations. Such profoundly disturbing experiences should occur at as rare intervals as is possible.

The school has four obvious duties in the matter. (1) It should avoid the arousal of emotions in the course of its own program; (2) it should provide for relatively harmless ways of working off such emotions as are unavoidable; (3) it should require that its teachers understand emotional manifestations and be able to recognize the symptoms as these appear in the schoolroom; (4) it should give definite instruction about the emotions. This section will deal with these four points.

Avoidance of emotional disturbances.—The school precipitates a large number of disturbances by its own procedures. A few of the more common may well be examined. First, come those concerned with administration.

For instance, many a school principal has become so imbued with the idea of differences in mental development that he has introduced "X, Y, Z" sections into his classes in all fundamental subjects in high school and has let everyone know on what basis these sections were formed. Such divisions should be made, because the teaching situation varies so much with the capacities of the pupils being taught, but there is no reason why the basis should be shouted from the housetops. The pupils in the X sections often become quite intolerable from conceit and those in the Z sections become justifiably annoyed for being branded publicly as stupid—a situation that is not their fault and about which they can do nothing. Such divisions can be made on constructive instead of destructive grounds. Those intending surely to go to college can be placed in the X sections, those hoping to go but not entirely sure of it, in the Y sections, and those who have only vague plans in the matter in the Z sections. With the aid of a vocational counselor who stresses the extra and often irrelevant work to be done by those preparing for college, the pupils in the Z sections become glad they are placed where they are, instead of being heartbroken about it. Dull pupils can be told, for instance, that in the Z English section they will be trained to read, instead of the "dull" classics, such things as trade journals, newspapers, magazines, novels, and directions of the type they will meet in their subsequent work. Such a plan of attack is constructive from their point of view, and they often develop a marked preference for their own type of instruction. Publicly branding adolescents, or children either, as "dumbbells" never does them any good. Children who are dull soon find it out, and they should find it out, since they have to adjust themselves to the world with what mental equipment they have. What is objectionable is publicity in the matter. The writer would even go so far as to tell pupils their I.Q.'s, but she would not publicly put up a list of I.Q.'s for all pupils to read and comment upon—which is, in effect, what is done by the division of pupils into X, Y, Z sections on the basis of ability alone. The stupid person cannot avoid incidental humiliations, but he should not be humiliated intentionally. The emphasis should be put upon different kinds of work—not upon different kinds of student.

Throughout the average school one finds discriminations, either intentional or unintentional. Such attitudes are fatal to the emotional equilibrium of those against whom the attitude is expressed. A few common situations may be quoted.

The writer has heard several teachers say they would never give a Negro more than a passing grade, no matter how good his work was. Similar attitudes are found against Chinese, Japanese, Mexicans, foreigners generally, Jews, or children coming from some particular section of a city. Teachers with such attitudes have no business in a public high school. Many emotional problems would be completely eliminated if administrators would insist upon a real equality in their schools. A high school should, for instance, never agree to sponsor any extracurricular activity, whether an athletic team, social club, or any other organization, that excludes anyone in the high school from admission. Naturally, social relationships that are purely personal would not be affected. That is, children would still choose their friends as they wished, eat their lunch in whatever company they preferred, ask those they liked to their own homes, and so on. Such activities are not backed by school authority and require no stamp of approval except from the pupils' own families. The point is that officially sponsored activities of a school should be open to anyone—and equally open to all. Clubs based on common interests—such as the nature study club, the radio club, the literature club, and so on—should require as the basis for admission nothing but a real interest in the matter under consideration. Athletic teams, debating teams, or honorary clubs should ask no more competency for admission from a foreigner, Jew, Negro, or Oriental than from an American white child. The official school dances should be open to everyone who wants to come; the school swimming pool should exclude only those who have infections that might be communicated to others and should never base their exclusions upon the silly notion that a black or yellow skin will pollute the water. In classes in which work is sometimes done by pairs or small groups of children, such units should be made up either by putting together those of equal standing in the subject or by sheer chance—as when one groups children according to the alphabetical arrangement of their names or by the row in which they happen to sit. School routine should be of a type which leaves no possibility for discrimination in its official procedures.

The results of unnecessary discrimination may be shown by the following case of a Negro boy who had been arrested for attacking white high school girls. He had, to be sure, merely put his arms around them and tried to kiss them, but his attacks would undoubtedly have gone further if allowed to continue. The boy, who was sent to the writer for examination, told the following tale. He had never, in his ten years of school, had a teacher who would call on him as often as she called on the white children. He had never been allowed to collect papers, erase blackboards, run errands, or do any of the other things that so delight the soul of the school child. He had always been made to work by himself whenever there were group projects, unless there happened to be another Negro in the room. He had been forced to work repeatedly with one very stupid Negro girl during the preceding year because she was in many of his classes. He had never heard one of his own compositions read and commented on in class, though he wrote well. In high school he had been excluded from the swimming tank. The football coach would not even allow him to try out for the team. When he tried to take his girl to a supposedly public school dance he was refused admittance. He was not allowed to eat in the school lunchroom. His teachers often passed him on the street without speaking to him. On the day before the first attack he had stumbled over a girl's foot in the aisle as he went toward the blackboard; she had slapped his face, and the teacher had scolded him for being careless but had not made the girl apologize. Finally, this patient Negro boy's tolerance simply gave out. Ten years of constant discrimination had worn him down until he had to assert himself or be crushed for the rest of his life. His manner of self-assertion might well have cost him more than an arrest. This boy's problems and attitudes were in the main created by the school itself; the blame is with the teachers and administrators who permitted a child's spirit to be broken with the load of countless small insults.

Any school that permits discrimination is letting itself in for trouble because it is developing warped personalities both among those who discriminate and those who are discriminated against. A spirit of tolerance can be built up in a school if those in charge will insist upon it. If parents object, as they probably will, they can be told their child must either learn to live tolerantly in the school world as it exists or else be sent to some private institution that is based upon discrimination.

A school should not be content with mere discouragement of discrimination but should take positive steps toward equality for all, not only by admittance of all children to activities for which they can qualify by either interest or ability, but by such relatively simple practices as regulating the clothes in which the children are allowed in school. One high school in which the writer has worked required that the boys wear either cords or jeans, any colored shirt they liked, and sweaters; neckties were permitted but by no means regarded as essential. The girls were allowed cotton blouses of any color and either cotton or woolen skirts, or any plain cotton or woolen dress; if they arrived in silk dresses they were sent home to change. Such a regulation makes a positive contribution to equality because discrimination on the basis of wealth is not possible. A child cannot acquire prominence through being better dressed than other children; he or she must stand out because of ability, not appearance.

The school also makes difficulties for itself in matters of discipline. The sarcastic teacher probably causes emotional disturbances all out of proportion to any good she may do. Sarcasm is an unfair weapon that the sophisticated adult in a position of authority uses against pupils whose respect she cannot obtain. The writer was once present when a sarcastic teacher commented once too often upon the well-intentioned efforts of an exasperated and poorly inhibited pupil, who forthwith smashed her book into the teacher's face and broke that lady's nose—a reaction the teacher

EMOTIONAL DEVELOPMENTS

had been simply asking for during years of sarcasm and scorn. If more disagreeable teachers were treated to such results, the emotional atmosphere in the classroom would be considerably cleared. Most administrators realize well enough the dangers of sarcasm, but they do not know how to find out which teachers employ this weapon against their pupils. Teachers are never disagreeable as long as an administrator, supervisor, or parent is in the room. And it is not safe to act upon tales brought to the principal's office by students, especially by failing students against whom the sarcasm is most likely to be used. An excited adolescent is prone to exaggerate his troubles, and he can rarely remember the exact wording of what was said to him.

To the administrator one of two lines of action are open. He can either wait until so many students have complained about a teacher that he begins to investigate by seeking statements from those pupils he regards as most level-headed and mature, or he can introduce a routine by which every teacher in the school gets rated anonymously by every one of her students every year. The plan is relatively simple and has been carried on with success in several places. At the end of each school year all the students in the school are provided with a sufficient number of questionnaires to rate each teacher with whom they have studied during the year. The questionnaires consist of inquiries such as those listed below:

1. How often was this teacher sarcastic?
   Answer: very often, sometimes, occasionally, never.
2. How often did this teacher have to punish students?
   Answer: very often, sometimes, occasionally, never.
3. How often did this teacher lose her temper and scold students?
   Answer: very often, sometimes, occasionally, never.

The questions to be included in such a series can be extended to cover matters of presentation, technique of teaching, methods of giving assignments, or any other topics about which information is desired. All the students have to do is to underline what they regard as the right answers. Since the ratings are anonymous (the teacher's name being already printed on the sheet), pupils may express themselves without fear of personal involvements. There will usually be for each teacher two or three unfavorable ratings, handed in by pupils who dislike the teacher and have taken this opportunity to express their feelings. Such results can always be disregarded. But if a hundred students report a teacher as losing her temper very often, fifty more as losing her temper sometimes, and another fifty as losing it occasionally, while only ten or a dozen report that she never loses her temper, the administrator can be very sure that the teacher under consideration is too poorly inhibited a person to be trusted with teaching. Any administrator or supervisor who wishes to find out exactly what teachers do daily in their classes and what they are like as individuals need only ask the appropriate questions of the students who sit in those teachers' rooms day after day.

Sarcasm has been mentioned first as a type of discipline based on fear because it is probably more frequent in high school than other unfavorable kinds of discipline. Any technique, however, that makes students come into a classroom in a state of emotional excitement is equally bad. Teachers should realize that fear in all its forms is a highly destructive emotion and always has an inhibiting effect upon learning. The boy or girl who does not learn Latin verbs cannot be frightened, nagged, or scolded into doing so. More learning would be accomplished if there were fewer efforts to bully children into mastery of subject matter.

To be sure, fear is sometimes useful as a deterrent to action. It is sometimes necessary if adolescents are to be prevented from doing things that will result in permanent injury of some sort. The pupil who is afraid to steal because of the punishment he will receive if caught is not acting from very high motives, but at least he is not building up a habit of stealing. There are some adolescents to whom an appeal on a higher level is not successful. With such pupils fear is perhaps the only feeling through which they may be held back from delinquency. It should be noted, however, that the effect of the fear is to prevent something from happening and not to cause something to happen. Although fear never brings about learning, there are occasions when it may be used. If a teacher has in the room one intractable child who is constantly disturbing other pupils and preventing them from working, she is quite justified in restraining him by the fear of penalties for misbehavior.

Good discipline for adolescents has five outstanding characteristics.[15] It is, first, the natural result of the misbehavior. For instance, if a boy loses his temper and throws an ink bottle at the wall, the natural punishment is to make him clean it up—

not to require him to solve six extra problems in arithmetic after school. Second, punishment must be certain; if an algebra teacher sometimes makes students remain after school to finish incompleted work that they have had plenty of time to finish before class and sometimes lets them go scot-free, the punishment for poor preparation is too variable to be efficient. Third, punishment should be just; the English teacher who gives a failing mark to a boy because, on the final examination, he split an infinitive is being so unjust as to defeat her own ends. Fourth, punishment must be impersonal; the history teacher who gets annoyed at a pupil's general inattention and assigns a penalty that springs primarily from her own exasperation will never succeed with adolescents. They know the penalty is only an outlet for the teacher's emotions and they blame her rather than themselves. Finally, punishment should always be constructive, so that it will lead to better self-control. Letting pupils suggest and carry out their own punishment is more likely to develop self-control than any penalty assigned from above.

Another source of disturbance in school comes from an overdeveloped emotional attachment between a student and a teacher. Since the teachers are mostly women and since they are enough older than the average boy in school that they do not attract him as possible love-objects, the most frequent and distressing manifestation is the "crush" of a girl in the early years of adolescence for some teacher. Many girls, during junior high school and the early years of senior high school, have not yet succeeded in developing heterosexual interests. They are, therefore, not yet ready to become emotionally fixated upon any boy and they find their teachers, because of greater maturity and experience, more attractive love-objects than most girl friends of their own age. The crush is, therefore, a fairly common phenomenon in a coeducational high school, and is so chronic as to be the expected thing in a girls' boarding school or college. The crush is undesirable, not because the teacher will usually do the girl any harm, but because the situation is prolonging a childish mode of response beyond the years of its usefulness and is helping to prevent the girl from developing interests which will fit her to be a normal adult.

The handling of an adolescent crush demands considerable tact and sympathy, but it demands even more an attitude of objectiveness and lack of emotion on the part of the teacher. It does not do at all to refuse the girl a normal degree of attention and friendliness, because if she does not get them she will probably develop intense emotional reactions that will only make matters much worse. Teachers often are quite brutal and cruel in trying to suppress a crush, but such behavior rarely has the slightest effect upon the intensity of the devotion. In fact, the brutal teacher succeeds only in adding a complete disorganization of personality to emotional drives which are already far too intense.

The exact details of a desirable treatment will vary, of course, with the temperament of the individual girl and teacher. But three general principles can be laid down for the guidance of the teacher. First, the teacher should never make the mistake of showing emotional interest in the girl, even though she may feel it. If she is herself a well-adjusted person, she will have no particular desire to fasten upon the emotional offerings of a half-developed adolescent. But even if she feels more or less desire to return the girl's affection, she must realize that a rigid objectivity is the only attitude of permanent value. The main idea is to redirect the girl's emotional interests, at the same time keeping her friendship and respect. The second general rule is that the teacher should never allow herself to be alone with the girl. Most of the embarrassing and difficult situations into which an adolescent girl with a crush may precipitate both herself and the teacher are prevented if other people are always present. Since the girl's devotion is only a temporary affair, any unpleasant situations are soon looked back upon with embarrassment by both the persons concerned. A teacher should therefore make certain the girl will never have an opportunity to see her alone. The third general rule is for the teacher to provide the girl with a great many helpful things to do. If she is an intelligent girl she may be allowed to become of real assistance in the classroom; in any case, she can be used to run errands, wash blackboards, and do other routine jobs. While the crush is at an intense stage the girl is burning up with energy and devotion and is only too pleased to have tasks assigned to her. If they are not assigned, she will probably think up more emotional ways to demonstrate her feelings. Two or three weeks of washing blackboards, cleaning erasers, counting out books, and so on are usually quite sufficient to calm down the emotional fires of the most intense crush. In this way a girl may succeed in working off her emotional energies through normally accepted channels. At the end of the intense stage, the teacher and the girl are still friends and there are no unpleasant episodes for either to look back upon.

A successful handling of such a situation is described below by a girl who had completely recovered from her emotional obsession.[13]

This teacher not only led me into industrious habits, but she seemed to understand me better than others. She encouraged me to go on with drawing and painting. I had always loved flowers and the out-of-doors. She liked flowers too and helped me identify many species common in our woods. She used to say that she never saw me without a flower, and it was largely through her influence, I think, that I finally decided to major in botany. My "crush" was so intense that I imitated my teacher in every way possible. I walked as she did, tried, without success, to learn the trick of raising one eyebrow in a way she did, and tried in every way, from writing to attending the same church, to be "like teacher." That teacher never lost faith in me and still is interested in me, although we seldom meet and never write.*

From time to time a teacher has as a pupil some boy who has never outgrown his infantile devotion to his mother. Such a boy may accept the teacher as a substitute and may fall quite completely and sincerely in love with her. If it happens that she returns the feeling, an extremely awkward situation arises. The two individuals not only belong to different generations, but they have met as teacher and student; no matter what their subsequent relations may be she will always remain the teacher and he the pupil. This relation, while entirely satisfactory during childhood and adolescence, is a poor basis for adult happiness. Usually, however, the teacher does not return the boy's devotion. In this case the same advice just given for the handling of crushes is applicable.

* This material is used by permission of the D. Appleton-Century Company.

The teacher should remain objective and unemotional, but at the same time friendly and sympathetic. She should never allow herself to be alone with the boy. Aside from the considerations already presented in the case of the girl with the crush, there is the wholly practical difficulty that if the teacher is caught in an emotional scene with a boy student she will undoubtedly lose her job. Finally, she should not attempt simply to crush the boy's feelings toward her, but should present him with a number of objective, normal ways in which he can work them off. In all probability the emotion will last for some period of time. During this period the boy is likely to write love letters, to waylay the teacher on her way to and from class, and to precipitate emotional scenes unless something is done to divert his modes of expression into more practical and less emotional lines. The writer recalls one high school boy who developed tremendous devotion to a Latin teacher. It happened the class was reading the fourth book of Caesar and had about reached the famous description of the bridge across the Rhine. The teacher seized upon this situation and asked the boy to build for her a really adequate model. He built a model about three feet long and completely correct in every detail. This work required the better part of his leisure time for nearly a month. By the time it was done he had recovered completely from his devotion, and nothing had happened to interfere with the establishment of normal relationships between the teacher and boy.

The school arouses emotion unnecessarily—through its administrative procedures, through discrimination of various sorts, through unfortunate discipline, through the personality of its teachers, and through undesirable emotional fixations. It also makes a large number of emotional problems for itself through its failure to adjust the curriculum to the needs of the pupils. The curriculum as it exists in most high schools today can be understood only when one realizes its historical development. It is composed partly of subjects left over from the former classical education, partly of subjects demanded for college entrance, partly of purely vocational subjects, and, to a very slight degree, of subjects with an immediate, intrinsic interest to adolescents. Moreover, many schools are inclined to fit the adolescent to the curriculum rather than the curriculum to the adolescent. As a result of all these circumstances, many boys and girls become emotionally distressed either over failure in their courses or their lack of interest. The high school could, if it wished to take the time and trouble, design a curriculum in which even the dullest pupils would find courses of interest with standards they could pass. More intelligent pupils, of course, would take different subject matter. Differences in interest could also be accommodated. It is mainly a matter of finding out what adolescents need and want and then taking care that the right child gets into the right course. There is to be a later chapter dealing with problems of the curriculum, so no further discussion will be given here; but it should be kept in mind that the school precipitates discontent, discouragement, feelings of failure, feelings of inferiority, and despair through the rigidity of its own requirements.

Provisions for outlets of the emotions.—A second contribution of the school to emotional stability is the provision of adequate outlets for such emotional situations as are inevitable during the adolescent period. It is an incontestable fact that a strong emotion will find some outlet, desirable or otherwise. If one avenue of expression is forbidden, another will be found. Simple suppression is never a permanent solution to any emotional problem; it may work for a while, but the final expression is likely to be the more violent because of the inhibition. The adolescent who becomes violently enraged because of some trivial happening in the schoolroom is usually not reacting to the single stimulus he has just received but is rather allowing pent-up feeling to burst out. It is better for all concerned if the school allows emotions to be expressed as they are generated by providing outlets that are unobjectionable in character and enter into school routine often enough so that a feeling which must, in the interests of others, be temporarily suppressed will soon be worked off. Such outlets are of various types.

Since emotions generate great nervous and muscular tension, anything that requires severe exertion acts as a relief. Games of all sorts give excellent opportunity to work off the pent-up feelings often generated during classes or at other periods during the day. It is not sufficient that a school provides only for the development of school teams. In fact, these are likely to cause more emotional upsets than they relieve because of the hard training, intense competition, and nervous strain involved. What is needed is exercise and recreation for everyone at regular intervals. If every pupil in a high school has some agreeable form of exercise during his last hour in school, he is automatically provided with an outlet of a socially accepted sort. Kicking a football is just as good as kicking a chair and much better than kicking the family cat. Sheer physical exertion uses up the extra supply of blood sugar with which the muscles are already well provided and allows them to relax again. Games may also act as compensatory activities for those pupils whose academic work is poor but whose athletic skills are superior. Unless undue competition enters into the situation, participation in active games is more likely to help than to harm.

Any kind of extracurricular activity may also function in the same way, even though little or no physical exertion is involved. For one thing, such developments distract the pupil's mind from worries, provided the activities are interesting to him and he does not find them too competitive or too difficult. One of the chief defects of the usual system in developing and maintaining extracurricular interests is that those pupils who need them most get them least and those who do not need them at all get the lion's share. As long as the pupils themselves control the situation the distribution is sure to be poor. The school can, however, exercise enough control over the situation to make sure that activities are distributed according to need. The best technique thus far developed seems to be to absorb the activities into the schoolwork by devoting certain periods each week to them. In such cases the various clubs all meet during school hours, but the pupils may choose which club they prefer to attend. If a boy has a lively interest in radios, for instance, he may be able to work off, during the time he spends with the radio club, the feelings of inferiority and discouragement he has developed earlier in the day because his English composition was unsatisfactory. Extracurricular activities will not automatically function as outlets for emotional stress, but they may be made to do so if they are correctly guided.

The human animal is extremely talkative. In fact, talking comes to be a substitute reaction to all kinds of situations; as already pointed out, talking is the chief substitute response to stimuli causing anger. Adequate opportunities for conversation are necessary as outlets for emotional strain. Talking between students and between teachers and students may act as opportunities for getting emotions expressed and out of everyone's system. Of the procedures already in existence in most high schools, the two that are most pertinent in this connection are the school assembly and the student government meetings. Both these assemblies can be utilized, as occasion demands, for the airing of emotional attitudes that have developed concerning some matter of general school interest. Instead of letting students argue among themselves and get themselves into all kinds of emotional jams, it is much better to call for a public discussion—in large groups or small, according to the situation.

If, for instance, the pupils generally regard the required reading in English as so much useless junk and are constantly fussing among themselves and to the teachers about the matter, they are generating considerable emotion to no very useful purpose. Such objections are based largely upon adolescent ignorance and prejudice, but the situation will not alter materially until better understanding is somehow brought about. In this particular instance, the English teachers should have a chance publicly to defend their choice of reading matter and the pupils to make their objections known. By means of sufficient talk back and forth the matter may get itself settled, and emotional strain will subside.

Finally, the school should provide plenty of opportunity for social adjustment—in the form of purely social meetings, dances, picnics, chances for groups to lunch together, and so on. Especially is there need for heterosexual social relations. The coeducational high school is particularly well equipped to promote normal development of sex interest and fixation. All that most young people need is a chance for plenty of association with each other under conditions that prevent, in so far as possible, the dangers of too great intimacy. School dances, bridge parties, and so on can serve as excellent outlets for emotional interests but they can also serve to precipitate more emotional stress than they relieve. In the first place, it is not sufficient by any means that the most socially inclined 25 per cent of the students should participate; these youngsters do not need social stimulation; they generate more than is good for them without any help from anyone. Unless everyone can participate, any social event is likely to bring into sharp relief all the discriminations and inabilities that exist in the school group. The unpopular boys and girls either shun the parties altogether or else hang around the edges, looking and feeling acutely miserable. It is these children who need the experience at social adaptation, but they will not get it unless the school steps in to modify adolescent loyalties to one's own clique and antagonism towards all other groups. The high school has the techniques already in existence for adequate social adjustment on the part of all its pupils. The point now is to utilize these techniques in such a way that they will relieve emotional strain instead of creating it.

Recognition of emotional disturbance.—People generally are rather inexpert in seeing signs of emotional disturbance. It is quite possible, however, for a school to insist upon having teachers who can recognize symptoms of emotional stress as these appear in the classroom. Partly, such ability is a matter of personal sensitivity on the part of the teacher; in so far as this is true, it cannot be taught. Partly, the ability is due to a type of training in which the common symptoms are explained. That is, a "course" in the appropriate subject matter will be of some assistance to any teacher and of great help to those who by nature or previous experience are already sensitive to human reactions. A school can at least insist that its teachers have a reasonable amount of training in the recognition of emotional peculiarities on the part of their students.

Quite recently the writer has had the opportunity to observe a teacher who was quite without such training and had relatively little natural aptitude in observation and diagnosis. This teacher believed she had in her room only one problem child. This pupil was reported as interfering constantly with class routine by talking, getting up from his seat, and general restlessness. Upon examination his condition turned out to be due to a light, chronic case of chorea, plus a general lack of discipline. He was therefore kept in bed for six weeks and upon his return to school placed in the room of another teacher whose discipline was notoriously strict. At the end of two weeks in her room, plus the relaxation from his long rest, he no longer presented any problem, during school hours at least.

EMOTIONAL DEVELOPMENTS

The teacher with whom he was originally placed showed her lack of insight, first, by assuming his behavior to be mere intentional mischievousness and, secondly, in assuming he was the only problem child in the room. Two others of much more serious character stood out like sore thumbs. One of them was a girl of markedly exhibitionistic tendencies. She was an intelligent child with a vigorous and dominating personality. Except for actual instructons, it was she and not the teacher who "ran" the room. She took full charge of all such routine details as passing out papers or collecting them, washing blackboards, cleaning erasers, passing out or collecting paints, and in addition took it upon herself to discipline and sometimes to instruct all the children on her side of the room. For a ten-year-old child she was an amazingly efficient individual and had made herself so useful that the teacher had not the faintest idea this girl was a problem child. Instead of arranging matters so the girl's exhibitionism would be discouraged, the teacher allowed the youngster to exhibit herself as the center of attention in the classroom twenty or thirty times a day. The child was already domineering, self-centered, conceited, and insufferably officious.

In a back corner of the room sat a small boy, under age for his grade but highly intelligent, whose only fault in the teacher's eyes was absent-mindedness. He was often found to be working on the wrong lesson and frequently failed to hear instructions. On several occasions he had gone home at the eleven o'clock recess under the impression that it was twelve o'clock and school was over. When his mother explained the situation to him, he always returned willingly to school. He apparently never noticed at such times that the other children remained on the playground, nor did he observe that the school traffic officers were not at their usual posts; in fact, this boy was wandering around in a fog most of the time. No child of nine has any business to be as absent-minded and full of irrelevant fantasies as this child showed himself to be. The teacher, however, rated him as a satisfactory pupil, her only complaint being that he sometimes did not pay attention to what he was doing. It would seem that a course dealing with emotional manifestations would enable a teacher to pick out two such obviously abnormal children as those just described. If schools insisted that its teachers be informed on such matters, there would be less emotional strain because teachers would observe the symptoms and make some effort at adjustment.

The teacher who would recognize emotional symptoms must first of all become adept at recognizing substitute responses. By the time children become adolescents they will no longer make obvious, direct, emotional responses unless intensely aroused, but will usually resort quite unconsciously to some kind of substitute mechanism that will permit them to avoid the emotional situation altogether. There are five of these substitute responses which appear so frequently the teacher should surely understand them.

When, for instance, a pupil has tried very hard to pass a course in English composition but finds he is failing, he is likely to resort to a convenient "projection" of the blame. He may say that his father is a foreigner and speaks little English at home, that his mother was always a poor speller and never liked to write compositions when she was in school, and that his older sister also had trouble with English. In this way, he can explain his own failure in terms of heredity and home environment, thus projecting the blame onto somebody else and relieving himself of the emotional discomfiture that comes when one feels oneself a failure. He no longer thinks he is to blame, he no longer makes any effort, and he thus avoids the emotional situation altogether.

Another frequent mechanism is called "compensation." It means simply that a pupil compensates for a poor showing in one matter by a good showing in another. A common example of this mechanism is seen in the pupil who is too small for athletic competition and too shy to be a social success, who therefore compensates by getting the best grades in class and receiving adulation as an academic prodigy. Actually, success in his studies may be only his third choice. His concentration upon academic work may serve further to alienate him from the social intercourse and physical exercise that he badly needs.[1] His compensation, however, makes him feel comfortable most of the time because he is no longer competing along lines in which he is a failure.

A third type of mechanism is called "sour grapes," the name being derived from the fable about the fox who could not reach the grapes he wanted and so comforted himself by developing the conviction they were too sour, anyway. The adolescent who states loudly that all fraternities and other secret organizations are worthless is probably displaying exactly the same mechanism. At an earlier time he has very likely wanted badly to be elected to such a society but failed to be among those chosen. It creates a most unpleasant emotional situation to desire membership in an organization to which one is not invited. In fact, if the emotion generated by such a situation continued for weeks the adolescent would become permanently crushed and defeated. Usually, however, this convenient sour-grapes point of view develops and the entire emotional problem disappears.

The fourth mechanism to be mentioned is the frequent and particularly universal daydreaming, shown by almost everyone from childhood on.[19] It is, however, more prominent during adolescence than at any other time. When one daydreams he turns his back upon reality and makes believe things are what they are not. The boy who has failed to get a prize he thought he had a chance for may be bitterly disappointed, but he can comfort himself to some extent by daydreams of himself receiving the same or another prize in the following year. If his daydreams are sufficiently clear, he may succeed in avoiding altogether his feeling of discouragement. While too much daydreaming is undoubtedly dangerous, a little is undoubtedly valuable.

Finally, there is the mechanism of "rationalization." A good rationalizer can think up a perfectly acceptable reason for doing any of the things he wants to do anyway, but for other reasons. If a girl feels she is unable to pass the college preparatory work in high school the chances are she will not admit the situation, but will produce some very plausible reasons why she would rather take some other course. Perhaps she says her friends are taking other subjects, or she believes another course of study will lead to greater financial returns, or she regards other lines of work as more interesting and modern—indeed, any reason may be given except her real conviction that only failure awaits her in the college preparatory course.

All these mechanisms have their value because they permit an individual to get rid of his emotional reactions towards situations about which he can do nothing. When used occasionally their effect is beneficial rather than otherwise. Their extreme use, however, indicates the existence of some unsolved emotional problem that the adolescent cannot face and is consequently running away from. All these mechanisms permit an individual to escape reality; it is not advisable that people do this all the time. Thus, the pupil who always projects the blame for everything onto something or someone else and never admits the blame on his own part is showing symptoms of constant emotional strain from which he is trying to escape by projection. The pupil is running away from something he cannot face and from something that must sooner or later be faced and overcome in some more rational fashion if he is to become a normal individual. An overindulgence in these mechanisms should be a danger sign to any teacher.

In addition to the mechanisms just described, pupils show other signs of emotional difficulty. Two extremes of behavior were described in the examples given above—the exhibitionistic type of response and the withdrawal behavior. These two types of behavior, which can be observed in any classroom, are probably two alternative types of reaction which may be made to the same kind of problem. The difference between two pupils, one an exhibitionist and one an introvert, is perhaps only one of vitality. If a person of vigorous health and dominating personality finds himself incapable of doing something he wants to do he is more likely to become an exhibitionist than an introvert. The exhibitionist is trying very hard to convince both himself and everyone else that he is adequate to any situation. The more intensely he feels he is not adequate, the harder he tries to make everyone think he is. Exhibitionism is usually the result of insecurity and inefficiency of some sort. It is the type of behavior that teachers should learn to recognize in its true significance.

The introvert, who withdraws from reality and lives in a world of fantasy, is showing another type of reaction to some central problem of insecurity or inability. Unlike the exhibitionist, he is usually a person of relatively low vitality and relatively weak personality. During his childhood years he has learned that he cannot impress himself as much as he would like upon other children, so he has simply stopped trying. He has withdrawn, in so far as he can, from social contacts with others and is making no effort at adjustment of his central emotional problem. There is no other type of pupil so likely to be overlooked by the average teacher. Introverts are not disciplinary problems, except for their occasional absent-mindedness. They are quite content to sit quietly and do their work as unostentatiously as possible. Usually the teacher is only too willing to have in her room one child who never makes any trouble, so

EMOTIONAL DEVELOPMENTS

she leaves the introvert alone and lets him continue his withdrawal behavior which will, if unchecked, eventually prevent him from a normal adult existence.

Finally there is the defiant, destructive type of response. A pupil showing such behavior is never overlooked, but the source of his difficulties is frequently not realized. After the attitude of defiance becomes fixed, there is great difficulty in overcoming it; any minor incident is sufficient to push the student into undesirable action. In the beginning, however, there was an adequate reason for the behavior. The time to investigate is at the appearance of the very first defiant response. This sort of behavior is, like exhibitionism, usually the response of a vigorous but inferior individual to an environment to which he cannot adjust normally. Defiance of authority is one form of outlet for emotional stress. Even though it often precipitates the individual into other troubles, it does relieve strain for the time being.

The high school teacher should learn to recognize the symptoms of emotional stress. They are danger signals. Wholly aside from general humanitarian considerations, recognition is essential because emotions are hindrances to learning. No pupil can master usages in English composition, operations in algebra, or irregular verbs in French if he is in a stirred-up emotional state. If a teacher wants her students to learn, she should avoid arousing their emotions by her own procedures, she should assist in the direction of such activities as help "work off" any emotional stress in an acceptable way, and she should be ever alert to symptoms of emotional stress.

One final caution seems desirable. The teacher should be especially careful not to confuse emotional with nervous symptoms. The child who is nervous and restless is not necessarily emotional at all. The fundamental trouble with many children whom the teacher regards as emotional problems is that they are too tensely nervous to sit still long. They need, chiefly, less vigorous exercise, more sleep, better balanced diet, and less intense competition. That is, their troubles are primarily physical, not emotional. They quickly become keyed-up and excited over anything that demands an alert mind, keen attention, and tense muscles. After the exertion or competition is over, they cannot relax. Such children often have no emotional problems, although they create disciplinary crises with considerable frequency. In a few individual cases of this type the author has succeeded in eliminating completely these disciplinary difficulties by having these children lie down in a room by themselves for an hour every morning and a half-hour every afternoon, by giving them one really good meal in the school lunchroom, and by exempting them from all competitive games, whether physical or intellectual. Usually a month of this treatment eliminates the restlessness and overexcited behavior that push these nervous children into difficulties. Nervousness is serious—but it is not synonymous with emotionality.

Instruction concerning the emotions.—A high school can and should teach adolescents about emotional phenomena. Pupils are old enough to understand the main facts, and certainly no information could be of greater practical, immediate usefulness. Presumably a course designated as "Mental Hygiene" would be the appropriate place for presentation of such information. In a later chapter a required course of this type is discussed and recommended, so no details will be given here. It is the school's duty to give its students scientific information in regard to emotional life. Adolescents need it so badly they will get it somehow, but they all too often have to depend upon quacks and pseudopsychologists for help. As matters now stand in the ordinary high school, any reference to emotional problems comes incidentally into class discussions or private interviews with teachers. Neither of these arrangements is satisfactory. Instruction concerning such important matters as emotional development and control should never be left to chance.

ILLUSTRATIVE CASE STUDIES

Stories of actual individuals have the advantage of being more interesting and more easily remembered than a general discussion. There will, therefore, be a generous use of such illustrative material. The studies below illustrate (a) emotional immaturity, (b) sexual maladjustments, (c) fear reactions, (d) the effects of sarcasm, (e) the characteristics of daydream-

EMOTIONAL DEVELOPMENTS

ing, and (f) the mechanism of projection. While reading the episodes described, one should try not only to get an understanding of adolescent emotions but also to analyze these samples to see what stimuli and responses can be found. These samples have been made brief in order to include as many types as possible. With a little thought any experienced teacher can supply from her own experience many instances of adolescent emotional storms.

Eugene [18] at the age of eighteen years was regarded by all his high school teachers as the most immature boy in the senior class.

Instances of his immaturity were cited as follows: His schoolwork was of a low grade; his interests seemed to be characteristic of younger boys in that he was still actively interested in the scouts and wore his scout uniform to school; he made few friends among the boys in his class and was seen about much of the time alone; and he seemed immature in his lack of emotional control. He had, for example, cried and begged the principal not to report some minor school delinquency to his mother, and he was given to violent outbursts of temper, demonstrated on one occasion by his picking up a chair and smashing his radio after hearing of a last minute touchdown in a tie football game.

Although Eugene had at times sold various products for premiums, he had not even made a gesture toward earning money after school hours. He excused his indolence on the grounds that he was unable to find the kind of job he wanted. He kept the yard and automobile clean, and occasionally helped with the dishes or making the beds, but there was no indication that he took any initiative or thought of assuming any responsibility.

Although this boy's mental equipment was rated as low average, it would appear that his activities, his choice of companions, his taste in books (he greatly enjoyed his small collection of boy scout and adventure books characteristic of the reading taste of the twelve-to-fourteen-year-old), and his general attitude toward life were on a level far below even his mental age. Fully conscious of the disparity between what was expected of him and what he was doing, he played aimlessly about without any plan of life—unhappy and needlessly inefficient.

Possibly Eugene got a bad start in making the adjustment from rural to city life, for it sometimes seemed as if he were pining away for his earlier environment. Again, his trouble may have been due in part to too much mothering and the lack of contact with someone more resourceful in introducing disciplinary methods. It is certain that his immaturity was not really due to an intellectual limitation but to the fact that he was finding, on a low level, certain satisfactions for which he would have had to struggle if he had tried to meet life on a level in keeping with his years.*

Elaine was a thirty-two-year-old woman. She had been the youngest of three sisters. Her father died soon after her birth. The mother and the three girls then went to live with an aunt who was a missionary in India. At the mission there were two other white women, but no men. The girls were not allowed to play with native children. When Elaine was fifteen she was sent to a boarding school in an Eastern state. The rules there were strict; she saw no boys; she spent her vacations at the school with two or three other equally isolated girls. After two years she entered a women's college. At both boarding school and college she was conspicuous for her crushes. At one time she fell in love with her history teacher, spent several entire nights sitting outside the woman's door, dogged her footsteps in the daytime, wrote her letters, talked of her continually until the other girls became too bored to listen. This affair lasted about six weeks, during which she lost over fifteen pounds. Later, she developed an equally intensive crush on a senior girl; in this case the feeling was mutual. The two girls were not allowed to room together, but they managed to spend the entire twenty-four hours of almost every day with each other. After graduating, Elaine returned to her alma mater as an assistant. Several other crushes occurred. Finally, at the age of twenty-nine, she decided to get a Ph.D. and matriculated at a large state university.

There are few women majors in physics (her department) so she was, for the first time in her life, in classes with men. At first she treated them with utter scorn. Two or three advances toward girls and women failed dismally. She was thrown more and more with men associates. During her second graduate year a marked change took place and she became boy-crazy in the silliest possible fashion. She chased every man in the department, had two rather scandalous affairs, stayed out nights with men, and generally made a perfect fool of herself. Her behavior closely paralleled that of a thirteen-year-old girl who has suddenly discovered that boys are nice instead of mean. But Elaine was too old for supervision by the time she reached the same stage. As the third year of her graduate work came along she began to realize she could never get a personal recommendation from the professors

* This case study is presented through the permission of the D. Appleton-Century Company.

EMOTIONAL DEVELOPMENTS

in her department. She developed spasms of weeping and complaining; for months she was an utter nuisance because she insisted upon telling all her troubles every day to everyone. All kinds of minor hysterical symptoms developed. Then a new young man enrolled in the physics department to get an M.A. He was several years younger than Elaine, inexperienced, fresh from a small denominational college in a rural community. Elaine fastened upon him with avidity. There was a whirlwind love affair, followed by their elopement. After her marriage Elaine settled down, had two children, and is still happily married.

This woman remained in a homosexual stage of development, probably through environmental influences, until she was twenty-nine. Then she passed, in three years, through the early period of mixed scorn and attraction toward men and boys, through the boy-crazy phase, through a flowering of romantic love, and into a final adult adjustment. All the early stages should have taken place before she left high school, while she was still under home and school supervision. A woman of thirty-one who makes eyes at every man she sees is as retarded in her emotional growth as a high school senior who still plays with dolls.

Donald is a boy of seventeen. During the past year he has developed a fear of riding in any auto unless he is driving it. The source of this obsession is not altogether clear but probably comes from an earlier claustrophobia which has been revived by several experiences of being packed into a Ford coupé with four or five others. Donald will go through the most extraordinary maneuvers to keep from riding with anyone else. Neither his friends nor his family know about the matter, for he has always been able to rationalize every situation and has never been forced to admit the truth. However, the fear is affecting his entire social life. Other boys think he is selfish with his car because he will not let them drive it. The girl he likes best has her own car and often quarrels with him because he insists on using his. Recently they had a terrific row: she had, with considerable effort, arranged to borrow her father's shiny new car for a school dance, under the restriction that no one but herself should drive it. When Donald appeared to escort her, she sprung her surprise on him; he refused to go to the dance in any car but his own ancient Ford. In the end, she called up another boy and went with him. Donald has several times been forced by his fear to withdraw suddenly from some picnic, party, or date because he foresaw the necessity of riding with others. This obsession is undermining and disorganizing Donald's entire life. In his social group, refusal to go in another person's car is a deadly insult. Donald is nervous, restless, worried, apprehensive; he knows his social prestige is rapidly slipping and he never knows from one moment to the next when he will be precipitated into the catastrophic situation of admitting the truth. In the meantime, he cannot sleep, eat, study, or relax.

In a certain school there was a Latin teacher, Miss B, whose reputation for biting sarcasm was well known. Miss B was, herself, an unhappy, unadjusted individual who found emotional release in abusing her students. The writer was in one of Miss B's classes. Beside her sat a girl named Josephine who was poor in translation and incredibly bad in Latin composition. Miss B was not long in signaling out Jo as a victim. One day she stood Jo up on the platform in the front of the room and fired at her exactly one hundred questions on grammar, marking on the blackboard the correctness or incorrectness of each answer. Jo lasted through the first ten questions, even getting three of them right, but then she began to disintegrate. She guessed wildly, she sobbed, she begged to be released, but Miss B was showing her power and would not excuse the girl. At the end of one hundred questions, Jo's score stood at 4 to 96. The remaining few minutes of the hour was spent in scolding Jo for her bad showing, fuming at the low level of preparation, and threatening the rest of the class with similar searching examinations. By the end of the hour everyone was alternately chilled with horror and bursting with fury. That afternoon and night several girls took turns sitting with Jo and keeping her from killing herself. For a week Jo would not attend class. Eventually the writer worked out a signaling system by which she could tell Jo the answers. In the meantime, no one else had been grilled, although there had been a few tirades. A month passed during which Jo had to be almost carried into class. She was in an agony of fear; she shivered every moment; her teeth chattered; if called on, she could not make a sound even when she could remember what the signal meant.

All the girls tried to distract Miss B's attention from Jo, but everyone knew the teacher would eventually concentrate again on her victim. Preparations were accordingly made. One girl who knew shorthand came daily with a stenographer's book under her arm; in this she took down the worst of the sarcasm verbatim. Pupils in Miss B's other classes had been approached; there had been two or three general indignation meetings. Then came the day that Miss B again chased Jo onto the platform and again threw one hundred questions at her. The stenographer's book flapped open and her pencil flashed across the page. With her friends'

EMOTIONAL DEVELOPMENTS

moral support, Jo stammered answers to about forty questions before dissolving in tears. Miss B commanded her to continue, but Jo wearily returned to her seat. This action started some magnificent verbal fireworks, that were also recorded. The period ended with a short lecture on the class's general ignorance and a severe scolding for everyone. The stenographer at once typed her notes, making several carbons, and all members of the class signed each copy—putting her name under a solemnly worded oath as to the truth of the account. The copies were sent to various school officials. Then all students in Miss B's classes went out on strike.

The strike caused great excitement. All other classes were poorly attended because the students could not tear themselves away from impromptu meetings and discussions. Various extroverts got up and made speeches; the failing students in Miss B's classes blamed their troubles on her. Half the faculty was in sympathy with the strikers. Emotion ran high on all sides. The affair lasted only two days and was then wisely settled. The girls returned to Miss B's classes—an appropriate requirement, since students should never be allowed to "hold up" the administration and faculty—but the Latin Department promised there would always be one of them in the room during every class period. Under this guard, the semester's work was finished. When classes convened for the second semester, Miss B had disappeared.

Mildred had been a roly-poly girl up until the age of thirteen, when she suddenly began a growth spurt that ended at sixteen, leaving her a tall, rangy, slender, awkward adolescent. She was unhappy, tired easily, felt herself conspicuous, and refused to continue the social life that had been hers during her childhood. Her low vitality led her to sit around, or read, or bask in the sunshine. This new scheme of things was far from satisfactory. She recalled good times she had had, envied other girls who were not plagued by self-consciousness, and imagined various episodes of more exciting character than her daily life. Her parents tried to laugh her out of her condition and her brothers teased her unmercifully. As a reaction, Mildred indulged in many daydreams of being sick, injured, or dead, with her entire family weeping from shame at their earlier treatment of her. She imagined herself stoically enduring years of hardship, and would sit and cry for an hour at a time in self-pity. Other daydreams dealt with situations in which she was an admired heroine. She would rescue someone from drowning or burning to death; then she would show her real nobility by refusing the Carnegie medal. She would win the school essay prize and then, at commencement, turn it over to the runner-up who was supposedly dying of a broken heart from her failure to get the prize. Such daydreams persisted until other girls and boys had grown up to Mildred's size; she became well co-ordinated, her family stopped teasing her, and she became too busy and too satisfied with school and clubs to have time or desire for daydreams.

Dick's chief and fundamental trouble [18] was due to the fact that he had been the center of attention in a large family circle for a period of nearly fifteen years. Three sets of grandparents, a mother and a father, and two older sisters made up an appreciative audience which was difficult to resist. In spite of this handicap, however, he had done better than might naturally have been expected. Although somewhat critical of others, he was a likable chap and made friends easily. He was especially considerate of those who were socially inferior and in no way competing with him, but he was rather inclined to deprecate the value of those who were his equals or superiors. He rode well, played a good game of tennis and golf, and always considered himself particularly efficient at baseball.

During his first year at boarding school, he got on with indifferent success. He had few close friends, and many of those with whom he made contact looked upon him as being stuck-up. His scholastic work was passable but inferior to what one had reason to expect of a boy of his intellectual equipment. It was later gathered from talking with his parents that he was simply hanging on till the baseball season opened so that he could demonstrate to the school that he was a regular fellow and that he had been misunderstood and underrated. This was the general theme of his conversation with the various members of his family when he was at home for Easter.

When the baseball season actually opened, he started out enthusiastically to demonstrate his superior ability in this particular field but he found competition keener than he had expected. He had made no allowance for the fact that the older boys would be given preference over the new ones and he soon began to talk about not getting a square deal. This attitude of mind did not improve his achievement on the baseball field, and it was not long before he was being called down by the coach and razzed by the other boys for not doing his best.

While he was in this state of mind he was accidentally hit in the head by a pitched ball during a practice game. It appeared to be nothing more than a glancing blow at the time. He was not unconscious, but it was thought wise to send him to the infirmary, where he was carefully examined immediately by the school physician and, that same night, by a neurologist as he had begun to complain of loss of vision. The neurological and x-ray examinations revealed nothing to account for his symptoms.

Two or three days later he was visited by the psychiatrist, who, in the meantime, had acquired from the family, the principal of the school, and two of his masters a fairly complete history of the boy and his general reactions to life. Being assured by a previous medical examination that the loss of vision was not due to injury or disease, the psychiatrist was able to determine that this boy's handicap was serving a very definite purpose in his life—that is, getting him much attention and sympathy on the one hand, and, on the other hand, keeping him out of what had unconsciously developed in his mind as being an intolerable situation—namely, meeting competition on the baseball field.*

BIBLIOGRAPHY †

1. Beck, A. G., "School Success as a Withdrawal Mechanism in Two Adolescents," *Journal of Abnormal and Social Psychology*, 1934, 29: 87-94.
2. Brown, F., "The Nature of Emotion and Its Relation to Anti-Social Behavior," *Journal of Abnormal and Social Psychology*, 1934, 28: 446-458.
3. Cannon, W. B., *Bodily Changes in Pain, Hunger, Fear, and Rage*, D. Appleton-Century Company, 1915, 404 pp.
4. Cason, H., "Common Annoyances," *Psychology Monographs*, Vol. 40, No. 182, 218 pp.
5. Dejean, R., *L'Émotion*, Alcan, Paris, 1933, 261 pp.
6. Furfey, P. H., "A Revised Scale for Measuring Developmental Age in Boys," *Child Development*, 1931, Vol. 2, No. 2.
7. ———, "Developmental Age," *Catholic Educational Review*, 1930, 28: 550-553.
8. Gates, G. S., "An Observational Study of Anger," *Journal of Experimental Psychology*, 1926, 9: 325-336.
9. Hesnard, A., *Strange Lust: the Psychology of Homosexuality* (Translated by J. C. Summers), Amethnol Press, 1933, 256 pp.

* This case study is used by permission of the D. Appleton-Century Company.
† See also the references in the Appendix.

10. Hurlock, E. B., and Klein, E. R., "Adolescent 'Crushes,'" *Child Development*, 1934, 5:63-80.
11. Landis, C., "Emotions: The Expressions of Emotion," in *A Handbook of General Experimental Psychology*, Clark University Press, 1934, pp. 312-351.
12. Meltzer, H., "Students' Adjustments in Anger," *Journal of Social Psychology*, 1933, 4:285-309.
13. Mudge, E. L., *Varieties of Adolescent Experience*, D. Appleton-Century Company, 1926, 134 pp.
14. Pressey, S. L., and Pressey, L. C., "Development of the Interest-Attitude Tests," *Journal of Applied Psychology*, 1933, 17:1-16.
15. Pringle, R. W., *The Psychology of High School Discipline*, D. C. Heath, 1931, 362 pp.
16. Richardson, R. F., *The Psychology and Pedagogy of Anger*, Warwick & York, 1918, 100 pp.
17. Ricketts, A. F., "A Study of the Behavior of Young Children in Anger," *University of Iowa Studies in Child Welfare*, 1934, 9:159-171.
18. Thom, D. A., *Normal Youth and Its Everyday Problems*, D. Appleton-Century Company, 1932, 361 pp.
19. Varendonck, J., *The Psychology of Day-Dreams*, The Macmillan Company, 1921, 367 pp.
20. Watson, J. B., *Psychology from the Standpoint of the Behaviorist*, J. B. Lippincott Company, 1929, 458 pp.

CHAPTER IV

SOCIAL DEVELOPMENTS OF NORMAL ADOLESCENCE

THE adolescent years are, pre-eminently, a period of social development and adjustment. During the preceding years of childhood there have been, to be sure, a beginning of socialization and some acquisition of fundamental social skills. The elementary school child learns how to get along with others of his own age and sex in such social situations as arise during his schoolwork or his play outside of school. He also develops some reasonable relationship between himself and his parents or teachers. It is quite necessary that these childish adjustments take place, since they serve as a basis for the more complete development of the adolescent years. The boy or girl who enters adolescence without being adjusted to the give-and-take of childhood is seriously handicapped. The social development of children is, however, limited both by their immature mentality and their inattention to many social stimuli.

With the oncoming of adolescence, the boy or girl becomes acutely aware of social pressures and relationships. There is no period of life during which the awareness of other people's opinions and attitudes is so keen. It is this sensitivity that leads the adolescent into the abject conformity characteristic of the period. Any deviation in dress or manners from the mode of the group is actually painful. The boy or girl must have the same kind of clothes, must use the same slang expressions, must do the same things in the same way, must study the same subjects in school, and must enjoy the same forms of amusements as his or her friends, or else there is great emotional strain. The adolescent is all too acutely aware of every possible social stimulus. As he grows older, he learns to react to some situations but not to others and consequently achieves a greater peace of mind. But during the early years of adolescence he rarely does or says anything without first considering the probable reaction of his group to his behavior. It is therefore essential that the teacher should realize the strength of these social drives.

In the present chapter there will be two main sections: The first deals with the spontaneous, unorganized social life of adolescent boys and girls, while the second is concerned with organized activities, such as clubs or games, by means of which the social drives of adolescence may find expression.*

SPONTANEOUS SOCIAL LIFE DURING ADOLESCENCE

In the relationships and activities to be described in this section, adults have practically no part. Indeed, they should not attempt to dominate the situation; if they do, they succeed only in alienating the affection and respect of the adolescents involved. Boys and girls of this age consider the selection of their own friends and leaders as their inalienable right. If parents and teachers would regard the period of early adolescence as a time for experiments in social relationships—while girls and boys are too young to make many irreparable mistakes—there would be less friction between the generations and an earlier maturity on the part of the adolescents.

Friendships.—Adolescent boys and girls insist upon choosing their own friends and are inclined to resent rather than follow adult guidance in the matter, unless the guidance is tactfully camouflaged. A child rarely persists in a friendship that meets with parental opposition; even if he does not understand the source of his parents' objections, he is afraid some vague, dreadful fate may overtake him if he continues on friendly terms with the prohibited child. This mixture of submission to parental authority and fear of consequences will no longer work

---

* Data concerning measurement of social attitudes has been included in the next chapter which presents the results of measurement for social, moral, and religious attitudes. Since a topic that is regarded by some people as religious may be regarded by others as social or ethical, it seemed best to keep reports of measurement in these three fields together.

when the child has become an adolescent. He considers himself old enough to select his own friends and mature enough to select them wisely. Of course, he does not choose wisely in all instances, but he can learn to make wise choices only by making *some* kind of a choice. He will never learn as long as his parents do his choosing for him. Normally, however, the adolescent's feeling of independence leads him to assert himself. Naturally, all adolescents make a number of undesirable friends, because of their inexperience in judging people. Their errors in estimating others are due chiefly to an overemphasis on externals. Even highly intelligent boys and girls will become for a time close friends with some relatively stupid child who wears nice clothes, has a nice appearance and a conventional line of chatter. Usually such associations do no particular harm and the adolescent eventually makes friends more like himself. When a boy or girl has developed an attachment with some undesirable adolescent, the parents would do well to regard this friendship as so much training in estimating character. If there is reasonable supervision, the adolescent will learn something about judging people and will not make that particular mistake again.

The small, pretty, empty-headed adolescent girl of every generation has caused altogether too much anxiety among the mothers of intelligent adolescent boys. Such attachments do not last long and represent a normal phase of masculine development. An adolescent boy is none too sure of himself at best and is usually acutely aware of his social handicaps. He cannot converse on equal terms with an adult, and he is rather fearful of attempting conversation with an intelligent girl of his own age; but the empty-headed little girl will give him the admiration he gets from nobody else. At least he is brighter than she is, and he takes great satisfaction in her adoration of his not especially remarkable exploits. As he gets older and becomes surer of himself, he will feel the need for feminine acquaintances who are more intelligent and less effusive.

There is one good rule to follow in dealing with the undesirable friendship formed sooner or later by practically all adolescents, and that is to invite the undesirable friend *as often as possible* to the adolescent's own home. Whatever the deficiencies in the guest, they are likely to stand out in high relief against the family background; even an infatuated boy or girl can see them. It may be taken for granted that the adolescent will see his or her friends somewhere. All the parents can do is to determine the place of meeting. The least desirable spots are public places of any kind where there is no stable background and no supervision. If the undesirable member of a pair of friends invites the other to his or her own home, the situation more often than not plays into the hands of the less favored person. If parents are willing to conceal their own aversion and to welcome into their home any friend their child wishes to bring, they will retain control of the situation and nothing serious will happen. It is only a question of time before their boy or girl discovers the crudities or other undesirable traits of the acquaintance and will terminate the friendship of their own accord.

There have been various studies made in an effort to determine which adolescents in a school are likely to become friends with each other. When an individual enters a new social group, numbering perhaps two hundred children of his own age, he will not distribute his affections equally among all of them but will select two or three as his most intimate friends. The bases on which his judgments are made are not particularly clear, except in their general outline. Close friendships usually develop between adolescents who have in common similar social and economic backgrounds and similar intellectual and nonintellectual interests.[9] There may be, however, in a school fifty adolescents who are potential chums of any given boy, in so far as these criteria are concerned; and yet he develops real friendship with not more than a few of the total number who seem, from any external point of view, equally appropriate. What is known about childish and adolescent friendships indicates much more clearly why certain children do not become friends than why certain other children do. Much more study of individual friendships is needed before one can state with any certainty what the reasons are for the growth of intimate personal relations between any two persons.

Normally, boys and girls develop friendships with each

other during this period. Sometimes the transfer from preadolescent friendships with members of one's own sex to the heterosexual interests of adolescence takes place gradually and easily. At other times the transfer is sudden and bewildering. A girl starts out after lunch to spend the afternoon with two other girls, meets some boy whom she has known—and treated with utter scorn—for years, and finds herself to her own amazement talking with him till suppertime. Such abrupt changes of interest are extremely trying, especially because they are sure to meet with ridicule from the previous intimates of one's own sex. The wise parent should not only refrain from comment or opposition, but should be thankful the transfer has occurred. Whether sudden or gradual, the boy-and-girl friendships of adolescence are essential to normal adjustment. Nothing that results from them could possibly be as serious as their failure to develop.[24]

Aside from the emotional maturity reflected by the interest of boys and girls in each other, these friendships serve a practical purpose. They give experience in courtship and provide the basis for subsequent ideals of mating and marriage. If a girl is "protected" from such youthful love affairs she is likely in later years to think herself in love with the first man who courts her. It is very difficult for young men or women who are too old for any parental supervision to think clearly about each other if they are intoxicated by their very first experiences in love-making. If they have already had a few attacks of puppy love they know how to discount mere excitement. Far from being dangerous, the somewhat sentimental boy-and-girl attachments are highly educative at the time and are essential for self-protection in the years after home supervision has been left behind.

It goes almost without saying that girls and boys will make some undesirable heterosexual attachments. No adolescent is mature enough to display much wisdom at first. Parental interference will merely precipitate clandestine meetings or an elopement. The only thing for parents or teachers to do is to provide a safe meeting place and then go away. The infatuation will soon wear itself out. The less fastidious of the two youngsters is certain to shock and revolt the other long before any harm is done. An adolescent who has had one such experience becomes wary about beginning another friendship of doubtful character. Parents or teachers may deplore such episodes, but human nature is not so arranged that one can learn without practice. Life cannot be lived in a vacuum.

The "crowd."—When the mother of an adolescent boy or girl asks her child where he or she is going, the answer is likely to be "just out with the crowd." A few years earlier the reply is "just out with the gang." From the adult point of view the "gang" and the "crowd" may be more or less synonymous, but the adolescent uses the terms to denote somewhat different groups. The gang is typically a spontaneous social unit of late childhood. Its members are of the same sex, and it is relatively small. The activities of a gang are, of course, influenced by the outlets provided in a given neighborhood, but its general objective is to seek adventure and excitement.[6] The crowd, on the other hand, is typically composed of both boys and girls, usually an equal number of each, and its unconscious objective is the establishment of normal social relationships between the two sexes. It differs from the gang in three respects: it contains both boys and girls, it is usually larger, and its objectives are not the same.

In successive classes in the psychology of adolescence, the writer has asked for written information from students in regard to the crowd they went with in their high school days. Questions were asked about the size of the group, its personnel, its activities, and its value. The facts below are based upon such reports from about four hundred students. The median number of adolescents belonging to such a crowd was eight, with the size varying all the way from four to twenty. The distribution of boys and girls was exactly equal in about 70 per cent of the cases and would have been in most of the remaining cases had an equal number of acceptable adolescents of both sexes been available. The activities of these crowds are very difficult to list, far more so than the activities of a gang. Aside from a few definite social functions, such as dances or parties, the crowd seems to do practically nothing. In the summer it sits around on someone's piazza, with occasional excursions to the neighborhood drugstore. In the winter it sits around in someone's house, plays the radio, and makes raids on the icebox. None of this comes under the heading of adventure as seen through the eyes of late childhood, but it is apparently exciting for the adolescent. It is adventure, not into the world of things but into the world of social relationships. An adult listening to the conversation of such a crowd for an evening has to admit the conversation has been about practically nothing. It does not seem to start anywhere, to go anywhere, or to be about anything. It is, however, highly satisfactory to the participants. It obviously gives them an opportunity to develop their conversational powers on other people whose abilities are no better than their own. They also achieve through these conversations some experience in judging people, although the judgments of the group as a whole are usually superficial.

The values obtained from such a crowd were listed as follows: experience in getting along with other people, experience in social skills, development of loyalty to a group, practice in judging people, and experience in love-making under circumstances in which the participants are protected from serious consequences. The only negative training mentioned was the development of antagonism toward all other crowds than that to which the individual belonged. For the most part, then, the crowd is a socially valuable unit of adolescent society and probably does more to bring about normal social growth than teachers and parents combined.

It is impossible to give any general rules for the way in which such social groupings take place, but it is possible to understand any given social grouping if one only knows enough about the individuals concerned. There are good reasons why a particular boy or girl is included in some adolescent crowd, while another particular boy or girl is excluded. These reasons, however, are probably quite different from those which result in the inclusion or exclusion of any other two adolescents. Because of this specificity of causes it seems desirable to give an actual example in which the reasons for inclusion or exclusion are known and can be demonstrated.

In a certain district of about a dozen blocks in a small city there lived a total of sixteen boys or girls between the ages of sixteen and nineteen. This particular example is taken from conditions before adolescents had automobiles; it therefore involves a relatively small amount of territory in the community. The intimate friendships among adolescents until recent years were necessarily limited to those who lived within a reasonable distance of each other. In this small city these boys and girls went to and from school and to and from one another's houses on foot. Those living outside the area shown on the accompanying map were therefore automatically excluded, except on very special occasions.

The center of the group was a pair of twin boys, numbered 1 and 2 on the map, and their sister, Girl A. These three children were members of a large and jolly family who lived in a huge rambling house where hospitality was always extended to anyone the children brought home. This family had the further advantage of living within two blocks of the high school. Moreover, the parents of this family were people of both money and judgment. They had fixed up the lower floor of the house with various kinds of equipment for the amusement of children and adolescents and had practically turned these rooms over to the "crowd." This house naturally became the headquarters of the group to which the three adolescent members of the household belonged.

For the remaining girls of the neighborhood, inclusion in or exclusion from the crowd was determined by the following reasons: Girl B had been a member of the childhood group out of which the crowd developed, but she had married when not quite seventeen. Although she still lived only a block away from the headquarters, she was excluded partly by her own interests and partly because the other members of the crowd did not like her husband, who was a man about ten years older than herself. Girl C, who lived directly across from the school and near the meeting place of the group, was excluded as completely as if iron bars had intervened between her and the others. She had "gone into society." Her family was wealthy and Girl C had "come out" as a debutante before she was seventeen. Thereafter she was caught up in a whirl of social activities in which the group as a whole could not take part. Although they may secretly have been envious, the group members protected themselves by developing the utmost derision for Girl C's social prominence; they laughed at her picture in the social columns of the Sunday paper and they credited her with snobbishness, whether she possessed it or not. It was a case of "thumbs down" as far as Girl C was concerned. Girl D was sometimes included in the crowd and sometimes not, depending upon

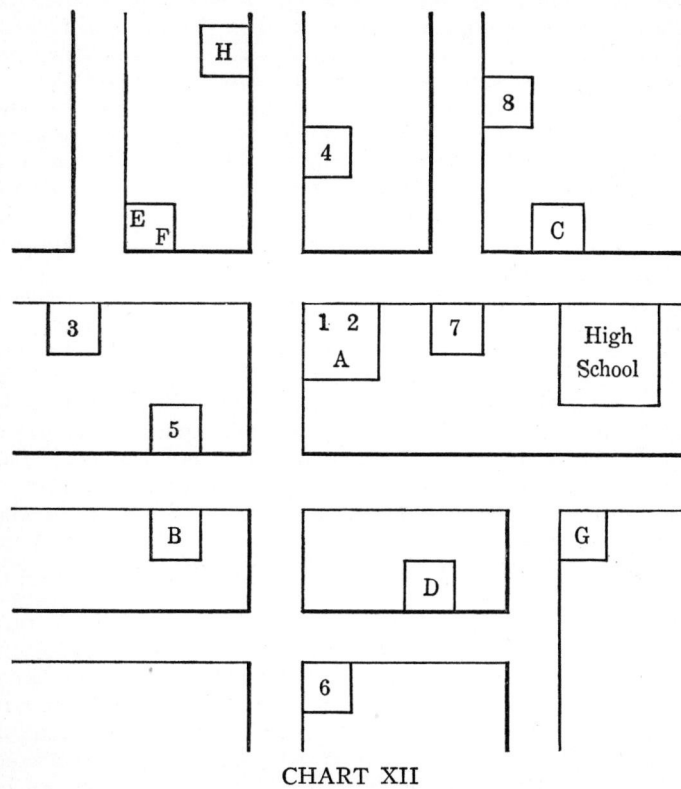

CHART XII
PLAN OF A NEIGHBORHOOD

how many girls were needed to go around. She, Girl F, and Girl I took turns as the fourth girl in the central nucleus of the crowd, although sometimes all three were included when a larger group was felt desirable. The objection to Girl D was her interest in religion. She had become converted and insisted upon talking about the evil ways of the world unless one could distract her attention from this engrossing topic. When she forgot about religion for a few minutes, she was an acceptable member of the crowd; but, although she rarely tried to impose her ideas upon the group as a whole, she showed a tendency to revert to religion as soon as she was paired off with some boy. While the girls had little objection to her, the boys had. Girls E and F were sisters. Girl E, the girl friend of one of the twin boys, was a regular member of the crowd. She was an attractive, well-dressed, wholesome girl who fitted well into the social group. Her sister, Girl F, however, was homely, studious, and not very lively company. It is probable that Girl F was seriously maladjusted and had turned to academic pursuits to compensate for the social inferiority she felt towards her sister. Girl F was, however, sometimes brought into the group when there were not otherwise girls enough. She understood her position and while she resented it she was more or less forced to accept it if she were going to have any social contacts in the neighborhood. Girl G was rather stupid, but she was a cute little child and the girl friend of the other twin. She came from a slightly lower social group than most of the others but had picked up the social manners and customs of the crowd and was one of its regular members. Girl H had been a close friend in the earlier years of adolescence, but when about sixteen she had become utterly boy-crazy and had amassed an imposing collection of dirty stories which she insisted upon telling. The boys were frankly embarrassed by her. To be sure, they occasionally went out with her alone, but they did not usually want her around with the rest of the crowd.

The boys in turn were included or excluded as follows: Numbers 1 and 2, the twins, were in the center of the group. Number 3, although living near, participated only rarely because he went to a private school. Although away during the week, he was at home week ends and therefore could have taken part in many activities; but he did not have the same things to talk about as the other adolescents, since his entire school life was different from theirs. Moreover, this private school was the chief football rival of the high school, and he fell heir to a certain amount of antagonism for which he was not in the least to blame. Although the members of the crowd often invited him individually to their homes, the crowd could not forgive him for being in the ranks of the traditional enemy. Boy 4 was the only adolescent in the neighborhood who was really stupid. He came of a good enough family, but he was so dull as to be three years behind others of his age. When there was a large party being given he was often asked, since what brains he had were all in his feet and he could dance, but for ordinary purposes he was altogether too much of a drag upon the general conversation. Boys 5 and 6 had been friends from childhood with the twin boys and had remained intimate members of the crowd. In fact, the four boys formed the backbone of the crowd, thus necessitating the inclusion of four girls. Since Boy 5 went around with Girl A, the sister of the twins, an extra girl always had to be found for Boy 6. Unless he brought in a girl from outside the district entirely, he had to choose among girls who were religious, homely and studious, boy-crazy, snobbish, married, or dull. It was only through the adolescent conviction that the number of boys must equal the number of girls that a fourth girl was included in the group. Boy 7 came from a family that had been in comfortable circumstances until the death of the father. The boy had then withdrawn from high school and gone to work. His new interests and friendships, plus different working hours, soon broke off his connection with the other adolescents who, after the fashion of youth, regarded him as a deserter from the crowd. Boy 8 was a victim of circumstances. When he was about sixteen, his father—who had always had a civil service position of some sort—was appointed as head of the city garbage collection. This situation precipitated endless ridicule by the adolescent population of the neighborhood. It was in vain for Boy 8 to prove vehemently that his father did not collect garbage but sat at a desk in the City Hall and never did anything worse than to get his hands dirty handling papers. The social prejudice was not to be overcome. After a year or so of violent protesting against the situation he ran away from home and joined the Navy, thus eliminating himself from the local scene altogether.

This typical adolescent crowd consisted, then, of a nucleus of four boys and three girls. These adolescents paired off as follows: Boy 1 with Girl E, Boy 2 with Girl G, and Boy 5 with Girl A. Boy 6 was therefore required to choose for any particular occasion a girl from the remaining number available in the neighborhood. For the ordinary social relationships of the crowd, however, an extra girl was not always necessary since Boy 6 played the piano while the others danced. For many evenings of general conversation and fun an extra boy made no particular difference, anyway. Boy 6 was essential to the crowd because he had been since his early childhood their natural leader. Although the twins had the undeniable advantage of living where the gatherings took place and of owning most of the material with which games were played, neither was the leader of the crowd. To be sure, on many occasions there was no definite leadership. The members of the group drifted into the house some time between 7 and 7:30 of an evening, amused themselves as they liked, and usually set out for home between 9 and 10. The parents of the twins always retired to the third floor of the house whenever the crowd got together, thus leaving the youngsters downstairs to do whatever they liked. When, however, the crowd was at a loss for something to do, it was Boy 6 who usually came forward with a proposal. It was he also who first wore new kinds of clothes and it was he who had by far the most sensitive eye for newness and originality in the girls' apparel. In fact, he was, without being in the least effeminate, almost the local dictator as regards what should or should not be worn. He fortunately had excellent taste and therefore prevented the crowd from wearing such extraordinary clothes as the other adolescents would willingly have worn if he had. This lad was neither especially intelligent nor especially handsome, but he had, in a far larger measure than his friends, mature judgment and resourcefulness.

It will be observed that inclusion or exclusion was settled upon the individual merits of each boy or girl. It was not a matter of family alliances, nor exclusively a matter of similar social backgrounds. The crowd was based primarily upon sympathetic personalities and upon particular boy-and-girl friendships. It was in most respects a typical, spontaneous, adolescent crowd.

Pupils do not group themselves spontaneously in such a way as to promote the mental health of the entire school population. Adolescents in particular tend to form small, compact cliques. Such groups are frequently competitive and, in some instances, have seriously interfered with the normal conduct of school affairs. In any event, these cliques rarely include more than two-thirds of the school members; many individuals are therefore left in social isolation.

The natural grouping of adolescents into "crowds" or cliques is well shown by the chart below.[14] Each square represents a boy enrolled in a boys' preparatory school. The lines indicate which boys are attracted to each other; for purposes of simplification, the antagonisms and attitudes of indifference have not been noted on this chart. There are a number of definite groups, the members of which have no voluntary social connections with other groups or with isolated members of the

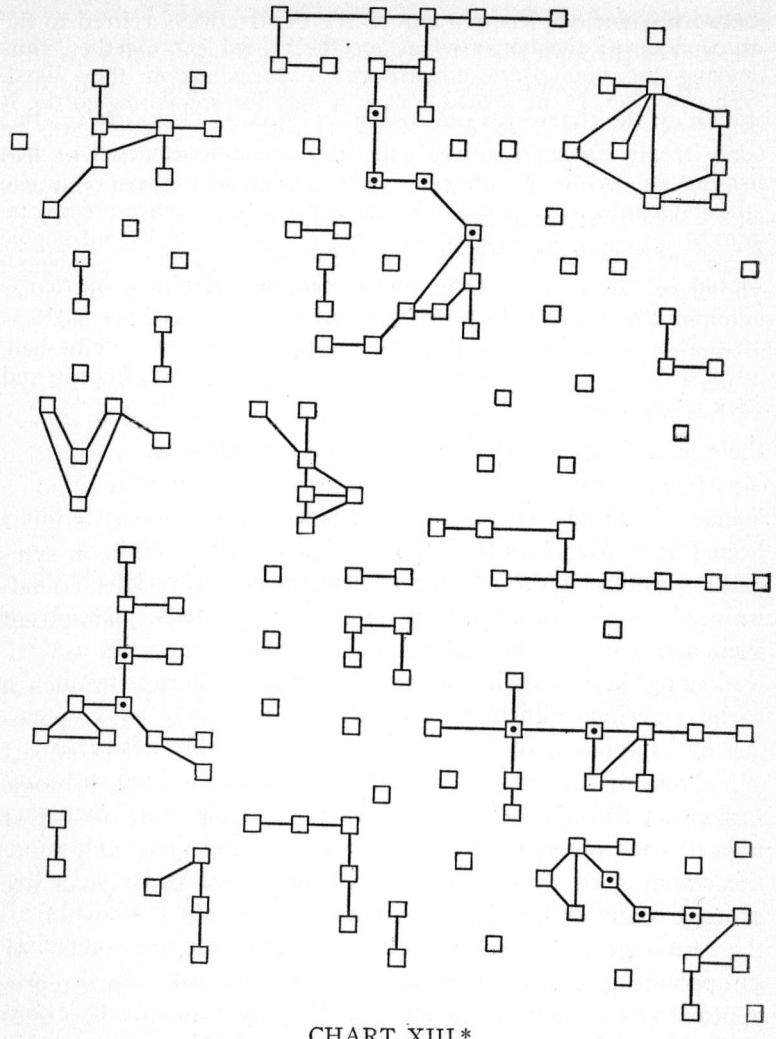

CHART XIII*

VOLUNTARY GROUPINGS OF 153 BOYS IN SECONDARY SCHOOL (Moreno [14])

*This material is presented by permission of the Nervous and Mental Disease Publishing Company.

school population. In only rare instances is there a joining of the cliques through the attractiveness of a single pupil to members of two separate groups; these "connecting" pupils are shown on the chart by a dot inside the square. There are thirty-three totally isolated individuals who are not attracted or attractive to anyone. In addition, there are several others who are partly isolated; these are friends with only one boy, who is already associated with a definite group. These pupils are represented by the squares that appear on the periphery of many groups. There are also seven pair of chums who have a deep attraction for each other but show either dislike or indifference toward everyone else. The situation here shown is typical of adolescent social relationships if pupils are allowed to make their own choices without supervision or guidance.

Leadership.—Because of the social prominence of the leader and because of his strategic position, psychologists have been trying for years to find out what qualities result in leadership. Although the number of leaders is always small, their influence is always large because of their strategic position in their own society. The high school that can influence its student leaders to exercise their power along desirable lines is not likely to have serious difficulties with the student body as a whole. An understanding of leaders seems, then, highly desirable.

Most of the studies of leadership have consisted in locating, either through observation or by the adolescents' own ratings of each other, the leaders in a school and then comparing the standing of these leaders in a number of traits with the average standing on the same traits of the other students of the same age in the school. The results to date are somewhat disappointing because they are so very general. The leaders appear to excel their fellow students slightly in practically every mental, social, and physical trait.[1, 2, 7, 15, 22] They are usually more intelligent than the average, they are taller and heavier than the average, they are in better health, they are older than the average, their athletic capacities are higher, and their social adjustment is better. These characteristics apply of course to

SOCIAL DEVELOPMENTS

leaders as a group; not all of them are true of any individual leader.

In some investigations high school pupils have been asked to tell what characteristics in their own leaders make them stand out. Such results are too generalized to be of much use; the adolescents making the ratings are evidently unable to analyze their impressions. In one such study, the list of traits characterizing leaders was as follows: [22] vitality, loyalty, enthusiasm, sportsmanship, versatility, organizing ability, tact, imagination, sense of humor, initiative, poise, originality, and sympathy. These are all obviously superior human traits, but the characterizations are much too general to explain why one generally superior girl is a leader and another is not. It should be noted that in the above list of traits intelligence as a characteristic does not appear at all, although it is probably rated indirectly under the headings of versatility, organizing ability, initiative, and originality. Still it is worth noting that the adolescent who impresses others of his age as undisguisedly intelligent does not become a leader. Another investigation,[21] in which sixteen student leaders in a junior college were studied individually, resulted in a classification of these leaders into types as follows: the social climber, the intellectual success, the good mixer, the big athlete, and the hyperactive individual. These classifications do not particularly help, since they too are evidently based on unanalyzed impressions. In order to characterize each of these five types one would merely need to take the list of thirteen traits given above and arrange them in varying order so as to give greater weight to one trait or another.

The leader is a fundamental source of social control because of his strategic position in the community. The potential power of the popular as compared to the unpopular student is well shown in the two figures below.[14]

Pupil A is a typical leader. Of the seventeen other pupils in his immediate group he shows mutual attraction for six; they choose him for an intimate and he chooses them. He is indifferent toward six others, who are, nevertheless, definitely attracted to him. He feels repulsion for four members of his group, but they are indifferent to him. Between him and one other pupil there is a mutual antagonism. In an emergency this student could command the unhesitating loyalty of two-thirds of his group and could hope by a little effort to win support from all but one.

Pupil B is an unpopular individual. He has a bond of attraction with only one student. He feels attracted toward three others, of

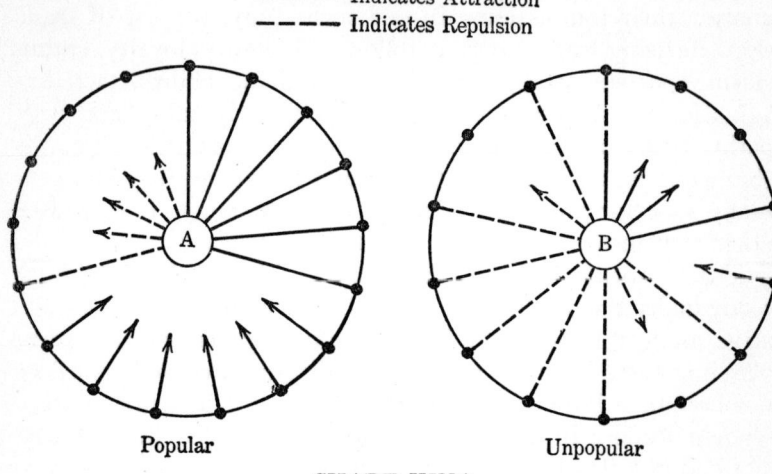

CHART XIV*

SOCIAL CONTACTS OF A POPULAR AND AN UNPOPULAR BOY (Moreno [14])

Each dot on the circles around A and B indicates an individual in the immediate social group.

If the attraction or repulsion between A or B and a group member is mutual, the connecting line extends from the dot to the center; if the feeling is on one side only, the arrow indicates the direction of the feeling. Absence of any line means indifference.

whom two are neutral toward him and one actively opposed. He dislikes two other pupils who are indifferent to him. Finally, he has formed bonds of mutual repulsion with seven out of the fourteen others in his immediate group. This pupil is clearly a focus of antipathy and indifference.

The effect of a leader upon her followers is well illustrated by the example below.[14] This chart depicts the emotional bonds between seven workers and the forewoman in charge of the

* This material is presented by permission of the Nervous and Mental Disease Publishing Company.

SOCIAL DEVELOPMENTS

work. Girl A is the real center of discontent; she has an active dislike for the forewoman. Girls C, D, E, F and G are positively attracted to Girl A—that is, they are her followers. With one of

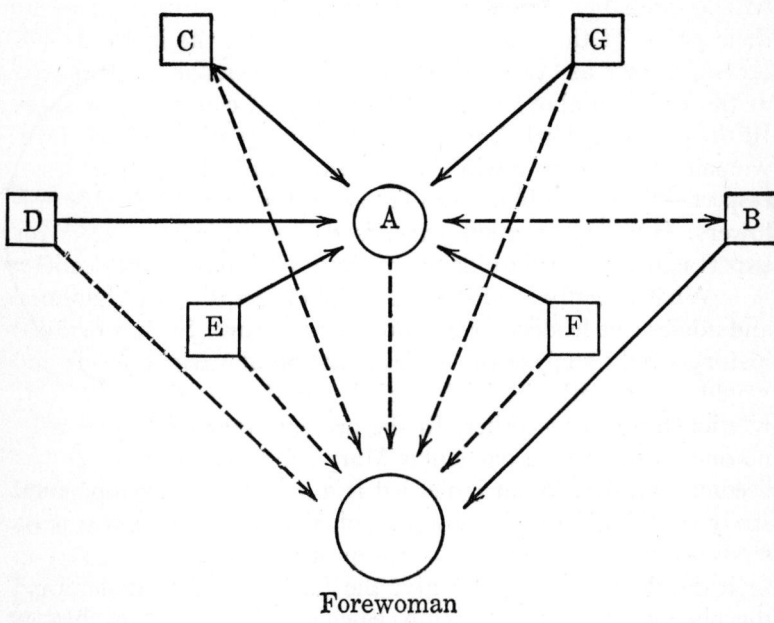

Forewoman

CHART XV*

INFLUENCE OF A NATURAL LEADER IN MOLDING PUBLIC OPINION
(Moreno [14])

them, Girl C, she has formed a bond of mutual attraction, but toward the others she is neutral, although she commands their loyalty. Between her and Girl B there is a feud; they are thoroughly antagonistic. Through the emotional bonds between Girl A and her followers, everyone in the group except Girl B has come to dislike the forewoman. The main loyalty of the

* This material is presented by permission of the Nervous and Mental Disease Publishing Company.

group is to Girl A, not to the constituted authority. Girl B, being rejected by the natural leader, has retaliated by showing affection for the forewoman. This same situation is all too common in the schoolroom. A single pupil of great popularity influences her admirers adversely toward the teacher. Only the socially isolated members of the student group like the teacher, having probably turned to her because they were rejected by their peers. If the teacher returns the liking, the isolated ones become known as "teacher's pets." Such emotional crosscurrents as those shown above wreck the serenity of classroom or shop. In the example, Girl A is the key to the situation. If the forewoman can somehow win this one girl's affection—or at least, respect—she will obtain similar attitudes from Girl A's followers. Here, on a small scale, is demonstrated the need for expert education and guidance of those who are natural leaders.

What is badly needed is a careful observation of childhood and adolescent leaders over a number of years. Such a detailed history would analyze the social situation at various levels and would study both the "followers" and the "leaders" in their relationship to each other. In the present stage of information no one knows why a particular Mary Smith or John Jones has become a leader. What is needed is a long-time, developmental study of a large number of individual leaders. No amount of study of these students as a group at a particular moment in their development will ever give the facts needed to understand the phenomenon of leadership. Such developmental studies as have just been suggested are entirely possible, since the student leader usually begins to show his or her characteristics at some age between ten and twelve and from then on merely develops more and more skill. It is the writer's conviction that a research fund could hardly be spent more wisely than in a study of leadership along the same comprehensive lines as the long-time study of genius now well into its second decade of work at Stanford University. With such a program it might be possible to determine what makes a leader and why he or she can lead. This knowledge would naturally result in an effort to educate adequately the leaders of the next generation. Through the training of leaders the situation offers unparalleled possibilities for influencing public opinion, both during the school years and into adult life.

ORGANIZED SOCIAL ACTIVITIES

So far as the high school is concerned, the organization of social activities takes the form of the extracurricular program. Although these activities should always be based upon the spontaneous interests of adolescent boys and girls, they are nevertheless to some extent organized and supervised. These activities of the school form an important part of secondary instruction. They are in most respects poorly named; they should be emphatically *inside* of the curriculum, not *outside,* because they assist materially in the achievement of the social objectives of the high school. One objective of any school is the mastery of subject matter; a second is the development of its students into acceptable and efficient human beings. For reaching these two somewhat divergent objectives the school needs two programs of procedure which should go hand in hand. Neither alone is sufficient for the training of modern youth.

For many years after its appearance, the high school was centered primarily upon the mastery of subject matter, with extracurricular activities appearing to a very slight extent. It must be remembered, however, that for several decades the high school was attended by a small and highly selected group of students who were there primarily to prepare themselves for college. These students came from good homes where they obtained an adequate socialization through personal contacts.

Since the recent expansion of high schools, the situation has markedly changed. As soon as the high school group became heterogeneous, extracurricular activities took on a new importance. The traditional curriculum was far too hard for many students and did not at all meet their interests. These students therefore turned to activities of a quite different character, perhaps as compensation for their relatively poor showing in the classroom. Various teachers soon noted how successful many of these academically inferior students were in their nonacademic activities and began to encourage the development of various clubs and other organizations. Because of the intense interest of all adolescents in social life, these extracurricular activities grew apace.

In many a modern high school the social life of the school has completely overshadowed the academic life. For some types of pupil this situation is probably quite justifiable. However, it would seem that a more rational balance between the academic and nonacademic programs could be found without danger to either. In a later section there will be a chapter on the curriculum; therefore, the academic program need not be discussed here, but it should not be forgotten during the forthcoming presentation of the nonacademic program. The two programs should work together in such a way that the high school graduate is not only a socially adjusted person but a socially adjusted person who knows something.

Theoretically, the extracurricular program should include opportunities for students to develop their interest and skill along any line not already adequately provided for in the program of classes. Actually, however, the theoretical expansion of extracurricular activities with only the interests of the students as a limit is always conditioned by the size and facilities of any particular school. A school cannot have a club in which children actually print their own stories, for instance, unless it owns a printing press. The extracurricular activities need not, however, be influenced by the practical objectives that dominate the academic program. Thus, if a girl with relatively slight artistic ability likes to draw and gets real enjoyment from it, even though she does not draw at all well, there is no reason why she should not exercise in a drawing club whatever meager talent she may have. In her academic work she might well be allowed to elect courses in art appreciation, but not the technical art classes; in these latter she would be a handicap to talented students and she herself would meet with discouragement instead of pleasure. Her interest and skill are not sufficient for the practical purpose of earning a living but they are sufficient for entrance into nonacademic activities. The extracurricular activities of the school grow, then, out of the spontaneous interests of the pupils and should be allowed to develop in whatever direction these interests tend.

Before taking up the different types of organizations which flourish in the American high school, a few words should be said in regard to the teacher's relationship to these activities. Most of the social clubs are outgrowths of the work in some department of the school; therefore, the teachers in that department are the individuals best equipped for supervision of these clubs or other activities. Naturally the boys and girls should be allowed control of certain details of management, but they are neither inventive enough nor mature enough to keep a club as interesting or as soundly managed as it will be if it has the assistance of a sympathetic teacher. It is not the idea at all that any teacher should dominate the activities of the students, but rather that she should help them to make their activities more interesting. Most teachers have fundamentally no objection to such participation in the nonacademic program of the school. Difficulty arises, however, when a teacher who has already taught seven or eight classes in a day is asked to remain after school to assist with some club. Adequate supervision cannot be done casually; it imposes a real burden upon time, vitality, and ingenuity. If a school wants teachers to develop the extracurricular program as well as the course of study, it must make time in the teacher's schedule for work of this sort. Indeed, one of the main handicaps in the healthy growth of extracurricular activities is the attitude that they are extra and unnecessary tasks imposed upon the teacher at the end of a hard school day when she is so tired she has no enthusiasm for anything. The two school programs will have to find some way of co-operating instead of competing with each other. If this can be done, there will be no difficulty in persuading teachers to work with groups of adolescents who have come into a club because of spontaneous interest.

Types of extracurricular activities.—The first type of activity to be discussed is the organization for governmental purposes of the homeroom, the class, the student council, and the assembly.[5] Through these activities, the pupils practice techniques of government and participate in the conduct of school affairs. They learn how voting is done, how laws are formulated and passed, how a court functions, how rules are enforced. These activities are clearly directed toward practical training in citizenship. It is not the purpose of the present book to consider in detail the different kinds of organizations and clubs, but rather to point out the value of these organizations to the adolescent boy and girl; matters of administration and management have therefore been omitted. Through these activities pupils get experience in working together for common purposes in such small groups as the homeroom and such large groups as the school assembly. The more students participate in their own government the better, but there are obvious limitations to their participation. In the first place, there are several matters that are not at all their business: for instance, the finances of the school, the repair of buildings, the employment of teachers, and, to a considerable measure, the curriculum. High school boys and girls are old enough to understand some points about the curriculum, but they are not yet mature enough to judge whether or not certain work should be given in the high school. There should, however, be some recognized means through which they can make known what curricular adaptations they would like; the curriculum committee of the faculty can make good use of suggestions from students. The main purpose in student government should be the control of behavior in the school, the punishment of the offenders against the students' own regulations, and the management of small units of government—such as the homeroom or any of the clubs developed by the school. These civic responsibilities usually appeal to adolescents because they feel themselves old enough to determine rules for their own behavior; they therefore participate spontaneously in the conduct of school government.

Adolescents express their numerous interests in organizations of a second type—the various clubs and activities that constitute the major portion of the school's nonacademic program. In order to demonstrate the wide variety in adolescent enthusiasms, a summary is given below of a recent investigation [5] into the types of clubs sponsored in several hundred senior and junior high schools. The following classification includes all nonathletic and nongovernmental student activities; the latter have already been discussed and the former will be given consideration later.*

  I. Language and Literary Activities: writing clubs, appreciation of literature clubs, contemporary writing clubs, public speaking and debating clubs, dramatic clubs, ancient language clubs, modern language clubs.
 II. Science Clubs: mathematical clubs; naturalist clubs, Audubon and Agassiz societies, astronomy clubs, geology clubs, agriculture clubs, surveying clubs, chemistry clubs, physics clubs, automobile clubs, aeroplane clubs; social science clubs, history clubs, current events clubs, biography clubs, Know-Your-City clubs, historic dramatization clubs, civic clubs, patriotic clubs, sociology clubs.
III. Art Activities:
   1. Music: orchestra, bands, glee clubs, school chorus, and musical appreciation.
   2. Drawing and painting: sketching, camera, cartoons, posters, art collecting, art appreciation, designing.
   3. Dancing: aesthetic dancing.
   4. Mechanical art activities: mechanical drawing, blueprinting, printing, carpentry, cabinetmaking, forging and metalworking.
 IV. Commercial Activities: business correspondence clubs, stenographic and typing clubs, office practice clubs, school banking, market clubs.
  V. Homemaking Activities: embroidering, crocheting, and knitting clubs; millinery clubs, sewing circles, fashion clubs, home nursing clubs, cooking clubs, gardening clubs, canning and preserving clubs, textile and basketry clubs.
 VI. Honor Organizations: Phi Beta Sigma Society, Cum Laude Society, Oasis Society, Arista Society, Memerian Society, Pro Merito Society, Ephoebian Society, National Honor Society, local honor societies: T.N.T. Club, Torch Club, Order of the Daisy, leaders' clubs.
VII. Welfare and Social Activities:
   1. Welfare activities: Boy and Girl Scouts, Camp Fire Girls, Junior Red Cross, social workers' clubs, hospital auxiliary.

*This material is used by permission of the Houghton Mifflin Company.

2. Religious and moral training activities: Girl Reserves, Hi-Y clubs, Junior Y.W.C.A. or Y.M.C.A.
   3. Social intercourse activities: parties and dances, college clubs, fraternities, etiquette clubs.
VIII. Publications: handbook, annual, magazine, school newspapers, school and departmental bulletins.

These clubs give an indication of the catholicity of adolescent interest. Theoretically, such a list is limited only by the number of things adolescent boys and girls want to know about and do.*

Although these clubs are obviously related to the curricular work of various departments in the high school, they do not have the same objective as the courses from which they undoubtedly developed. Therefore, the clubs have values quite different from those of the regular classes. Since there are no particular requirements to be met in these nonacademic activities, students may use them for purposes of exploring various untried fields. In the regular class schedule such exploration is relatively difficult because a student, once enrolled in a course, must either continue through the semester or else lose several hours' credit by withdrawing from the class. Moreover, a club can keep up to date far more easily than the curriculum. Thus, an aeroplane club can be formed and functioning long before data on aeroplanes get into the textbooks in physics. These activities are valuable in the development of avocations and of profitable and interesting uses of leisure time. Through club work, boys and girls are provided with many opportunities to develop normal social relationships with each other. The organizations serve also to furnish practice in self-direction and self-government on the part of the members. Finally, the activities

* With one exception the organizations above listed are conducive to desirable personal development on the part of the participant. The high school fraternity, however, is to be condemned. Adolescents are, even at best, strongly inclined to prejudice; social barriers are high enough without the fraternity. Such organizations emphasize the natural antagonisms within a high school group, develop totally unjustified airs and snobbishness among the members and become a source of distress to the outsiders. The fraternity is the quintessence of all the worst traits of adolescence.

SOCIAL DEVELOPMENTS 125

serve as outlets for the emotional drives and interests of adolescence.

A few examples of extracurricular activities may make clearer their value. In secondary school the writer belonged to a nature study club. During one year, by vote of the members, the club collected rocks. Every Saturday morning about twenty girls tramped over hill and dale looking for specimens. By the end of the year, several hundred had been gathered, classified—with considerable help from the instructor—and properly labeled. There was then an exhibit, with introductory remarks and explanations by the president of the club. During another year, the writer belonged to a Latin club whose members decided to write a play in Latin. The supervising teacher however persuaded the group to dramatize a fairy tale instead of attempting original composition. For reasons long since forgotten, the girls voted to dramatize Bluebeard. The Brothers Grimm were therefore consulted for a correct version of the tale, which was turned into execrable Latin by one of the girls; after that it was examined and rewritten—in even worse versions—by each successive member until all had had a chance at it. Eventually, the instructor intercepted the manuscript and managed to persuade the group to eliminate the worst of the errors. Not content with the mere dramatization, the girls rehearsed their production and gave the play in Latin for the school. Since everyone knew the story anyway, nobody was inconvenienced by the use of Latin words. The writer was wife Number 2 who died a grueling death, probably from an overdose of bad syntax. At a still later period, there arose among the girls in the school a feeling that the faculty and students did not understand each other and needed more social contacts. For some obscure reason the means taken to bring about a *rapprochement* was the production by the students of a one-act play, in which the teaching of a particularly stupid class was portrayed. Over this chef-d'œuvre, a committee labored on and off for weeks; the members then assembled a cast of characters and trained them; they requisitioned the embryo artists of the school to create appropriate posters and invitations; eventually they gave their play—which was extremely funny, but not for any of the intended reasons. On another occasion several girls decided to publish a book of poems. They bullied something out of practically everyone in the school; next they persuaded two or three girls who could print nicely to write the poems on fancy paper; then they bound the sheets together and presented the volume to the principal of the school—who nearly wept—but that was before she read the verses, most of which were pretty dreadful. Toward the end of the last year, about a dozen girls suddenly developed a bad attack of religion and formed the habit of meeting with one of the teachers every Sunday between breakfast and church. In the course of these meetings they discovered many beautiful passages in the Bible, reached numerous naïve conclusions on theological matters, and acquired the beginnings of a philosophy of life.

The outstanding point about all these partly spontaneous, partly organized activities is the value received by the participants. Aside from social experience in getting along together, the girls who collected rocks learned some geology, those who wrote the Latin play learned some Latin, those who engineered the book of verse and the school play held the school together for a time by directing its combined efforts toward a common end, and those who developed religious enthusiasm discovered an integration of life not presented to them in any high school class. Upon looking back, the writer is amazed at the countless hours voluntarily dedicated by the pupils to these activities and by the educational values received.

Athletic activities form a class by themselves. In the past they have shown a tendency to overshadow all other elements in the nonacademic program of the high school. Because of interschool games, athletics stir the adolescent imagination profoundly. The intense competition between schools has probably done far more harm than good, however. It has served to burn out the vitality of the participants at an age when they are willing to exhaust themselves under the emotional strain of competition. The social prestige and general publicity given the high school athlete have combined to produce abnormal personalities in many boys who were entirely normal until their period of athletic prominence. Intense competition in high school athletics has led to the development of a few experts rather than to the rounded development of every pupil in the school. It has acted unfavorably upon the curriculum through the comparative social standing of the successful scholar with a successful athlete and through the powerful pressure brought to bear upon teachers to lower their standards and pass members of any school team. In recent years more and more people have realized that high school athletics were having a damaging effect upon morale and were preventing rather than promoting the development of good sportsmanship. Football and baseball in particular have in many schools become professions, not games. To combat this situation, the intramural athletic program has been developed, in some schools most successfully.

As a means of physical development and as a preparation for leisure time every adolescent should learn to play reasonably well at least one game for which the equipment will be available in later years. This provision immediately rules out football, except for the professional player, because the equipment is too expensive and the risk of injury too great for the game to be played in adult life. Basketball, baseball, hockey, tennis, golf, swimming, and skating, on the other hand, may be continued after the adolescent years. In addition, there are a number of minor sports such as badminton, deck tennis, ping-pong, volleyball, handball, etc., that should be added to the above list of major sports. Except for those with high vitality such violent games as hockey and basketball are not continued after the late years of adolescence, because they burn up too much energy. As training for an adult use of leisure, the less vigorous games and sports should always be given precedence.

For the adolescent the chief values of athletics should never be forgotten—and they often are in the excitement of too great competition. He or she should, first of all, develop a sense of fairness and sportsmanship. To be sure, the athletic department has no mortgage on these particular virtues. Games and sports are merely two ways in which fair play and leadership may be developed; they are by no means the only two ways. Secondly, the adolescent learns to control his own body and his own temper. And thirdly, he has one more opportunity for learning how to submerge his own personal desires for the good of the largest number. Athletics should take their place as one element in the extracurricular program of the high school, but they should never be allowed to develop a prominence that makes them seem the only activities through which certain personality traits can be developed.

The clubs and other activities of the school should, then,

be the means for developing interests, for giving training in the wise use of leisure, for providing practice in self-government, for allowing leaders to practice leadership, and for building character. It is not to be supposed that no progress toward these objectives is ever made in the classroom; however, the nonacademic program is in some respects better equipped for their realization.

Distribution of extracurricular activities.—It has always seemed to the writer that the pupils who most needed extracurricular activities for their own development were the ones who had the least opportunity of participating. If it is the function of such activities to develop the personalities of adolescent boys and girls and to train them in social adjustment, then those who *most need* this training should be the ones to receive it. Instead, the activities all too often become merely the means of self-expression for adolescents who are already examples of perfect social adjustment. The boy or girl who is shy, self-conscious, and repressed rarely has much opportunity to participate in activities and thus to achieve the social ease that he or she lacks. The adolescent who is already definitely queer from too much isolation never has a chance to obtain the only kind of experience that might save his sanity. Adolescents show spontaneously a blind loyalty to the few people they admire and a complete intolerance towards everyone else. These emotional characteristics cause pupils to elect the same leaders over and over again and to refuse absolutely any participation to those who seem queer or unusual. There is no sin so grievous to the adolescent spirit as a difference in manners, appearance, or speech from the mode of the group. He who deviates is lost.

An interesting example of this tendency to accord more participation to those who already have enough is shown in a recent investigation of fraternity and nonfraternity men in a college.[12] For five consecutive years a record was kept of all students participating in cultural, ethical, athletic, political, or social organizations. During this time the membership rolls of such clubs showed 1,774 fraternity men and only 468 nonfraternity men, even though the total number of men in fraternities was 10 per cent smaller than the total number outside. Membership in extracurricular

SOCIAL DEVELOPMENTS

clubs was, then, four times as great for those men whose fraternity connection indicated an individual already acceptable socially, besides providing considerable opportunity for further social adjustment. Moreover, these men could well have spent more time in study, since only 37 per cent of the high scholarship records (those averaging B or above) during this five years were made by fraternity men. It is a sad commentary on education that so many people who achieve social adjustment do not master subject matter, while so many who master subject matter remain socially unadjusted. There ought to be some way of passing around the favors a bit more evenly.

In many schools the authorities, realizing the situation, have tried to regulate participation by a point system. This technique alone has been quite ineffective for two reasons. In the first place, the number of points—indicating the number of positions a pupil may hold simultaneously—is always too high. Secondly, pupils who love to expand their egos by participation in nonacademic activities usually resort to the following trick: They use up their own points and then they get their friends elected to any other positions they covet, whereupon they proceed to shelve the obliging friends and do the work themselves. The mechanical limiting of participation by means of points is not successful because it is too easy to get around. What is needed is a constructive educational policy of distributing participation in terms of needs, not in terms of personal enjoyment.

The usual situation in high school is well illustrated by the two graphs shown on p. 130.[8] In this study, 313 pupils kept count of the amount of time spent during a given week in nonacademic activities; the same pupils also listed the number of organizations to which they belonged. The time spent shows first that 34 per cent participated in no extracurricular activities during the week of the investigation. Another 49 per cent spent one to ten hours on such activities. The remaining 17 per cent spent from eleven to twenty-two hours. To put the matter another way, this group of 313 pupils spent a total of 1,508 hours, of which 51 per cent were spent by only 14 per cent of the pupils. A similar situation is shown by the number of groups to which these students belonged. Thirteen pupils belonged to no club. On the other hand, there were two who belonged to eight different clubs. In this entire group of 313 pupils there was a total of 946 club memberships. Of this

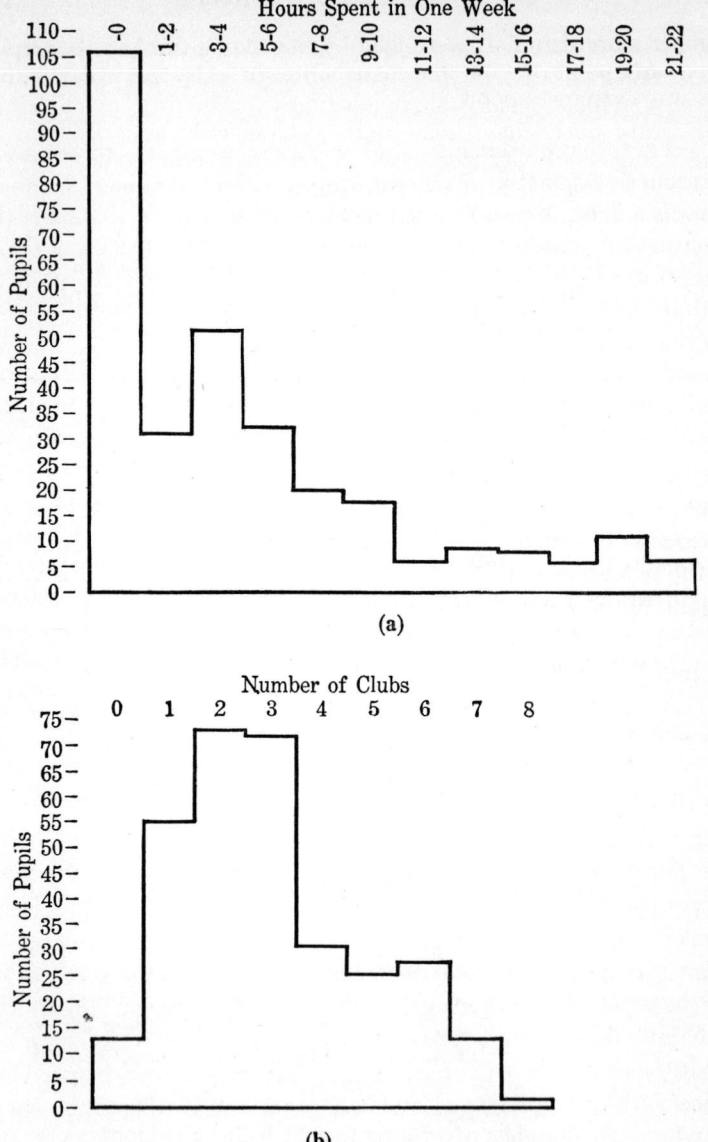

CHART XVI*

DEGREE OF VOLUNTARY PARTICIPATION IN EXTRACURRICULAR ACTIVITIES
(Hayes [8])

  *This material is presented by permission of the Bureau of Publications, Teachers College, Columbia University.

number more than half were held by less than a third of the pupils. From any point of view the distribution of extracurricular activities was extremely poor.

There have been here and there a few efforts to organize extracurricular activities along more constructive lines. In some schools a definite period is set aside once or twice a week for the meeting of school clubs. Every student in the school attends some meeting. Each pupil is entirely free to select the club he will attend and is also permitted to change from one group to another whenever he wishes. The only requirement is that he should attend some group meeting during the time set aside for club activities. This technique brings many "outside" activities inside the school where they belong. In other schools a similar arrangement has been made by extending the school day for an hour or more after the completion of classes and carrying on various activities during this additional period of time. Thus, if the academic work closes at 2:30, the pupils do not leave school until 4:00. Such arrangements are, of course, a step towards an educational use of nonacademic activities, because all pupils in the school are automatically involved.

A second step consists in making arrangements whereby the responsibility for managing various activities devolves upon a variety of students instead of upon a very few. In some schools the following arrangement has been found to work well: In each club there is a central committee of three pupils. Each week one pupil resigns and a new one is added. Each member thus serves for three consecutive weeks before he resigns. Continuity is provided for, since in any given week there are two members from previous weeks. A dispersion of control is also provided for because, in the course of the year, every member in the club will be on this central committee. This arrangement is greatly preferable to the election of three or four permanent officers. In the interests of continuity and student prestige, there may be a permanent president for each club—in addition to the central committee—but no official is really necessary.

Another step in a constructive program consists in the

playing of intramural tournaments between teams so arranged that every member of the school is on some team and many teams have an equal chance of winning. Few schools, however, have solved in a satisfactory manner the problem of choosing teams. What usually happens is that about half the pupils organize themselves as they please, and then those who are left over are assigned to makeshift teams which have no natural cohesion. A much better arrangement consists of the plan described below.

If a school in which three hundred boys are enrolled decides to have an intramural basketball tournament, there is material for sixty teams. The first thing is to nominate sixty captains. These captains should be selected from all social groupings within the school and can best be appointed by a teacher who is aware of what personal affiliations exist among the boys. Each captain then submits to the faculty member in charge of the tournament the names of the boys he would like to have on his team. If the captains have been so chosen as to represent all groups within the school, there will be relatively little overlapping among the lists. There will, however, inevitably be some pupils chosen by two or more captains and some boys not chosen at all. The faculty member settles the assignment of boys chosen on more than one team by placing them with their friends. The next step is to send back to each captain the list he has submitted with a line drawn through the names of boys already assigned to another team. Each captain whose team is not yet complete is asked to see the instructor in charge. When he appears he is shown a list of the boys not yet assigned and makes up his team from this list. By such a procedure the majority of boys will be satisfied with their placement and every boy will be on some team. If the instructor in charge exercises reasonable tact, he can prevent the best players from getting together in a single group. In a school tournament arranged in this manner there are at least a dozen teams who have an equal chance of winning. The trouble with most intramural contests is the concentration of all especially capable pupils on one or two teams; such a tournament is simply an opportunity for successful athletes to express themselves at the expense of less talented individuals. It is not in any sense a school tournament. Naturally, a school cannot have more than two or three such comprehensive contests in the course of a year, but it is better to have a single tournament run on educational lines than a number of smaller affairs in which only the athletically superior participate. Moreover, such contests as are held should involve games anyone can play; highly specialized games like football are automatically eliminated.

Finally, for the really educational use of nonacademic activities, it is necessary that someone should be charged with the responsibility of bringing about participation on the part of those pupils who most need the trainng and socialization and who are least likely to get it of their own accord. It takes a good deal of tact and quiet persistence to persuade an introverted adolescent to participate in anything; and it takes more tact and an occasional show of authority to prevent the exhibitionist from indulging in the tactics most harmful to his development. There must also be some sort of compromise between the adolescents' natural following of leaders and the personal requirements of the nonleader. Yet all these adjustments have to be made if the extracurricular program is to function in the development of normal personalities.

On the other hand, one must not neglect the natural leader to whom adolescents turn spontaneously. These individuals are sure to lead others and they need practice in the wise controlling of their followers. They are the pupils who have the natural authority to assume such positions as the head of te student government, the president of the senior class, the president of the athletic association, the chief editor of the yearbook, etc. There are relatively few such prominent and exacting positions in a school, but there are also relatively few leaders to fill them. The problem is chiefly that of getting the natural leaders into these difficult positions. Such important posts are obviously no place for the inexperienced; it will not help the introverted pupil to be elected to an onerous position, even if school politics could be so managed as to elect him. The situation is best arranged when the natural leaders fill the outstandingly important posts in a school, where the authority they exercise will influence the largest number, while the less important positions are used for the development of personality among those who need, for their own mental health, a little prominence and a little responsibility. Such a situation can be brought about only through the management of a tactful adult who knows a good deal about adolescent psychology and even more about the individual adolescents enrolled in the particular high school under consideration.

In deciding how many activities a given pupil may safely carry, one must be guided by each student's needs rather than by any rules or regulations. There may conceivably be some students in a high school who should take no academic work at all. Certainly there are many who would develop much better if they were entered in only one academic class and spent the rest of their time in nonacademic activities. The proportion of non-verbal, nonintellectual, nonbookish students in the average high school is increasing every year. For many of these the usual curricular training is totally inappropriate. For them the chief value of the high school lies in the ability to give training in citizenship. There are some introverted pupils who need socialization badly; their class schedule should be so lightened that they can participate in as many activities as may seem wise. At the other extreme there are some perfectly adjusted students who come from homes which furnish more than adequate opportunities for socialization outside of school. The extracurricular program for such pupils is largely duplication. There are, moreover, matters of health, personality, and emotional attitudes which inevitably enter into the decision as to how many and what extracurricular activities are appropriate for a given student. Only by individualizing participation—exactly as the classroom teacher has learned to individualize instruction—can the extracurricular program grow constructively into a means for the development of healthy personalities and for the expression of the social inclinations, emotional drives, and varied interests of normal adolescence.

ILLUSTRATIVE CASE STUDIES

The histories below illustrate a number of the points already emphasized in general. The reader should look for evidence of adolescent social developments and attitudes. In this material adolescent loyalty, prejudice, excessive enthusiasms, snobbishness, and interests have all been illustrated. No high school teacher can safely disregard these characteristics of her pupils.

Mary Wilkins [18] came of a family that lacked sufficient means to send her to the small college to which all her friends were going. However, she had an aunt who kept a restaurant in a town about fifteen miles away from the state university. This aunt made the proposal to the family that if Mary would help her in her restaurant during the evening dinner hour, and on Saturdays and Sundays, she would give the girl room and board and let her attend the university during the day. Mary's family agreed to this arrangement and so sent the daughter away from her friends to a totally new environment.

Mary's day began at about 5:30 in the morning, when she got up and helped with breakfast before riding an hour and a half on the streetcar to reach her classes. She was so pressed for funds she brought with her a sandwich, or some other light lunch, which she ate in one of the women's rest rooms on the campus. Her time was occupied by classes or work or some laboratory until about 2:30 in the afternoon, when she traveled home for an hour and a half on the streetcar, then worked in her aunt's restaurant until about 8:00 in the evening. Because of the distance from her former home, the arrangement for Mary's education disrupted her former high school friendships. Because of her evening work in the restaurant and her absence during the day, she made no friends in the town where her aunt lived. And since she could not afford to go to any of the college lunchrooms and could not stay on the campus long enough to participate in any campus activities, she made no friends at the university.

As a result of this combination of circumstances, the girl was by the end of her first year almost completely isolated and homesick; she felt decidedly injured that her former happy life had been so badly interrupted. She wept much of the time and seemed utterly miserable. She had failed most of her work. She very much wanted to go to the small college where her friends had gone but saw no way of financing this plan. During the entire year she had not attended a single social event, or been out with a boy, or made a friend, or seen a movie. Most days at the university did not produce more than a faint smile of recognition from students next to her in class. Mary appeared to be fairly intelligent, but had been so completely transplanted to an unfamiliar environment, so badly overworked, and so starved socially that solution of her problems without radically changing the whole situation seemed impossible.

The first step in getting Mary "back to normalcy" consisted in writing to the small college she wished to attend and arranging for her to do some work there to help her financially. She next wrote to her friends and found they could include her in their plans for an apartment the following year; by doing some of the housework she could cut down her living expenses. Correspondence with her family showed they were willing to supply such additional funds as would be involved under this new arrangement. It was agreed that Mary should make the change after the summer vacation. When these arrangements were finally completed, the middle of the spring term had been reached and Mary was failing in every course she was taking. It was pointed out to her that her period of loneliness and homesickness was nearly over, provided she could make good enough grades for admission to her new college. So Mary applied herself with new energy and hopefulness and brought all her work up to a satisfactory level. She thereupon left the university, as planned, and entered the college of her choice—where she is happy with her friends and doing good work.

The case is an example of what is perhaps the greatest danger faced by the student working her way—the danger of unhealthy and narrowing social deprivations. In the present instance the girl had been well socialized before going to college, and circumstances were extreme. In consequence of these two facts, her misery was so acute as to lead to an early crisis, forcing remedial steps. More often there is unfortunately no crisis, but instead chronic emotional discomfort and a growing sense of social estrangement and ineptitude which may poison the whole adult life.

Fee Wong was a Chinese boy of fifteen who had been in this country less than a year. In China he had learned some English and had quickly enlarged his vocabulary after his arrival, but an accent was still prominent in his speech. His parents were old-fashioned Chinese who insisted Fee wear native clothes. Each morning one could see Fee walking slowly and unobtrusively toward the school, his arms folded in front of him, his eyes on the ground, his face immobile. His manners were nothing short of perfection, but they were inordinately amusing to American pupils. His costume evoked only ridicule, although his clothes were of most elegant silk. Fee did not understand the situation. He tried hard in his classes, received average or better grades, never spoke unkindly to anyone—and yet he could make no friends and his tentative smiles were rarely returned. He had been warned to expect some discrimination, but the brutality of adolescent scorn and ostracism was almost more than he could bear. One afternoon a group of boys seized him on the way home from school, took him to a near-by garage, and stripped off his silk clothes. Fee was desperate; his carefully acquired English was forgotten; he begged them in Chinese for the return of his clothes. The boys had never heard

Chinese before and the nasal singsong struck them as excruciatingly funny. Finally, they exhausted themselves with laughter and went away, leaving Fee almost naked in the garage. It was hours later, after an alarmed family had notified police and school authorities of the boy's continued absence, that a doctor coming home from a night case found Fee huddled in a corner of his garage, terrified and incoherent. The doctor led the boy at once into his house, pushed him into a hot bath, extracted the family's name, and telephoned the parents. The next day the school authorities were told of the episode. Fee did not ask for revenge; like most Chinese he was peace-loving, and all he wanted was to be left alone. But the principal was not satisfied with anything so mild. He insisted on knowing the names of the boys, made them apologize to Fee, and punished them severely. The boys, however, were indignant that Fee had "squealed" on them. They felt he had outraged their sense of "sportsmanship" by tattling. They did not dare to attack him again, but they did everything they could to make his life miserable. The principal was distressed; in the end he persuaded Fee's parents to send their son to a central high school attended by considerable numbers of Chinese pupils where he would make friends of his race. Adolescent cruelty in such cases is almost incredible to adults.

A few years ago the writer was asked to act as referee for an intramural hockey tournament and to assist, on the basis of the games seen, in choosing a school team. There were eight teams, making a total of eighty-eight girls. Since there were well over three hundred girls in the school, the writer wanted to know where the others were and was told the others were all so hopeless no one wanted them on a team. Throughout the tournament, which lasted for two afternoons, these unwanted maidens had to put on their gymnasium clothes and stand on the sidelines to serve as audience. The first two games on the first day were uneventful; only one girl seemed to be worth consideration as a prospect for a school team and the writer was beginning to wonder if her standards were too high. Then came the third contest; but this was not a game—it was a slaughter of the innocents. On one side were eleven excellent players; on the other were eleven girls who had never played together, did not know each other's names, and had little skill with a hockey stick. The writer stopped the game at the end of ten minutes, with the score standing at twelve to nothing. The next day, this same team ran up ten goals on another group in less than fifteen minutes; that game also was stopped. The final contest was less one-sided, but the one team of good players won by a score of seven to nothing, the score being held that low chiefly by the efforts of a stellar fullback on the opposing side. The entire performance was merely an opportunity for one group of girls to trample on everyone else; it was no tournament. There was never a moment's doubt as to who would win. Incidentally, the good players were furious because their Roman holiday was twice brought to a sudden close by the referee's decision; they had certainly derived no ideas of sportsmanship from their athletic training.

Doris is a sixteen-year-old girl. For several years she has had two intimate girl friends from whom she is practically inseparable. The three confide all their hopes, dreams, ideas, and ambitions to each other. No one of them is brighter or more dominating than the other two. All are interested almost exclusively in boys and clothes, with school experiences a poor third. They walk to school together every morning, spend recess together, have a common lunch basket which is filled by each mother in rotation, go to movies together, play the same games, walk home in a group, and spend most of the evening at the house of one or the other. Every boy in school has been discussed by them at one time or another, and every dress worn by any girl has been analyzed and criticized. Their favorite entertainment is for all of them to try on successively all the clothes of any one of them. This performance will keep them interested for three or four hours at a time—usually until they get hungry. They are forever making over their dresses. Before they go to a dance they spend every available moment for a week in getting their dresses ready, their hair curled, their nails manicured, and so on. Any girl who is not as nearly as possible like themselves is regarded as queer. All three are thorough snobs whose fundamental tenet is the social ostracism of everyone who is "different." Within the last two years, life has been much complicated by the need of a boy friend for each of them. At any given moment one of the three is certain to be in the midst of a quarrel with her particular boy. During such episodes the two not immediately involved are told all the details of the estrangement. If a new boy comes into the school or neighborhood, all three look him over and decide which one should try to fascinate him, in case he is worth it. Their plans for the simplest activity are incredibly involved. If one decides to give a swimming party at a near-by tank and asks the other two, plus three boys, there is endless discussion as to who will go in what car, which bathing suit should be worn, what new caps can be bought with the remains of their allowance, where and what the crowd should eat after their swim, and so on. Nothing is ever done without plans down to the ultimate minutiae. Once there was an episode of some kind that led one girl to think Doris had "stolen" her boy friend; no one was ever able to get the details straight, but the affair reverberated for months, although an open break was avoided. Within the past two or three months the group has begun to show subtle signs of disintegrating. One girl plans on going to the state university, one to a business college, and one to a private finishing school; already the differences in objective are beginning to be felt. Moreover, they are discovering that more than three interesting people exist in the world. It is now only a question of time till this tight little clique breaks up. It has done its duty in furnishing social training, in educating taste, and in bringing about natural relationships with boys. Further persistence would lead to a continuation of adolescent intolerance into adult life.

In a small boarding school there was a freshman class composed of only seven girls. In the senior class there was an immensely popular girl named Marjorie who had been captain of the basketball, hockey, swimming, and skating teams; she also had won both the singles and doubles tennis tournaments during the previous year. Marjorie was also president of student government and of the senior class. Every one of the seven freshmen practically worshiped the ground Marjorie walked on. They could think of no more thrilling experience than to be allowed to do Marjorie a favor. One of them acquired social prestige because Marjorie once offered her a bite off her sandwich! During the fall there was a practice tennis tournament, played off during the regular gymnasium periods. Marjorie and one of the freshmen, Elaine, were playing a match. Elaine was excited and embarrassed at finding herself actually playing with this idol of the community. Some other seniors came past and called out, "Well, well, look at our little girl now." The freshman, unused to mannerisms of speech in the school, supposed of course the remark was made about her; so she responded pleasantly, "Yes, but she won't be here long." This remark was meant to be a compliment, the best she could think of on the spur of the moment, but it was interpreted as sheer insolence, since it turned out the "little girl" referred to was the senior! The chilling silence with which her comment was greeted completed Elaine's disorganization, and Marjorie beat her by a large margin. By the next day, Elaine's remark had been told to everyone in school as an instance of how conceited a freshman could be. For several days Elaine was ostracized, but she eventually made her classmates at least understand the situation.

Throughout the year devotion to Marjorie ran high; the feeling was nothing but sheer hero worship, however. Marjorie was a sweet, mature, capable girl who attracted followers and worshipers without any effort whatever. In the spring, the real tennis tournament took place. Elaine and Marjorie met in the finals. The match took place on the day before commencement as part of the final program of events. It happened that someone had just given the school a cup; the winner's name would be the first to be engraved on it. Everyone in the school was eager for Marjorie to win—even Elaine. But Marjorie was tired from the round of final exercises and the conclusion of numerous activities. After Elaine had won the first set and four games in the second, she began hitting balls out on purpose, but Marjorie had completely lost her usual serenity and was unable to keep the ball in play long enough for Elaine to make a sufficient number of mistakes to lose. When she had five games, Elaine served four intentional doubles in a row, so as to give Marjorie at least one game. Her freshmen friends sitting on the sidelines were begging her to lose; tears began to stream down everyone's face. It had simply never occurred to anyone that Marjorie *could* lose. When only one more point was needed for victory, Elaine, acting upon advice from behind her, went up to the net and defaulted the match! The whole school clapped loudly and for a moment it looked as if Elaine would be a heroine and not the villain who was keeping the school idol from realizing her last ambition. At this point the principal put down her foot and insisted the match should be played out. Marjorie and Elaine were both crying but obedient. Under the pressure of authority Elaine did not dare to throw the point away openly and she did not have enough skill to be subtle about it. Consequently she won. The principal shook her by the hand, but the entire school rose en masse and left. That afternoon it was necessary to take Elaine out of an exhibition of folk dancing because no one would dance with her. The next morning feeling was still high. The head usher had to hunt for some time before she could find any girl who was willing to march with Elaine in the commencement procession. The only thing that saved Elaine from permanent ostracism was the end of school. After a summer of intense worry, she returned to find her friends more mature and the whole episode largely forgotten.

SOCIAL DEVELOPMENTS

BIBLIOGRAPHY *

1. Bellingrath, G. C., "Qualities Associated with Leadership in the Extracurricular Activities of the High School," *Teachers College Contributions to Education,* No. 399, Bureau of Publications, Teachers College, Columbia University, 1930, 59 pp.
2. Brown, M., "Leadership among High School Pupils," *Teachers College Contributions to Education,* No. 559, Bureau of Publications, Teachers College, Columbia University, 1933, 166 pp.
3. Bykowski, L. J., "Figle i psoty mlodziezy szkolnej," (Tricks and Practical Jokes among High School Students) *Kwartalnik Psychologiczny,* 1933, 4: 41-191.
4. Clem, O. M., and Dodge, S. B., "The Relation of High School Leadership and Scholarship to Post-School Success," *Peabody Journal of Education,* 1932, 10: 321-329.
5. Fretwell, E. K., *Extracurricular Activities in Secondary Schools,* Houghton Mifflin Company, 1931, 552 pp.
6. Furfey, P. H., *The Gang Age,* The Macmillan Company, 1926, 189 pp.
7. Garrison, K. C., "A Study of Some Factors Related to Leadership in High School," *Peabody Journal of Education,* 1933, 11: 11-17.
8. Hayes, W. J., "Some Factors Influencing Participation in Voluntary School Activities," *Teachers College Contributions to Education,* No. 419, Bureau of Publications, Teachers College, Columbia University, 1930, 82 pp.
9. Jenkins, G. G., "Factors Involved in Children's Friendships," *Journal of Educational Psychology,* 1931, 22: 440-448.
10. Jenkins, L. B., "Mental Conflicts of Eurasian Adolescents," *Journal of Social Psychology,* 1934, 5: 402-408.
11. Lippert, E., "Diebstahl in einer Jungmädchenklasse," *Zeitschrift für Jugendkunde,* 1934, 4: 125-129.
12. Maney, C. A., "The Distribution of Memberships in the Extracurricular Activities of the Liberal Arts College," *School and Society,* 1934, 39: 63-64.
13. Mills, H. C., "Subject and Activity Load of High School Juniors," *University of Buffalo Studies,* 1934, 9: 87-102.
14. Moreno, J. L., *Who Shall Survive?* Nervous and Mental Disease Publishing Company, 1934, 437 pp.
15. Partridge, E. D., "Leadership among Adolescent Boys,"

* See also the references in the Appendix.

Teachers College Contributions to Education, No. 608, Bureau of Publications, Teachers College, Columbia University, 1934, 109 pp.
16. Pfleger, E., "Sociale Verhaltensweisen eines körperlich entstellten Halbwaisen," *Zeitschrift für Jugendkunde,* 1934, 4: 129-132.
17. Pound, O., *Extracurricular Activities of High School Girls,* A. S. Barnes Company, 1931, 97 pp.
18. Pressey, L. C., *Some College Students and Their Problems,* Ohio State University Press, 1929, 97 pp.
19. Roberts, A. C., *Extra-Class and Intramural Activities in the High School,* D. C. Heath Company, 1928, 529 pp.
20. Schliebe, G., *Reifejahre im Internat,* Klinkhardt, Leipzig, 1934, 144 pp.
21. Spaulding, C. B., "Types of Junior College Leaders," *Sociological and Social Research,* 1933, 18: 164-168.
22. Stray, H. F., "Leadership Traits of Girls in Girls' Camps," *Sociological and Social Research,* 1934, 18: 240-250.
23. Sullivan, C., "A Scale for Measuring Developmental Age in Girls," *Studies in Psychology and Psychiatry,* 1934, Vol. III, No. 4, 65 pp.
24. Williams, F., "Confronting the World," in *Concerning Parents,* New Republic, Inc., 1926, pp. 137-159.
25. Zillig, M., "Beliebte und Unbeliebte Volksschülerinnen," *Industrielle Psychotechnik,* 1933, 10: 378-379.

CHAPTER V

MORAL AND RELIGIOUS DEVELOPMENTS OF NORMAL ADOLESCENCE

A CHILD's behavior is based almost exclusively upon the specific habits in which he has been trained. He regards as "right" those things he has been allowed to do; he regards as "wrong" both those actions of his own that have met with punishment and whatever other behavior he has heard condemned verbally by elders in whom he has confidence. Thus, a child will mark as "wrong" such deeds as "forgery," "divorce," "adultery," "blasphemy," or "sin" for which he can give no definition whatever; but he has heard such words spoken in a tone of voice already associated with his own misdeeds. During childhood, the boy or girl acquires more or less meaning for commonly used moral terms: honesty, charity, modesty, purity, and the like. The meanings given these words by children are not, however, those used by adults. Thus, a number of children asked to define "honesty" will produce such a series of responses as those given below:

> doing what your mother says
> telling the truth
> marking your arithmetic papers right
> not cheating on examinations
> keeping your score right in a game
> admitting wrong things you have done
> not copying from other children.

These definitions are obviously based upon the particular circumstances in which the word has been met. If a child is questioned sufficiently, he can often give more than one partial meaning for an abstract term, but he is not able to give a generalized definition that will include all his partial concepts.

The adolescent can improve upon the child's performance in two ways. He can, first, identify the common element in all his previous experiences with honest behavior and can therefore obtain a generalized meaning of "honesty"—that is, a concept of the term. This improvement is due partly to growth in intellectual power and partly to an increased number of practical experiences. Because of his ability to generalize, the adolescent can take a second step: he can apply his concept to new situations. When this stage is reached, the adolescent has achieved an "ideal" of honesty—whether his behavior conforms or not. His ideal, when fully developed, becomes then a "guide to conduct" in situations that are new.

Every normal adolescent has ideals, and he judges his own conduct in terms of them. It should not, however, be supposed that the ideals need to be socially acceptable. The boy who sees, in many diverse situations, the ability of the strong to coerce the weak may develop the ideal that "might makes right." He may then use this ideal to guide his own conduct or as a basis for judging new situations. His generalization is just as truly an "ideal" as a conviction that the strong should protect the weak.

Since concepts grow out of experiences, the child with socially acceptable habits usually grows up into the adolescent with socially acceptable ideals. Hence, the vital importance of training children in desirable habits. The small boy who "swipes" other pupils' erasers, buys candy with money given him to put on the collection plate, and cheats in games is laying the basis from which he will develop the ideal that dishonest conduct is wrong only when it is detected. No other general principle could reasonably be deduced from his earlier behavior. To be sure, the period of adolescence may bring new experiences and these will, in turn, lead to modifications. However, the essential connection between experiences and ideals should never be forgotten.

Dull people, like children, do not have the intellectual development necessary for seeing the common element in diverse situations. Consequently, they have only partial meanings and

MORAL DEVELOPMENTS

habits. They get along in the world as well as they do because most of one's life is lived on the basis of habit. No sane person uses up energy invoking an ideal in a situation for which an established habit is quite sufficient. Those who have charge of defectives train them to meet ordinary situations by consistent drill on appropriate habits and to meet unusual conditions by coming at once to an official adviser. With such training a defective can and often does live a normal social life without the assistance of any general concepts at all. The dull pupil in high school will not spontaneously develop consistent, integrated ideals; he needs help in generalizing his experiences sufficiently to see any interrelationships at all, and even then his "guides to conduct" will be relatively specific.

Ideals do not "jell" during adolescence; they keep on developing because life does not stand still. As long as one has new experiences one's ideals continue to modify. The adolescent is, however, more interested than adults in the development of attitudes. He has just discovered their existence and likes to exercise his new mental powers in further development. The resulting mental gymnastics are comparable to the small child's manual manipulation of a new toy. The adolescent becomes enormously concerned over such concepts as "democracy," "honor," "humanity," "sexual purity," or "prohibition" largely because he has so recently discovered their existence. The delinquent of the same age becomes equally thrilled over such concepts as "highjacking," "gang loyalty" or "racketeering." No essential difference appears in the underlying mechanisms. All ideals are generalizations of past experiences, used for the purpose of assaying present or future conduct.

In the course of the adolescent years, a boy or girl acquires a considerable assortment of attitudes. During the last decade there have been many investigations into the range of attitudes, beliefs, and ideals shown by young people. The specific items of information that have emerged concern three types of concept: (1) attitudes toward social or political movements, (2) attitudes toward ethical or moral questions, and (3) attitudes toward religious matters. The remaining sections of this chapter will present data on these three points.

Before considering the results in detail, however, an explanation concerning the type of "test" generally used seems desirable. Pupils are sometimes presented with (a) a series of statements; they are to check those which best represent their opinions. Other tests consist (b) of a series of questions with objective responses; the pupils are to mark the one response that best expresses their own attitude. In general, these results demand no writing and are thus entirely anonymous. There naturally arises some suspicion as to the reliability of reports gained in this manner. First, the reader must realize that chance "errors" due to flippancy, mischievousness, overconscientiousness, or simple misunderstanding will always cancel themselves out if enough opinions are collected and averaged. Second, the results must be evaluated by common sense; thus, if only one in a thousand high school pupils admitted he had ever cheated on a test, the results would be entirely unbelievable. Third, if a series of personal questions has been given to a class and the instructor has offered to talk over any student's paper with him if he can identify it, a considerable proportion of students will voluntarily come for an interview, locate their own papers, and frankly discuss their answers. Such discussion almost invariably proves the checking to have been carefully done, any errors being due to the kind of misunderstandings that will not influence results if enough pupils are tested. Finally, the reader should not suppose that questions concerning sociological or ethical opinions are given to a class without any explanation or preparation. The investigator uses one or more class periods to lead up to the actual administration of an "attitude" test. The students know their reports will be treated with confidence; they know nothing they say will influence their grades; they know the results are to be used in scientific research. Under these circumstances they have little if any reason to lie. Although the group questionnaire is not a precise instrument of measurement its use with large numbers of pupils does give results that are reliable, significant, and indicative of average opinion.

ATTITUDES ON SOCIOLOGICAL MATTERS

During recent years efforts have been made to measure attitudes on various questions. The majority of results have been

MORAL DEVELOPMENTS

obtained from undergraduate students whose ages were between eighteen and twenty-one. The results to be presented reflect, therefore, the attitudes typical of late adolescence. What data there is in regard to high school pupils indicates a greater conservatism during the earlier adolescent years. The total range of opinions is about the same for high school and college students, but the average opinion of the former is more conventional than that of the latter.

It is obviously impossible to present in a single chapter all the results obtained with tests that measure attitudes. For this section, therefore, the writer has selected a few typical investigations. These fall roughly into four groups: attitudes on such general social problems as prohibition, communism, and birth control; attitudes reflecting racial prejudice; attitudes indicating social prejudice within the adolescent group; and finally, attitudes toward popular superstitions. The results will serve to show the general nature of adolescent opinion along a number of different lines.

Attitudes on social problems.—These attitudes are usually measured by presenting pupils with a series of statements ranging from conservative to radical and asking each pupil to check those statements that best express his own opinion. From such a list of statements in regard (a) to prohibition,[21] the following items received the largest number of checks; that is, they represent the average opinion of undergraduate students.

> It should be a person's own business whether he drinks or not.*
> Prohibition should come as a result of education, not legislation.
> Liquor should be allowed under government license.

At one end of the total distribution of scores, 10 per cent of the students—those who most strongly opposed prohibition—marked the following statements:

* These responses and those listed on the next few pages in regard to communism and birth control, are used by permission of the University of Chicago Press.

> Prohibition should not be forced upon a people whose majority oppose it.
> Manufacture of liquor should be permitted without restrictions as to alcoholic content.
> Prohibition is making our young people lawless and degenerate.

At the other extreme of the distribution, approximately 10 per cent of the students favored such statements as:

> On the whole, the prohibition laws are satisfactory.
> Prohibition is fundamentally sound in principle.
> Prohibition has been a great lesson to our country.

The distribution of opinion shows about the variation found in the adult population. What evidence there is from groups younger and older than undergraduates in college indicates a steady but gradual trend from support of prohibition to opposition towards it. The tests used in the above investigation involve a vocabulary too difficult for children. Other tests and personal inquiries, however, show children to be almost 100 per cent in support of prohibition, probably because in school and at home they are taught the dangers of alcohol. The increasing opposition toward prohibition is probably the result of a realization that the problem is far more complicated than a mere abstinence from drinking.

(b) The average undergraduate attitude toward communism [21] is reflected in the following three statements that stand at the median of the distribution:

> Both the evils and benefits of communism are greatly exaggerated.
> We should be open-minded about communism.
> We should not reject communism until it has been given a longer trial.

The 10 per cent most strongly opposed to communism checked such statements as the following:

> It is only the ignorant and incompetent that want communism.
> If Russia today is a sample of how communism works, we don't want it.

MORAL DEVELOPMENTS

> If a man has the vision and ability to acquire property, he ought to be allowed to enjoy it himself.

At the other end of the distribution, 10 per cent marked the following statements, which show a strong support of communism:

> The communist may be rough, but he has the right idea.
> Give Russia another twenty years and you will see that communism can be made to work.
> The ideals of communism are worth working for.

Again the distribution is roughly that of reasoned adult opinion. It must be remembered, however, that these results were obtained from the highly selected group of students who attend college; opinions expressed by working adolescents of the same ages might be quite different. In all probability high school pupils would generally condemn communism—partly from ignorance, partly from intolerance of anything unusual, and partly from imitation of what they hear around them. Communism, being a total mode of life, is too complex a matter to be understood by adolescents.

(c) The average attitude toward birth control [21] is expressed by college undergraduates in the following statements:

> Birth control is a legitimate health measure.
> Birth control increases the happiness of married life.
> Birth control is necessary for women who must earn a living.

The 10 per cent most strongly opposed to birth control marked such statements as:

> The practice of birth control evades man's duty to propagate the race.
> Birth control is morally wrong in spite of its possible benefits.
> The practice of birth control may be injurious physically, mentally, and morally.
> Decency forbids the use of birth control.

The 10 per cent of students most strongly in favor of birth control marked the following statements:

Only a fool can oppose birth control.
Birth control is the only solution to many of our social problems.
Uncontrolled reproduction leads to overpopulation, social unrest, and war.

The entire range of opinion on this subject is unusually wide. There are several factors which might lead to such a result. First, the moral issues involved have been emphasized more than in the case of prohibition or communism. Communism is regarded as a social and economic rather than a moral reorganization of society, while prohibition has become so bogged down in graft, politics, and crime that its original moral implications have almost disappeared from view.

The relative newness of discussion concerning birth control inevitably influences the range of opinions regarding it. When any social question first arises, it is opposed or supported by extreme and vehement opinions; but as time goes on one extreme defeats the other, what was once an advanced view becomes the average opinion, and this belief is handed on to future generations as a social heritage. For example, when the doctrine of evolution was first advanced, it was supported and attacked with equal vehemence. For approximately two generations the conflict continued, but as more scientific data were assembled in support of evolution there came to be a greater acceptance of the theory until today few adolescents even question the evolutionary point of view. A test of attitude on evolution, given in 1850, would undoubtedly have shown violently opposed extremes of opinion such as are now expressed in regard to birth control. Today the average man holds many beliefs for which he would, in earlier generations, have been burned at the stake.

Finally, the range of attitude on any problem is influenced by the degree of organized opinion in back of the extreme viewpoints. Thus, in the case of birth control, organized religion strongly supports one extreme. This support, especially through its emphasis upon moral values, is efficacious in producing and maintaining the conventional point of view. At the other extreme are the experts in social science. One can only guess which attitude will eventually be victorious. But whichever it

MORAL DEVELOPMENTS

is, it will consolidate itself and be handed down to successive generations as the truth.

Racial prejudice.—There have been several investigations of attitude toward both Orientals and Negroes. The average adolescent shows strong racial prejudice. Youth is notoriously intolerant, and nowhere does this characteristic show more clearly than in the relationship between races. The antagonism is not merely a reflection of parental opinions. During the years of childhood the same individuals from the same homes do not show this attitude. White, colored, and Oriental children play together on the school playground, or work together in the classroom with little, if any, prejudice. The real basis of the marked antagonism is the profound adolescent dislike for anyone who is different from the average of the local social group. This desired uniformity prevents the social absorption of minor races into adolescent society.

A recent study [15] has investigated the racial attitudes of over one thousand children and adolescents in a middlewestern state. The test used included questions dealing with attitudes towards Jews, Negroes, Filipinos, Chinese, Japanese, Mexicans, Italians, and foreigners in general. These tests were given from the seventh to the twelfth grades. They were scored in two different ways. The first score showed the extent to which each pupil's opinion on impersonal questions approached the average opinion of adult, competent observers. The averages per grade based on this score are shown in the chart below. It will be noticed that this curve rises slowly through the tenth grade and then shows a slight decrease. It is at no time within sixty points of the scores made by the competent adult observers. The second score is based simply on those items that have a personal implication. Such a question as "Is the Negro more likely to be yellow in a fight than a white man?" was excluded from the second score while such questions as "If you were on a high school baseball team, would you just as soon have a colored boy for captain?" were included. The averages of these items showing personal reactions toward different races and nationalities decreased steadily from the seventh grade to the twelfth. That is, the personal intolerance became greater with every passing year. During the first four grades covered by the experiment there was, then, a slow gain in what might be called intellectual tolerance; there was a steady decrease in personal

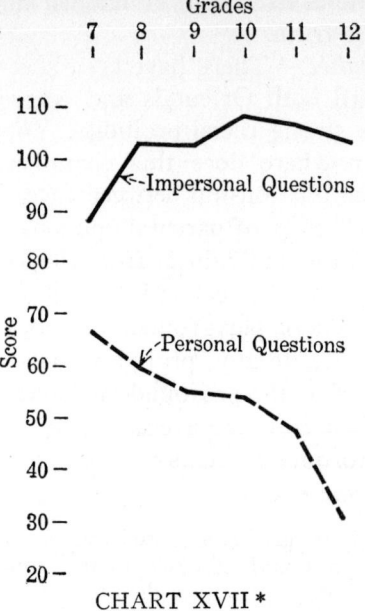

CHART XVII*

DEVELOPMENT OF RACIAL PREJUDICE (Minard [15])

tolerance which, in the last two years, evidently began to affect intellectual reactions as well. In both the intellectual and emotional fields the junior high and high school pupils are far from approximating competent adult opinion.

In another study,[1] a large group of Negroes was asked concerning any racial prejudice they had felt to be exerted against themselves. A few had never experienced any humiliation based on racial discrimination but most of the Negroes reported the appearance of discrimination at about the age of twelve; practically no prejudice was felt during the childhood years. The situations in which discrimination appeared were social in character. The most frequent reaction on the part of the Negroes was a complete withdrawal from sports, companionships, clubs, or any activities requiring social relationship with whites. The realization of prejudice against themselves was a severe blow to the Negroes'

* This material is presented by permission of the University of Iowa Press.

sense of security. Most Negroes involved in the study reported profound resentment against white pupils, with a consequent increase in the emotional attachments formed with other Negro adolescents. Racial antagonism thus began to manifest itself in the early years of adolescence and resulted in complete cleavage between the races in social activities, except those over which the school had control. As a result, the members of different races withdrew completely from each other, became utter strangers, and eventually developed deep and permanent antagonism.

One explanation for this permanence of racial prejudices is found in a study of prejudice toward Orientals.[25] Two types of tests were used; the first measured information concerning Oriental life and customs while the second measured attitude toward the Chinese and Japanese. The correlations between the scores on information test and attitudes varied from .65 to .82. In other words, those who knew most about Oriental life and customs had the least prejudice, while those with the most complete prejudice knew practically nothing. Over three hundred of the students tested stated they had one or more fairly close Oriental friends. These students averaged nine points higher than others on the information test and eleven points higher on the attitude test, again suggesting that knowledge and tolerance go hand in hand.

The implications from the above studies are fairly clear. Adolescents become easily intolerant of those not like themselves. This attitude at once terminates any intimate relationships with other groups, and this termination leads to ignorance. As a result, there is permanent prejudice on the part of white children and permanent resentment on the part of Orientals and Negroes. Each group withdraws to itself, and only the unusual individual ever succeeds in maintaining social relationships with those from any other group. If racial prejudices formed during adolescence were not permanent, they would not be so serious. The public school is the one institution most likely to succeed in breaking down unjustified antagonism, especially through its extracurricular activities.

Student snobbishness.—The data to be presented below are taken from a study of attitudes shown by fraternity and sorority members.[11] These attitudes not only reflect an intensification of normal adolescent prejudice and antagonism, but also show the effect of fraternity life in molding adolescent opinion.

In the course of the investigation, this question was given to over three thousand fraternity members: "Provided members of the groups listed below were otherwise good fraternity material, would you admit the following types of students to your own fraternity?" There then followed a list which included the names of various religious, national, racial, and social groups. Those who would be excluded from fraternity life are listed below: Jews, queer-looking students, atheists, Italians, American Indians, agnostics, Slavs, Armenians, Greeks, students with unconventional morals, Orientals, Turks, Hindus, Bolshevists, anarchists, students of low intelligence, loafers, Negroes. In this list are reflected racial and national prejudices; there is also the usual adolescent antagonism to anyone who is "queer"—in appearance, religious beliefs, or moral attitudes.

Another item presented to members of fraternities or sororities was the following:

> Check one of the two following statements which more nearly expresses your general feeling in regard to your fraternity or your sorority: (a) "My fraternity is a group standing for high ideals. The active personnel changes from year to year but the fraternity goes on, always upholding the same standards. A disgrace to my fraternity hurts me and reflects on all its members. A high standard of conduct should be required of its members so that the fair name of the fraternity should be upheld." (b) "My fraternity is a group of individuals and its ideals are no higher or no lower than those of the individuals. The fraternity and its standing really exist only in the personnel active at the time. A high standard of conduct should be required of the members because since they are associated in the fraternity a disgrace to one might affect the reputation of each of the others."

Approximately 70 per cent of the undergraduate fraternity members checked the first statement; even in the graduate school it was checked by half the students with fraternity connections. This idealizing of a group of individuals is a typically adolescent attitude that is crystallized and perpetuated far beyond its normal limits by the fraternity or sorority. In fact, the attitude expressed is often permanent. The writer was once chairman of a committee composed of herself and two forty-year-old women who, in their student days, had belonged to rival sororities. At the end of several meetings the writer was forced to request a new committee because the other two women refused absolutely to agree on any point and alternately visited the chairman secretly to enlist her support. Each of the two sororities involved had so inculcated loyalty to itself and antagonism to other groups that twenty years later the rivalry was interfering with matters having no relationship whatever to college life.

A further reflection of fraternity influence was shown by answers to a question about the probable effects on the university of continued losses by the local athletic teams to outstanding rivals. Approximately 20 per cent of the fraternity members believed such losses would not affect the merit of the university at all and the reputation only slightly, if any. Another 30 per cent believed the reputation would be considerably lowered but the merit unaffected, while 40 per cent believed the reputation of the university would be utterly lost and the merit considerably reduced. The most extreme 10 per cent believed both reputation and merit would be "completely destroyed." These attitudes are not due to mere youthfulness because students of the same age but not belonging to fraternities showed a far more balanced attitude. Only one-fourth of them believed the reputation would be seriously affected by athletic losses, while the majority discounted any effect at all of such losses upon merit and more than a moderate effect upon reputation.

On this, as well as on other opinions collected during this investigation, the members of fraternities and sororities showed an emotional and social immaturity distinctly below that of unattached students. Adolescents are admittedly intolerant and snobbish, but they gradually acquire mature attitudes if their earlier tendencies are not re-enforced by outside influences. Fraternities undoubtedly extend the period of unthinking loyalty and blind acceptance of group attitudes far beyond their normal limits.

Superstitions.—Despite the general dissemination of scientific knowledge, many superstitions are still firmly believed by pupils in high school. One study [3] investigated the extent to which two hundred unfounded beliefs were held by 854 high school pupils. The average per cent of superstitions marked as believed changed from thirty-five in the seventh grade to only twenty in the ninth. Superstitions about black cats, getting married on a rainy day, the unluckiness of the number 13, haunted houses, howling dogs, breaking mirrors, and picking up pins show a continuing belief on the part of an appreciable number of pupils. Even in college, some degree of superstition remains.[22] Lighting three cigarettes from the same match, stepping on the cracks of a cement walk, knocking on wood, wearing a "lucky" piece of apparel, carrying a fetish to examinations, and the like, are admitted by a group of intelligent, highly selected, well-educated college students. A recent book [20] lists fifteen hundred unfounded beliefs, which are grouped under twenty-five different headings. The per cent of adults believing each is, of course, not given, but it is a curious situation that so many unsupported and erroneous ideas should be believed at all by people living in a modern scientific world. One would think there must be something wrong with the teaching of science in both elementary and secondary schools. A definite attempt to uproot superstition might well be included somewhere in the curriculum.

Average adolescent attitudes on sociological questions as measured by these tests are a blend of ignorance, conservatism, immaturity, superstition, and prejudice. The range, however, is as wide as that for adult opinion. It will be interesting to find out, ten or twenty years from now, if the intensive teaching in the social sciences now developing in high schools will have had any measurable effect upon such attitudes.

ATTITUDES ON MORAL AND ETHICAL PROBLEMS

The results to be reported in this section have been accumulated through three different types of investigation. Most outstanding are the studies concerning the extent of dishonesty shown by school children in different situations. This research used only "performance" tests; that is, actual behavior under controlled conditions, not statements of opinion. In a second type of investigation, students checked statements in regard to cheating in examinations, either by themselves or by others.

These results refer, of course, to a particular phase of honesty. The third type of investigation was made by submitting to groups of school pupils a descriptive account of some criminal act and then asking them questions which revealed their insight into the nature of the behavior described. These studies are, admittedly, only samples from a large field. A comprehensive picture of normal moral development cannot at the present be given because not enough is definitely known. These scattered samples may, however, prove enlightening.

Development of honesty.—In some schools the extent of dishonesty increases with age; in other schools, it decreases; in still others, dishonesty in schoolwork decreases, while other types of deceitful behavior increase with maturity.[14] When results of all types are put together, there is a very slight decrease in dishonesty from year to year. This result may be due to greater maturity or to the elimination of the dullest and most delinquent members of the school population. The writer is inclined to believe the change in honesty represents little more than the normal elimination of dullards from grade to grade. The decrease is relatively small, and the variability of performance from one group to another relatively great. Certainly there is no such decrease as one hopes might result from education.

The extent of dishonest behavior correlates directly with a number of factors.[14] The intelligent pupil cheats less on school tests than the unintelligent, but both the intelligent and stupid cheat more in social situations than the child of average mental ability. Educational maladjustment leads to dishonesty, as shown by increased cheating on the part of retarded children. Emotional instability and suggestibility both correlate positively with dishonest behavior. The level of honesty tends to be similar among friends, or among members of the same family. Finally, honesty correlates highly with the economic and cultural level of the homes from which children come.

These relationships may be brought out clearly by the statistics given below. The first table shows the per cent of cheating shown on school tests, co-ordination tests, and social tests, by children of different levels of intelligence. The second table presents a rating of homes as to their economic and cultural levels, and the per cent of dishonesty shown by children from these homes, both on school tests and on homework. The third shows, for two sample grades, the relation between suggestibility and dishonest behavior. Other tables, showing the relationship between dishonesty and educational or emotional maladjustments, are too long for presentation here, but are equally convincing as regards the relation of maladjustment to deceit.

TABLE III

Relationship between Honesty and (a) Level of Intelligence, (b) Type of Home, and (c) Degree of Suggestibility * (May and Hartshorne [14])

(a) INTELLIGENCE

Classification †	Per Cent Cheating on		
	School Tests	Co-ordination Tests	Parties
A	27	32	57
B	31	58	62
C+	30	70	33
C	46	73	46
C−	49	88	42
D	70	89	53
E	82	100	50

(b) HOME

Score on Sims Score Card ‡	Per Cent Cheating on	
	School Tests	Home Tests
16	16	22
15	16	34
14	20	35
13	50	42
12	52	60
11	50	55
10	55	50
9	69	86
8	100	100

(c) SUGGESTIBILITY

Score §	Per Cent Cheating in	
	Grade 5	Grade 6
80-89	.7	33
70-79	3	40
60-69	5	57
50-59	7	67
40-49	8.5	77
30-39	14	93
20-29	14	89

* Use of this data has been made possible through permission of The Macmillan Company.
† This classification is based on the grouping of test results used in the army; A is the highest and E the lowest.
‡ The higher the score, the better the type of home.
§ High scores indicate resistance to suggestibility.

It would appear, then, that honesty was largely dependent upon four factors: intelligence, home background, resistance to suggestion, and adequate social adjustment. To some extent these factors are, of course, interrelated. The dullest parents usually maintain the poorest homes and the dullest children are both suggestible and more likely than not to be maladjusted.

MORAL DEVELOPMENTS

The implications of this research for the teacher are clear. She can expect cheating in schoolwork from about 35 per cent of children having average ability, about 75 per cent of dull pupils, and even from 25 per cent of the brightest children. In athletic contests and parties she can expect dishonest behavior from somewhere between 30 and 50 per cent of adolescents, without much respect to intelligence. She can expect greater dishonesty from retarded than from accelerated pupils and more from those who do poor work than from those whose work is satisfactory. If a given pupil's friends or siblings are known to be deceitful, she can anticipate dishonesty from the pupil concerned. She can also expect dishonest behavior in proportion to the amount of direct training in the particular situation being tested. Thus, in a group of children of whom 80 per cent will peek through their fingers in order to get a drawing traced more accurately, not more than 30 per cent will cheat in scoring their own papers, and not more than 3 per cent will steal money. Both home and school give intensive training concerning the honest handling of money. The school struggles from the kindergarten through graduate school to produce honesty in classroom work. However, it is only in a few games, such as hide-and-seek, that children receive training in inhibiting peeping through their fingers.

Cheating in schoolwork is more frequent than most teachers realize. It does not appreciably decrease as the pupils grow older. There is always a group of pupils at the bottom of the class, no matter how much elimination has already taken place. The pressure put upon those below the average becomes, if anything, greater with the passage of years. By the high school period, the childish motives for cheating have been re-enforced by the emotional drives of adolescence. Failure in school is distressing enough to children, but often means to the adolescent boy or girl a total collapse of both social and academic standing. It is no wonder that adolescents cheat; considering the strain put upon them by a too-difficult curriculum, it is surprising so many of them learn to be honest.

Cribbing.—In one extensive investigation,[11] over three

thousand undergraduates were presented with a series of questions in regard to their own cheating upon quizzes and examinations; they were asked to check whichever of the listed answers most nearly approximated their own reactions. The returns were entirely anonymous. Naturally, these results depend upon what the students were willing to admit. There were, however, undoubtedly more students underestimating than overestimating their cheating. The results may, therefore, be regarded as representing the minimum amount of cribbing one can expect in the college classroom. Of the 3,515 students, 30 per cent admitted no cribbing, 8 per cent reported cribbing only once, 24 per cent admitted cribbing on quizzes but not on final examinations, 33 per cent confessed cribbing on several examinations, while 5 per cent reported constant cheating on all types of work. These responses indicate the situation with which one has to deal.

To understand the motives and attitudes underlying the degree of admitted academic dishonesty, further investigations were made.[11] These same students were asked to indicate their degree of satisfaction with their college work and the extent to which their classes gave them opportunity for developing their main interests. Those who felt perfectly satisfied with their course of study cribbed little if any, while 75 per cent of the dissatisfied students cribbed more or less. Cribbing was then, to some extent, a product of discontent.

Nearly twice as many fraternity members as nonfraternity students were habitual cribbers. Approximately one-half the nonmembers admitted no cribbing, while only one-quarter of the fraternity members denied cribbing. There is in these results a suggestion that cheating on examinations is to some extent a type of social behavior handed down from one generation to another in certain social groups. From the writer's own observations she would suspect the fraternity results to be dependent upon an unfavorable social tradition on the part of a few fraternities, practically all of whose members cheated regularly. The unorganized students cheat less, perhaps because they do not have any integrated tradition and may therefore follow their own preferences.

One further investigation revealed several interesting facts.[4] The degree of cheating upon the Otis Intelligence Test and upon course examinations increased from the freshman to the graduate

MORAL DEVELOPMENTS

years in college. Discussion concerning problems of honesty had no effect on the results. Cheating was lowest when the instructor stayed in the room, increased if he absented himself occasionally, and rose still further if he were not present at all. The amount of cribbing shown by students who came from high schools having honor systems was greater than that shown by graduates of schools not having such plans. The honest and dishonest students showed no differences in chronological age, intelligence score, or academic standing. Here again there is a strong suggestion that cheating is a type of social behavior for which the motivation is more complicated than teachers generally suppose. It is entirely possible that honor systems give practice chiefly in dishonesty.

Further light was obtained from a question asking students to explain why they cheated. The main reasons given were matters of expediency: unfair grading, the necessity of competing with cribbers for grades, and negligent proctoring. These situations are remedial. With the present extent of dishonesty in classwork, an instructor is encouraging rather than discouraging cheating if his proctoring is lenient. Many teachers make sincere efforts to develop honesty among the pupils by putting them on their honor and then leaving them without supervision. Unfortunately, such behavior merely gives dishonest students a totally inexcusable advantage and encourages those who are willing to be honest to cheat in order to compete on an equal basis with the cribbers.

Cheating, once started in a group, quickly spreads. The writer recalls one examination in which she received a B while students on either side of her, who copied all answers from the textbook, received A's. On this occasion the instructor was out of the room during the entire period of the examination. A few students opened their books and notebooks as soon as the teacher was out of sight; within a half hour, two-thirds of the students were consulting their notebooks; by the end of the examination, only a few who were extremely honest, extremely well prepared, or entirely without notebooks were answering the questions honestly.

As long as the dishonest student can get better marks than the honest, cribbing is sure to continue on a large scale.

Still more information [11] was gained from questions designed to show the opinions of these same 3,515 students. They were asked to estimate the seriousness of cribbing in the entire university by checking one of a series of statements, beginning with "Cribbing is as bad as lying or cheating," and ending with,

"Every student should take what he can get. If he can get his degree by cribbing, that is the thing to do." The relationship between the expressed seriousness of cribbing as an offense and the confessed indulgence in this form of dishonesty is shown in the table below. Obviously, the extent of cribbing is in some

TABLE IV

Expressed Attitudes of Cribbers and Noncribbers *
(Katz and Allport [11])

(a) ATTITUDE TOWARD CRIBBING

	Per Cent of Those Who Admitted No Cribbing	Per Cent of Those Who Admitted Frequent Cribbing
1. It is as bad as lying	52.2	14
2. It shows defect of character	9.7	5
3. It is unfair but not wrong	20.2	21
4. One cannot maintain honesty in practical situations	8.6	23
5. One has to crib in order to gain one's rights	7.7	30.7
6. Cribbing is a game between teacher and student	1.1	6
7. One has a right to get all he can any way he can	.5	.3

(b) OPINIONS ON FREQUENCY WITH WHICH ALL COLLEGE STUDENTS CRIB

	Per Cent of Those Who Admitted No Cribbing	Per Cent of Those Who Admitted Frequent Cribbing
1. No college student cribs	3.4	.9
2. About one-fifth crib	34.8	13.1
3. About one-third crib	23.3	17.1
4. About one-half crib	17.4	20.4
5. About two-thirds crib	13.1	24.7
6. About four-fifths crib	7.5	20.8
7. All college students crib	.5	3

* These materials are published by the permission of the authors.

measure a result of one's "ideals." The majority of the noncribbers condemn cribbing, while the majority of the habitual cribbers report it as acceptable behavior. One further question asked these students to estimate what proportion of college students in their estimation actually did cheat on examinations. The relation between the estimated extent of the practice and the confessed behavior is shown in the second part of the above table. Those who did not admit any cribbing were inclined to discount the extent of such behavior in others. Few of the habitual cribbers thought less than one-third of students in general cheated on examinations, and many of them thought all students cheated. These results may, in part, be due to a desire for justification; but they undoubtedly reflect, in some measure, sincere beliefs. Students who cheat do not regard the practice as wrong or unusual.

Insight into criminal behavior.—It is generally assumed that adolescents have, by the age of eighteen, a reasonable degree of insight into the nature of criminal acts. Adolescents are supposed to know right from wrong, not only in familiar situations but also under new circumstances that call for reasoning. A recent investigation [7] demonstrates the actual extent of insight with regard to a criminal act of such a type that the adolescent must decide for himself whether the behavior was right or wrong. In this study the following story was given adolescent boys to read:

> A boy of seventeen planned to make a bicycle trip during a two weeks' holiday. For this he obtained parental approval and a sum of money which should last him for the duration of his trip. Before leaving the city in which he lived, however, he concluded to hire a motorcycle. So he stored his bicycle and hired the motorcycle, paying out most of his expense money for the hire. By the end of the second day, he had no funds left. He did not write home because he knew his father would not approve of the motorcycle and because the money already furnished had not been used as his father had intended. The boy did not want to lie to his father by writing he had lost the money already given him, so he decided to get it in some other way.
>
> He registered at a good hotel, had dinner and breakfast served in his room, and then sent the porter out to buy him a ticket to a near-by city. With some small change he tipped the porter, telling him to charge the amount of the ticket to his account at the desk. The boy then went to the railroad station. Here he explained that he had been forced to change his plans and could not use the ticket. The ticket seller therefore refunded him the money. Leaving his hotel bill unpaid,

the boy again set out on his motorcycle. The money thus gained lasted him for several days. When it was gone, he again raised money in precisely the same manner. At the end of the vacation he returned, left the motorcycle at the shop, and rode his bicycle home. In the course of the next two or three weeks he earned some money doing odd jobs and sent the appropriate amount to each of the two hotels where he had left an unpaid bill.

Concerning this story the children were asked four questions: first, if there were anything illegal or immoral in the boy's behavior; second, if there would have been anything illegal or immoral if the boy had never returned the money; third, if the transaction with the ticket involved dishonesty, without consideration of the unpaid hotel bill; and fourth, what punishment they would consider appropriate, supposing the money to have been returned. The average age of those answering the questions was seventeen. Fourteen per cent thought the boy's actions illegal and wrong. Forty-eight per cent thought his behavior neither illegal nor wrong. The remaining 38 per cent regarded his behavior as more or less wrong, but saw nothing illegal in it.

Assuming the boy had never returned the money, the per cents ran as follows: Forty-eight per cent still saw nothing immoral or illegal in the situation, but the proportion regarding the behavior as both wrong and illegal rose to 40 per cent, leaving only 12 per cent who thought the behavior morally wrong but entirely legal. The proportion who saw nothing wrong in the situation was the same whether the money was or was not returned. About two-thirds of those who previously had thought the behavior wrong but legal changed their opinions and regarded it both immoral and illegal.

The children were also asked their opinion regarding the operations with the railroad ticket, leaving out of consideration the unpaid hotel bill. Fifty-eight per cent saw nothing wrong or illegal in the behavior. Twenty-three per cent thought the manipulations wrong but nothing one could be arrested for, leaving only 19 per cent who regarded the episode as illegal.

Finally, the children were asked what punishment they would give the boy, basing their judgment on the story as it stood. Twenty per cent thought he should be punished, 64 per cent thought he should not be punished at all, and 16 per cent were doubtful.*

* This material is published by permission of *Zeitschrift für Kinderforschung,* Berlin, Germany.

The above story described a situation which, while clearly illegal, is unusual. The children whose opinions were asked had probably not previously heard of such an adventure. If the story had concerned the murder of one man by another—a situation for which they have already been taught an attitude—the results would have been different. This situation was new. Although the pupils answering the questions averaged within a year of the legal age of responsibility, one-half of them displayed no insight into the illegal nature of the behavior described.

All experimental evidence points to a justification of many juvenile offenders who state they did not know what they did was wrong. The more one investigates the ideals of adolescence, the more one appreciates the failure of the average youth to generalize. Even slight variations in a familiar situation seem to color the matter quite differently. Thus, the boy who will not steal money from his mother's pocketbook or his father's pockets may take money that has been left on the table or has fallen on the floor; he may then justify his behavior by saying that the money at the moment belonged to nobody and therefore he could not be stealing. Such statements sound like rationalizations, but they are sometimes the actual truth. The ideals of youth as revealed in biographies and diaries represent far too high a standard for the ordinary boy or girl. Until more is known in regard to *average* moral and ethical attitudes in the adolescent population, teachers would be wise to assume a lack of clearly defined ideals until towards the end of adolescence, and perhaps not then.

One further point may be emphasized. It has often been assumed that knowledge of criminal behavior would automatically deter one from criminal acts. In a recent study,[19] groups of 200 prisoners in penitentiaries and 272 schoolteachers were asked to arrange a series of forty-five criminal acts in order of their seriousness. The convicts' and the teachers' ratings correlated .95; in other words, there was essentially no difference between the groups in their understanding of the situations. From such evidence as this, one is inclined to doubt the efficacy of character training by means of verbal instruction. Direct teaching serves to identify a given situation with certain ideals of conduct, but it does not necessarily result in any modification of behavior. The main road to character development does not lie through the classroom.

ATTITUDES ON RELIGIOUS MATTERS

Traditional attitudes.—As one reads the biographies or autobiographies of famous adults from earlier generations, one is impressed with the religious conflicts characteristic of the adolescent years. The farther back one goes toward the Middle Ages the more conspicuous are these conflicts; conversely, the more recent the biography, the less conspicuous. In the life histories of men whose maturity fell within the last thirty years, adolescent conflicts seem to be more sociological than religious. There is, therefore, some indication that the intense religious doubts generally reported from previous generations may have been largely generated by tradition. Just as the adolescent Indian boy was expected to obtain a vision or personal revelation, so the adolescent European boy was expected to consider the salvation of his soul. The resulting conflict was between a personal God and a personal Devil, each of whom was trying to obtain possession of the adolescent. In more recent times the conflict was between the traditional beliefs of any church and the newer doctrines of evolution. The dogmas of science and those of the church stood in sharp contrast to each other, and the adolescent—at all times inclined to extremes—found it necessary to accept only one. As a result of these various social forces, one finds revolt and conversion as two typical experiences of adolescent youth in earlier generations.

Within the last fifty years, religious attitudes and customs have markedly changed. At present, the majority of adolescents have no religious doubts at any time. For those who do have difficulties, the conflict seems to be just as intense and preoccupying as ever, but these pupils form a minority in the total population. There are many reasons why intense conflicts over religious matters no longer appear among more than a fourth of all the intelligent young people in America. Present-day adolescents have been brought up on science. They acquire a materialistic and naturalistic outlook during their childhood years. Many have had no religious training whatever; they may have gone to church and Sunday school, but the content of the latter consisted of Bible stories plus a little ethical training, while the sermons in church concerned themselves primarily with social evils. Of church doctrines, most adolescents have no knowledge whatever. The American public school has also done its share in eliminating conflicts. Any discussion of religion is completely banned. On the other hand, elementary schools encourage children to do as much independent thinking as they are capable of. The American spirit is, in general, opposed to philosophical considerations of any kind. The American child and adolescent therefore rarely come across written matter that stimulates them to an interest in philosophical questions. There has also been in modern times an almost total escape from the fear of hell after death. Not over 35 per cent of college freshmen admit a belief in either hell or the devil.[11] The motivation played by fear has therefore disappeared and, with it, much of the concentration upon religious thinking. The adolescent of today is far more concerned with doing other people good in this world than he is with saving his soul in the next. In fact, not more than half the adolescent population believes in immortality.[11] Finally, there has developed a naturalistic point of view toward the three events that earlier were the three important sacraments of the church—birth, marriage, and death. No one of these three is commonly regarded in America, outside the Catholic church at least, as being in any sense sacred. The laws concerning them require their registration, but there is no need for any religious consideration unless one is prompted by one's own desires.

As a result of the combined pressure from all the above sources, the Protestant adolescent usually does not pass through any severe religious crisis. The Catholic child is also protected from a crisis but in not at all the same manner.[24] He is taught the forms of religion at an early age, and he learns verbatim a statement of doctrines. At the time, none of this means anything in particular to him. As he grows older, the empty forms gradually take on meaning until by the end of his adolescent period he has developed, by a continual process of acquiring deeper and deeper insights, the beliefs of his church. To the Catholic child, confirmation with full admission to the church is merely a logical development of a process started the day he was baptized. Catholic adolescents who do have severe doubts are those who find their education and their church conflicting, but unless one has a rather philosophical mind there is no clear-cut opposition between the two. The church deals with religious matters and the school with secular matters. The two sets of facts and beliefs remain in two mental compartments, between which there is not the slightest communication. The Catholic child who gets into difficulties is the one who lets ideas from one compartment get into the other. In his case the conflict is no different from that experienced by Protestant adolescents, except that it is often more severe, since rejection of his beliefs means a voluntary excommunication from a highly organized group to which he has been sincerely attached.

A psychology of religion.—There have been volumes written in regard to adolescent religious experiences. Some of these are obviously an expression of what an author believes or would like to believe, without the support of any objective facts. Others are written on the basis of diaries, autobiographies, or other writings. Such data are, of course, valuable, but by their very nature the results are limited to the experiences of exceptional or highly literate individuals, who make up not more than one per cent of the total population. There is not yet a coherent psychology of religion, based upon the actual experiences and beliefs of the average adolescent boy and girl. There are, however, certain beginnings of such a psychology.

Because belief in a Supreme Being is an essential religious concept, the majority of modern investigations have been concerned with adolescent belief in God. In addition, there have been a few scattered investigations into the environmental conditions or personal characteristics that are likely to influence the development of religious beliefs.

The usual technique for investigating attitudes toward God has been to present unselected groups of adolescents with a series of statements ranging all the way from complete belief to complete atheism. The students are asked to check those statements which best represent their own beliefs. One curious point about the distributions thus obtained is their bimodal character. That is, the beliefs do not distribute themselves in a normal curve, but rather group themselves around two central tendencies. In one investigation,[21] the following two sets of beliefs both showed an equally high frequency.

(1) I trust in God to support the right and condemn the wrong.
I think I believe in God but have not thought much about it.
I believe in God but my idea of God is vague.
My idea of God develops with experience.
I have a strong desire to believe in God.

(2) I do not believe in God and would be a coward if I were to say I did.
I am tolerant towards those who still believe in God.
Although I do not believe in God, I am open-minded about the mysteries of life.
The idea of God seems quite unnecessary.

These students have separated themselves into two groups—those who accept traditional belief and those who reject it. At the very extremes of the distribution there are about 5 per cent who marked such statements as those below:

God is the underlying reality of life.
I am quite convinced of the reality of God.
I am thrilled in contemplation of the Divine Creator.

The idea of God is a hindrance to clear thinking.
God has no place in my thinking.
It is absurd for any thinking man to use such a concept as God.

In these results it is again possible to see how the extreme beliefs of a former period have become the generally accepted beliefs at present. The most interesting point, however, is the clear antagonism of the two groups of adolescents—those who believe in God and those who do not.

In another investigation,[11] undergraduates in college were asked to express their beliefs by checking one of several statements concerning the nature of God. In general, 63 per cent regarded God as a person; 22 per cent regarded God as an impersonal force; 13 per cent were agnostic, while 2 per cent believed there was no God and the world was a machine. The relationship of these four points of view to earlier religious training is made quite clear in the chart below. Of the Catholic students, 51 per cent regarded God as a Divine Creator, and another 40 per cent as a friendly and intelligent Being. Only 6 per cent thought of God as an impersonal force, only 3 per cent had any doubts in the

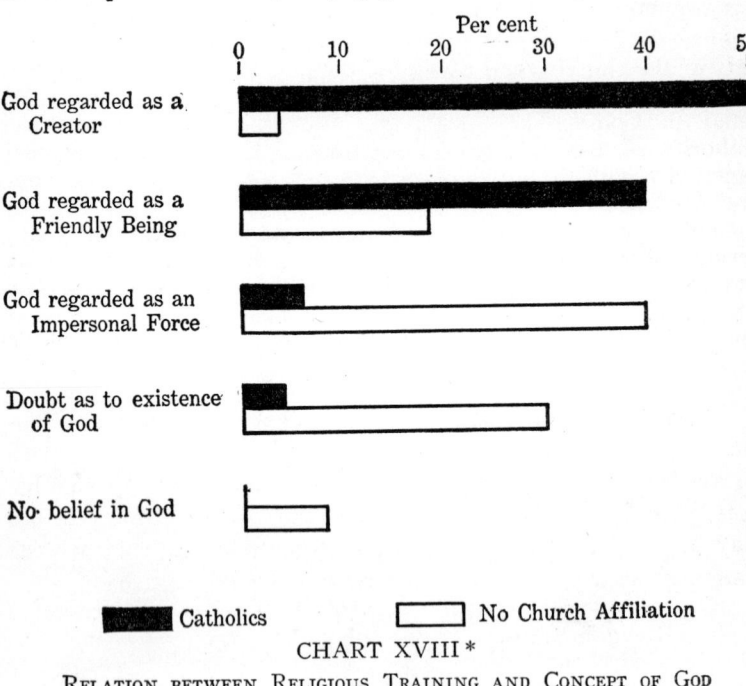

CHART XVIII *

RELATION BETWEEN RELIGIOUS TRAINING AND CONCEPT OF GOD
(Katz and Allport [11])

* These materials are presented by permission of the authors.

matter, and no one accepted a naturalistic view of the universe. Of those who had no religious affiliations, only 22 per cent thought of God as any kind of a person, 40 per cent regarded God as an impersonal force, while 30 per cent were agnostic—leaving 8 per cent who thought the world a machine. The Protestant and Jewish students expressed opinions about halfway between these two extremes, with the largest number believing God to be a friendly and intelligent Being.

Another study of college undergraduates,[6] covering much the same data, shows the change in beliefs through the college period. The freshmen were divided exactly evenly between belief in a personal and an impersonal God. By the senior year, however—either through elimination or through a change of opinion—25 per cent believed in a personal God and 75 per cent in an impersonal force.

A few other interesting points emerged from these various studies. Students usually credit educational influences with the responsibility for the loss of their childhood convictions.[11] The chief conflicts are reported as centering around the traditional beliefs of the church, the infallibility of the Bible, and the existence of God.[11] Students have been asked to give evidence for their belief in God.[18] The outstanding reasons presented were the authority of parents or of the Bible; a few listed a personal experience with the presence of God as evidence. Of several hundred students, 65 per cent reported a gradual growth of religious conviction with no sudden conversions and with no particular period of doubt.[11] Twenty-two per cent reported a period of doubt and emotional strain, with some degree of later reconstruction. The remaining students had no belief in God, but had arrived at this attitude by the same leisurely growth as characterized the first group.

The foregoing studies have investigated the religious convictions of later adolescence. One study of 646 children with an average age of thirteen gives some insight into earlier beliefs.[13] The statements used in this study are not analytic but may be of some interest; the per cent indicated marked each statement as true:

	Per Cent
1. Religion consists of obeying God's laws.	70
2. God is simply imagination.	21
3. We learn about God through dreams and visions.	28
4. God made us, the animals, the stars, and the flowers, and everything in the world.	82

		Per Cent
5.	God knows everything we say or do.	78
6.	God cares what we do.	89
7.	God has a good reason for what happens to us, even when we cannot understand it.	92
8.	God protects from harm those who trust him.	70
9.	God cares whether we repent of our sins or not.	82
10.	God hears and answers our prayers.	85
11.	True prayer consists of thinking of the wonderful ways of God in the world.	66
12.	It is possible to get things by prayer.	31
13.	The soul lives on after the body dies.	71 *

For the most part, these young adolescents accepted whatever religious beliefs they had been taught, but even as early as thirteen there was some degree of doubt and opposition. The idea, popular in childhood, that one can get things by prayer had been largely outgrown. A few children were already doubting God's existence. A considerable per cent had lost their confidence in God's omniscience and protection, and there was a far from uniform belief in immortality. These results are interesting in suggesting the age at which doubts first arise. These particular items do not indicate any belief in an impersonal force because all items assumed God as an individual.

Another group of investigators have sought to determine what factors are related to the development of religious beliefs. The relationship between chronological age and accepted beliefs is always negative.[13] Girls usually revolt against accepted beliefs less frequently than boys, less profoundly, and at a later age.[13] The correlation between the educational and economic level of homes and the acceptance of religious beliefs is also negative;[13] that between religion and intelligence is either slightly negative or close to zero.[2, 13] The relation between acceptance of religious dogmas and religious observances in the home or attendance of the entire family at church is relatively high.[13] With religious education or knowledge of the Bible there is no relation whatever.[8]

* This material is used by permission of the Bureau of Publications, Teachers College, Columbia University.

MORAL DEVELOPMENTS

On the side of personality even less is known. One investigation has attempted, however, to locate personal differences between thirty-six students who completely rejected traditional religious beliefs and thirty-four students who completely accepted such attitudes.[9] These extreme groups were tested for physical, intellectual, and emotional differences. There is no question of the difference in intelligence. Those who rejected religious authority averaged at the seventy-third percentile on the intelligence tests used; those who accepted averaged at the forty-eighth percentile; the lower end of one distribution overlapped with the upper end of the other. In physical traits there was no discernible difference. Two emotional differences were, however, found: The conservatives were far more suggestible than the radicals and reported three times as many intense emotional experiences. Too little is known about either religious or irreligious individuals to permit of any conclusion as to the fundamental differences in personality which lead to belief or rejection.

Emotional crises.—Although conversion or any other sudden realization of God's existence is not a particularly common experience, it is worth while to understand something of its importance to those who do experience it. There are many records in regard to sudden conversion. In fact, such an experience is found in the development of practically every great religious leader. To those who have had such an experience, the matter needs no description; to those who have not had it, the whole thing remains a mystery. As far as the emotional content is concerned, the descriptions of a conversion do not vary materially from those given by great scientists of their moments of discovery. The chief components appear to be an emotional exaltation, an abnormal physical fatigue, and a sudden, sure understanding of one's problems. Whether the insight is given into matters divine or matters scientific does not seem to be psychologically important.

The number of conversions is steadily becoming smaller. Except among a certain class of Negroes, it is no longer the fashion in America to "get religion." Conversion is undoubtedly quite as much a pattern of social behavior as a spontaneous individual experience. In the past, situations have often been deliberately arranged so as to produce conversions; people remained in church for many successive hours, in the midst of singing, praying, shouting, and general excitement. The first result was extreme physical and emotional fatigue. Any person in such a condition is highly suggestible. If one member of a group experienced a sincere and more or less spontaneous conversion, all those who were sufficiently fatigued to be oversuggestible would follow. While they had similar emotional experiences, the conversion was usually not lasting because it was based upon fatigue and suggestibility without any deep personal conviction or revelation. What the true convert sees at the moment of his conversion is a sudden reorganization of the world in terms he can understand and believe. The individual who by such an experience suddenly rejects religious beliefs has experienced a conversion—exactly as the individual who suddenly accepts such beliefs.

It is extremely difficult to obtain information or evidence in regard to the average individual's emotional experiences on religious matters. Ordinary contacts discover only those who are anxious to talk about themselves. Clinical observations are based exclusively upon those who have had serious conflicts. Evidence from diaries concerns only those who write well and easily enough to keep a diary. Thus far, hardly any beginning has been made in this matter. There are only a few scattered studies which may be quoted as evidence.

In one such investigation,[12] a group of 148 girls between the ages of fifteen and seventeen were asked to tell when and where they first experienced a feeling of reverence. Before this assignment was made, the meaning of "reverence" was carefully studied and an understanding of the concept reasonably assured. The matter was so developed in the preparatory periods that the pupils knew the experience need not have any relation to formal religion. Of the 148, twenty-two had never experienced an emotion they could honestly call reverence. Sixty-eight reported such feelings as arising at a time when they suddenly realized the beauty of nature. The feeling was not experienced if there were people around or if the evidences of human occupation were at all obtrusive in the landscape. Thirty-one pupils reported their first feeling of reverence or awe to be connected with some religious observance. Eighteen had experienced reverence toward some person they had known; usually, this individual had been badly treated and yet had not become embittered by life. Finally, there were nine pupils who had had such feelings while listening to music or looking at some especially impressive artistic masterpiece. The diversity of stimulus and the relative lack of connection with religious services is interesting. The results, slight though they are, certainly suggest that anything impressive and beautiful may arouse this particular type of emotional experience.

SIGNIFICANCE OF ADOLESCENT MORAL AND RELIGIOUS DEVELOPMENT FOR THE TEACHER

The public school teacher is forbidden to teach religion. She does, however, come in contact with moral problems because she is often the one adult in whose unprejudiced attitude an individual adolescent has confidence. She must, therefore, have some understanding of adolescent religious developments so that she may appreciate the nature of the problems experienced by her pupils and may be able to give reasonably sound advice. Although the material in this chapter is all too diverse and scattered, there still remain certain points of particular value for the teacher's consideration.

She should expect immature and prejudiced points of view, especially on matters that concern personal contacts between individuals. In her instruction, the English teacher should try to develop acceptable ideals of conduct, the science teacher to eradicate superstition, the social science teacher to bring about greater racial tolerance, and every teacher to decrease the present extent of social antagonism. A more concerted attack on honesty in schoolwork is needed. If examinations are so arranged that one dishonest pupil can get a good mark by cheating, the practice will soon spread, and before long the majority of students will have built up a habit of dishonesty that will function whenever there is opportunity. Adolescent ideals are not well developed, and the high school curriculum is too difficult for the average pupil; the teacher who sentimentally "trusts" her pupils and therefore fails to supervise them is giving them practice in habits of dishonesty—exactly the reverse of what she earnestly intends. The honest pupils want the teacher to stay in the room and protect them.

A school can do a good deal in breaking down student snobbishness. The school that lets pupils wear any clothes they like, establish any secret organizations they desire, work in laboratories or elsewhere only with their own friends, play on teams or belong to clubs only with their intimates is producing—not eliminating—snobbishness. Teachers should make definite efforts to break up small cliques by assigning the members to different classes; they should definitely foster democratic behavior by keeping all activities equally open to everyone and free from domination by a few.

The writer feels dissatisfied with the level of moral development shown in several of the studies, but does not know what might be done about it. She would, however, suggest that groups of teachers in large high schools consider ways of improving the situation. The students are clearly acting in a manner considerably below their knowledge of right and wrong—and their knowledge is none too good. The situation can be improved only by teachers who are willing to discover facts, face them—unemotionally and objectively—and then try out one method after another until some successful techniques are found for increasing adolescent understanding and improving adolescent behavior. With the greatly increased mental powers, to be discussed in the next chapter, there would seem every reason to expect a higher level of generalization and applied knowledge than is indicated by the results from most of the studies quoted.

ILLUSTRATIVE CASE STUDIES

The diverse nature of the material presented and the necessary omissions of some topics through lack of definite data make the chapter rather hard to illustrate. After some consideration the writer decided to concentrate on religious develop-

MORAL DEVELOPMENTS

ments, honesty in school, drinking, and sex morality; racial discrimination has already been shown by two previous examples in other connections. The first four short excerpts below are taken from statements of girls concerning their religious experiences.[16] The next two histories describe college students who were intoxicated or dishonest;[17] special attention should be paid to the causes of these manifestations. Finally, there is a description, taken from the sane, shrewd writings of Miriam Van Waters, of adolescent attitudes on sexual matters.[23]

Our interest was not only aroused concerning religious affairs, but we became deeply interested in society and those about us. Social responsibility rested heavily upon our shoulders. We organized a club for charitable purposes. We elected officers and each week gave a certain amount of our spending money. At one time there was nearly ten dollars in our treasury, and how rich we felt and how we planned to spend our money! With it we were going to help the poor not only of our own community but of the state. There was no limit to what we could do, and our idea of helpfulness soared to great heights. However, we did buy some cloth and made some clothes for the children of one poor family for Christmas, and with those and a few toys and candy ended our social welfare work. The material aid which we rendered was slight, but the encouragement we received from our parents and their interest in our plans for helpfulness were great. I think it was through the ideals which our little club had at that time, impractical though they were, that I realized what a need there was for kindness and helpfulness in the world and what social responsibility really meant.

The change in regard to my religion was perhaps the most intense and noticeable. From the careless, indifferent childhood, when I attended to my religious duties almost unconsciously, I passed into a period of great religious fervor. It was a time when I began to worry as to the right and wrong of things. I became very conscientious on the subject of lying and would scarcely ever be positive about anything for fear I might be wrong. I began to think a great deal about God and the principles of my religion. In church I was more attentive than hitherto. I prayed now with more meaning and thought. At one time I felt that I was quite wicked and not living up to my religion as I ought. I thought that I did not pray long and fervently enough. My night prayers came to occupy such a long time that my sister would often make me cease and go to bed. I considered this a great injustice and an interference with my duty. Often I would wake up in the night and feel obliged to rise and pray. I frequently desired that I might become very holy and pious. I felt sure that I would become a nun when I grew up. I took great interest in reading the Lives of the Saints at various intervals and would resolve earnestly to imitate them.

I never made a public exhibition of myself by being converted. I was most secretive and reserved as to my feeling. For a year I tried very hard to be good and did succeed in slightly improving my disposition. At the beginning of my fifteenth year I believed myself a hardened skeptic, a tragic doubter. This I kept from my family, for I feared my father's wrath and my mother's tears. Undoubtedly mother would be so disappointed that she would waste away and die. Nothing could be more tragic than this, except my own sad life. After sixteen I quieted down considerably and did not find life such a trying affair.

I do not know how to speak of my religious experience in the teens. I had gotten along very well without a "religion" before, but when I was about fourteen there was a series of revival meetings held in the different churches; and going to the Methodist church one evening, more out of curiosity than anything else, I was so frightened by the evangelist's statements as to our sinful condition that I became quite excited and would probably have "gone forward" if I had not had such a decided dislike for the woman who came to urge me to "take the deciding step now," and also for the fact that this church was neither "father's church" nor "mother's church." A week later there was another revival, this time in "mother's church," and I let myself be swept off my feet by the enthusiasm felt for it. One noon seven of us girls were going home and saying, "I'll go if you will," so that is how I came to "go forward," that night. I do not remember feeling more virtuous, "cleansed from sin," "resurrected to a new life," or any change whatsoever following my baptism, except that now instead of having Sunday at home in peace (I say this intentionally) I had to get ready and go to church or else be thought backsliding. Later on I very much regretted this "conversion," because if I had been let alone until I could think things out for myself I would have thought "father's church" the one I believed in and really cared for.*

* This and the three preceding paragraphs are presented through the permission of the D. Appleton-Century Company.

Hilda Davis [17] had been caught cheating. She could not deny she was guilty, but she did declare she was no worse than many other students who had not been caught, and she practically demanded a hearing of her side of the case. Before talking with Hilda, the interviewer looked up the girl's record and found she had a low intelligence, a poor comprehension of reading matter, and a record of failure in four courses out of the fifteen she had taken. Evidently, Hilda was hardly likely to graduate if she were allowed to remain in college. But expulsion on the basis of cheating seemed a less satisfactory finish than removal because of poor grades.

Hilda stated frankly that she had cheated in every course except the four she failed, and in those the instructors had watched her too carefully. She had at her entrance to college worked hard to master her subjects; but she had found by experience that her only chances for a passing grade lay in copying someone else's work, though she was not willing to admit she had to cheat because of inferior ability. She excused her conduct on the basis that everyone else did the same sort of thing. Hilda was a popular member of a sorority. This group had copies of term papers, book reports, topics, and previously used final examinations for all the courses commonly taken in the university. Any written work to be done outside of class was simply copied from some earlier paper. In addition, various members had made "cribs" of sundry sorts for the use of themselves and others. There was also "teamwork" in the classroom; if two of the sisters were in the same class they arranged to sit next to each other, to write large enough on examinations for each other to read, to have a set of signals, and so on. In other words, Hilda had come to know cheating as the common, clever, and "sporting" means of passing work. Her friends all knew she was not very bright in her studies and everyone was willing to help her "put one over" on her teachers.

Hilda wanted desperately to remain in college. She came from a home that was unpleasant to her. Her people were hard workers, steady and honest, but without much refinement. Hilda loved the social life of the university. Through her sorority she met many girls and became acquainted with many boys who were considerably above her own social class at home. If she returned to her parents she knew she would have to go to work—especially if she was sent home because of cheating—and to mingle with a class of people distinctly inferior in tastes, social skills, and wealth to her group at college. Being sent home meant being sent into social exile; meant that her whole future life would probably be on a social, economic, and cultural level distasteful to her; probably meant the end of opportunities to make the kind of marriage for which she had hoped. When everything is considered, it is small wonder that Hilda had cheated; it would have been more remarkable if she had not.

Hilda's case is pathetic, and her future discouraging. Here is a girl who has developed interests, desires, ambitions distinctly above the level of her abilities. She has been successful in deception so often that in the face of any difficulty she will probably again turn to dishonesty. She dislikes her home and she will dislike every job that she can possibly hold. In contrast with her sorority life, any other social group she is likely to enter will be without interest. Unless she is fortunate enough to marry a man of some means, she is as likely as not to enter the oldest feminine profession in the world, in order to gratify the desires which have been nourished in her by her college experiences. Even should she remain honest it will be years before she will be content with the social level to which her inferior ability would naturally confine her. For Hilda, separated from her too-clever friends, there are rocks ahead.

Theodore Wilkins [17] turned up for a class one morning, wobbly on his feet and smelling of whiskey, and proceeded to precipitate quite a scene. His instructor was horrified and, in spite of the boy's satisfactory academic record, was about to send him to his college office for discipline when someone suggested that careful and sympathetic study of the case, instead of immediate disciplinary action, might be the more constructive step.

After Theodore had had time to sleep off the effects of the whiskey, he presented himself for study, somewhat bewildered and embarrassed. At the first interview it became evident he was keeping back something that was troubling him. As his confidence was gained and his embarrassment decreased, he told the following story. He had been brought up in a home where he saw adults drink more or less, although he had never seen any member of his family actually drunk. He knew, however, from both observation and experience that a glass of liquor helped a person through emotional crises. He had come to the university from a large city high school where he had been reasonably popular. He was a Jewish boy, although he had hardly any of the usual facial characteristics. At college he had hoped to "make" a fraternity, and to that end had tried to disguise the fact of his nationality. Knowledge of it leaked out, however, with the result that he was blackballed in two different fraternities where he was being considered; at the same time he was offered membership with a group of Jewish boys. This latter offer he was unwilling to accept, and the failure to gain admittance to such a group as he desired hurt him far more than he was willing to admit. In his emotional depression he turned to a consoling glass of liquor. At first he drank in moderation—just enough to make him forget his troubles and to help him mix genially with others. As time went on he became deeply despondent because he could neither find friendship among non-Jewish boys nor adapt himself to the somewhat narrow social outlook of many of his own race. The final straw came when some fanatic Jewish student accused him vehemently of being a traitor to his people and tried to make him return to the fold. Theodore became thoroughly disgusted. He could see no future for himself with either Jews or Gentiles. In a mood of despair he drank himself into unconsciousness—as an escape from an intolerable reality. From time to time his troubles again mastered him, and he sought the same escape and oblivion.

Theodore's case was difficult of adjustment, although his story makes his dissipation understandable enough. His problem was to learn somehow to get along with the only people with whom intensive social contacts were likely. He was persuaded to build up friendships with the few Jewish students he did like and with a few men of other groups who were attracted to him. As a matter of fact, he was quite acceptable to many non-Jewish students, though not to most fraternity men, and in consequence he was able to make a fairly satisfying social adjustment. He still wishes his social dreams might have been realized, and he still feels the injustice of social discrimination. He has, however, been able to turn his feelings on this matter to practical use by electing courses in the study of racial problems and by joining a group especially interested in this subject. He is achieving some position in the college world as a thoroughly likable Jew. The drinking has stopped; Theodore is intelligent enough to see that he was merely running away from difficulties instead of facing them and finding a solution. He is now accepting reality and trying to find satisfaction in things as they are. It is probable that he will, after he leaves college, get along well in some profession.

Four girls, fourteen, sixteen, fifteen and seventeen years of age are next on the calendar.[23] They are high school students, healthy young Americans of "good" families. They are involved in a "school scandal." One was discovered by her teacher to possess a notebook of dull obscenities, sex jokes and drawings, together with improper parodies of popular songs, and what would have been, if true, a casual, supposedly witty account of rape on a school girl. These she had obtained from another girl, the delicate daughter of a minister, who in turn had received them from a taxicab driver. This young fellow, on being brought to court, was discovered by psychological examination to be feeble-minded. The notebook had circulated among students, brilliant, dull, rich and poor.

The four girls now before the court were the popular, well-dressed daughters of good families. They smoked, drank (when they could get it), rode home from dances in taxicabs with young men, took all night joy rides, used a great deal of paint and powder, swore at their parents. Each had a "daddy," although the tenure of office and length of service of these young lovers were precarious. The girls were sophisticated, tired; any exertion, besides dancing, wore them out. They detested athletics, books, and housework. They stood about average in high school work.

Three boys were also before the court, as witnesses, aged fifteen, seventeen, and twenty. They were prominent students in scholarship and activities. They were not, it seems, "daddies" of these girls, but there was some imperative, diplomatic reason why they should "help" the girls who were in a "scrape" or impending unpleasantness at home. So, the youngest boy obtained the parental automobile, the three boys and four girls "eloped," that is to say, went to the neighboring county seat to procure marriage licenses. En route gasoline gave out. Thereupon the parental car was abandoned and a strange one commandeered. In talking it over at leisure it was decided not to marry, the parents would probably "fuss," if one thing more than another was to be avoided it was "fuss." Now these girls were pretty and delicate, daintily reared, and the boys were "manly," "regular fellows" in good society, yet in court they admit, not only sexual familiarity, but promiscuity and disregard of [the] simplest requirements of decency and affection which would arouse honest contempt in the mind of a longshoreman. Early in the morning they had arrived at a roadhouse, and being without funds or gasoline, one of the boys telephoned to his parents. Now, charged with theft and immorality, they are before the court.

They presented an amazing contrast to their parents. One would have thought it was the parents who were laboring under burden of guilt, while the children were calm and rather disinterested. Clearly the parents behaved as if the pillars of their family esteem had suddenly collapsed; dazed with surprise and humiliation they sat with bowed heads, utterly pitiable. On the other hand the young people were courteous, frank, submissive to questions of court, but there were frequent smiles and impatience at the futility of it all.

MORAL DEVELOPMENTS

There are two tasks for the juvenile court: first to pierce the crust of composure, to reach in these girls and boys those central tissues that are still sensitive, to awaken them to insight of their actual human predicament; and second to assist these adults, the parents, teachers and neighbors, to an understanding sympathy.

The parents of the girls wish to take them home, but they demand punishment of the boys. [The] parents of the boys obviously view these girls as the mother of Samson would gaze upon Delilah. Their sons have never spent a night away from home, they are girl-shy, their morals are unimpeachable. Someone must be *guilty* they think, but they cannot believe it is their boys.

The juvenile court explains to the parents that the girls, equally with the boys, are responsible. Equally guilty are parents, school and court; clearly we are part of a human family which has failed in the elemental duty of bringing up our young. It is now a question not of degree of guilt, or weight of punishment, but of understanding and helping young people. The school has expelled them, the neighbors stripped them naked with talk, but they would be made welcome in every dance hall, cabaret, or brothel in town. Suddenly the court is conscious of responsibility of the instrument which the state has created to fulfill the duties of socialized parenthood and wonders how the public can be content with any but the wisest men and women in that place.

Sex is not sacred to these youngsters, or terrifying; it is merely fun. While their attitude may be less harmful than that of some of their critics, it is still dangerous, inadequate and abnormal, running swiftly into perversions. The court will send each young person with his or her parents, if possible, to a socially minded physician to be instructed in the elements of sex hygiene, for be it well understood [that] all their glib, seeming information is spurious. They do not know the body and its rules, any more than they know the spirit of the creative force which they have been destroying. The court, by probing, simple questions, tries to bring to them a sense of birth, child-rearing, nursing, illness, love, courtship, self-sacrifice, discovery, struggle and happiness, parenthood, and death. Not fear, but understanding and pity are sought, and since in race history human situations have not changed much, these young people are often genuinely impressed after their visits to orphanages, children's hospitals, and the like. Their parents have shielded them and have veiled reality, but the court has never faced a "flapper" who has not been somewhat touched by a true life situation, squarely presented. Funny parodies in the notebook become not quite so funny, if the mystery is removed, and biological sequences revealed. The court, however, would be guilty of a wrong did it not see that in sex instruction furnished these young people by doctor and probation officer, emphasis was on health and joy, rather than upon disease and pain.

To parents the court must stress [the] need of studying their individual children, of not blaming other young people for their children's delinquencies; of [the] need of vigor in parenthood, not alone physically, but in ideals of family life which make child-rearing a genuine fulfillment.

Surprising as it appears after hearing evidence, the largest proportion of these boys and girls from high schools and good neighborhoods, if taken to court early for first delinquencies, where they are wisely handled, and then put under adequate probation officers, if home, school, church, and court co-operate, make good. They do not repeat delinquencies, they look on their former conduct as a fad they have dropped; they become rather sober-minded, critical young American citizens.*

BIBLIOGRAPHY †

1. Beckham, A. S., "Study of Attitudes of Negro Adolescents," *Journal of Abnormal and Social Psychology*, 1934, 29: 18-29.
2. Boynton, P. L., "A Study of the Relation between the Intelligence and the Moral Judgments of College Students," *George Peabody College for Teachers*, No. 51, 1929, 49 pp.
3. Caldwell, O. W., and Lundeen, G. E., "Further Study of Unfounded Beliefs among Junior High School Pupils," *Teachers College Record*, 1934, 36: 35-52.
4. Campbell, W. G., "Student Honesty in a University with an Honor System," *School and Society*, 1930, 31: 232-240.
5. Carlson, H. B., "Attitudes of Undergraduate Students," *Journal of Social Psychology*, 1934, 5: 202-213.
6. Dudycha, G. J., "The Moral Beliefs of College Students," *Journal of Applied Psychology*, 1933, 17: 585-603.
7. Fischer, S., "Über die Einsicht der Jugendlichen," *Zeitschrift für Kinderforschung*, 1932, 40: 497-516.
8. Hightower, P. R., "Biblical Information in Relation to Character," *University of Iowa Studies in Character*, 1930, Vol. III, 72 pp.
9. Howells, T. H., "Comparative Study of Those Who Accept as against Those Who Reject Religious Authority," *Univer-*

* This case study is used by permission of New Republic, Inc.
† See also the references in the Appendix.

MORAL DEVELOPMENTS

     sity of Iowa Studies in Character, Vol. II, No. 2, 1928, 80 pp.
10. Jenkins, L. B., "Mental Conflicts of Eurasian Adolescents," *Journal of Social Psychology,* 1934, 5: 402-408.
11. Katz, D., and Allport, F. H., *Students' Attitudes,* Craftsman Press, 1931, 408 pp.
12. Kupky, O., *The Religious Development of Adolescents,* The Macmillan Company, 1928, 138 pp.
13. MacLean, A. H., "Idea of God in Protestant Religious Education," *Teachers College Contributions to Education,* No. 410, Bureau of Publications, Teachers College, Columbia University, 1930, 150 pp.
14. May, M., and Hartshorne, H., *Studies in Deceit,* Vol. I, The Macmillan Company, 1928, 306 pp.
15. Minard, R. D., "Race Attitudes of Iowa Children," *University of Iowa Studies in Character,* 1931, Vol. 4, No. 2, 101 pp.
16. Mudge, E. L., *Varieties of Adolescent Experience,* D. Appleton-Century Company, 1926, 134 pp.
17. Pressey, L. C., *Some College Students and Their Problems,* Ohio State University Press, 1929, 97 pp.
18. Searles, H. L., "An Empirical Inquiry into the God Experience of 140 College Students," *Religious Education,* 1926, 21: 334-341.
19. Simpson, R. M., "Attitudes of Teachers and Prisoners toward the Seriousness of Criminal Acts," *Journal of Criminal Law and Criminology,* 1934, 25: 76-83.
20. Thompson, C. J. S., *The Hand of Destiny,* Rider and Company, 1933, 303 pp.
21. Thurstone, L. L., *Scales for the Measurement of Social Attitudes,* University of Chicago Press, 1930.
22. Tozzer, A. M., *Social Origins and Racial Continuities,* The Macmillan Company, 1925, 286 pp.
23. Van Waters, M., *Youth in Conflict,* New Republic, Inc., 1925, 293 pp.
24. Vorwahl, H., "Die Religion der Jugend," *Vierteljahrschrift für Jugendkunde,* 1933, 3: 143-152.
25. Watson, G. B., "Orient and Occident," *Report of the Institute of Pacific Relations,* 1927, 92 pp.

CHAPTER VI

INTELLECTUAL DEVELOPMENTS OF NORMAL ADOLESCENCE

SINCE the very earliest studies of adolescence, stress has been placed upon the characteristic intellectual developments of the period. Anyone who has watched the growth of an individual between the ages of thirteen and twenty-one has been impressed by the rapid gains made in ability to handle ideas. Any high school teacher knows that subject matter too difficult for freshmen is easily learned by the same pupils when they are seniors. There is an evident increase in judgment, reasoning, comprehension, speed of performance, memory, concentration, or any other mental function. No doubt exists in the mind of observers in regard to the rapid intellectual development during these years.

Neurological evidence, however, is somewhat contradictory. Since the total number of neurones is complete at birth, this intellectual development cannot be due to any increase in the number of nerve fibers, as was once supposed. The nervous system acquires its adult weight during the early years of childhood. What changes take place during adolescence must, then, be due to growth in the length or thickness of the neurones. There is some evidence that such a development does take place in the neurones of the brain. A single nerve fiber would, through this process, come into contact with many more neurones than it could touch when it was shorter; thus a far greater complexity within the nervous system would develop. The neurologists themselves are still arguing over the matter, but the balance of evidence favors an assumption of longitudinal neural growth and a resulting increase in neural complexity. On the other hand, the neurological basis may have existed since birth, awaiting adequate stimulation from the environment.

Some of the observed increase in mental power is doubtless due to the piling up of experience and knowledge. By the end of the eighth grade a child has accumulated a store of basic information and has reduced many simple skills to such an automatic level that he can use them in his thinking. He has, for instance, acquired meanings for about ten thousand words; he thus has a vocabulary with which to think. Several mathematical skills have become habitual, many elementary scientific facts have been thoroughly absorbed, and there has been considerable experience with the relationship between cause and effect. The childhood years may thus represent a long, gradual development of sufficient experience to serve as a basis for more complicated thinking. In all curves of learning one finds long plateaus covering the periods during which basic skills are being acquired. At the end of such plateaus there is usually a sudden and marked rise in learning capacity, due presumably to the co-ordination of simple skills and not to any neurological development in the learner. This integration of experience, with childhood serving as a long plateau, is doubtless one cause of the relatively rapid intellectual development during adolescence.

Tests of intelligence have been widely used for the last twenty years; literally millions of children have been tested, at all levels in school. Several thousand children have been re-tested several times. There have been investigations of the mental growth of brilliant, average, and dull children. One can now prophesy from a reliably determined intelligence quotient what a child's mental capacity will be during succeeding years and what intellectual level he will reach in his maturity. The main evidence in regard to adolescent mental development has come through the use of objective tests. The first section of the present chapter will deal with the adequacy of existing mental tests to measure the intellectual growth of the period.

A second section will present data concerning the distribution of mental ability in the high school population. The purpose of this presentation is to show the teacher what "pupil material" she may expect in her classes.

Adolescent growth is shown not only in general intellectual level but also in specific abilities. The ordinary intelligence test measures primarily verbal capacity; other tests have been used to investigate mechanical or social intelligence. Still further investigations have traced growth in memory, reading comprehension, imagination, or reasoning ability. Results along these lines will be presented in the third section of this chapter.

There is also a broadening and changing of intellectual interests during adolescence. This change is reflected in the type of books read, the type of games played, and the type of school subjects preferred. There have been investigations of these matters, with results adequate to reflect the general trend. A fourth section of this chapter will deal with the development of intellectual interests during adolescence.

Finally, there will be a summary of the entire situation, pointing out to the teacher the practical significance of the various studies made. Daily procedure in the classroom should be based upon scientific research. The last section is designed to assist the teacher in transferring the essential points of the chapter out of the book and into her classroom.

There will be no discussion of theories of intelligence. They have purposely been avoided, partly because the whole matter is controversial and partly because such theories are of relatively little value to the classroom teacher. The reader who is interested in general principles will find a theory implicit in the presentation; for others it may well be omitted.

MEASUREMENT OF ADOLESCENT INTELLIGENCE

The table below shows the age norms from three widely used intelligence tests.[16, 20, 28] The score is simply the average number of correct answers marked by the pupils. The number of correct answers obviously increases from year to year throughout the period of adolescence. There are, however, at least three important considerations in the interpretation of such results.

TABLE V

Norms from Tests of Intelligence

Ages	Otis Higher Examination *	Terman Group Test *	Pressey Senior Classification †
10½	..	15	..
11½	..	40	15
12½	26	60	25
13½	30	80	33
14½	34	100	42
15½	38	125	50
16½	40	145	57
17½	42	167	64
18½	..	187	..
19½	..	210	..

* Reproduced by written permission of the World Book Company, Yonkers-on-Hudson, New York.
† Reproduced by written permission of the Public School Publishing Company, Bloomington, Illinois.

Difficulties of test construction.—The first point (1) concerns the nature of the tests used and the difficulties of selecting appropriate material for them. The fact that they are group tests is probably of no importance. To be sure, a group test does not give as reliable results as an individual test for any single student, but for norms based upon thousands of students the group test is entirely satisfactory. An individual child may do poorly because he was sick, did not really try, or misunderstood directions; he may get a higher score than he should because he copied or worked longer than the appropriate length of time. But all of these incidental matters cancel themselves out and do not affect the validity of norms based on several thousand results. There are, however, other and more important characteristics of a test than its mode of administration.

Intelligence tests supposedly measure innate ability. Everyone knows, however, that they actually measure innate capacities plus experience to date. Theoretically, such a test should contain questions dealing only with things children have had a chance to learn but have not been taught. Naturally, a test involving schoolwork reflects the quality of the teaching quite as much as the ability of the children. Material specifically learned in school should supposedly be eliminated from intelligence tests. Actually it cannot be, if group tests are used, because the pupils must read the test items, and reading skill is a product of teaching. A question such as "At what point does the Missouri River flow into the Mississippi?" would not be at all appropriate for an intelligence test because it is too closely associated with school teaching. Such a question as "What phrase is used in advertisements for Lucky Strikes?" is a much better question because all pupils have had opportunity enough to observe the slogan, and certainly no teacher has ever taught them the answer. One trouble with present tests of intelligence is the lack of material that is independent of school teaching and still not too easy for high school pupils to answer. What most tests actually include is material so commonly taught in school that all pupils have had adequate opportunity for learning it. They are, therefore, more nearly "classification" than "intelligence" tests.

A further difficulty in selecting appropriate questions arises as soon as pupils have begun to diversify their work. Making a test for adolescents is far harder than making one for children. In the early years of childhood, for instance, one can assume children have been taught to count from 1 to 20. On the basis of this common knowledge one can use as a test of intelligence the ability to count backward by 2's from 20 to 0. This process calls for a rearrangement of commonly known facts, and although it is based on school achievement, it requires a mental manipulation of the items learned. By the time pupils reach high school, however, their course of study has become so varied there is no such common content as exists in the early years of elementary school. One cannot use a question requiring manipulation of positive and negative numbers because some pupils have not had algebra. One cannot present a question asking for judgment of some character in a story because there is no story everyone has read. One cannot use anything but the simplest and most basic facts about history because the nucleus of information available to all pupils is so small. Items derived either from the general environment or from elementary school training are usually too easy to measure the upper limits of adolescent intelligence, and those based upon more recent training and experience give an advantage to pupils who have had good preparation. A test of readiness to enter high school or college is much easier to construct than a test of intelligence for pupils of the relevant ages.

The effect of widely divergent experience on test scores may be illustrated from results obtained with the Army intelligence tests.[35] When the scores made by recruits were grouped according to civil occupations, the stenographers and private secretaries scored at the top of the distribution while locomotive engineers scored near the bottom. A stenographer's business is the handling of words; he must write fast, read rapidly, and have a wide vocabulary. The locomotive engineer reads little except his orders and the daily papers; there is no need for verbal skill in his daily tasks; his job gives him no verbal training. The difference in fundamental intellectual ability between stenographers and engineers is certainly not as great as indicated by the test results. Concentrated training in handling a language automatically produces a high score in any intelligence test because of the common element involved.

Similarly, in high school the large numbers of nonverbal children are severely handicapped by the ordinary intelligence test, while the academically trained are more than adequately prepared. The fact is that as soon as children emerge from childhood their experiences become so varied that few common elements exist. Consequently, a test based on items everyone has had a chance to observe and no one has been taught is practically impossible.

Further evidence in regard to the nature of intelligence tests is obtained by anyone who works with children of different races or from different environments. Thus, a worker with Polynesian children reports complete uselessness of a test in the Binet scale that requires children to choose the prettier of two faces, one of which is very ugly. The Polynesian children refused point-blank to make any selection until they knew the social caste of each of the two individuals. They then unerringly chose the one belonging to the higher caste. It made no difference whether the higher caste were assigned to the prettier or the uglier of the two faces.

Workers with Indians are unanimous in testifying that time limit tests cannot be used. Native Indian life puts no premium whatever upon time; in fact, no one has ever succeeded in hurrying an Indian. Indian adolescents make scores closely approximating those of white children of the same age, if they are allowed to complete a test at their own rate.[9] Children from rural backgrounds always score poorly on tests of intelligence. They too are in no particular hurry. Moreover, many items of the average intelligence test are based on experiences one has in a city but does not have in the country. Thus the answer to the question on the Binet scale, "What would you do if you were going some place and missed your car?" depends upon whether the cars run once an hour or twice a week. Norms for widely used intelligence tests are based almost exclusively upon results from children in large cities. The entire nature of the usual test automatically handicaps pupils coming from any other type of background.

Essentially there are no tests of intelligence for use with adolescents. The tests which exist are excellent in their ability to measure academic potentialities; they are therefore extremely useful in classifying pupils for school purposes. Naturally they do measure native ability to some extent—just as any test measures the alertness of a pupil—but they also measure the training a pupil has received. The character of the ordinary intelligence test should never be forgotten in estimating the value of the results.

Influence of elimination on norms.—There is a second factor (2) that affects one's interpretation of such norms as are above presented. These norms are based on surveys of entire school populations. The results are then grouped by age and a median or average found for all pupils of a given age, regardless of their grade placement. However, with each passing year there is more and more elimination of children from school. Thus, of all the sixteen-year-old girls, for instance, about 65 per cent are in high school, 5 per cent are still in junior high school, 5 per cent are married, 1 per cent is in college, 1 per cent is out of school because of ill health, 3 per cent are defective or in institutions of some kind, and the remaining 20 per cent are working. If a test is used only in high school not more than 65 per cent of the entire distribution is tested. Even if the investigator includes all children of adolescent years still in junior high school or the grades, the distribution remains inadequate. Careful investigators determine the total number of children of a given age in a community, then they count as above the median those who are in college and as below the median all those who are defective, in grades below high school, or at work. Such a calculation, of course, assumes that pupils eliminated from the school are below average in mental capacity; probably some of them are not. A median found by using such scores as are obtained and assigning the missing scores to their probable half of the distribution is, however, of reasonable validity. The investigator next plots a curve from the norms of the fourteen-, fifteen-, sixteen-, and seventeen-year-old children from whom he has test results, and then projects the ends of the curve to indicate the probable score of twelve-, thirteen-, eighteen-, and nineteen-year-old pupils. In other words, there is no such thing as an age norm based on an entire distribution of any age above twelve.

If, as is most usual, the investigator does not take into consideration the missing pupils, the test norms reflect both increased intellectual ability *and* increased elimination. As more and more pupils terminate their schooling, the average score made by those remaining will rise whether there is an increase in intellectual capacity or not. There have been a few attempts made to measure intellectual development of the same pupils from year to year by using the same tests or duplicate forms of the same tests. Such results indicate a certain degree of growth but not nearly as much as is obtained by the usual technique of the school survey, which inevitably measures elimination. No one knows whether the rise shown by norms on group tests is merely a measure of elimination. Where it is small it may be. The main point to remember is that the rise due to elimination is always inherent in test results.

Limits of mental growth.—A final point (3) in regard to the interpretation of test scores concerns the assumed cessation of mental growth by the middle years of adolescence. During the entire period from thirteen to twenty-one, norms show relatively little increase, in spite of the elimination. The shape of the growth curve as derived from intelligence tests is shown below.[31] The increments after the beginning of adolescence are small, and progress appears to stop entirely by the middle of the period. Additional light on this point is given by the Army results.[35] The average score made by the adult recruits falls half-

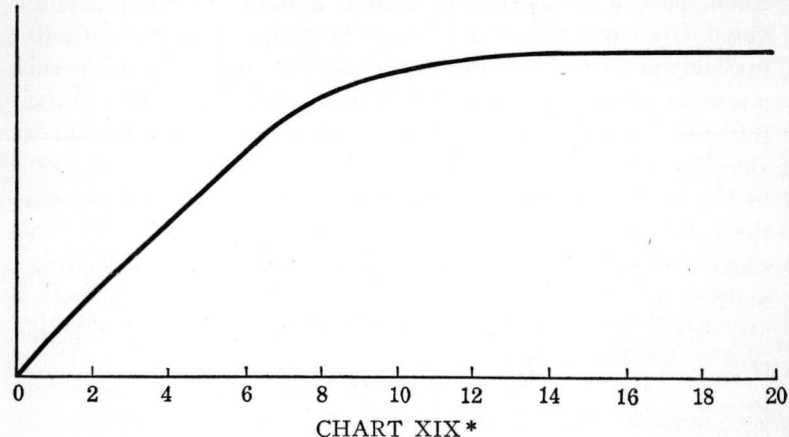

CHART XIX*

STANDARD GROWTH CURVE OF INTELLIGENCE (Thorndike [30])

way between the average scores made by thirteen- and fourteen-year-old children in school; that is, the average adult mental age is reckoned as thirteen and a half. Any high school teacher, however, has difficulty in accepting such findings at their face value. Any parent who has watched the mental development of a son or daughter from early to late adolescence also finds the relative lack of development—as indicated by test results—hard to believe. Growth in mental power certainly seems to be rapid during adolescence and to continue throughout the period. The test results do not square with everyday observation.

Those who have confidence in the existing tests of intelligence assume that all increase in ability along any line after the age of sixteen is due to greater experience and not to

* This material is presented by permission of the Bureau of Publications, Teachers College, Columbia University.

greater intellectual power. This is undoubtedly a possible explanation. It may be that maximal ability has matured by the middle of adolescence and only awaits sufficient stimulation. It is the writer's own conviction, however, that no one has ever adequately measured the growth or the distribution of adolescent intelligence. The kind of abilities measured by the present intelligence tests very likely do reach their adult level of development by the age of fifteen or sixteen. But this situation may be due merely to the character of the tests. The impression a teacher obtains of increasing mental power from year to year throughout adolescence and perhaps later may be only an illusion, but the writer believes there is such a growth, though it has never been measured. The same thing applies to growth through the earlier years of maturity. A man of thirty obviously differs from himself at the age of twenty in experience and knowledge; but it would appear to the observer that he has also developed in mental capacity. The upper limits of adolescent intelligence have certainly never been adequately measured because the tests do not give the most intelligent individuals any chance to show their ability. Tests could, and presumably will, be devised to measure the kind of growth in intellectual power which takes place during these years. The existence of such growth is at present only an assumption; intellectual growth may well continue—perhaps along new lines—at least throughout adolescence.

In spite of the shortcomings above indicated, results with tests of intelligence are illuminating. They do serve to give the teacher a rough idea of the "pupil material" with which she must work. One should neither believe without reservations the results of present-day tests nor should one refuse to accept them at all. A sane observer uses such findings as are at hand, always remembering they are far from being the law and the gospel. The present section was placed first in the chapter to make the reader thoughtful and cautious, not to destroy all confidence in tests. Most teachers are too gullible rather than too critical.

THE HIGH SCHOOL POPULATION

Distribution of abilities.—A typical freshman class in a large city high school shows a range of mental age about like that given below:

TABLE VI
A Typical Freshman Class * (Portenier [17])

I.Q. Derived from a Group Test	Mental Age †	No. Cases	Per Cent
150-159	21 years 4 months	4	.1
140-149	20 " 4 "	51	.8
130-139	18 " 10 "	155	2.
120-129	17 " 6 "	541	9.
110-119	16 " 1 "	1,192	18.
100-109	14 " 8 "	1,847	28.
90-99	13 " 3 "	1,797	27.
80-89	11 " 10 "	837	13.
70-79	10 " 6 "	139	2.
60-69	9 " 1 "	4	.1
		6,567	100.0

* This material is used by permission of the Bureau of Publications, Teachers College, Columbia University.
† The mental ages indicated have been calculated by assuming a median chronological age of fourteen and by taking the central I.Q. of each interval (65, 75, 85, etc.). These mental ages are therefore only approximations but will serve to show the range of intellectual level in an average entering class.

Here the mental age varies from that shown by the average fourth-grade child to that expected from seniors in college. The average I.Q. is 105—typical for entering freshman classes, although a quotient of 110 is average for those who graduate. If the upper ranges of adolescent ability were more adequately measured, the variability would be even greater than now appears. In any case, the school must make adjustments to this entire range of abilities.

Variability continues throughout high school, becoming slightly less as the dullest pupils are eliminated. Thus, one high school group that started with 1,721 freshmen, showing a range of scores from 25 to 184, ended with 621 seniors whose scores varied from 55 to 204. The median scores for the group rose from 96 in the first year to 126 in the last.[17] One cannot tell how much rise was due to mental growth and how much to the elimination of 64 per cent of the original group.

It is customary to present distributions of ability by sex and to point out differences between boys and girls in average or range of mental capacities. The writer has not done this, for a variety of reasons. Data concerning preschool or elementary school children are not relevant to this text. Differences shown among high school pupils are always reflections of the selective factors that have brought about elimination from school. Thus, as a general thing, more dull boys than dull girls drop out of school; consequently, the average score of high school boys frequently surpasses that of the girls, although the latter have been superior throughout the lower grades. In some communities, however, the exact opposite is the case, because there happens to be some local industry in which girls but not boys are employed. All comparisons of pupils beyond the compulsory school age are influenced by such matters of selection. Even if thousands of students are tested, the other thousands who are working are omitted; the results show merely the comparative standing of those boys and girls who have remained in school. For the adult years results are no more satisfactory. The Army test measured a large, unselected group of men, but there has never been any such measurement of women; hence, one does not know how the distributions would compare. If someone would give the same test to *every* individual from thirteen to twenty-one years of age in a community and if the test used were equally appropriate for boys and girls, it would be possible to determine average standing and variability of the two sexes.

Nor is the incompleteness of the distributions the only source of trouble. A test that is ververbal favors the girls; one that lays undue stress upon mathematics and mechanics favors the boys. The usual type of intelligence test undoubtedly gives girls a better chance than boys. Hence, any deductions from test results must be interpreted in terms of the particular test used.

Most differences that have been reliably demonstrated have little significance for the teacher, partly because the differences are small and partly because they are irrelevant. Thus a teacher proceeds in the same way whether 55 per cent of the girls exceed the boys or 55 per cent of the boys exceed the girls in a given type of test. Even if it were accurately shown that six or seven out of every ten brilliant students were boys, still the desirable education —presumably a firm foundation for university training—would remain unaffected. Obviously, experimental results showing, for instance, that girls have a more or a less sensitive skin than boys are quite irrelevant to the teaching situation. Indeed, the majority of reports dealing with sex differences are irrelevant. From a careful survey of the literature the writer can find only one difference that seems to be of sufficient size and importance to mention. Girls are undoubtedly superior in verbalism and boys in mathematics. These differences may be native or acquired; in any case, they seem to exist. An English teacher may, therefore, expect more girls than boys among her "A" students, while a teacher of geometry may expect the opposite.*

Changes in distribution.—Where records have been kept over a sufficient length of time, there is evidence of a steady decrease in the average ability of entering high school classes.[17] The table below gives the average I.Q. and mental age for enter-

TABLE VII

MEDIAN INTELLECTUAL LEVEL IN ONE SCHOOL, 1921-30 * (Portenier [17])

Year	Average I.Q.	Average C.A.	Average M.A.
1921–22	107.6	14 years 3 months	15 years 3 months
1923–24	105.2	13 " 9 "	14 " 4 "
1925–26	101.5	14 " 0 "	14 " 2 "
1927–28	101.2	14 " 0 "	14 " 1 "
1929–30	101.0	13 " 10 "	13 " 11 "

* This material is used by permission of the Bureau of Publications, Teachers College, Columbia University.

ing freshmen in one school system for the ten years between 1921 and 1931. These figures do not begin, of course, until after the enormous increase in enrollments during and after the World War. Nevertheless, there has been a loss of over a year in average intelligence. This situation is undoubtedly due to the increasingly greater persistence of pupils from the elementary grades into high school. For example, the enrollment in the ninth grade of a large school system in 1908 was only 14 per cent of the average number of pupils in the first four grades of the same system; in 1928 the enrollment in the ninth grade was 88 per cent of the average for the first four grades.[14] This method of reckoning persistence eliminates the factor of gen-

* Attempts to measure sex differences in the important field of personality must be viewed with even more skepticism than in the case of intelligence. Objective measures of personality are new, the results are not yet clearly interpretable, and no totally unselected groups of sufficient size have been measured. There is, therefore, no indisputable evidence that girls are, for instance, more docile than boys; they may very well be, but the proof does not yet exist. Any teacher does well to experiment sometimes with measures of personality, but she also does well to view the results of such tests with extreme caution.

eral growth in the population, since any increase would affect the lower grades even more than the higher. The obvious fact is that thousands of children who in 1908 would never have reached the ninth grade are now there.

The actual increase in the proportion of dull pupils is illustrated in the following figures, showing the per cent of entering freshmen from 1921 to 1931 who had I.Q.'s of eighty-five or below.[17] The mental ages of these dull pupils have been grouped into six-month intervals from eleven and one-half to thirteen and one-half, as shown in the graph below. Although

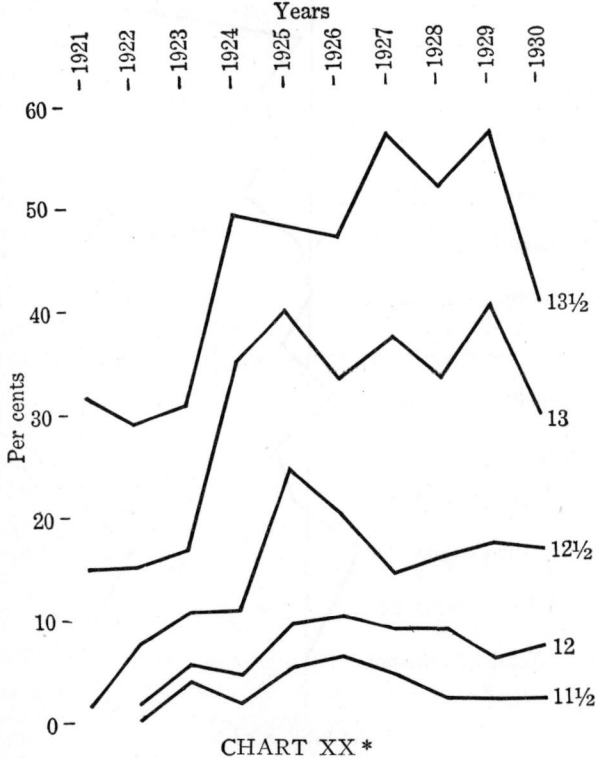

CHART XX *

PER CENT OF FRESHMEN, 1921–30, WITH MENTAL AGES OF THIRTEEN AND ONE-HALF OR BELOW (Portenier [17])

*This material is used by permission of the Bureau of Publications, Teachers College, Columbia University.

the change from year to year is somewhat irregular, and although the figures for the last two years reported were doubtless influenced by the depression, there seems no doubt that the number of relatively dull pupils in high school is steadily in-

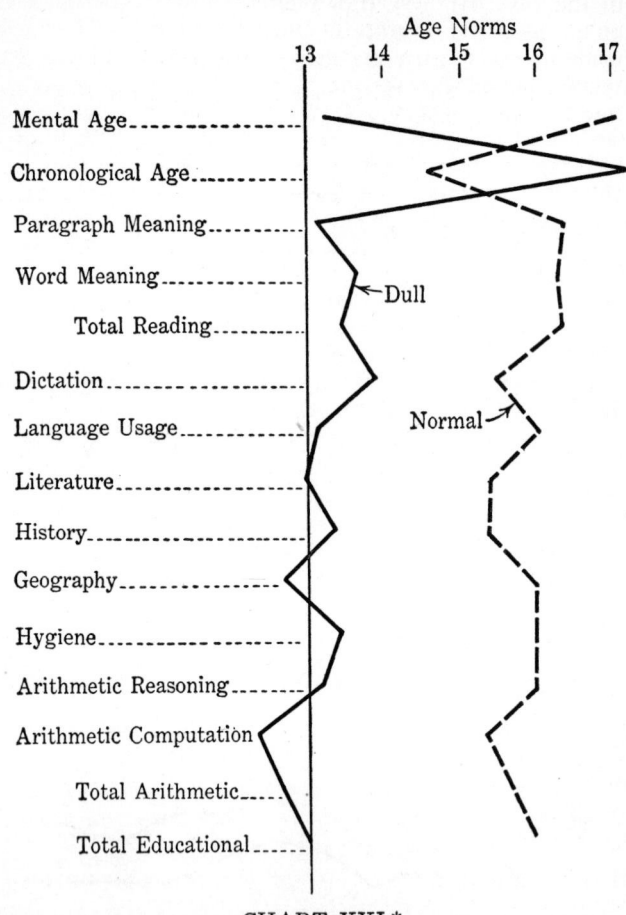

CHART XXI*

EDUCATIONAL PREPARATION OF SIXTY-SIX DULL PUPILS IN HIGH SCHOOL
(Portenier [17])

*This material is used by permission of the Bureau of Publications, Teachers College, Columbia University.

INTELLECTUAL DEVELOPMENTS

creasing. In this school system, fully 25 per cent of the freshman class is of too low mentality to profit by the usual academic curriculum, no matter how modified.

The educational foundation on which the high school must build, in the case of these dull pupils, is well illustrated by the graph on p. 200.[17] This graph shows the mental and educational scores made by sixty-six high school children with an average I.Q. of eighty-two and an average mental age of thirteen. Their chronological age is high (seventeen years, three months), indicating several retardations in the elementary grades. On no educational test do they average as high as the eighth grade; on four tests they are at or below the seventh grade level. Their total educational standing averages exactly normal for the seventh grade (equivalent of age thirteen). This graph gives a good picture of the situation with which the high school has to deal. It can often count only on an educational development normal for seventh grade children. The second curve on the page shows the standing of a group of freshmen with I.Q.'s of ninety-nine or above, chosen at random; this profile represents ordinary ability and achievement at entrance to high school.

Failures and eliminations.—No general discussion of these matters could give as clear a picture of the situation as is presented by the results of a recent study which traced the high school careers of 6,141 entering freshmen.[15] The figures below tell the story:

TABLE VIII*

HIGH SCHOOL CAREERS OF 6,141 FRESHMEN (O'Brien [15])

	Graduates		Nongraduates	
	No Failures	With Failures	No Failures	With Failures
No. Cases	811	1,125	1,757	2,448
No. Failures	0	5,823	0	12,137
Average	0	5	0	5

* This material is presented by permission of the Bureau of Publications, Teachers College, Columbia.

Of the original 6,141, 811—or 13 per cent—finished high school without failures. Another 1,125—18 per cent—graduated eventually, but averaged five failures apiece. A total of 31 per cent graduated. Of the nongraduates, 1,757—28 per cent of the total—showed no failures. The remaining 2,448—41 per cent—left school before graduating, with an average of five failures each. There are two striking points in this situation: the elimination is heavy, and failure is not a primary cause. The proportion of nonfailing to failing graduates is almost exactly the same as that of nonfailing to failing nongraduates. The frequency of failure among pupils who fail at all is no heavier among those eliminated than among those who graduate. Failures cause despair, but they do not cause withdrawal.

Further light on this point is shown by the persistence of those who do not graduate.[15] The table below presents the elimination by semesters for the failing and nonfailing groups.

TABLE IX

COMPARATIVE ELIMINATION OF NONGRADUATES WHO FAIL OR DO NOT FAIL *
(O'Brien [15])

Semesters	Nongraduates Without Failures		Nongraduates With Failures	
	No.	Cumulative Per Cent	No.	Cumulative Per Cent
1	1,073	61.	345	14.
2	297	78.	533	36.
3	129	85.	256	46.5
4	119	92.	454	64.5
5	42	94.	196	72.5
6	69	98.	302	85.
7	19	99.	137	91.
8	8	99.6	166	98.
9	1	100.	36	99.
10	..	..	19	99.8
11	..	..	4	100.
Total	1,757	100.	2,448	100.

* This material is presented by permission of the Bureau of Publications, Teachers College, Columbia.

By the end of the third semester, 85 per cent of those who have never failed have left school; but it takes six semesters—twice as long—to persuade a similar proportion of the failing students to leave. These facts seem contradictory to one's common sense; they certainly require interpretation. It is the writer's guess that the nonfailing pupils are those who soon realize their lack of ability or desire to complete a high school course. They get disgusted with the work presented and drop out of their own accord without waiting for failure to overtake them. They are probably brighter than the failing nongraduates; certainly they are shrewder. They evidently do not like their sample of high school life and do not continue with it. The story of the failing students is here shown in cold figures, but behind the per cents lie disillusionment and despair. These are the pupils who want to graduate but lack the ability. Failure hurts them, but they cling tenaciously to their educational careers. In the end, it must be something else that drives them out of school, for they fail no oftener than many other pupils who graduate. These youngsters who drag along from year to year, often failing and never graduating, constitute 41 per cent of the total. In them the writer sees regiments of largely wasted youth, from an educational standpoint; their history cries aloud for a revision of high school procedures and subject matter. Any pupils who persist with their educational plans as this group does are worth training—but along lines that will lead to satisfaction and success.

Failure is not, then, any such outstanding cause of elimination as is commonly supposed. The need or desire to make money, boredom with schoolwork, marriage, desire to enter special schools for art, music, dramatics, dancing, gymnastics, and the like, all play their part. In a later chapter there will be a discussion of a revised curriculum with greater holding power.

The high school teacher may know in general what to expect when she walks into her freshman classes in September. There will be a range of mental ages from eleven to twenty-one, with a mean between fourteen and fifteen. Nearly half the pupils will be too immature mentally to profit by the traditional high school subjects. Only about one in ten will graduate without failures, and only three in ten will graduate at all. Of the entire group, 59 per cent will fail some subject sooner or later. Instead of being discouraged by these vital statistics, a teacher should concentrate upon ways of bringing about a better articulation between capacity and requirements than exists at the present time.

DEVELOPMENT OF INDIVIDUAL MENTAL CAPACITIES

It is no longer the mode to speak of "mental faculties." There was a time when memory, imagination, and reasoning were regarded as inividual mental abilities more or less independent of each other. The popular conception postulated a mind divided off into areas, each of which functioned by itself and each of which could be trained independently. From this concept, by a series of logical steps, one arrived at phrenology, which assumed each function to be located in a particular part of the brain which, by being over- or underdeveloped, would cause protuberance or depression in the skull. Although this time-honored view has been abandoned in the light of modern research, such mental characteristics as imagination, memory, or reasoning still remain. These capacities are not, however, separate "mental functions." What differentiates reasoning from memory, for example, is the purpose towards which the integrated effort of the entire intelligence is directed. Presumably all these abilities involve use of the whole intelligence rather than of any isolated portion. But the end in view varies from one "function" to another. It is thus possible, in spite of certain destructive criticism, to employ these terms with this somewhat changed meaning.

In all probability, no test from which results will be quoted requires the use of any single capacity in isolation, but certain tests measure predominantly the ability of an individual to organize his mental efforts toward one purpose rather than another. The investigations rarely take elimination into account; hence, some of the improvement noted is due to the gradual weeding out of the less efficient by the increasing difficulty of the curriculum. With these two cautions in mind, the reader may profitably consider the results obtained from efforts to measure one intellectual capacity at a time. The data are both interesting and valuable.

Memory.—According to popular misconception, children have much better memories than adolescents or adults. What is true is that they are much more willing to memorize; adults do not like monotony and therefore prefer logical to rote learning. The typical adolescent distaste for rote memorizing is even more intense. Although children like monotony and usually like to memorize, they are not particularly efficient. During one semester, in the average school, a half hour is spent daily in learning addition and subtraction combinations. There is thus a total of fifty hours for this task. Counting the zero combinations, there are one hundred facts to be learned. The child has thus a half hour for each fact such as "4 plus 5 equals 9." Naturally, not all the class time is spent on formal drill, but the problems given necessitate the use of these same facts. At the end of the semester, not more than one-third of the pupils can give these one hundred facts without error. Any normal adult could certainly learn such items in much less time.

Test results also show increases in ability to memorize as children grow older. The graph on p. 206 presents three curves for different types of memorizing: one for abstract words,[24] one for concrete words,[23] and one for recall of a story.[22] In none of them is there decrease in ability to memorize. Evidence from the Binet examination gives similar results: a child can repeat four numbers after hearing them once; an adolescent can repeat five or six.[28] Presumably a final plateau is reached in the adult years, but during adolescence at least the ability to memorize increases, just as every other intellectual power develops during this period. This growth is often obscured by the adolescent's distaste for monotony and for isolated details. However, if any material to be memorized is so presented as to seem a logical step in gaining a desired end, an adolescent can be counted on to learn more rapidly than a child.

Concentration.—Children concentrate very badly; their attention is distracted by anything whatever. If one child in the room walks across the room to get a fresh sheet of paper, the intellectual activities of the other children come to an end for the moment. There is no question that adolescents can concentrate much better than children. In fact, it is during these years that a boy or girl first becomes so absorbed that he or she does not notice what is going on. The child will usually drop his book

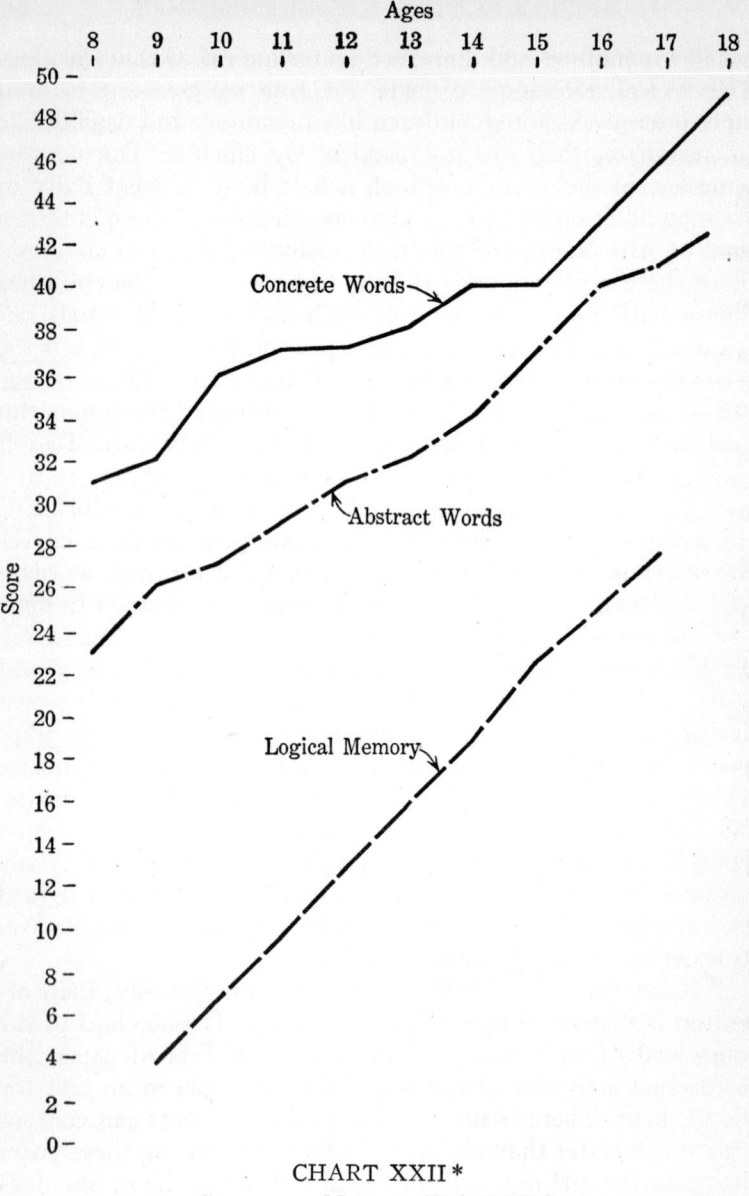

CHART XXII*
GROWTH IN MEMORY (Pyle [22,23,24])

*This material is presented by permission of Warwick & York, Inc., and The Macmillan Company.

when his mother calls him to dinner, but the adolescent often fails to hear the summons. The graph below shows the results of a test in concentration during these years. The marked increases during adolescence should be noted.

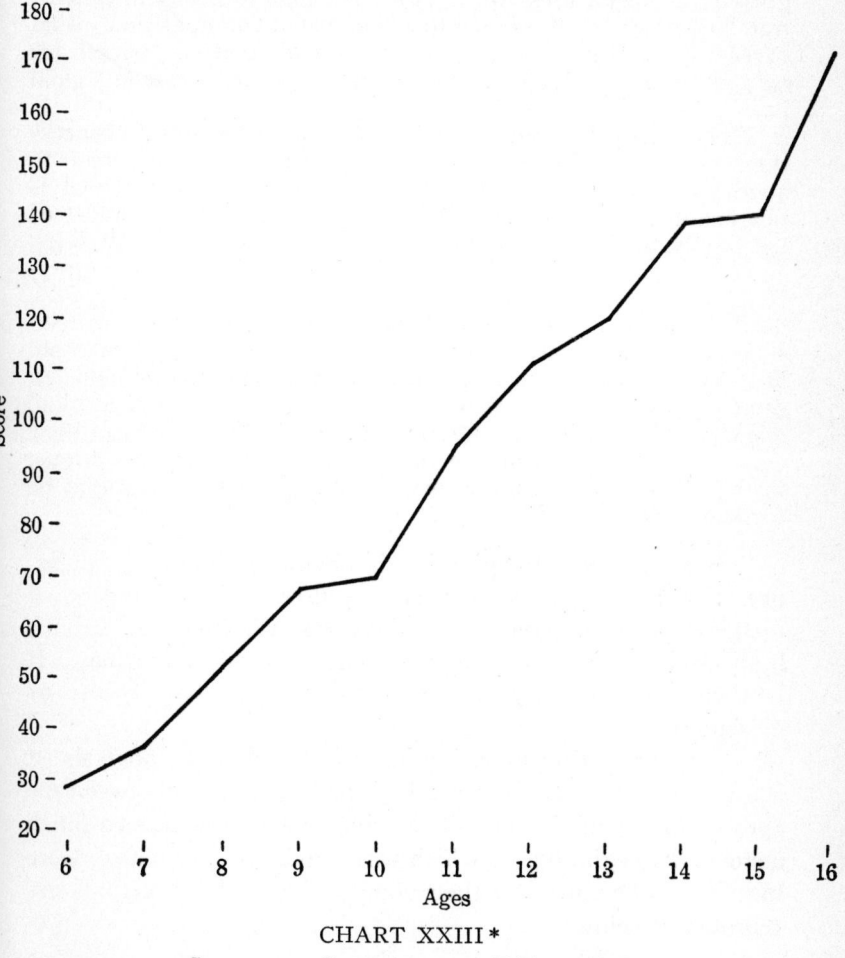

CHART XXIII*
GROWTH IN CONCENTRATION (Bickersteth [2])

*This material is presented by permission of the *British Journal of Psychology*.

Certain adolescents seem to a teacher to be quite incapable of concentration. The difficulty is usually that they are concentrating on something else than the desired stimuli. A boy who is emotionally upset concentrates badly upon his schoolwork. A girl neglects the housework she is supposed to do because her full attention is given to making a dress for a party. The gain in ability to concentrate is not necessarily shown by additional attention given to what parents or teachers want; however, an adolescent can pursue his own interests with far greater resistance to distraction than a child has.

The physical surroundings which help adolescents to concentrate, especially when studying, vary greatly from one person to another. Observation of the "A" students in a high school is illuminating on this point. One youngster studies in the midst of his family, with conversation going on continuously on all sides. Another turns on the radio full blast and then concentrates perfectly on his schoolwork. A third studies in between odd jobs, doing his work in periods not more than ten minutes long with constant interruptions. A fourth isolates himself in a quiet room and cannot concentrate if there are any competitive stimuli. In estimating what is a good or bad environment for concentration, one can judge only by results. If students get high marks in their work and if they accomplish this work without unusual fatigue, their environment is satisfactory for them, whatever it might be for somebody else.

Imagination.—Imagination is obviously difficult to measure. Yet, any high school teacher senses the development of imagination during the adolescent years. What few tests have been used for measuring this capacity are quite inadequate. It is therefore necessary to resort to less objective forms of measurement.

One interesting investigation [32] is based on an analysis of compositions written by 2,642 boys and 2,138 girls between the ages of nine and eighteen. The problem set them was to finish a story, the beginning of which was provided; given, also, were hints as to the nature of their compositions. The directions are reproduced below:

This is the beginning of a story about the moon.
"On a recent night," narrated the moon, "I was sliding through heavy clouds of snow. My beams tried to pierce them in

order to see what was happening on earth. Finally, the clouds parted before me and . . ."

You are to finish the story. You may choose any one of the five themes suggested below:

1. The moon saw a shipwreck.
2. The moon had a conversation with the giant, Roland, at the town hall of Bremen.
3. The moon comforts a sick man who is lying in bed.
4. The moon tells about a camp of hikers in the neighborhood of Bremen.
5. The moon talks with a pupil who cannot prepare his lessons.*

By these directions, every pupil was led into a situation in which he had to use his imagination. He could, however, choose a topic around which his fancy played most readily; and he was free to introduce whatever embellishments and minor incidents might occur to him.

There were three outstanding differences between the themes of child and adolescent. The children represented the moon primarily as an acting being, while the adolescents described the moon's thoughts and emotions. The older pupils enlivened their stories with various minor episodes, droll happenings, and artistic touches. The children's style was bald, but that of the adolescents showed numerous embellishments. The girls showed evidences of maturity earlier than the boys. The differences specifically in imagination are revealed in the two excerpts below, which are typical, respectively, of good childish and good adolescent imaginative power.

Because of the great distance the moon must sometimes use a spyglass, an opera glass, or glasses, or else send out his beams as messengers, for men appear to him as little ants and their lanterns as tiny glowworms. Up above in the heavens he flies through the clouds or in the clouds. Sometimes he allows a schoolboy to come up to him. Once he said, "Ah, my boy, can't you do your schoolwork well?"

"No, dear moon," answered the boy.

"Well, then, come on up here to me."

* This material is presented by permission of the *Zeitschrift für Angewandte Psychologie.*

The boy took his schoolbooks in his brief case and journeyed to the moon. Once he had arrived there, the moon indicated a room that looked exactly like a schoolroom. The moon then came into the room to the boy in order to help him with his lessons. The moon was willing to help him and sat down on a chair, took a pen, and did some arithmetic for him. Then he told the boy not to lose courage about his work. Later he picked up a book and read aloud from it.

One evening I was making my usual rounds in the heavens. The little angels had polished me till I shone, so that I was quite satisfied with myself. The little stars, my courtiers, had been cleaned by the heavenly guards and filled with oil, for it would be a shame if these sources of light were ever to fail. Although I am an old man, my stride was very elastic, and in my joy I didn't notice at all that I came too near a little star. Suddenly! Crash! Bang! We had smashed into each other and a tiny piece of the star roared off in a wide, fiery arch. All at once we heard a wee, distant voice saying, "Oh, look! A shooting star! Shiver my timbers! Now I wish for myself a hundred thousand dollars." It was indisputably one of those tiny little men on the earth who call such a thing a "shooting star" and, when they see one, wish for themselves the most wonderful things. I was sunk deep in thought but was aroused by the complaints of the injured star that rubbed its head and wailed, "Oh, my lovely hat! Oh, my lovely hat!" I calmed him down and asked him what his name was and how long he had been in service as a guard in the sky. He answered, "My very respected Lord, I have not been very long in service here, only about eight hundred years." [All of this preceded the actual story told—an illustration of the adolescent tendency to introduce minor incidents.]

The child's composition shows certain elementary imaginative touches—the spyglass, the glowworms, the moonbeams used as messengers. But, on the whole, the story is prosaic; the tale would not have varied essentially if the boy had been helped by his uncle. The adolescent shows not only imaginative touches, but a truly fanciful situation in the concept of a heavenly collision with its droll consequences. The effect of the mishap on humans, moon, and star occupies more space than the description of the action.

In the course of years, objective tests of imagination will

doubtless appear. In the meantime, one must be content with the indications of increased imaginative power as revealed by such evidence as that shown above.

Organizing ability.—There are undoubtedly various kinds of organizing skill. The person who can organize a group of individuals for the production of a play has a different type from that possessed by the individual who can organize a scattered group of ideas into a coherent argument. The skills that might be called social organization have never been measured and not more than a beginning has been made upon the ability to organize ideas. This ability leads, however, to the sudden insights characteristic of adolescence; by arranging ideas in a logical sequence a pupil comes to what is for him an entirely new point of view. High school teachers are well aware of an increase in organizing capacity. They therefore make such assignments as the writing of a composition for which material must be gathered from a half-dozen different sources and organized into a coherent presentation. In elementary school such assignments would be impossible, except for a few unusually brilliant children. The only measures of this capacity are all too inadequate. There is, however, one test which requires the pupil to rearrange a miscellaneous set of ideas into outline form.[13] The results from this test show an increase in score from 3.8 in Grade 9 to 13.8 for college seniors; the total possible score is sixteen. Even in this restricted type of organizing ability there is marked improvement through the adolescent years.

Ability to rearrange and reorganize ideas does not by any means stop with the end of adolescence. The leaders of mankind have usually become prominent after they were forty. Accounts of their youth or writings during their early maturity indicate considerably less ability to organize than they later show. It is no accident that the philosopher, the great financier, or the outstanding scholar is middle-aged. The ability to think coherently is one mental capacity which shows marked growth in adolescence and then continues developing into the years of adult life.

One element in organizing is the ability to distinguish the essential from the nonessential. In the case of paragraph reading, this ability has been tested by asking children to read, at their own rate, sixty short paragraphs and to underline the one sentence they thought contained the main idea.[19] The norms obtained to date are as follows:

TABLE X
Growth in Ability to Find Main Points in Reading Matter *
(Pressey [19])

Age	8½	9½	10½	11½	12½	13½	14½	15½	16½
Average number of paragraphs correctly marked ..	8	14	20	26	32	38	44	51	56

* This material is used by permission of the Public School Publishing Company, Bloomington, Illinois.

This test is not hard enough for the upper years of adolescence, but it shows a steady increase in ability to isolate the central thought of a paragraph.

Reasoning, thinking, judging, generalizing.—Tests dealing ostensibly with one of these capacities usually tests the other three as well, so it seems wisest to present results from these materials in a single section. There is, all told, a considerable amount of evidence to show the improvement made in ability to think logically, draw conclusions, or see hidden meanings; but the test results to be presented are somewhat scattered and piecemeal. Nevertheless, they are of real interest.

There is, first of all, the Binet examination [28] with its series of "comprehension" questions. Growth is reflected by successive steps from, "What would you do if you were hungry?" to "What would you do if you had broken something belonging to someone else?" to "What would you do if you were asked your opinion of someone you did not know very well?" The tests in years fourteen, sixteen, and eighteen are based mainly upon ability to reason, to think, to have insights, to judge, to organize, and to draw inferences. Many years ago Binet and Terman realized the value of such tests in measuring adolescent intelligence.

In one recent study, pupils were asked, first, to watch a series of simple physical and chemical experiments.[8] Then, they were asked to answer a number of questions as to how they

INTELLECTUAL DEVELOPMENTS

explained the phenomena. A second part of this test described a series of social situations for which explanations were asked. One item from this part is presented below:

> Raymond is a ten-year-old boy. He is very small for his age, however, and is not very strong. Raymond's favorite game is to play that he is a policeman. Best of all, he likes to pretend that he is going to arrest some of the other boys in his grade who tease him, and that he is going to take them to jail. Why do you suppose he likes to play policeman so well?

The answers were all written spontaneously and are reproduced later in the pupils' own words. The first group of answers shows the interpretations preferred by sixth and seventh grade pupils. Some are irrelevant, some merely restate a point in the story, and a few show some glimmering of insight. The next group are those preferred by tenth and twelfth grade students; these interpretations are logical and relevant, but show only a partial understanding. The answers preferred by college sophomores are reasonably complete interpretations.

Grades 6–7

Irrelevant	Restatement	Some degree of interpretation
His father is a policeman.	The other boys tease him.	He wants to be a policeman.
He has no one to play with.	He is not very strong.	He wants to escape from teasing.
He doesn't like the other boys.	He is small.	
He may have a policeman's suit.		

Grades 10–12

   He wants to get revenge on the other boys.
   He wants to show he is better than the other boys.
   He likes to imagine he is strong.

College Sophomores

   He wants to be strong.
   He wants to make up for his small size.
   He has a desire for mastery.

The growth in insight is too obvious to require comment.

The entire test—physical, chemical, and psychological items taken together—shows real gains in ability to reason, and probably would show more if the items dealing with natural science had not been so dependent upon the possession of scientific information. The answers given to all questions were rated by a number of judges on a four-point scale; all ratings of all judges on all questions were averaged to give an individual's score. The scale used is given below:

> Score 1: An answer that is completely erroneous, irrelevant, or concerned with facts not given in the story.
> Score 2: An answer that gives a simple repetition of facts in the story.
> Score 3: An answer that is logical but just misses the point or else does not completely explain the situation.
> Score 4: An answer that is logical, scientifically sound, and really explains.

The average score of 345 sixth- and seventh-grade children (ages between ten and thirteen) was 2.0; no score was higher than 2.7. That is, no child was able to give consistently logical answers. The average of 118 tenth- and twelfth-grade pupils (ages from fourteen to nineteen) was 2.65; these adolescents must have given many logical answers, although some were still childish. The range was from 1.9 to 3.2. The forty-two college sophomores average 3.1, with no score below 2.6. Between junior high school and college the average pupil's spontaneous interpretations of a wide range of simple natural phenomena and simple social situations rise from a mere repetition of facts given to something better than a logical but slightly incomplete understanding.

Problem tests in arithmetic are customarily used to measure ability to reason. They are not, however, satisfactory because the scores reflect chiefly a knowledge of fundamental operations. The only widely used objective test [27] that requires no calculations gives norms for successive grades rising from ten points in Grade 4 to twenty-one in Grade 9. The increases are small and are little more than mere elimination would bring about. It is the writer's opinion that tests in arithmetical reasoning are quite useless as measures

INTELLECTUAL DEVELOPMENTS 215

of ability to think. They have the same value as other tests in estimating the results of teaching—nothing more.

Adolescent ability to obtain insights, to judge, or to think are well measured by two distinctive and interesting experiments. The first of these studies [6] presents results of a test designed to investigate comprehension of the sayings and parables of Jesus. In this investigation, a series of objective tests were given to 637 children and adolescents, who were then classified on the basis of mental age. The study reports the per cent of children at each mental age who were able to understand each saying or parable. As illustrations, results of two parables will be shown: "The Sower," and "The Two Foundations." The development of comprehension for four famous sayings will also be presented: "What shall it profit a man if he gain the whole world but lose his own soul?" "Judge not that ye be not judged," "If you love God, keep his commandments," "Men love darkness rather than light because their deeds are evil." The next graph is illuminating. The curves are characterized by a sudden increase, at the mental level of early adolescence, in ability to understand allegories and double meanings. The gains between the mental ages of eight and eleven are gradual. Then there are large increases up to about fourteen; after fourteen the gain sometimes continues and sometimes not, depending largely on the height already reached by the curve at that time. In this investigation one finds a reflection of that increase in understanding always sensed by teachers and so rarely found in investigations using objective tests.

The second investigation [26] concerns the ability to interpret the meaning of cartoons. Although this study was designed originally to determine the appropriateness of cartoons for inclusion in history texts, the results are equally useful in the present connection. The children were shown the cartoons and were asked to select from a number of possible statements the best interpretation of each picture's meaning. Results from three sample cartoons are reported in the graph on p. 217. The results were grouped according to the mental age of the children

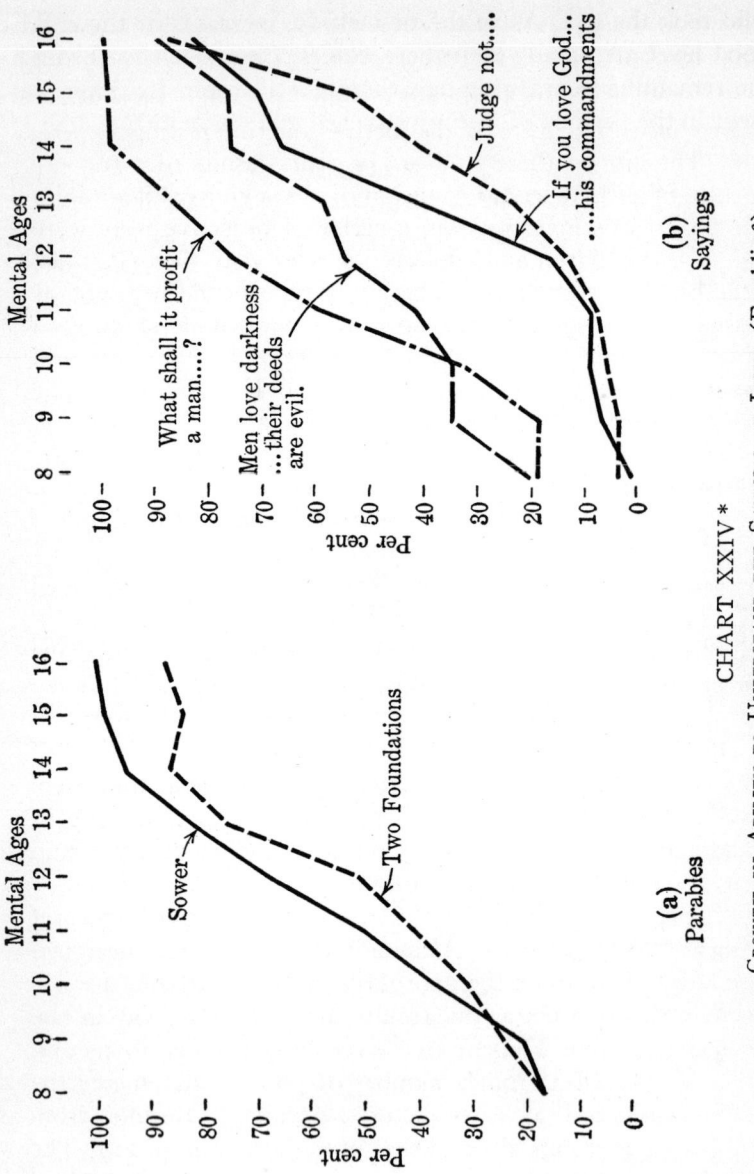

CHART XXIV*

GROWTH IN ABILITY TO UNDERSTAND THE SAYINGS OF JESUS (Franklin[6])

* These materials are presented by permission of the University of Iowa Press.

who took the test. As in the first study, increases at the childhood level are small; then there comes a marked rise through the remaining years, although there is still room for improvement in the periods of late adolescence and maturity.

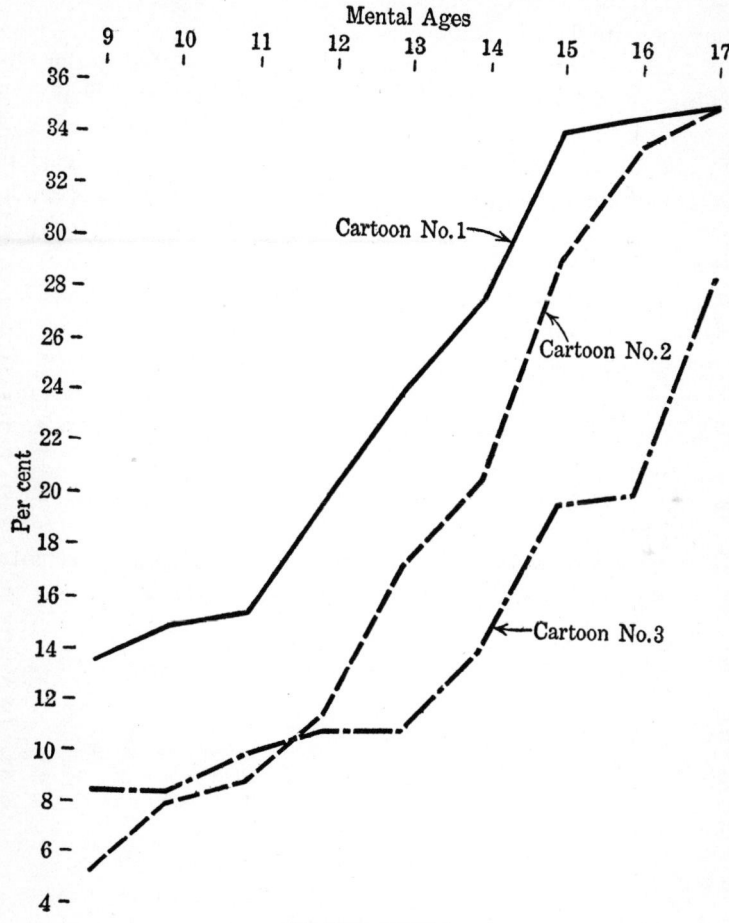

CHART XXV*

GROWTH IN ABILITY TO INTERPRET CARTOONS (Shaffer [25])

*This material is presented by permission of the Bureau of Publications, Teachers College, Columbia University.

Both these studies show the increase in power to "see through" a situation. It is in such ability that the adolescent is distinctively different from the child. Further measures of ability to judge, think, reason, and generalize will appear—with resulting improvement in one's understanding of intellectual developments during adolescence.

Special abilities.—The material to be presented under this heading is admittedly diverse. Development in mechanical skill, in appreciation of art, music, or prose, and growth in vocabulary are all included. The best objective tests for these various aptitudes have been selected and the norms observed. Especially interesting are the results with a test of mechanical aptitude, as shown in the graph on the opposite page.

The growth during childhood is fairly rapid, but there is a marked increase in late adolescence. Unlike the usual curves for verbal intelligence, mechanical aptitude shows no sign of decreasing increments during these years. Perhaps one trouble with intelligence tests is that they include only a narrow sampling of skills already well developed by the early adolescent years and they neglect entirely those abilities that do show marked improvement at this time.

For purposes of condensation, the results from the remaining tests have been grouped together in a single table:

TABLE XI

DEVELOPMENT OF VARIOUS SKILLS AND APPRECIATIONS *

Grades	3	4	5	6	7	8	9	10	11	12
General vocabulary [18]	12	26	38	48	56	64	72	..	..	..
Prose appreciation [5]	..	..	..	..	21	24	29	33	36	38
Art [12]	..	..	60	64	78	82	86	89	97	98	98	102
Music † [25]	..	..	..	63	67	70	73	74	75	76	77

* Norms for these four tests are used by permission, respectively, of the Public School Publishing Company, Bloomington, Illinois; the Educational Test Bureau, Minneapolis, Minnesota; the Research Service Company, Los Angeles, California, and the Silver-Burdett Company, New York.
† Norms are given only for Grades 5, 8, and adults, but a method of inferring intermediate grades is provided. The scores given are for the total score.

The gains in general vocabulary—the actual size is estimated by adding two ciphers to the norm—rise more rapidly during elementary than junior high school. Possibly children have, by the early adolescent years, about as much purely verbal acquisition as they are likely to develop. The norms for ability to appreciate prose selections show nothing remarkable. In both art

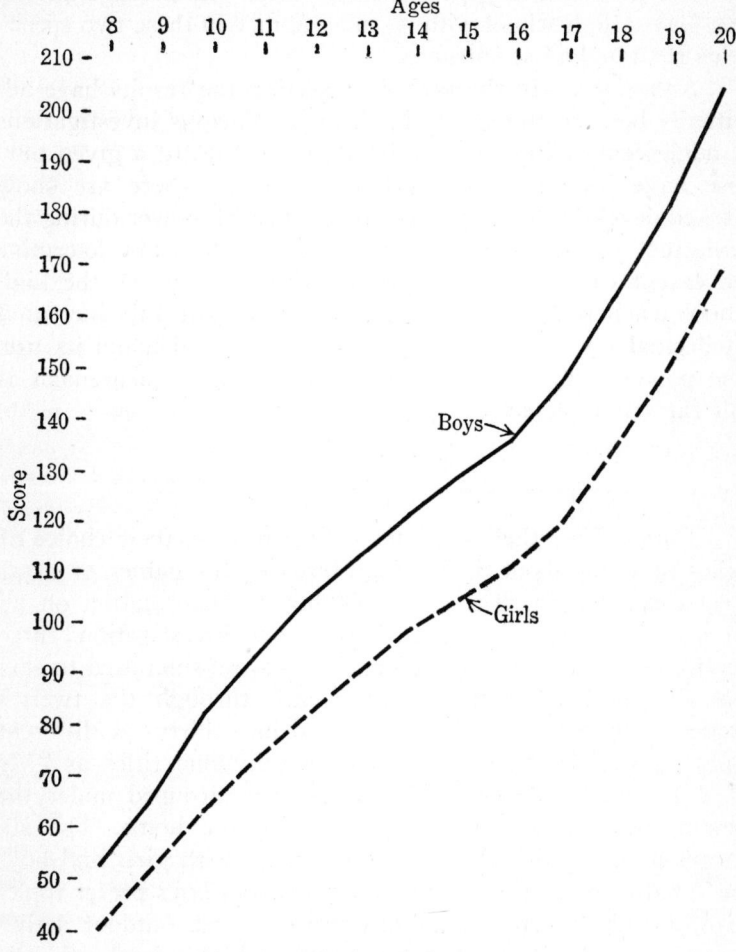

CHART XXVI*

GROWTH IN MECHANICAL APTITUDE (Baker[1])

*This material is used by permission of the Public School Publishing Company, Bloomington, Illinois.

and music, however, there is a marked slowing down of growth in such abilities as the tests measure. The few children with talent certainly continue to develop, but the rank and file seems to reach its maximal growth rather early. The average adolescent leaves high school with no more ability in these two special fields than he had at entrance.

Summary.—In the preceding section the results have admittedly been scattered and inadequate. Various investigations of adolescent ability to organize thinking toward a given purpose have been reported. What indications there are show marked development in all types of intellectual power during the adolescent years. Future investigators will probably determine the extent of such developments. In the meantime, the high school teacher should attempt to make use of this increased intellectual power by giving assignments that demand its use. The power is undoubtedly there, even if its measurement is still far from perfect.

SPONTANEOUS INTELLECTUAL INTERESTS

Pupils show their spontaneous interests in their choice of topics to write about, in their preferences for games or other diversions, and in their choice of books. Information on all three of these topics is available. In one investigation, three hundred possible titles for compositions were submitted to several thousand children in the seventh through the twelfth grades.[4] These titles could be grouped into thirty-six different types of subject matter. Thus, such individual titles as "My Ideal House" or "Our Back Yard" were grouped under the general heading of topics dealing with the home. The six groups showing the highest preference of both girls and boys are listed on p. 221. The junior high school boys prefer topics dealing with current events, adventure, travel, outdoor activities, or animals. By the last two years of high school, athletics have taken first place, topics dealing with travel, machinery, or outdoor activities come next, with vocational matters bringing up the rear. For the girls, the first preference at all ages is for

TABLE XII
COMPOSITION PREFERENCES OF 7,309 BOYS AND 7,232 GIRLS * (Coleman [3])

Grades	Boys	Girls
7	Current Events Outdoor Activities Adventure Travel Animals Famous People	Travel Adventure Animals Getting Rich Literary Topics Leisure Activities
8	Current Events Adventure Travel Outdoor Activities Athletics Animals	Travel Adventure Getting Rich Outdoor Activities Ethical Topics Literary Topics
9	Travel Outdoor Activities Adventure Athletics Famous People Current Events	Travel Adventure Personal Experiences Ethical Topics Literary Activities Outdoor Activities
10	Athletics Travel Outdoor Activities Adventure Ethical Topics Current Events	Travel Adventure Personal Experiences Outdoor Activities Ethical Topics Literary Topics
11	Athletics Machinery Travel Outdoor Activities Adventure Vocational Topics	Travel Personal Experiences Adventure Outdoor Activities Athletics School
12	Athletics Travel Machinery Outdoor Activities Pupil Employment Vocational Topics	Travel Personal Experiences Athletics Home Life Humorous Topics Ethical Topics

* This material is used by permission of the Bureau of Publications, Teachers College, Columbia University.

topics dealing with travel. In the earlier years, adventure is a close second; in the seventh and eighth grades, topics dealing with "How to Get Rich" show a surprisingly high preference. Literary topics also are popular. By the end of high school, topics dealing with purely personal experiences such as "A

Temptation I Resisted" have taken second place; athletics have appeared among the preferences, and topics dealing with school and home life have become popular. These preferences are in the main what one would expect but are still interesting as reflecting the intellectual interests of adolescents.

Spontaneous play activities [11] also reflect the interests of children and adolescents. The five most popular play activities at five, ten, fifteen, and twenty years of age are listed below for

TABLE XIII

THE FIVE MOST POPULAR PLAY ACTIVITIES AT AGES 5, 10, 15, 20 *
(Lehman and Witty [11])

BOYS

5 Years	10 Years
Playing with a ball	Football
Playing with blocks	Baseball
Playing with a wagon	Boxing
Playing house	Just playing catch
Playing horse	Riding a bicycle

15 Years	20 Years
Basketball	Having "dates"
Football	Football
Baseball	Basketball
Driving an automobile	Watching athletic sports
Tennis	Listening to the radio

GIRLS

5 Years	10 Years
Playing house	Playing the piano
Playing with dolls	Going to the movies
Playing with a ball	Looking at the "funny" paper
Playing school	Playing with dolls
Drawing	Roller skating

15 Years	20 Years
Reading books	Social dancing
Going to the movies	Playing the piano
Social dancing	Having "dates"
Playing the piano	Going to entertainments, etc.
Riding in an automobile	Just "hiking" or strolling

* This material is used by permission of the A. S. Barnes Company.

both boys and girls. The general development is clear. Small boys spontaneously play by manipulating different objects and by imitating the life they see about them. The ten-year-old boy plays extremely active games. Although the names he gives to some of his games are the same as for later years, he does not play them the same way. What he calls "baseball" is usually a game played by perhaps four boys against five others. His form of football consists of a group of from ten to thirty small boys first choosing sides; then everyone runs and jumps on everyone else without much regard to teamwork or to the progress of the game. At fifteen the three favorite activities are highly organized group games, played with established rules. At twenty the spontaneous activities show two changes. First, some of them are social and involve relationship with girls. Second, some of them are passive rather than active. Already at twenty the average boy has developed the attitude of the average man and derives his pleasure from watching sports rather than participating actively in them.

With girls, there are parallel developments. The little girl plays with objects or imitates life about her in much the same way as a boy of her age. Differences between the sexes have begun to show, however, by the age of ten. The girl's spontaneous activities are already more social and for the most part more passive. The only active play is roller skating, which comes at the bottom of the list; aside from social dancing there are no items during the later years involving physical exercise. At fifteen years the preferences are either social or of a passive recreational type such as reading, playing the piano, or going to the movies. There is almost no difference between the preferences of the fifteen and twenty-year-old girls except for a shift in emphasis. Girls' favorite activities are completely lacking in athletic interest and show a much earlier social maturity than boys'.

Intellectual interests are reflected also in the type of books children like to read.[30, 33, 34] In the elementary school years the interest of boys is in such stories as deal with war, boy scouts, athletics, or strenuous adventure. With the beginning of adolescence, however, many boys develop a craze for reading an entire series of books; the topics deal mainly with adventure and athletics. It is not until the later years of adolescence that the romantic novel makes any appeal to boys. Girls show a somewhat different development. During elementary school their interest is chiefly in fairy stories and tales of home or school life. With the beginning of adolescence, they become almost immediately interested in romantic literature; most girls of thirteen are already reading love stories. Once this interest has developed, it continues through the adolescent years almost to the exclusion of all other types of reading. There is no more marked intellectual difference between boys and girls than that shown between the thirteen-year-old boy who is reading "On the Plains with Custer" and the thirteen-year-old girl who is reading "The Rosary."

A teacher may expect an adolescent girl to prefer composition topics dealing with travel, personal experiences, home life, and, to a lesser degree, adventure and athletics. She can expect an outstanding preference for the romantic novel. Finally, the teacher can anticipate relatively passive diversions, a relative lack of enthusiasm for athletic participation, and a profound interest in all kinds of social activities. The average adolescent boy can be trusted to choose theme topics or books dealing with athletics, travel, machinery, outdoor activities, or occupations. His play preferences show similar developments. He shows socialization in his adherence to teamwork and rigid rules, but he does not have as much interest in social affairs as the girl of his age, nor does he develop such interests as early. Information on these points should be useful both in the classroom and in connection with extracurricular activities.

PRACTICAL SIGNIFICANCE FOR THE TEACHER

This chapter has been long and has presented highly diverse materials. Numerous details are of obvious value to teachers, who may be trusted to note these as they read. What are not so obvious are certain more general ideas implicit in the discussion.

The teacher should have some consistent attitude toward intelligence tests at the secondary school level. Those in existence are good enough measures of the kind of thing they measure at all; they are extremely useful for purposes of classification. However, the teacher should not be too trusting; she should realize their limitations and should expect more adequate and comprehensive measures to appear.

Teachers should always keep in mind the probable distribution of intelligence in high school, the probable direction of any changes in this distribution from year to year, and the undeniable presence of many definitely dull children in every entering class. The percentage of failure is far too high when only 13 per cent of freshmen graduate unscathed. The answer to this situation is not a lowering of standards in present classes; teachers are quite justified in their refusal to pass large numbers of students in the subjects now forming the backbone of the high school curriculum. These courses are totally inappropriate for about half the pupils. A simplification would do only harm—even if the subject matter could be sufficiently simplified, which is doubtful—because most students in the upper half of the distribution have vital need for these courses as preparation for later work. The answer lies, rather, in a curricular revision that will give these failing students material with which they can be successful.

The teacher should change the nature of her assignments as the pupils mature. The growth in mental power is there; it merely awaits adequate stimulation by classwork. Readings that demand organization, experiments that require close reasoning, writing that calls for vivid imagination, and even assignments, properly presented, that demand memorizing, should be stressed. Opportunities for getting insight into social, scientific, aesthetic, moral, or practical problems should be numerous.

Types of learning other than the purely verbal should not be as neglected as they usually are. Boys and girls are steadily developing abilities and skills along mechanical lines. To these, the traditional high school classes give no scope; most secondary school subjects were developed to meet educational needs in a premachine era. The modern school has inherited and, to some extent, sanctified them. But modern life is based on a "machine" civilization. The school should not neglect mechanical aptitudes—not if it wants to send out graduates equipped to face the world of today. Incidentally, more use of mechanical ability and less use of verbal ineptitude would probably cut down the number of failures.

Finally, there is the matter of adolescent intellectual interests. The wise teacher will utilize them to get work done. Certainly, she will not make the mistake of appealing to interests that have been outgrown.

The modern high school often emphasizes social and emotional adjustment to the detriment of intellectual progress. The classroom has become a side show, attached to the main tent where the extracurricular life of the school is in full swing. With all the intellectual growth and change that takes place during this period, the relatively minor role played by classwork in the lives of adolescents is inexcusable. These vital powers are poured without stint into other kinds of work. It is the teacher's job so to utilize them in her daily assignments that her classes stimulate eager interest and promote adolescent growth in intellectual power.

ILLUSTRATIVE CASE STUDIES

This chapter contains such diverse materials and so much material that illustration of all points would be both difficult and tedious. The writer has tried, therefore, to illustrate two or three important and significant points in order further to emphasize them upon the reader's mind. A simplified example of test construction has also been introduced; there was no room in this chapter for a discussion of test construction, but it seemed undesirable to omit this matter entirely. In reading this illustrative material, the teacher should consider how she would apply the general principles to work in her own field.

Everett entered high school when he was fifteen. During his first semester he took English, French, algebra, and history; he failed the algebra and received barely passing marks in the other courses. For the rest of the year he continued three courses and substituted mechanical drawing for the mathematics. At the end of

INTELLECTUAL DEVELOPMENTS 227

the year he failed French, passed history and English, and made a good grade in drawing. At this point he decided to quit the classical course. The next fall he elected mechanical drawing, shopwork, English, and commercial geography. In the first two he received average grades; English he barely passed, and geography he failed. For his second semester he again tried algebra, continued his English and shopwork, and repeated history. He passed all his courses but received a good mark only in shopwork. At the beginning of his third year he transferred to the mechanical course, although he knew he would lose a semester because he had not taken the right courses, and elected algebra, chemistry, and two shop courses. Before a month was over he was hopelessly lost in algebra and was allowed to drop it. He scraped through chemistry but did good work in his other courses. For the second semester he elected chemistry, physics, and English—having been warned to take a light schedule because of probable difficulties. He did surprisingly well in physics at first, although his mathematical deficiencies eventually reduced his grade to only a passing mark, but he failed the second semester of chemistry. Perusal of his course of study showed he still had several doses of science and mathematics ahead of him. He realized he would never be able to graduate in the technical courses. The business course did not attract him and, anyway, he would have to start all over with freshman subjects if he tried to enter that curriculum. The academic course offered him nothing that was interesting. After talking matters over with his teachers and parents, Everett left school and went to work in a garage where he is highly successful.

This boy was not dull, nor is his history unusual. Four failures are within normal limits. Floundering about is unfortunately the rule rather than the exception. Withdrawal from high school is more frequent than graduation. Subsequent success in a line of work independent of high school courses is the usual thing. Everett's academic experiences are essentially those of the average American boy in the average American high school.

There is no room in a book of this sort for a discussion of how intelligence tests are made. However, the teacher should have some information on this point if she is to understand them. The construction, as usually described in technical books, is submerged in a welter of statistics; few teachers ever discover the essential steps in test construction. It occurred to the writer that the history of a test would be desirable as a "case study."

Suppose, then, a research worker wishes to construct a test of intelligence for high school pupils. The technique, shorn of its statistical refinements, may be described simply. One first studies the school record of all pupils in a large high school, obtains estimates of their ability from all their teachers, inquires into their reputation among other students, and perhaps obtains from each pupil a sample of spontaneous writing. None of these results is an absolutely valid measure of ability. However, all of them taken together do point out reasonably well the extremes of the distribution. For test construction the middle may be forgotten. The research worker next goes over all the data and selects one group of pupils—about one hundred, probably—who seem from all pragmatic indications to be superior and a similar number of the same ages who seem markedly inferior. These pupils may be interviewed, in case there is any doubt as to their allocation. By this method one may not get all the brilliant pupils in a school but at least one gets two extreme groups whose performance can be compared.

The next step is to construct items. The worker makes up all the questions he can think of and pesters everyone he knows for further questions, most of which will be of little use because they are too dependent on school information. In all probability the worker continues for weeks with his collection of items. If he wants a test containing two hundred questions he will need at least four hundred to start with, and he will make a better test if he uses five hundred. When he has finally accumulated as many as he thinks he will need, and has tried to arrange them from easy to hard, he gives the entire number to his two extreme groups of pupils, allowing every pupil to use as much time as he needs, but to answer every question. To prevent fatigue from influencing the results, he breaks up the initial tests into five forms of one hundred items each.

With the data thus obtained he retires into the silence of his office for several weeks. The papers are marked and the scores tabulated by item. That is, the investigator finds out what per cent of each group passed each item. The ideal item would be one that was passed by 100 per cent of the bright group and failed by 100 per cent of the dull; unfortunately, there is no such animal, but one tries to approximate this standard as closely as possible. When the results are all tabulated such facts as those on p. 229 emerge.

Items 48 and 395 are excellent and 241 is satisfactory; they differ from each other in the difficulty of the item, as revealed by the per cent passing it. Items 130 and 314 must be thrown out because they do not show enough differentiation between the extremes. Items 10 and 63 are unsatisfactory because they are too hard; if the vast majority of pupils cannot answer a question at all it is obvious the question will not measure anything. Item 436 is far

TABLE XIV
Per Cent of Subjects Passing Each Item

	Brilliant Group	Dull Group
Item 48:	87 per cent	12 per cent
Item 130:	54 " "	48 " "
Item 10:	11 " "	2 " "
Item 436:	99 " "	91 " "
Item 222:	38 " "	47 " "
Item 395:	78 " "	5 " "
Item 63:	7 " "	0 " "
Item 241:	43 " "	8 " "
Item 314:	59 " "	51 " "

too easy. Item 222 shows one of the reversals that occasionally occur—no one knows why. From these nine questions, two only are really satisfactory.

The investigator selects all the items that seem to be usable. He then makes a trial form of his test, which he gives to the entire school. These results he correlates with teachers' estimates of every child's ability, with marks, or with the results of tests already established. There are further refinements of a technical nature about which one need not bother here. The essential procedure has been demonstrated.

Miss Judson was an English teacher. She had been impressed with the diversity of abilities in her freshman classes; one year she decided to make an accurate investigation of their extent. For this purpose she gave, during the first two weeks of school, a whole series of tests. When she had scored her papers she was amazed at the range of abilities shown. She constructed the graph on p. 230 to show to her associates. The lines indicate the extent of variation from the highest to the lowest score on each test given.

Miss Judson should not have been as surprised as she was. These results are perfectly typical of the distribution of abilities in the average freshman class. They illustrate the absolute need for some form of differential treatment.

As an example of the dangers involved in the use of tests with groups for which they are inappropriate, there seems no better material than that presented in the quotation below.[21] Too many people are inclined to regard "intelligence" as a quality that is independent of cultural background and can be measured everywhere with identical instruments. Nothing is further from the truth. Tests are usually developed through administration to urban groups, since it is far easier to accumulate thousands of cases for norms from city than from country children. Whenever such tests are applied to children coming from other backgrounds, the results must be interpreted with care. In the case of adolescents, this cau-

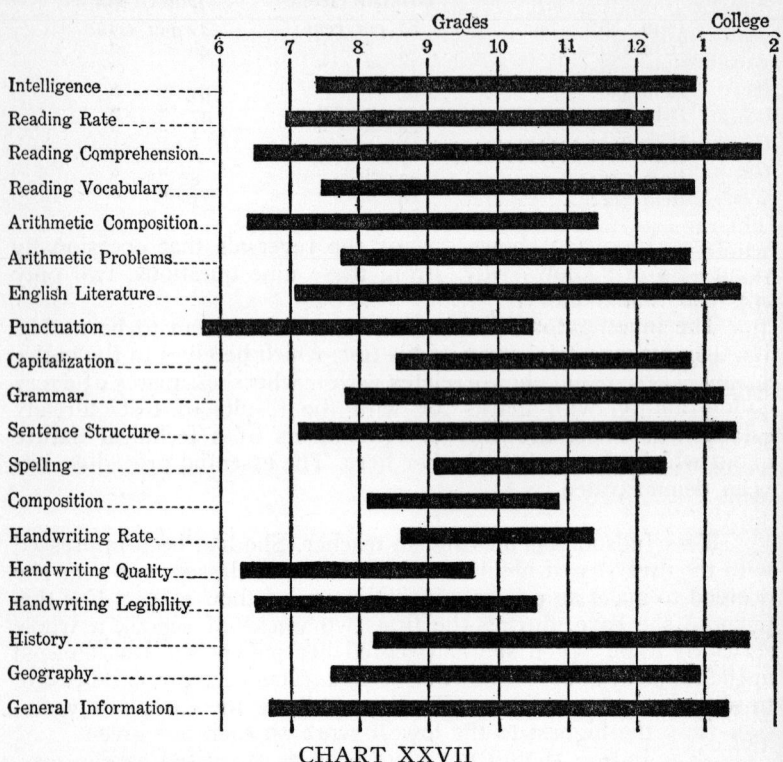

CHART XXVII
DISTRIBUTION OF ABILITIES IN ONE HIGH SCHOOL CLASS

tion is even more necessary, since older pupils are more influenced by environmental factors than children.

The experience of a friend, while giving Binet examinations to some "poor whites" in Kentucky, will further illustrate the possible explanation in terms of environment of what appear at first to be innate differences. One question of the series is, "If you went to the store and bought six cents' worth of candy and gave the clerk ten cents, what change would you receive?" One small urchin, upon being asked this question, replied, "I never had ten cents and if I had I wouldn't spend it for candy, and anyway candy is what your mother makes." Still wishing to find out if the boy could subtract six from ten, the examiner departed from the directions and asked, "If you had taken ten cows to pasture for your father and six of them strayed away, how many of them would you have left to drive home?" Replied the child, "We don't have ten cows, but if we did and I lost six, I wouldn't dare go home." This reply indicated a probable knowledge of the subtraction; but the examiner was not satisfied, and tried once more with the inquiry, "If there were ten children in a school and six of them were out with the measles, how many would there be in school?" This answer came even more promptly: "None, because the rest would be afraid of catching it too." To say that this boy had not the native ability of an average nine-year-old—the year for which this test is intended—is absurd in the light of his shrewd replies. But the examiner still did not know if he could subtract six from ten when the need for the skill was imbedded in a practical problem. The incident illustrates neatly the great difficulty of administering to one group of children an examination originally constructed from replies given by a totally different group. The nonverbal tests are less subject to this criticism than the verbal, but wide differences in home and community background always enter into the results.*

The development of imagination is well illustrated with the following samples, which were written by the same person at different ages. The first excerpt below is from a fairy tale written at the age of nine. No one can accuse this child of wasting words. The account is wildly improbable—the only possible episode being that of the second man, at which point the child seems to have run out of ideas—and entirely without adornment.

> Once upon a time a king sent three men out each to find a princess. A golden carriage was given each of them to bring back the princess in. The first was going by a lake when he saw a tongue of a man laying by the roadside. This tongue he took to a fairy who turned it into a beautiful princess. The second found a lovely girl without any trouble. The third slew a dragon and rescued a princess who had been chained to a rock for five hundred years. The king was so pleased with all three girls that he let each son marry one and divided the kingdom between them. And that is all that happened.

* This material is presented by permission of Harper & Brothers.

The second sample is an excerpt from a "Farewell Ode" written at the age of seventeen on the occasion of graduation from boarding school. It is characterized chiefly by sentimentality and a complete lack of humor. Form and vocabulary are more mature than in the first sample, but the writing is lamentably verbose.

> Fair B——, to Thy fame
> We dedicate our lives! But now the time
> To leave draws nigh and with that strength of heart
> Thy influence has made to grow in us
> We need not fear for what the future holds;
> For nothing here or in the world to come
> Can from our hearts dispel our love for Thee,
> And loving Thee we *cannot* go astray.
> Thou Spirit that hast inspired our lives and led
> Us ever forward on our way,—Farewell!
> But in the future days we shall return
> And lay upon Thine altars fair a gift,
> An offering of love a thousand-fold
> Increased, and thanks unbounded. But for now,—
> Farewell.

The third sample was produced four years later, as part of an assignment that required the writing of a diary by a Florentine who visited Venice in 1532. Here there is a profusion of detail; the imaginative element is under better control than earlier. Sentimentality has disappeared, although the writer still tends to use too many words and to emotionalize.

> Monday evening
> Venice—at last! The journey from Florence has been tedious despite the two breaks at Ravenna and Padua, but if Venice charms upon closer investigation as she fascinates at first sight, the time and money expended to get here have been well spent. I feel as if I had been transported into a roseate land of dreams, where even the old are young and fair; where the stream of life is full of smooth eddying whirlpools which pull the ship of individual fate quietly down within its depths and smother it. I am accustomed to fierce rapids and dangerous shoals—we have them in Florence—but where else is felt the pulling of worldly desire which silently ties its bonds around the soul and draws it down? I am bewildered by the warm luxury and glowing beauty of this city. She is well clothed and colored to be the Eastern bride in her yearly marriage with the Adriatic. As I came into the harbor this eve-

INTELLECTUAL DEVELOPMENTS

ning the sun was setting and the coloring was beyond the imagination of any who have not seen it. At home we stand upon a hill outside the city and look at the sun dipping into the sea—you are in one place, the sun in another. Here you are *in* the sunset—it shines about you, it envelopes you. Wherever you look—*there* is the sunset; the whole sky is suffused with shimmering, glorious-colored lights, the water gives a glad reflection—or is it that upon the floor of the sea there is another sunset casting its beams up through the wavering water and smoothly rolling waves? Over the city hangs the vaporous sunset clouds of opalescent hues amid which the city floats and winds about itself its nightly veil of golden haze. The all-engulfing sunset strangely colors the faces of the boatmen and the passengers. To be *in* the sunset, to glide slowly ashore to a dream-city in a narrow boat that smoothly and noiselessly cuts the water, propelled by men who handle an oar as skillfully and deftly as a housewife her spindle, and who chant in full, sweet voices a sort of song as they pull—'tis all of this—this pleasing almost to surfeit, of the senses—for a foreigner to arrive in Venice at the hour of sunset. After days of exhausting travel, to find this beauty is to be filled with a new kind of joy which terrifies while it allures. We have plenty of vice and lust throughout Florence, where in these days riot is rife, for the Medici are back again, but at least such atrocities are the result of man's appetites and weakness—Nature does not set a trap with beauty as a bait, as here in Venice she seems to do; and while I am charmed I feel that I must keep watch upon myself or the beauty will lure my mind from serious thought.

On the whole I am well content and favorably, though rather forcibly, impressed by Venice, and am anxious for tomorrow to come when I can investigate closely the apparent splendor of the public buildings. But although my mind is here, my heart is still in Florence and I turn away in my imagination from this city of brilliant, resplendent jewels to my city of flowers blooming in her emerald frame.

BIBLIOGRAPHY *

1. Baker, H. J., and Crockett, A. C., *Detroit Mechanical Aptitude Tests,* Public School Publishing Company, 1928.
2. Bickersteth, M. E., "Application of Mental Tests to Children

* See also the references in the Appendix.

of Various Ages," *British Journal of Psychology*, 1917, 9: 23-73.
3. Carroll, H. A., "Generalization in Bright and Dull Children," *Teachers College Contributions to Education*, No. 439, Bureau of Publications, Teachers College, Columbia University, 1930, 54 pp.
4. ———, *Prose Appreciation Test*, Educational Test Bureau Incorporated, Minneapolis, 1932.
5. Coleman, J. H., "Written Composition Interests of Junior and Senior High School Pupils," *Teachers College Contributions to Education*, No. 494, Bureau of Publications, Teachers College, Columbia University, 1931, 117 pp.
6. Franklin, S. P., "Comprehension of the Sayings of Jesus," *University of Iowa Studies in Character*, 1928, 2: 1-63.
7. Hopkins, L. T., *Intelligence of Continuation School Children in Massachusetts*, Harvard University Press, 1934, 132 pp.
8. Keen, A., *Study of the Growth of Concepts and of Reasoning concerning Physical and Psychological Causation*, Ph.D. Thesis, University of California, 1934, 111 pp.
9. Klineberg, O., "Racial Differences in Speed and Accuracy," *Journal of Abnormal and Social Psychology*, 1927, 22: 273-277.
10. Layton, W., and Hennigar, A., "A Follow-Up of Drop-Out Boys," *Vocational Guidance Magazine*, 1932, 10: 202-207.
11. Lehman, H. C., and Witty, P. A., *Psychology of Play Activities*, A. S. Barnes & Company, 1927, 242 pp.
12. Lewerenz, A. S., *Tests in the Fundamental Abilities of Visual Art*, Research Service Company, Los Angeles, 1927.
13. McClusky, F. D., and Dolch, E. W., *Outlining Test*, Public School Publishing Company, 1926.
14. Meek, C. S., "What a Superintendent Has a Right to Expect of an Institution Training Teachers for Secondary School," *N. E. A. Proceedings*, 1930, 67: 740-746.
15. O'Brien, F. P., *The High School Failures*, Teachers College, Columbia University, 1919, 97 pp.
16. Otis, A. S., *Self-Administering Tests of Mental Ability: Higher Examination*, World Book Company, 1922.
17. Portenier, L. G., "Pupils of Low Mentality in High School," *Teachers College Contributions to Education*, No. 568, Bureau of Publications, Teachers College, Columbia University, 1933, 109 pp.
18. Pressey, S. L., *Diagnostic Reading Tests: Vocabulary*, Public School Publishing Company.

19. Pressey, S. L., *Diagnostic Reading Tests: Paragraph Meaning*, Public School Publishing Company.
20. ———, *Senior Classification Tests*, Public School Publishing Company.
21. ———, *Psychology and the New Education*, Harper & Brothers, 1933, 594 pp.
22. Pyle, W. H., *Nature and Development of Learning Capacity*, Warwick & York, Inc., 1925, 119 pp.
23. ———, *Examination of School Children*, The Macmillan Company, 1913, 70 pp.
24. ———, *Psychology of Learning*, Warwick & York, Inc., 1921, 308 pp.
25. Seashore, C. E., *Psychology of Musical Talent*, Silver Burdett & Company, 1919, 288 pp.
26. Shaffer, L. F., "Children's Interpretations of Cartoons," *Teachers College Contributions to Education*, No. 429, Bureau of Publications, Teachers College, Columbia University, 1930, 70 pp.
27. Stevenson, P. R., *Problem Analysis Test*, Public School Publishing Company, 1924.
28. Terman, L. M., *The Intelligence of School Children*, Houghton Mifflin Company, 1919, 317 pp.
29. ———, *Group Tests of Mental Ability*, World Book Company, 1920.
30. ———, and Lima, M., *Children's Reading* (Second edition), D. Appleton-Century Company, 1931, 422 pp.
31. Thorndike, E. L., *et al.*, *The Measurement of Intelligence*, Bureau of Publications, Teachers College, Columbia University, 1926, 616 pp.
32. Valentinier, Th., "Die Phantasie im freien Aufsatze der Kinder und Jugendlichen," *Beihefte zur Zeitschrift für angewandte Psychologie*, 1916, 168 pp.
33. Washburn, C. W., and Vogel, M., *What Children Like to Read*, Rand McNally & Company, 1926, 286 pp.
34. Watson, S. M., *A Study of High School Students' Literary Interests*, M.A. Thesis, University of California, 1925, 97 pp.
35. Yerkes, R. M., "Psychological Examinations in the United States Army," *Memoir of the National Academy of Sciences*, No. 15, 1921.
36. Yoakum, C. S., and Yerkes, R. M., *Army Mental Tests*, Henry Holt and Company, 1920, 303 pp.

PART III
TYPES OF ADOLESCENTS

INTRODUCTION TO PART III

Thus far the book has been concerned with the general developments observed among adolescents as a group. There has been discussion of adolescent growth along physical, emotional, social, moral, and intellectual lines. The effort to date has been to get a general and somewhat de-personalized picture of adolescence as a period of life. There have been, to be sure, case studies here and there and some emphasis upon individual differences along each line considered, but the discussion has been confined mainly to developmental trends without respect to individual pupils in the school.

The second section of this book will be devoted to a description, with illustrated cases, of different types of individuals found with some degree of frequency in the adolescent group. Obviously, the first type to be discussed is (1) the "normal" adolescent. Abnormal types of pupil demand a disproportionate amount of attention; therefore teachers often forget that the majority of individuals are normal. Following this first chapter will come chapters on (2) the delinquent adolescent, (3) the neurotic adolescent, (4) the brilliant pupil and the pupil of low intellectual level, and (5) the vocationally maladjusted adolescent. All these types appear in the general school population. The teacher should, therefore, be able to recognize them, even though most of the remedial work involved in dealing with these pupils does not lie within the teacher's province.

The public school teacher occupies a strategic position for observing which pupils are not developing normally. She has three advantages over the parents. First, she sees hundreds of pupils and so has a basis for knowing what is normal and what is not. Second, she sees these pupils far more objectively than parents can see their children, because she is not tied to them by bonds of emotional sympathy. Finally, she sees all pupils under the same school conditions; that is, the environment is "controlled," and the teacher can note the reactions made to this standardized school situation. She has, therefore, particularly good opportunities to observe deviations from normal behavior as soon as they occur. She is not, however, at all well placed for the remedial treatment of abnormality. In the first place, she cannot possibly be a doctor, a social worker, a juvenile court officer, a psychiatrist, a teacher of special classes, and a vocational counselor, as well as a classroom teacher. She can, of course, co-operate with such individuals and assist in carrying out remedial measures, but she is not an expert diagnostician nor a specialist in remedial treatment, except along strictly educational lines.

The training of teachers should, therefore, be concentrated upon the *recognition* of unusual types, not upon diagnosis nor upon the details of remedial treatment. A teacher's main duty is completed when she has recognized an unusual adolescent and has set in motion the agencies designed for the expert handling of such cases. The emphasis in the following sections will therefore be placed upon the description of atypical adolescents, plus some explanation, where it seems desirable, of the causes leading to such deviations.

CHAPTER VII

THE NORMAL ADOLESCENT

EVEN from a most pessimistic point of view, 80 per cent of the school population falls into the normal group, and probably about 85 per cent. Normalcy covers much more ground than many people seem willing to admit. The expression "normal person" is often used synonymously with "average person." Everyone knows that an average is the exact middle point, mathematically computed, for a group of individuals; hence an average is definitely a point, not an area. Because of the interchangeable use of "average" and "normal" in ordinary speech, many people have derived the idea that normal people are only those located at the exact center of a distribution for any given characteristic. Thus, in the field of intelligence, many teachers regard as perfectly normal only those children with I.Q.'s of exactly 100. Such an I.Q. is the mathematical "average." The normal group, intellectually, includes those with I.Q.'s from 85 to 115. The same situation may be seen in other traits. Normalcy is an area, not a point. It could be statistically defined as that area of a distribution within which 80 to 85 per cent of the cases fall.

Normal people are not alike, however, in regard to any characteristic which may be mentioned. They show variations, but these are relatively small when compared to the total possible amount of variation. For instance, it has already been stated that adolescents as a group are given to daydreaming. The amount of daydreaming from none at all to the patient in the insane hospital who lives in a world of fantasy, would, if accurately measured, show an unbroken distribution from zero to 100 per cent. At some point along this line the amount of daydreaming ceases to be normal and becomes abnormal, but within the normal amount there still remains considerable difference among individuals. Normal people may, therefore, be expected to show a wide range of variation in all characteristics and to be distinct individuals, quite unlike each other.

The real criterion of what is normal and what is not is the pragmatic test of what "works." For only a few human traits has it thus far been possible to develop objective and accurate tests. Normality is therefore defined in terms of what happens to an individual in his daily attempts at adjustment, rather than in terms of a test score. Thus, individuals of defective mentality are often defined as "those who cannot conduct their affairs with ordinary prudence." Emotional deviates have been defined as "people who cannot get along in ordinary social relationships." The moral deviate is a person who "cannot conform to the moral standards set by the society in which he lives." The test of normality is, then, whether or not an individual can adjust to the world. Conversely, all those individuals who *can* and *do* get along in society must be rated as normal, even though in some particular trait they may show considerable variation from the average. No one has a perfect adjustment to life, but the bulk of mankind manages to conform well enough to the conditions around them that they can maintain themselves as accepted individuals in their social group.

It is not to be supposed that the normal individual has no problems. He or she will probably find difficulty in choosing a career, in acquiring social skills, in mastering academic subject matter, in making ambitions fit capacities, in developing acceptable emotional attachments, in controlling prejudices, in deciding moral questions, and so on. There is no lack of problems in the life of a normal adolescent, but usually he is able to find an acceptable solution to the problems. In the case studies to be presented later it should be noted that each individual has a reasonable number of problems, some of them quite severe.

A few years ago a very simple investigation [8] was made as to the number and types of problems reported by a group of college freshmen. The students were asked to state (a) whether or not they had had in college problems along seven different lines, (b) whether or not these problems had been serious, (c) whether or not they were still unsolved, and (d) if solved, from what sources they had received assistance. The per cents below speak for themselves.

TABLE XV
PER CENTS OF ONE HUNDRED COLLEGE WOMEN REPORTING PROBLEMS *
(Pressey [8])

	Vocational Selection	Social Adjustments	Relations with Family	Methods of Study	Worry over Being Queer or Abnormal	Worry over Social Conventions	Worry over Moral or Religious Matters	Averages
Problems	74	52	24	80	27	25	57	48
Serious Problems	51	32	18	66	16	17	27	32
Unsolved Problems	41	24	15	57	16	16	32	29
Sources of Help								
Classes	11	1	1	29	5	0	6	7
Personal Conferences with Instructors	21	1	1	19	2	2	5	7
Friends	23	26	4	5	9	4	10	11
Family	14	7	3	3	0	2	7	5
Books	0	1	0	7	2	1	4	2
Sorority	1	10	0	0	0	1	1	2
Church	1	2	1	0	1	2	1	1

* This material is used by permission of the Public School Publishing Company, Bloomington, Illinois.

There may, of course, have been in this group of college students two or three abnormal individuals, but the great majority of them were normal; yet they report a total of 387 problems, of which 259 were serious. One may conclude, from this and other evidence, that an adolescent is not abnormal merely because he finds difficulties of adjustment to his environment.

THE RANGE OF NORMALITY

The normal adolescent in secondary school can be fairly well described by synthesizing the developments and abilities already discussed. The paragraphs below should be interpreted to refer to the middle years of adolescence: from fifteen to eighteen years of age, approximately.

Physically a normal adolescent in high school may be described as follows: If a boy, he is a person between five feet five inches and six feet in height, with a weight from 115 to 145 pounds. The normal adolescent girl has a height from five feet two inches to five feet eight inches, with a weight from 120 to 140 pounds. The boy has either recently passed through the period of puberty or else is still pubescent; the girl is already sexually mature. For both sexes the period is one of rapid growth. Boys and girls may be expected to be awkward and to be embarrassed over their increasing size. Gains in muscular strength for girls are substantial; for boys the increase is very large. The adolescent's face is distinctly out of proportion, the lower part being usually too small for the upper. The skin is more likely than not to show eruptions. The typical adolescent complains of cramps and pains in his muscles. His bodily proportions are quite characteristic: he or she has a high waistline, a high hipline, broad shoulders, long arms and legs, and large hands and feet. Most girls become quite distressed about the size of their hips.

The average adolescent has a heart too small for his arteries and is therefore liable to strain his heart. Practically all boys and girls experience faintness, dizziness, and heart palpitations at one time or another. Digestive disturbances can be expected. So also can one anticipate large but peculiar appetites. Queer selections and avoidances of food are the rule rather than the exception. The average adolescent's diet would produce digestive difficulties in a goat. Both boys and girls perspire all too freely and use up much emotional energy worrying about it.

The sex glands are usually mature but the sexual functions have not been established on an adult level. Both boys and girls may be expected to worry over sexual manifestations, to become self-conscious, and to have an interest in obscene stories and jokes. The average adolescent boy has just begun to shave, and his voice is not yet under control. The average girl has relatively little menstrual pain, although she does have some discomfort and very soon learns to capitalize on this discomfort to get out of work she does not want to do.

Emotionally the normal adolescent shows a great sensitivity to social stimuli of all sorts. The characteristic stimuli that make adolescents angry are those that insult his dignity, or make him seem ridiculous, or make him feel he is being treated as a child. His fears are a curious mixture of the most persistent fears of childhood and those characteristic of adults. Adolescents are afraid of social situations in which they may appear to a disadvantage; they also fear disease and accidental violence. Partly through his lack of physical equilibrium and partly through his sensitiveness to environmental pressures, the normal adolescent has many and profound emotional experiences. A chronically wrought-up condition is typical, not abnormal.

Normal adolescent boys and girls have broken away from any intense emotional fixation upon either parent, upon older individuals of either sex, or upon members of their own sex. That is, heterosexual interests have been established. This is one of the few changes absolutely essential to normality.[10] At one time or another every adolescent may be expected to develop an intense love affair. In fact, parents or teachers should be much more worried about a boy or girl who does not fall in love a half-dozen times than about one who does.

In all probability, the normal adolescent will have occasional trouble with school discipline. He is restive and from time to time wants to leave school altogether. About one-third of his teachers he will violently dislike, and only one or two are likely to arouse him to his best efforts.

The average boy or girl finds the demands of life rather difficult to face and develops techniques for escaping from uncomfortable situations. Of these, daydreaming is undoubtedly the most common and can be expected in all normal pupils in secondary school. As long as the individual distinguishes clearly between daydreams and reality, no harm is done. Daydreaming is a source of constant irritation to parents and teachers, but it provides a simple outlet for the disappointments and bewilderment incident to adolescent adjustment.

Socially the normal adolescent is deeply concerned about his appearance, his clothes, his social standing, the reputation of his friends, the appearance of any girl he is seen with, his behavior in social situations, etc. He is acutely miserable unless his clothes are of exactly the model that is currently fashionable. Often he or she will stay away from some social event rather than go in last year's clothes.

The normal adolescent belongs to a group of boys and girls who go about together as a crowd. The proportion of boys to girls is not always exact, but if acceptable individuals can be found, the number of each sex is more likely than not to be identical. Such a group receives the adolescent's chief devotion and loyalty. The normal boy or girl is not a leader except in minor enterprises; he is a willing and loyal follower of the few who have initiative and leadership. He is blindly loyal to his own friends and utterly intolerant of people from other social groups.

The normal adolescent belongs to two or three school clubs and plays several games. He also has one or two hobbies which he pursues somewhat erratically. He has vastly more enthusiasm for his games and hobbies than he has for his classwork and voluntarily spends many hours in such pursuits. The normal adolescent boy, indeed, is likely to become completely absorbed in athletics. Sometimes it is a single game that excites him; sometimes it is any game. It is the boy who is not thrilled about athletic contests who is abnormal, not the boy who is.

Morally the normal adolescent may be expected to develop his own ideals of conduct. These will probably not be identical with those of his parents and will certainly differ markedly from those of his grandparents.[1] His ideals may or may not be socially acceptable, but he does develop some general criteria for estimating conduct.

His opinions upon such general social matters as prohibition, communism, war, crime, birth control, or capital punishment are still immature. His attitude toward individuals of other races shows an increasingly marked and deep-seated prejudice throughout the secondary school period. He still believes many common superstitions, whether he will admit it or not. Normal adolescent boys and girls are more likely than not to crib on examinations unless they are supervised, although they are willing to be honest if the situation is so controlled that others cannot possibly cheat. Ordinary adolescent insight into criminal behavior, except of the most obvious types, cannot be trusted; they apparently see nothing wrong in many situations which to the adult are obviously illegal.

A normal boy or girl of adolescent years has religious doubts, which arise usually in science classes, but these doubts do not seem to have deeply disturbing effects. The youngster realizes there is a discrepancy between what he has been taught by his church or his parents and what he is taught in school, but he does not feel any great emotional crisis on this account; the whole matter seems intellectual rather than emotional. Doubts exist, but they tend to resolve themselves gradually and without excitement. A normal adolescent may or may not believe in the existence of God; the chances are approximately equal between these two standpoints. If he believes in God at all, he usually regards Him as a friendly and intelligent Being rather than as a Supreme Creator. It is no longer probable that the average adolescent will experience a sudden conversion. Indeed, any violent reactions or serious emotional preoccupation with religious questions are abnormal rather than typical.

Intellectually adolescents show a mental age somewhere between 13 and 19. The normal high school pupil has an I.Q. from 95 to 115 on the ordinary intelligence tests. The chances are about even that an adolescent of average ability will complete high school or will leave without graduating because of failure, his own preference to go to work, or his desire to attend some other type of school. Any number of failures between two and five is perfectly normal for a four-year high school course. The average adolescent has a good memory but is not fond of using it. He has good powers of concentration upon what interests him, but he often fails to concentrate upon what other people want him to do. His imagination is vivid but is shown primarily in daydreaming, rather than in any written form. If an average adolescent is given a short passage to read, he can get the main heads of an outline from it and some of the subheads. He can find the main point in about one-half the paragraphs he reads, if he bothers to look for it. He can give explanations for simple, natural or social phenomena, but his explanations though logical are not likely to be complete. He can give an adequate interpretation of about one-half the parables, allegories, or fables read to him. He cannot interpret correctly the meaning of more than one political or historical cartoon in three.

The normal adolescent's verbal intelligence is not in a state of rapid development. He is acquiring relatively few new words and restricts both his spoken and written vocabulary to a small assortment. His progress in appreciation of art, music, poetry, or prose is very nearly at a standstill, but his mechanical aptitude and ability are showing rapid increases. These facts are true for both boys and girls. A turning away from the aesthetic and the verbal toward the mechanical and practical may be regarded as a normal development of this period. Indeed, the average high school pupil of today is a nonverbal, nonacademic individual.

Adolescents normally have no great interest in their schoolwork, although an occasional class arouses enthusiasm. The normal boy does not like to write any kind of composition; if he must write something, he prefers athletics, travel, outdoor activities, machinery, or vocational matters for his topics. The adolescent girl is a little more willing to write; she prefers travel, personal experiences, and topics dealing with home or school life as her subjects. Both groups like games in which teamwork is important and complicated rules are enforced. Feminine enjoyment of such games is, however, more likely to be passive than active. Interest in all kinds of social affairs that bring together members of both sexes is high for both boys and girls, although the normal girl shows such interest a year or two sooner than the normal boy. During the entire adolescent period, in fact, the girl has a far more intense interest in social matters than her brother. The normal boy will read books dealing with adventure, a few novels, a fair number of detective stories, travel articles in magazines, and the sporting page of the newspaper. The normal girl reads chiefly romantic novels, a few detective stories, and love stories in magazines. Devotion to the classics is distinctly unusual, not typical.

Normal boys and girls show such characteristics as those summarized above. One may wish the average development were higher or in some way different, but an assumption not based on facts leads only to trouble. Teachers must learn to accept facts as they are. Few people realize (a) how relatively low the average ability of a high school group is and (b) how different from one another boys and girls can be and still be "perfectly normal."

ILLUSTRATIVE CASE STUDIES

Two types of material are presented in this section. First there are two comprehensive studies, based on questionnaire results and personal interviews, of a normal girl and a normal boy. Then come several excerpts from diaries. These latter should be read with caution. The adolescent who keeps a diary is highly literate, more intelligent, more repressed, and better educated than the average. However, the descriptions of one's own feelings and attitudes are best written at the time they are experienced and by the individual concerned. From what one can observe of normal adolescent behavior and reactions, these samples from diaries reflect reasonably well the ideas and emotions of normal adolescence. Of course, the number of samples given is far from adequate to illustrate all phases of adolescent behavior within normal limits; those selected are merely typical.

Case No. 65 [6] presents the picture of a perfectly normal girl. The opinions given on various points are the answers she made to a detailed questionnaire that was given to her and a number of other girls. A summary of her answers reveals her attitude towards her family, friends, vocational objectives, and religion.

She states that she thinks her parents have higher standards than the parents of her friends, and that she is prouder of her father than they are of theirs. She likes the friends of her parents, thinks her mother unselfish, and has been impertinent to her father. Her parents believe in God, and she knows of their belief regarding Jesus. They talk over their plans before her, and she underlined doubly her responses that they did not quarrel, that they did deceive one another, and that her father took good care of her mother. They do not disapprove of her smoking. She has an older sister whom she is very fond of, has been jealous of, has worried about, has quarreled with, has been proud and ashamed of. She has had secrets with her sister that they did not share with their mother.

Of her social life she states that she visits friends, belongs to a club, and goes on picnics, but she has never been to a girls' camp nor been an officer in a club or class. She has done some charity work, and has cheated in a contest. She has had a "crush" on an older friend; and she doubly underscored her response that she did not like to flirt and had never been in love. She has had helpful friends, older friends with whom she has had serious talks, and friends who have been unfair. She has been in trouble with friends at schools, has done things she was ashamed of, has had secrets she was ashamed of, but has had no friend who had a really bad influence on her. She has kept her friends' secrets inviolate.

Of herself she states that she wants to go to college, has good health, is not nervous, has been ill and badly frightened, but has been in no disaster. She doubly underlined her response that she did not try to smoke, but says she discusses it. She likes to daydream and has imagined herself doing things she would not really do. She has imagined herself as she hopes to be at twenty-five years of age, successful, clever, and happy. She longs to help those less fortunate than herself. She especially admires her musical friends, she has been to concerts and likes classical music and hymns, but not jazz. She likes poetry and writes some. She has been to art exhibits, loves pictures, and has been thrilled by lovely scenes. She is interested in movie stars, and has been shocked by immodest pictures (doubly underlined).

Of her religious life she states that she goes to a religious school and to church habitually, and has wanted to join the church. She believes in God, knows some Bible stories, and does not believe sickness is God's punishment of sin nor that God answers prayer directly. She prays habitually and thinks it helps one. She has heard lovely prayers, wanted to write a prayer-poem, and has discussed prayer with friends. She has wondered about the nature of God, evolution, the Holy Spirit, Jesus, and life after death.

This girl's attitude towards her mother shows in general a dependence upon her mother's judgment and a deep affection for her. In the questionnaire used several typical adolescent incidents were described; the girls were then asked how much they would tell their mothers about each of these incidents. In answer to most questions this girl stated she would tell her mother everything because her mother understood and was interested. Sometimes apparently she would tell her mother only casual details and for a few of the sample situations presented she replied she would not tell her mother anything for fear of being scolded. Her relations with her mother are evidently not entirely free of restraint because she occasionally gave as her reason for not discussing certain topics with her mother such reasons as: "I don't know how to bring it up," "I don't like to talk about such things," or "I feel sensitive or silly." Other answers indicate her mother's relation to her; to some of the questions she responded she would tell her mother everything because, "She likes me to confess," "She likes to hear my ideas," "She likes me to be brave, good, helpful, and happy." But she evidently got much from the relationship. She wrote, in answer to some questions, that she would confide in her mother because: "Mother would comfort me," "Mother would sympathize with my hurt feelings," "I like to confide in her," "Mother could tell me what is right."

This girl gives a picture of normal family relationships. She has not developed independent habits of thought, since she responds to questions regarding confidence in her mother in the negative when her doing so is a mode of protection from some form of discomfort, and in the positive when the response takes some form of propitiation or dependence.*

The suddenness of the adolescent change [5] is well illustrated by the case of Eugene. At the age of fifteen years and one month he was an enthusiastic member of a local boy scout troop. He was very proud of his scout uniform. Having long since attained the rank of second-class scout he was working hard to become first class. The incipient change first showed itself by some minor disorders at a scout meeting. Evidently Eugene was beginning to lose

* This case study is presented by permission of the Bureau of Publications, Teachers College, Columbia University.

interest. Soon after he began to object to wearing the scout uniform. He felt that it made him look conspicuous. However, at the age of fifteen years and three months the boy was still interested enough in scouting to take the trouble to pass his map test; but he was beginning to spend more and more time with a group of older boys in the high school which he attended and with another group of older boys who lived on his block. He liked to talk about these new friends and their exploits, and took a rather patronizing attitude toward his fellow scouts.

A month later at the age of fifteen years and four months, he finally became a first-class scout, but after another week he was very disrespectful toward his scoutmaster at a patrol meeting. The next day he apologized and went on a hike. He now began to spend more and more time with the other boys on his block. One of them bought a very old Ford and the group began the task of overhauling it. For the next month Eugene hesitated between the two groups. He divided his spare time between working for merit badges with the scouts and working with his new friends on their Ford. He began to grow cold toward Francis, his former bosom friend, and spoke of the latter as being somewhat too childish for his attention. In another month the change had become complete. Eugene had definitely severed his connection with the scouts and had thrown in his lot with the boys on his block. He was very much interested in the process of remaking the Ford and spoke about taking up automobile repairing as a vocation—something which he later actually did.*

Girl, Age 16:[7] In the very earliest part of this [adolescent] period I had a queer feeling toward boys. I did not care for their company; in fact they rather bored me, yet I rather liked to be noticed by them. I considered it the proper thing to disagree with boys continually and rather prided myself upon my continual wrangling. A favorite scheme of my chums and myself was to pretend that we did not see the boys but put ourselves where they would surely see us. But on the whole we considered them a silly lot. Some of the girls of our age went to dances, and we considered this the most stupid and silly thing possible. Often, while I was sitting on the porch in the evenings with mother, many boys would pass and naturally speak. Mother would answer, but I coolly cut them and considered it very smart especially when, afterward, people remarked what a stubborn person I was. Until I was fifteen

* This case study is used by permission of The Macmillan Company.

I loudly asserted that I would be an "old maid," and then in my sophomore year I suddenly changed my mind.*

Girl, Age 15:[7] The sex knowledge caused a very sad and disturbed feeling in my heart. I thought about it for days, wondering and wondering why life had to be that way and talking it over with some of my friends who were equally puzzled. I did not ask any older person. If I had gone to my mother or some other older person in whom I had confidence I could probably have been helped very much, but every time I had asked before I had been told not to think about such things, and I was too ashamed and embarrassed to ask. I felt that I was doing wrong in thinking of this but continued to do so. This, however, caused no reaction against older people except an amazed feeling of misunderstanding.

Girl, Age 16:[2] Everything is so artificial in school; I laugh and carry on and am so unsatisfied; I feel so awful. Every day when I wake up, if it happens to be a free day I am disgusted. And every day of school, I get disgusted but not so much, for in school I forget and get completely stupified. But when I am supposed to go home I have a horror and dawdle about for a while in the street. . . . When other human beings are sad they know why; I don't know why I must torture myself this way.†

Boy, Age 18:[2] I still recall that once our whole family was taking a walk. Going home we met a father with his daughter. I could not turn away my eyes from her beautiful figure, her attractive dress. I still recall that I was amazed and saw nothing but her. Then I heard Mother saying to Father, "Just look at our Fritz." Thus, I was dragged back into grim reality, only furtively so that no one noticed it, I had to glance back again and again toward the heavenly child.

And when I kissed the first girl! In the evening I wanted to go to Röders'. On the way, I met my longed for Anna. She wanted to go to a gardener in order to bring a little flower pot to a friend. I said, "Oh, Anna, this suits me swell. I can go along." I still hear her expectantly consenting voice, so bashful, chaste, and yet yielding. When we were halfway, I said, "Come, Anna, let us go out there." And I laid my arm around her childlike form. Thus we walked along happily. She also liked to hold me in her clasp.

* This and the following paragraph are used by permission of the D. Appleton-Century Company.
† This and the remaining paragraphs of the chapter are presented by permission of G. Fischer, Jena, Germany.

In the meadow in front of the wide street—I still remember quite distinctly—I stood still. Her head rested on my cheek, but I could not muster up courage to kiss her. I recall the sensation of this first uncertain groping toward an experience. Oh, and when on the way home, I pressed, clasped, and kissed her, there was no such intoxicating bliss as I had expected. I was overwhelmed by embarrassment because I seemed now to be responsible for this girl.

And today, again, the maddening craving for a yielding feminine body. What can I expect from a yielding girl unless I control myself now? I definitely require relations with girls whose presence quenches my craving.

Boy, Age 15:[2] Nowadays when I am alone I often have a strange feeling. *I long for something but I don't know for what.* For a friend? For freedom from school? I don't know. Perhaps it is only because of the springtime, for the feeling always returns when there is a proper spring air and when I hear the birds begin to sing. When I have this feeling in school, I am nauseated by all life so that I must take care not to hurl my books into a corner or give an impudent answer if I am asked to recite. I believe people have committed suicide when they have felt this way. It is a pity I have no one to whom I could read the nonsense I write into this book. Kate and Ernest [sister and brother] would mock me, Roehl [chum] does not listen, and there is no one else. But I believe that it is my own fault, for others do find friends. Or, are there some who are also looking, like myself, for someone? If I met them perhaps we'd understand each other.

Boy, Age 16:[2] It is most disagreeable for me to have to say to myself, "No one understands you," for that really sounds as if I wanted to play the part of a hermit in a theatrical way and were an odd fish who insists on being different. Either of these I consider silly. But the fact remains that I am really not understood. Is it my fault or that of the other people? I always used to get along best with Father. Now that has changed somewhat because he is not satisfied with my schoolwork. Mother, as I notice at every opportunity, pictures me in every way as the exact opposite of what I am. She has no conception of me. Kern at least behaves passively. He does not understand me either, but he admits I have a right to exist as I am. He is at least better than the people who constantly tell me I am straying from the straight and narrow path. At last I thought I had found in Bergmann a boy who could think with me, and this misled me into talking frankly with him.

At once he was horrified; he declared I had sunk in his esteem, without his taking the least trouble to understand me. These four are the only persons who could be considered. . . . At bottom, we are what we often called ourselves in jest or in earnest—lonely souls.

Boy, Age 13:[2] It is evening. My watch is ticking softly. Everyone is asleep. I closed a just-finished book and wiped two tears from my eyes. Whether this was weakness or nothing to be ashamed of, I don't know. The book tells the story of a boy who at the side of a friend struggles and obtains work and faith. This friend dies and the boy ceases to develop. I always feel that I lack a friend, one who can completely enter into my personality, to whom I could utter all my thoughts, and who would be fond of me. . . . I also know that few people love me, but I shouldn't care about that if I had one who was willing to be my friend. Then I should say I am of value to one person and could ignore others with indifference, but, as it is, knowing that I have not completely won over anyone, knowing that there is no one who likes me better than all the rest of his comrades, it seems to me as though I were worth very little. I should not, like Socrates, like to look for men, but for one man. *I think it is a disgrace to be without a friend.*

Boy, Age 19:[2] That quotation is right—"joyous to the heavens and downcast unto death!" I picture to myself how long it would probably take until I would find Eva a nuisance, even repulsive! Hannah with her madonna face and her looks full of renunciation, and yet for that very reason inviting, I don't care about any more. It is a fortunate thing that I immediately stifled my sprouting love for Bertha. Otherwise, I suppose I should not be able to dance with her at all in the folk dance courses. I feel something like a rapture when I meet Fannie. In her I divine a spiritual leader. Yet, I dare say, she isn't that either. The point is I don't want a girl who allows herself to be kissed and is ready for necking; toward such girls I should become insistent and sensual. I know that. Therefore, hands off; I'm better off alone. My eyes look across the sea toward the woman who is to be the core of my life. Shall I find her? Pure body, pure lips, devout heart, and clever spirit!

Girl, Age 16:[2] I often have a yearning to get acquainted with wholly strange people. It comes suddenly, possibly when I am walking on the street or sitting in the electric car. I see a face, a quite ordinary face, but when I look into his eyes and at the fine marks left by mental work or spiritual struggles, I suddenly realize there is one of my soul comrades. Like me, he has bumped against the same stumbling blocks, pondered over the same questions, tried to leap over the chasms made by prejudice and stupidity. Why is it impossible to talk at once to such a person? Instead of that, we sit decorously and only stare at each other and are glad, and yet nothing is done to prevent our losing sight of each other forevermore within a few minutes' time. How stupid! Who knows how much that is beautiful we might give and reveal to each other.

Girl, Age 18:[2] I don't know what awakened in me this great yearning for beauty. I have never looked for that sort of thing. I kept away from art because I understood nothing about it, because I knew I had no desire for it. Then it seemed as if I could hardly get along without the choral singing in the cathedral and longed for it from one time to the next. Then I began to revel in nature and liked nothing more than steeping myself in its beauty. The desire simply overwhelmed me. Then I ardently yearned for drawing, for accurate study of art, for beauty of color and form. Everywhere I would sit with my sketchbook and dog. All of this came unsought and so full of life. When I came home from my journey, I completely rearranged my room, for I did not like it any more.

BIBLIOGRAPHY *

1. Anderson, A., and Dvorak, B., "Differences between College Students and Their Elders in Standards of Conduct," *Journal of Abnormal and Social Psychology,* 1928, 23: 286-289.
2. Bühler, Ch., *Das Seelenleben des Jugendlichen,* Gustav Fischer, Wien, 1927, 215 pp.
3. Burdge, H. G., *Our Boys: A Study of 245,000 Sixteen, Seventeen, and Eighteen-Year-Old Employed Boys in the State of New York,* J. B. Lyon and Company, 1921, 345 pp.
4. Edwards, A. S., "A Theoretical and Clinical Study of So-Called Normality," *Journal of Abnormal and Social Psychology,* 1934, 28: 366-376.
5. Furfey, P. H., *The Growing Boy,* The Macmillan Company, 1930, 192 pp.
6. Leonard, E. A., "Concerning Our Girls and What They Tell Us," *Teachers College Contributions to Education,* No. 430, Bureau of Publications, Teachers College, Columbia University, 1930, 192 pp.

* See also the references in the Appendix.

7. Mudge, E. L., *Varieties of Adolescent Experience*, D. Appleton-Century Company, 1926, 134 pp.
8. Pressey, S. L., et al., *Research Adventures in University Teaching*, Public School Publishing Company, 1927, 152 pp.
9. Smithies, E. M., *Case-Studies of Normal Adolescent Girls*, D. Appleton-Century Company, 1933, 284 pp.
10. Williams, F., "Confronting the World," in *Concerning Parents*, New Republic, Inc., 1926, pp. 137-159.

CHAPTER VIII

THE DELINQUENT ADOLESCENT

FIRST and last, a good deal is known about delinquent adolescents and the environments that produce them. Research has been going on for some years but has recently received fresh stimulation from the increase in the number of juvenile delinquents and the inability of the juvenile court alone to deal with the problems before it. In so far as the high school teacher is concerned, delinquency is a minor problem statistically because most delinquent adolescents have already left school. However, the teacher needs to understand the fundamental causes of delinquency, to realize the part the school sometimes plays in actually promoting delinquent behavior, and to be acquainted with the most promising treatments thus far devised for dealing with pupils who are on their way to becoming criminals.

Obviously, delinquency is a type of social behavior. It is the result of certain types of environment working upon certain types of individuals. In very few cases is the delinquency either wholly "inherited" or wholly "acquired." While individual and environmental influences will be considered separately, it should never be forgotten that they work together, as will become clear in the case studies to be presented.

CHARACTERISTICS OF DELINQUENT ADOLESCENTS

It was once supposed that there were certain, clearly recognizable "criminal types" of individual. Apparently, nothing is further from the truth. There are, however, a few personal traits, either native or acquired, that are more likely than other characteristics to lead to criminal activity. The degree of rela-

DELINQUENT ADOLESCENT

tionship between these various traits and delinquency should first be considered.

Level of Intelligence.—There have been numbers of studies made concerning the distribution of intelligence shown by groups of delinquents. Such facts as those given below emerge.

> The I.Q.'s for several delinquent groups (one of 3,584 cases) have been found to distribute themselves in a normal scatter,[25] but with the center at some point between 82 and 88 instead of at the theoretical 100. The extreme I.Q.'s usually vary from below 60 to about 120.[13] There is no relationship between recidivism and intellectual level.[6]

From such studies it is clear that low intelligence is a causative factor in only certain cases at best and is almost never the only factor. For every delinquent adolescent with an I.Q. at any level above 70—or even below if proper education has been given—there are any number of perfectly normal adolescents of the same intellectual level. Since all levels of intelligence produce both delinquent and socially normal persons, low mental ability alone cannot be considered as a main cause of delinquent behavior. The majority of delinquents fall into either the "normal" or "low normal" classifications.

Physical condition.—There seems some evidence that physical abnormalities sometimes act, probably indirectly, as contributing causes to delinquency. Usually, about 50 per cent of any delinquent group shows physical handicaps of some sort. Thus in one group of 967 delinquents, 57 per cent were in good health, 30 per cent in fair physical condition, and 13 per cent in poor health.[13] However, about the same per cent of normal children have some physical abnormality. An erroneous conclusion may be drawn unless one keeps the entire situation in mind. An unusually careful study has done so.[5] For this research, 282 delinquent boys were given physical examinations; then, 282 nondelinquent boys of the same age, grade, and intelligence were similarly examined. The excess of the former over the latter group for each type of physical abnormality varied from 45.8 per cent for dental caries to .3 per cent for deafness. Only three items—dental caries, poor dental hygiene, and defective tonsils—showed differences of more than 8 per cent between the two groups. Although there were several slight differences between the delinquents and nondelinquents, these were by no means sufficient as sole causes of the differences in behavior between the two groups.

It is probable, however, that physical condition acts in two ways as a contributing cause, in a certain number of cases. A chronic deficiency of almost any kind makes a person restless and uncomfortable. Pupils with physical defects may therefore get into disciplinary difficulties because they cannot concentrate as well as more healthy children can, or because of general restlessness. This theory is made more tenable by the increase in delinquency during the most common period of puberty—ages thirteen and fourteen years.[35] At this time the organism is under unusual stress. In other cases, the atypical behavior seems to be the response of a person with an obvious defect, who is overcompensating for his deficiencies. However, poor physical condition without complicating emotional factors cannot be regarded as an independent cause of delinquency. There are too many adolescents who are physically defective or sick, but who show perfectly normal behavior.

Educational record.—For the most part, delinquents stop their schooling in the upper grades of grammar school. Out of one thousand juvenile offenders, only ninety-six were ever in high school at all and only twenty-eight were there at the time they were brought into court.[18] Of the remaining number, 681 were either in elementary school or had left before reaching the seventh grade, while 223 were or had been in junior high school. Delinquency among those children who reach high school is, therefore, not common. Indeed, the degree of educational retardation shown by delinquents is far greater than can be explained by the degree of mental retardation.

In general, delinquents—whether or not actual truancy is one of their offenses—are irregular in their school attendance. They do not like school, and they do poor schoolwork. Thus, out of 1,343 delinquents, 61 per cent showed irregular attendance.[35] Out of 977 juvenile offenders, 85 per cent were retarded from one to five years, 12 per cent were at age for their grade, and only 2 per cent were accelerated.[13] The average attitude toward schoolwork and the lack of success shown by delinquents cannot be explained upon the basis of inferior intelligence. There are many children of no better ability who love school, attend regularly, study hard, and are reasonably successful. Delinquents are not usually delinquent because they are uneducated; they are much more frequently uneducated because they are delinquent.

Social competency.—There seems to be little if anything the matter with the social capacities of delinquents; indeed, many of them would be better off if they did not so easily make friends and so easily become members of gangs. Many delinquents even have distinct qualities of leadership. Although the forms of expression are usually inacceptable, the underlying social competency seems at least average.

In a recent study [1] the participation in social activities of one hundred delinquent and one hundred nondelinquent boys of the same ages and intelligence was observed. The delinquent boys showed greater increase in participation from the lower to the higher ages than the nondelinquents and a consistently higher average participation at all ages. Common observation gives similar results. Delinquents are unpopular enough with their teachers and other school officials, but once they are on the playground or in the gymnasium they participate freely and naturally in whatever is going on. They show a capacity to get on with their peers that academically successful children would do well to imitate. Delinquents do not often get into trouble because of any withdrawal from society.

There is plenty of evidence that the delinquent is not a person of academic competency. He often has shrewdness, knowledge of the world, and a considerable *savoir-faire,* but he finds nothing stimulating between the covers of a schoolbook. He does, however, have a social capacity upon which the traditional school makes little demand. Since ordinary schooling does little good it would seem that a curriculum based almost wholly upon developing social capacities along acceptable lines should be substituted. Social competency is the average delinquent's sole talent. The school should capitalize on it and train it, whether the youngster ever learns long division or not.

Emotional maladjustment.—Everyone who has studied delinquents regards them as emotionally unstable and unadjusted individuals. They are not reconciled to society as it is constituted. They like the wrong people and want to do the wrong things. They are bored with the ordinary ways of living and want excitement and change. They react to the stresses of everyday life in unusual ways. They resent discipline, and discipline leaves little or no effect upon them. They will not submit to normal social restrictions but set about making their own society. All observations and tests produce the same results: that delinquents differ from normal children mainly in their social and emotional adjustments. Thus, in one careful study, it was found that, of 1,343 delinquents, 97 per cent showed social maladjustments, 83 per cent maladjustments in school, and 77 per cent inability to adjust to their homes.[35] Further points in regard to the emotional instability and lack of social adaptation shown by delinquents will be stressed in a later section.

The predelinquent child needs, above all, training in acceptable forms of emotional expression. Usually he seeks through the activities of his gang or other play group the satisfaction that he fails to find anywhere else.[27] By his contacts with such groups he receives his major training for life.[28] The modes of expression thus taught are generally antisocial. Since one method of expression can be substituted for another, if it yields the same degree of satisfaction, the problem becomes one of finding acceptable outlets for pupils who are unable or unwilling to use those outlets found adequate by normal children. As will be seen shortly, part of the maladjustment is due to the nature of the delinquent child's environment, which usually deprives him of many possible outlets while providing him with many that are undesirable.

The fundamental difference between the normal and the delinquent child is to be found, not in intelligence, health, educational level, or social competency but in the force of emotional drives, the failure to conform to society's demands, and an emotional instability that makes ordinary training in correct responses ineffective.

CHARACTERISTICS OF A "DELINQUENT" ENVIRONMENT

Three elements in the total social situation seem to be of utmost importance in conditioning the behavior of delinquents —the home, the neighborhood, and the school. Because of their outstanding importance they will be dealt with in some detail.

The delinquent home.—Homes may be characterized from various points of view, all of which deserve consideration. The most obvious characteristic of a home is its physical condition. Out of 734 delinquent children studied by one investigator [13] 62 per cent lived in homes in which the physical conditions were distinctly poor; 25 per cent came from homes of fair condition, and only 13 per cent from homes that were sanitary, well equipped, and reasonably prosperous. The moral tone of a home shows an even closer relationship to delinquency. Of 908 delinquents, 74 per cent lived in homes where the moral tone was bad, 19 per cent in homes of fair moral level, and only 7 per cent in really good homes.[13] The moral condition of these homes is further shown by the fact that in 84 per cent of the cases, some member of the immediate family was also delinquent— one parent, both parents, or one or more siblings. In 52 per cent of the cases, one or more members of the immediate family was insane, feeble-minded, epileptic, or syphilitic; such defects were suspected in the families of another 30 per cent. The poor condition of the home and the incompetency of the parents is further revealed by study of the fathers' occupations.[13] In 43 per cent of the homes the father was a day laborer, in 39 per cent he was a semiskilled artisan, in 12 per cent he was a small shopkeeper or clerk, and in only 6 per cent was he a semiprofessional or professional individual. In a more recent study,[6] 72 per cent of chronically delinquent children came from homes that were on poor relief. In a study of truants,[14] 46 per cent were found to be children of day laborers.

In another investigation [35] of 1,343 children who were problems in school, 77 per cent came from homes in which one or both parents were of low-grade mentality, illiterate, diseased, or immoral. From the above data it is clear that delinquents come from poorly equipped homes in which the parents are of low capacity, inferior economic status, and questionable morals.

There are two further characteristics of these homes, however. In half of those studied the parents were separated—by death, desertion, divorce, or absence of one parent from chronic illness or imprisonment.[30] The natural family constellation was thus broken. In 70 per cent of the homes the discipline was either sadly lacking or quite unsound.[13] The parents of delinquents are evidently people who have little control over themselves and even less over their children. When one considers the staggering odds against any child's developing normally in such homes, one is surprised that delinquency is not more frequent than it is.

The delinquent neighborhood.—Of 911 delinquents, 86 per cent are classified as coming from "bad" neighborhoods, 11 per cent from "fair" neighborhoods, and only 3 per cent from "good" neighborhoods.[13] In evaluating what is meant by such statistics, one must obviously define the terms used and must determine exactly what elements go to make up a "bad" neighborhood.

During the last few years many studies have been made in different places in regard to this point.[15, 21, 29, 36] The approach has been entirely pragmatic. Investigators have first taken a detailed map of the city or area under investigation and have tabulated upon it the location of those homes from which delinquents came. In all cases these homes centered in a few districts, usually in not more than two or three. Having located the neighborhoods in this way, the investigators next made a careful survey of these localities. The "bad" neighborhoods turn out to be one of three types. They are (1) business districts, (2) manufacturing districts, or (3) districts in which the population is in the process of changing. In no investigation is there more than a tiny scattering of cases from strictly residential neighborhoods.

A business district is typically a place where adults are busy with work or amusement and have no time or attention for children. The adults there, except possibly policemen, feel no responsibility for what children are doing. Consequently, the youngsters have none of the supervision that comes to all children who are living or playing in a residential district, where the mothers especially pay attention to anything any child is doing. Manufacturing districts are not much more acceptable than business districts as places in which to bring up children. In the first place, the smells and sights are likely to be so unsavory that only those who cannot afford to live elsewhere will live there. Only cheap houses are built and the inhabitants are those who work in the near-by factories—mostly families of unskilled or semiskilled laborers. A business district usually abounds in forms of amusement intended for adults, but a factory district is rather worse in this respect because the amusements are of a lower type—poolrooms, cheap theaters with burlesque shows, houses of prostitution, saloons, men's "clubs," hangouts of gangs, and so on. Neither factory nor business district offers the protection or the normal outlets for activity that children need.

The third type of district presents a somewhat different problem. Suppose the houses in a few blocks have been tenanted primarily by Hungarians, for instance; while this situation lasts, there is formed a little, closed-in colony, the members of which feel responsible for its children. Suppose then these people begin to drift away—perhaps toward some new place where the men are employed. The cohesion begins to break up almost at once, and is further broken if, for example, Italians start moving into the vacated houses. If the process goes on and the neighborhood becomes entirely populated with Italians, there is again social cohesion. But during the period of the shift, the district is pulled apart by antagonistic social forces. The adults of the two groups do not get on with each other; the children inherit these antagonisms and develop competing gangs. The looseness of social control is furthered if the adults of both groups speak much less English than do their children. In any case, the neighborhood has lost one set of standards without acquiring another. While the change is in process it becomes an area in which the rate of delinquency is higher than the rate in near-by districts that are inhabited solidly by members of either nationality alone. Thus, in one study of two hundred sexually delinquent girls and their partners,[8] it was found that over half the homes and places where sexual relations occurred were located on the boundaries of community areas, while 86 per cent were located on the boundaries of language areas. Such data suggest that "mixed" districts—regardless of the elements entering into the mixture—are also unsettled districts in which delinquency is likely to flourish.

Perhaps the outstanding characteristic of all these "bad" districts is that they offer no social cohesion, little protection, and only warped outlets for childish activities. The "good" district presents the opposite picture. It is one in which there are social traditions, excellent protection (in the form of observant adults), and adequate outlets for the restlessness and emotional drives of childhood and adolescence. In all investigations "bad" neighborhoods or "bad" companions are found to be important elements contributing to delinquency in the great majority of cases.

The delinquent school.—The public school is in general a contributor to mental health rather than to delinquency, but there are still a few characteristics of the average school that may produce abnormal behavior. The chief adverse element is the rigidity of the curriculum. It must be remembered that the curriculum is, at all levels, an inheritance from a previous time when only a few children went to school beyond the first four or five grades. It is at present a compromise between the training needed by bright children and that needed by duller children and, like most compromises, it does not accomplish either of its two objectives. For children of average and more than average ability the curriculum contains too little and for those of less ability it contains too much. The delinquent is typically a nonbookish, nonintellectual, nonacademic, nonverbal individual. In the regular grades of school he is taught too much about books and too little about life. If he is put into a special class he is usually taught the same things, but at a slower rate. Presently the predelinquent becomes a truant because he will not attend a school in which there is nothing of any interest to him. In the early stages these truants often simply wander harmlessly about, watching bricklayers build houses and day laborers dig up sewers. The school contributes to delinquency because, instead of presenting a curriculum around those things to which a predelinquent child *will* pay attention it tries to suppress such interests and to substitute a desire for academic learning. By now it is certainly evident that delinquent children revolt against the school—and their one hope of salvation is lost. Neither their homes nor their neighborhoods are good enough to keep them stable. When they leave school they usually abandon the only constructive influence in their lives. If schools would learn that saving children is more important than saving the curriculum there would be less delinquency.

Summary.—A "delinquent" environment consists, then, of three main elements: (1) a home in which parents are ineffective in discipline, unsuccessful economically, of not more than average native ability, of undesirable personal habits, and of questionable morality; (2) a neighborhood that is devised for adults, totally without safeguards for children, and largely without safe outlets for emotional and social life; and (3) a school that tries to make scholars out of nonacademic material. When all three elements are affecting the same unstable child at the same time, a delinquent is practically certain to be produced.

THE PREVENTION OF DELINQUENCY

Various investigations have shown how hard delinquency is to "cure." Thus, in one study of 905 juvenile offenders, 88 per cent were again arrested (from one to twelve times each) within five years of their first appearance in juvenile court—62 per cent of them on very serious charges.[13] Of the 628 delinquents who were old enough to be brought into the adult courts by the end of the five-year period after their first appearance as juvenile offenders, 94 per cent had already appeared there. This study is only one of many—and all of them tell the same story.

Delinquency is a type of social behavior. It is handed down from one generation of people to the next—and from an older group of boys or girls to a younger group.[27] In some environments children of average or dull mentality learn to play truant, to shoot craps, to resent authority, to swipe what they want, to swear expertly, to tell filthy stories—by exactly the same techniques that lead them to eat with their knives, blow their noses into their hands, or wear dirty clothes. Such behavior is their social heritage. Within any neighborhood there is a "society" made up of children who play together. This child society is often quite at variance with the adult society on all sides of it. In typically "bad" neighborhoods it becomes the ruling force in the lives of delinquent children until it has undermined the loyalty normally felt toward home and school.[27] It is chiefly through the efforts of teachers, mothers, and social workers that any children from undesirable neighborhoods escape the manners and morals of their social group. Delinquency is hard to cure because it is a mode of life—not a single bad habit. Efforts must therefore be centered upon prevention.

One cannot alter the physical and mental inheritance of those who may become delinquent. It would, of course, be entirely possible to prevent the birth of many potential criminals if the public would outgrow its sentimentalism about birth control and would help instead of hinder in the spread of such information. Schools and other social agencies are handicapped in their struggles by the sheer weight of numbers. Society must, however, deal with whatever potential delinquents it will allow to be born. From birth on, it is a matter of modifying environment.

Foretelling delinquent behavior.—In this connection, it is essential to consider the possibility of foretelling which children will become delinquents and which will not; otherwise there is no way of knowing for whom the environment should be modified. The next table is of interest. It shows, in the first column, the ages at which one thousand children were first brought into juvenile court and in the second the ages at which delinquent behavior was first noted.[13] The per cents given are cumulative. Thus, between ages seven and nine, 7.1 per cent of the entire group had been brought into court; between ten and twelve another 24.5 per cent was added, bringing the cumulative total up to 31.6. The other per cents are to be read in similar fashion.

TABLE XVI
HISTORY OF ONE THOUSAND JUVENILE OFFENDERS *

Age of First Appearance in Court			Age of First Observed Delinquent Behavior		
Ages	Number	Per Cent	Ages	Number	Per Cent
7–9	71	7.1	1–2	3	0.3
10–12	245	31.6	3–4	21	2.4
13–15	512	82.8	5–6	110	13.4
16–18	172	100.0	7–8	223	35.7
			9–10	266	62.3
			11–12	214	83.7
			13–14	125	96.2
			15–16	38	100.0

* This material is presented by permission of the Harvard University Press.

Although only 31.6 per cent of these children had been brought into court before their adolescent years, 83.7 per cent had showed symptoms of delinquency before that tme. By the end of the first two school grades, 35.7 per cent of these children could have been recognized. In fact a trained observer could doubtless have recognized more, since these figures are based on behavior observed by parents or classroom teachers. As investigators study delinquency more and more it becomes increasingly evident that this mode of behavior shows itself early.[10] Predelinquent children can be recognized while there is still time to make adjustments to their needs.

In recent years there have been many efforts to measure any tendency toward delinquency before actual misdemeanors have taken place. To some extent these efforts have been successful. A detailed description of the measuring instruments used will not be given here. In general, they are of two types: the rating scale made out by teachers or parents and the questionnaire made out by the pupils themselves. Rating scales contain such items as: *

* For a complete list and description of over two hundred tests of various sorts for the measurement of personality, the reader should consult P. M. Symonds, *Psychological Diagnosis in Social Adjustment,* American Book Company, 1934, 362 pp.

1. Often does little things to make others happy.
2. Often starts fights.
3. Often makes disturbing noises.
4. Often cheats.
5. Often asks teacher unnecessary questions about assignments.
6. Often starts a conversation with another pupil during free periods.
7. Often undertakes extra work voluntarily.
8. Often asks questions showing interest when the majority of the class is also asking questions.
9. Often sits in a slouched position during class.
10. Often reads good books in free time in school.
11. Daydreams in class.
12. Often destructive of school property.
13. Often deceitful.
14. Usually plays with younger children.
15. Acts tired most of the time.

The teacher using such a rating scale checks those items which describe a given child; in the scoring the number of items indicating undesirable traits is combined with those indicating desirable traits in such a way that the score gives a measure of the total social adjustment of the pupil rated. The particular items used in these scales have been selected on the basis of careful previous research as being those that differentiate between the behavior of pupils known to be delinquent and pupils of the same age and intelligence known to be normal in their social adjustment.

Until children are old enough to read easily and to see themselves with some degree of objectivity, the rating technique must be used. However, with adolescents, the ratings of others may be supplemented by questionnaires answered by the pupils themselves. The items for the questionnaires in use were selected in the same way as those appearing in the rating scales. A series of such items, taken from various questionnaires, appears below:

1. Would you rather be with those of your own age than with older people?
2. Do those who play with you say you quarrel or fight too much?
3. Have you often been punished unjustly?

4. Are you unhappy most of the time?
5. Do you like to go to parties?
6. Do you like to recite in class?
7. Do people say you are disobedient?
8. Do you ever stutter or stammer?
9. Do you frequently get your feelings hurt?
10. When you see a group of students whispering together do you usually think they are talking about you?
11. Do you often get excited over unimportant details?
12. Do you usually worry about unfinished work?
13. Do you often feel a buzzing inside your head?
14. Do you usually have difficulty in getting to sleep?
15. Do you think you are less popular than other pupils of your age?

It can be seen from the nature of the inquiries that the questionnaire adds something to the rating scale. The latter reports only on overt behavior; the former reports mainly on the pupil's thoughts and feelings. Used by itself, either type of test will give a one-sided picture, but used together—particularly if supplemented by individual interviews—a good picture of the degree of social adjustment may be obtained. Naturally, a positive score on a single item does not mean much, but when a pupil is consistently rated as indulging in antisocial behavior and when the same pupil reports himself as having consistently abnormal feelings and ideas, the total result is highly reliable. In fact, these measures of personality are sufficiently valid to enable an investigator to pick out of the school population a considerable proportion of problem children before they have become delinquents.[35] With such further developments as are almost certain to come in this field of personality measurement, it should soon be possible to locate predelinquents at an early age and consequently to start remedial work much earlier than is now possible, when the delinquent is usually not brought to the notice of experts until after he has committed some serious offense.

The work in measuring personality has already developed one concept that is proving of real usefulness in understanding delinquents—the concept of "emotional age."[23] As already discussed in an earlier chapter, emotional reactions change with increasing age and are made to different stimuli as an individual grows older. It is certainly true in some cases that the delinquent is a person who is reacting to social situations in a way that is quite normal for children much younger than himself but quite abnormal for an individual of his maturity. Thus, if a two-year-old child takes property that does not belong to him, he is acting normally; if the same individual when twenty years of age takes property not belonging to him, he is behaving as if he were only two. Everyone knows by now that the mental ages of a thousand ten-year-old school children, for instance, will vary all the way from about six to about sixteen; it is probable that their emotional ages will vary quite as much, if not more. And there is already some evidence to show that the delinquent child has either a very low or very high emotional age.[23] For years educators have insisted that the educational treatment to be given ten-year-old children must take into account the differences among them in mental development. Social treatment should vary to an equal extent, in terms of the differences in emotional maturity. Perhaps the relative success of the school in dealing with its intellectual deviates is due to its experience in modifying the training given pupils of varying degrees of ability, whereas its relative failure in dealing with delinquents is due to its lack of experience in modifying social stimuli.

Naturally, the use of tests for measuring personality will not locate every predelinquent child, but their use—together with measures of ability—will point out a large proportion of those who may be expected, under the stress of adolescent adjustments, to develop delinquent behavior.

Treatment of predelinquents.—With this point in mind the question naturally arises as to what adjustments should be made, once the children have been selected. These adjustments divide themselves rather naturally into the necessarily limited possibilities of the school and the almost unlimited possibilities of society. A school can, first, recognize its potential delinquents early. Then, it can abandon its traditional curriculum and build a new one on the nonacademic interests these children undoubtedly do have. The objectives of this new curriculum should be to train the children in acceptable behavior and for earning their living at the levels open to them. It should emphatically not try to "educate" them, in the ordinary sense of the word.

These children should be under supervision of the school from early morning until bedtime; they should be fed at least two meals at school; their play activities should be carried forward on the school playground, with excursions under school control. Their homes and neighborhoods usually offer nothing but deteriorating influences; the one chance of preventing delinquency lies in allowing the school to take the place of both home and neighborhood. Such a program is by no means as impossible as it may sound. And it would prevent a considerable amount of delinquency. Surely nothing the school could do along such lines is likely to be less effective than the usual concentration on mastery of subject matter.

Society could do much more, if it really wished to prevent delinquency. It could, for instance, simply abolish all dwellings now located in business or industrial districts. It could pass and enforce a law that people having children must live in residential areas, and it could, by zoning restrictions, keep these districts permanently residential. It could instruct its police to keep children away from business and industrial areas, returning them to their homes if they stray away. It could provide adequate recreation grounds, with some degree of supervision. There is no reason, except society's indifference to children, why any child should grow up in an unsupervised environment. For adults without children, life in the center of a big city is all right enough, in case one cares for it, but for children it is dangerous. Such legislation as that proposed could obviously be enforced if passed; there are, in every large city, whole blocks of apartment houses in which no child is allowed to live because the owners object. If private enterprise can keep children from living in certain districts of a city, a general law could do the same. Society could also—if it would—make it impossible for children to enter places of amusement unsuited to them, to obtain stimulants, or to undertake occupations that are harmful. Society brings about its own human deterioration because it is too indifferent to pass and enforce the measures necessary for the elimination of unsuitable districts and for the training and protection of children.

Recent research has shown the possibilities of training problem children, once they have been found. The first step was to locate parallel groups of problem and nonproblem children. The first group was then given analysis and treatment. Scores on a highly valid test of emotional and social adjustment are shown below:

TABLE XVII

SCORES OF PROBLEM AND NONPROBLEM CHILDREN * (Martens [22])

Score	Before Treatment Problem	Before Treatment Nonproblem	After Treatment Problem	After Treatment Nonproblem
550–99	1	..	..	..
500–49	1	..	..	..
450–99	3	..	..	..
400–49	2	..	3	..
350–99	4	..	2	..
300–49	6	..	8	..
250–99	12	..	6	2
200–49	16	3	5	5
150–99	10	6	12	11
100–49	9	12	19	15
50–99	3	25	12	19
00–49	1	22	1	16
Total	68	68	68	68
Median	247	81	185	107
Difference	..	..	−52	+26

* This material is used by permission of the U. S. Bureau of Education.

Among the nonproblem children, the degree of maladjustment increased, but the decrease among the problem children is marked. Presumably appropriate education could help materially in eliminating maladjustments.

THE HIGH SCHOOL AND THE PROBLEM OF DELINQUENCY

Delinquency is not primarily a problem of the high school. However, there is gradually coming into existence a group of delinquents whose ability is fundamentally good, whose educational record is at least average, and whose misconduct does not manifest itself until the years of adolescence. Thus, in one recent study,[4] 68 per cent of the delinquents had progressed to the seventh grade or beyond, 85 per cent of them had no previous record of maladjustment before this period, and practically none of them came from "poor" homes. With this group, as well as with the small number of chronic delinquents who continue in school, the schools above the elementary level have to deal.

The main adjustments consist merely of an adaptation, at a higher level of intelligence, of the same principles already set forth. (a) These pupils should study themselves and society—not algebra, Latin, English literature, or chemistry. (b) They should receive direct vocational training and subsequent placement. (c) They should be under constant supervision of the school. These are the essentials. True, such a procedure would not prevent all possible delinquencies, but it gives a promise of relative effectiveness. These intelligent predelinquents should emerge from their last years of schooling with some understanding of their own problems, adequate training for earning their living, and prolonged experience in supervised social and recreational activities. Even though the number of juvenile offenders in high school is never large, it is sufficient to demand careful consideration.

ILLUSTRATIVE CASE STUDIES

In reading these accounts, the following questions should be kept in mind: What were the symptoms shown? How far back in the pupil's history were the first symptoms observable? What did the school do to help these delinquents? What else could have been done? What factors outside the school helped either to produce the delinquency or to control it?

Arthur was a delinquent boy thirteen years old. He had been a truant on and off for the last four years. He was reported to be surly, aggressive, dishonest, and distrustful. Recently he had been arrested by a policeman who saw him knock down a middle-aged woman. When brought into juvenile court Arthur would not speak. Everyone connected with the court tried to get from him some account of his behavior but all questions met with a sullen and defiant silence. The court decided it must have an investigation before any judgment could be passed. Arthur was therefore sent to a detention home for examination. When examined by the doctor, Arthur refused to open his mouth. The doctor disliked using force, so he let the matter rest until the social worker should have collected some information about the boy. The boy's parents reported he had been staying out nights and absenting himself from school on and off for several years. When he was at home he was usually well behaved. There was no evident maladjustment in the home to account for Arthur's absences from it. The parents vouchsafed no reason for his surly attitude, but just as the social worker was leaving the home, the mother said she thought perhaps the other children picked on Arthur because he had no palate!

The social worker next visited the school. Every teacher from kindergarten on had commented on Arthur's chronic "grouch"; he had been seclusive, unco-operative, and surly. Other boys in the class teased him, mimicking the sounds of a person with no palate. Arthur never tried to answer, but his fists flew on the slightest provocation. Arthur was enrolled in the fourth grade; he had been in this room with the same teacher for three years. The teacher reported that Arthur could not read and that she had kept him in the fourth grade until he could read well enough to pass the work of the upper grades. An examination of Arthur's permanent record card showed he had made a score on a silent reading test at the average for the sixth grade children. When confronted with this evidence, the teacher said she meant oral reading, not silent. It then developed that she made every pupil stand up in front of the room and read out loud. With twenty-five pupils in the room she got around to each one about once every three weeks. Arthur, of course, could not enunciate a single word clearly. When he saw his turn approaching, he stayed away from school until he thought the danger was passed. His teacher had apparently no idea that Arthur's customary silences and odd noises, when he was bullied into speaking, were due to anything but sheer obstinacy.

With this information at hand the social worker talked to Arthur, persuaded him to let her look at his palate, and succeeded in getting his friendship. When asked why he had run into the woman and knocked her down, he said she looked like the teacher he had had for the last three years. Arthur eventually let the doctor finish his examination. It appeared that the boy had a rudimentary palate to which an artificial palate could be attached, by means of which his speech became practically normal. He was at once promoted to the sixth grade where he continued his school career without further delinquencies.

Edward,[18] aged 15, had repeatedly stolen small sums of money. Once he had run away. He had recently stolen a large amount and had been referred by the court for investigation.

Edward came from a home in which the father was an irregular worker of moderately alcoholic habits. His mother had been dishonest as a girl and still had a reputation of possessing only indifferent morals. The parents had been divorced for years. Edward's mother was indifferent toward him and had left him with his grandfather and uncle. This home was definitely good, but it had not been able to compensate for the indifference of Edward's mother. She made no effort whatever to care for him.

When he was first sent to his grandmother, he had been content to have his mother visit, write, or give him presents, but for two years his attitude had changed to irritability and indifference. He had continued to steal indiscriminately from relatives, neighbors, or anyone who had left money visible to him. He spent it on pleasure and shows. His school record had been good until recently, when he failed consistently; he was a leader among the boys. All the adults with whom he came in contact, except one teacher, believed his tendencies to criminality thoroughly established and recommended that he should be sent to reform school.

His unhappy, sensitive expression seemed significant to the Judge Baker Foundation. In his own story it came out by chance that he had a "sore spot," the knowledge of his mother's delinquencies in stealing. He had never done any stealing until he heard his mother twice accused. In spite of the continual admonitions of principal and relatives, he never tried to get over his dishonesty, evidently having no intention of so doing. What he spends the money for does not seem significant. He does not know certainly that his mother is stealing now, but he thinks about what she did before, and when he has opportunity to steal he thinks of her and he feels reckless, as if it did not matter if he stole.

As a first step in treatment he was placed on a farm twenty miles from town, where he worked for board and small pay. He would not go with fellows from the farm to the movies, but he did his work very well and was much interested. The mother was asked to talk the situation out with her son, promised, but never did. The first foster home was the well-kept farm of two young men; the mother of one of them kept house. Edward was treated pleasantly, but no one succeeded in winning his confidence.

The second temporary home was in town, where he neither went to school nor worked steadily. He stole several times. The visitor brought mother and son together, since the mother did not do anything about him herself, and it was the visitor who had to tell the boy his mother was sorry for the past; she merely acquiesced.

In spite of more opposition to putting Edward anywhere but

in the reform school, he was placed in another foster home with the B's, a couple without children and anxious for help and a companion. Here he did well and was well liked, although he was hard for Mrs. B to approach. This time there were no complaints; Edward had been growing very fast, had gained in weight and strength. Mrs. B was very happy because one day he had asked to talk with her and had told her a great deal about himself and his problems. Not a single serious complaint had been received about him; not once had he stolen; his sulky spells have practically disappeared. His mother evidently is jealous and demands money from him, which he does not send, since she did not help him when he needed it and he is planning for his future needs.

The change in the boy through the influence of Mrs. B is very remarkable, not so much because his delinquency has ceased as that there has been such a change in personality trends. It is clear it was not merely a good home and the ordinary pleasures of boyhood, or even family affection other than parental, that the boy needed. Nor was the companionship of wholesome men, such as he found in his first foster home, sufficient. What he had needed all along was a mother substitute. The relatives did not succeed in this. There is no reason to believe that if a satisfying family relationship could have been built up earlier, either in the boy's own home or through earlier placing, Edward long before would have ceased his delinquent trends.*

Abigail [18] was an energetic girl of good ability and generally attractive personality. Abigail had been well known for over four years to the staff of "The Boston Young People's Institute," an educational and recreational institution for young people. She had been a great favorite and was entrusted with the handling of considerable money. She was suspected of stealing a large sum of money from there, and of stealing a piece of jewelry and other articles from a store where she had worked the previous summer. Moreover, she had recently been fabricating and exaggerating her own importance. Other girls in school did not like her because of her airs and her lying.

The family life of this girl was far from happy. Her father was a habitual drinker, deteriorated in character, bad-tempered, and indifferent to his family. The mother is reported as fanatically religious, believing all pleasure a sin. She is very difficult to live with, being a great nagger and scold. She has a furious temper

* This case study is used by permission of the Judge Baker Foundation, Boston.

and has been seen even beating her grown-up girls with a broom handle. She is saving to the point of parsimoniousness and she demands all of her children's earnings. She talks of money continually and displays a hard attitude toward her children, looking upon them as economic assets. At home there was much unhappiness and dissension. The girl's disagreeable characteristics of bossiness, etc., probably arose from her feeling of authority in the Institute and the absence of any expression at home.

In the girl's own story, she said she never stole before that summer when she took the jewelry and clothes; she worked with a girl who talked about the unfairness of rich people's being able to buy all the things they were selling. When she later had a chance to take the money from the Institute, it flashed into her head that she wanted the money, and she took it.

She was put into a foster home where she became almost one of the family. After a while she got over her antagonisms to girls at school but, in letters to friends, she continued to lie about the clothes she had and the money and good times.

Abigail continued to go to high school, until in the third year she went home to help out in some serious trouble; later she went to work steadily and to school part time; finally she succeeded in entering kindergarten-training where she did well.

Interesting to a student of the psychology of conduct is the gradual evolution of this girl's character tendencies from attempted ego satisfactions, through fantasy and dishonest acquirement of possessions, through outside help and through her own efforts, to obtain a place for herself in the world.*

Theo was a fifteen-year-old girl of good ability who had been involved in repeated sex immorality from early childhood. Subsequently she had run away from her foster home and had again been immoral. When sent to a reform school she had been disobedient, willful, and impertinent.

Theo's mother was insane and immoral. During her pregnancy with Theo she had repeatedly attempted abortions. Theo's father was unknown. The home was dirty and the girl quite uncared for. Neighbors had complained about the mother when the girl was only six years old. At the time Theo had seen sexual intercourse and had had men play with her.

Placement in a foster home was not very successful. Theo was unruly and was often caught writing obscenities to boys. From

* This case study is used by permission of the Judge Baker Foundation, Boston.

time to time she ran away and returned to her mother. But she rarely remained for long because her mother was so slatternly and nagged her so badly.

At junior high school—which was held in a centralized building—Theo became acquainted with a gang of young hoodlums who ran wild all over the business part of town, stayed out nights, were chased by policemen, were immoral, and often stole small amounts of money.

After a time Theo was arrested and sent to reform school. Here she was disobedient and frequently tried to send out filthy letters to her former friends. She is still in the school, but no obvious reform has yet taken place.

Jim was the "bad" boy of the seventh grade. He fought continually, picked on smaller boys, tortured animals, swaggered about unbearably, was insolent, and did failing schoolwork. Several teachers had tried to help him, but he apparently wanted no assistance from anyone. Indeed he assured everyone he could look out for himself. One of Jim's favorite boasts was that he would take any "dare" any boy could think of. One day someone dared him to intercept the boy who was carrying money to the office on bank day, knock him down, and steal the money. From later accounts it was clear that Jim had no stomach for this job, but he felt his prestige as the "worst guy in the room" was challenged. As a finishing touch Jim got an old revolver from a junkman. With it he staged a convincing and hair-raising holdup. But once he had the money he did not know what to do with it or where to go. While he was still wandering about the streets trying to decide, the police arrested him.

Jim was shaking with fright when he came to the psychologist for examination. At first he could only stammer incoherently. To put him more at his ease the topic of the holdup was abandoned and some general questions asked about Jim's childhood and how he had come to fight so much. Then the boy's fundamental trouble came out. He was terrified all the time that certain older boys that dominated the neighborhood between Jim's home and the school would "gang" up on him and kill him! He had once seen a boy beaten by this gang and had lived in an agony of fear ever since. He did not consciously plan to become "bad"; this reaction was due partly to his frantic response if another boy so much as pushed him and partly to a hazy desire to have such a bad reputation other boys would be afraid of him. Descriptions of Jim's fights strongly suggested that he simply went into a panic of fear so intense as to give him unusual strength and complete indifference to his own injuries. Jim's bluff had certainly worked; he was thought to be afraid of nothing—hence, the dare.

Jim did not want the money he had taken, he was scared of the gun, and he had no desire to have more prestige. All he wanted was to be left alone. Since his reputation was so secure in his school and neighborhood, it seemed unwise to keep him there and "show him up" as only a harmless boy, since other children had rather admired his apparent recklessness. His parents were therefore encouraged to move across the city where Jim could make a fresh start in a new school. They were also instructed in the real nature of their boy's difficulty and asked to bring him back to the court the moment any unfavorable symptoms reappeared. Jim promised to make a new start. At first he reported to the psychologist once a week, then once a month; there were no more fights or delinquencies. Jim is now a normal young man of twenty-five whose height of six feet three inches—backed up by over two hundred pounds of bone and muscle—has furnished the confidence and courage that the undernourished, undersized Jim of fourteen so badly lacked.

BIBLIOGRAPHY *

1. Atwood, B. S., "Social Participation and Juvenile Delinquency," *Indiana Bulletin of Character and Correction,* 1933, No. 210, pp. 208-211.
2. Berk, A., Lane, L., and Tandy, M. C., "Follow-Up Study of Thirty Habit Clinic Children Who Manifested Delinquency Problems before the Age of Ten Years," *Bulletin of Massachusetts Department of Mental Diseases,* 1933, 17: 61-81.
3. Butcher, W. M., Hoey, J. M., and McGinnies, J. A., *A Study of Problem Boys and Their Brothers by the Sub-Commission on Causes and Effects of Crime,* Crime Commission of New York State, 1929, 409 pp.
4. Caldwell, M. G., "Recent Trends in Juvenile Delinquency," *Journal of Juvenile Research,* 1933, 17: 179-190.
5. Christie, A., "Physical Defects in Adolescent Boys," *Journal of Juvenile Research,* 1934, 18: 13-22.
6. Cochrane, H. G., and Steinbach, A. A., "Fifty Recidivists in the Norfolk Juvenile Court," *Mental Hygiene,* 1934, 18: 576-591.
7. Courthial, A., "Emotional Differences between Delinquent and Non-Delinquent Girls of Normal Intelligence," *Archives of Psychology,* 1931, No. 133, 100 pp.

* See also the references in the Appendix.

8. Crook, E. B., "Cultural Marginality in Sexual Delinquency," *American Journal of Sociology*, 1934, 39: 493-500.
9. Elkind, H. B., and Taylor, M., "One Thousand Delinquents," *Mental Hygiene*, 1934, 18: 531-552.
10. Fisher, M. L., "Measured Differences between Problem and Non-Problem Children in a Public School System," *Journal of Educational Sociology*, 1934, 7: 353-364.
11. Ford, C. A., and Balen, H., "The Effect of Stopping Supervision of Certain Department of Recreation Play Areas upon the Delinquency Rates of Older Boys," *Psychological Bulletin*, 1934, 31: 639-640.
12. Furfey, P. H., *The Gang Age*, The Macmillan Company, 1926, 189 pp.
13. Glueck, S., and Glueck, E. T., *One Thousand Juvenile Delinquents*, Harvard University Press, 1934, 341 pp.
14. Haase, E., "Zur Kenntniss der Schulschwänzer," *Zeitschrift für pädagogische Psychologie*, 1932, 33: 15-18.
15. Hayner, N. S., "Delinquency Areas in the Puget Sound Region," *American Journal of Sociology*, 1933, 39: 314-328.
16. Healy, W., Bronner, A., Braylor, E., and Murphy, J. P., *Reconstructing Behavior in Youth*, Alfred A. Knopf, Inc., 1929, 325 pp.
17. Healy, W., "Practical Value of Scientific Studies of Juvenile Delinquents," *Children's Bureau of Publications*, Washington, D. C., 1921, 31 pp.
18. Judge Baker Foundation, "Case-Studies," Series 1, 1-20, 1922-1923.
19. Laslett, H. R., and Manning, J., "A Delinquency Survey of a Medium-Sized High School," *Journal of Juvenile Research*, 1934, 18: 71-78.
20. Loofbourow, G. C., and Keys, N., "A Group Test of Problem Behavior Tendencies in Junior High School Boys," *Journal of Educational Psychology*, 1933, 24: 641-653.
21. Maller, J. B., "Delinquency Areas in New York City," *Psychological Bulletin*, 1934, 31: 640-641.
22. Martens, E. H., "Adjustment of Behavior Problems of School Children," *Bulletin of the United States Department of Education*, 1932, No. 18, 77 pp.
23. Pressey, S. L., and Pressey, L. C., "The Development of the Interest-Attitude Tests," *Journal of Applied Psychology*, 1933, 17: 1-16.
24. Rogers, C. R., "Measuring Personality Adjustment in Children Nine to Thirteen Years of Age," *Teachers College Contri-*

butions to Education, No. 458, Bureau of Publications, Teachers College, Columbia University, 1931, 107 pp.
25. Rogers, K. H., and Austin, O. L., "Intelligence Quotients of Juvenile Delinquents," *Journal of Juvenile Research,* 1934, 18: 103-106.
26. Selling, L. S., "Psychopathology without Functional Change as Shown in a Delinquent Group," *Journal of Juvenile Research,* 1933, 17: 153-162.
27. Shaw, C. R., "Juvenile Delinquency—A Group Tradition," *Bulletin of the State University of Iowa,* New Series, 1933, No. 700, 14 pp.
28. ———, "Juvenile Delinquency—A Case History," *Bulletin of the State University of Iowa,* New Series, 1933, No. 701, 11 pp.
29. ———, and McKay, H. D., "Social Factors in Juvenile Delinquency," *Report on the Causes of Crime,* Vol. II, Government Printing Office, 1931, 401 pp.
30. Sullenger, T. E., "Juvenile Delinquency, a Product of the Home," *Journal of Criminal Law and Criminology,* 1934, 24: 1088-1092.
31. Symonds, P. M., *Psychological Diagnosis in Social Adjustment,* American Book Company, 1934, 362 pp.
32. Terman, L. M., *Measurement of Intelligence,* Houghton Mifflin Company, 1916, 362 pp.
33. Thomas, C., "Results of the Sims Socio-Economic Rating Scale, when Given to Delinquent and Non-Delinquent Juveniles," *American Journal of Orthopsychiatry,* 1931, 1: 527-539.
34. Tramer, M., "Lebensschicksal eines jugendlichen Rechtsbrechers," *Zeitschrift für Kinderpsychiatrie,* 1934, 1: 66-68.
35. Williams, H. D., "Survey of Pre-Delinquent School Children in Ten Midwestern Cities," *Journal of Educational Sociology,* 1934, 7: 365-370.
36. Wilson, R. T., "Delinquency Areas in San Jose," *Psychological Bulletin,* 1934, 31: 588-589.

CHAPTER IX

THE EMOTIONAL DEVIATE

VARIOUS investigators have estimated the number of neurotics, or emotional deviates, in the adolescent population as anywhere from 15 to 3 per cent. The exact figure depends upon where one draws the line between what is normal and what is abnormal and upon how complete a survey of the population was made before the investigator made his estimate. Obviously, no one knows exactly what proportion of people at any age are neurotic. However, any teacher knows that the group of emotionally abnormal adolescents provides most of the problem cases which come to her attention. Neurotics have fundamental difficulties in "getting along" with others and are therefore liable to be in constant trouble with school routine.

In this single chapter it is obviously impossible to present a large accumulation of facts about abnormal types of individual. However, the teacher should have some idea of the behavior shown by emotionally unstable pupils. The writer has therefore attempted some thumbnail sketches of various types of emotional deviate. These descriptions are necessarily somewhat dogmatic and oversimplified. The effort has been to stress chiefly the conduct characteristic of instability, so that the teacher may gain a clearer idea of what behavior is "peculiar." No teacher, unless she has had special training, should attempt the treatment of emotional abnormality, any more than she should attempt to cure physical disease. The present discussion is therefore strictly limited to descriptions of behavior. When a teacher recognizes reactions as peculiar she should send pupils showing them to an expert for diagnosis and treatment. The teacher is, however, the only person so situated as to make early recognition of mental and emotional peculiarity possible. If teachers do not notice abnormalities no one else is likely to do so until the condition has become highly acute—and probably incurable. Some comprehension of abnormal types is, therefore, desirable.

A neurotic person is essentially an overemotional person. Neuroses, although usually accompanied by both physical and intellectual symptoms, are emotional in origin. They appear when someone of emotional instability is confronted by a problem to which he cannot find any normal mode of adjustment. It is not necessary here to consider whether the emotional instability is native or acquired. One does not need to be a firm believer in heredity, however, to see that within the neurotic individual himself there are certain characteristics which prevent him from normal adjustment. All people are faced with problems of high emotional intensity, and most people find acceptable solutions. The problems facing the neurotic are often no more severe than other people's problems, but the adjustment made is unsatisfactory. It therefore appears that the neurotic's own temperament must furnish one of the contributing elements to the development of a neurosis.

The other element in the situation is the existence of a chronic and severe emotional strain. In all probability the duration of the strain is more important than its intensity. Thus, the child who has grown up in a home in which there was constant, but never extreme, antagonism between the parents is more likely to develop a neurosis than the child whose parents have quarreled and completely separated. The situations which confront neurotics are such that the particular individual involved cannot solve them. Either they are matters over which he actually has no control or else they are situations about which he thinks he can do nothing. In either case, he seems to be up against a stone wall.

When people find themselves confronted by an emotional situation to which there seems to be no solution, the reactions they may make are varied. There are, however, five types of behavior and attitude that are commoner than any others. They appear so often that the teacher should be able to recognize them. These five types will be presented shortly. It should first be understood that any type of response may be associated with any sort of situation. The identical situation which produces in one person one type of behavior may produce in another a totally different type. These five types described below differ from each other then in the behavior shown, but not in the situations to which the responses are being made.

NEURASTHENIA

The first emotional deviates to be considered are the neurasthenics. The behavior of neurasthenic adolescents is mainly of the withdrawal type. The most pronounced impression they make upon the observer is that they are already defeated by their environment and have stopped struggling against it. They are negative, quiet, repressed individuals. In general, three definite characteristics are outstanding.

Neurasthenics are always in a somewhat exhausted physical condition because of the prolonged emotional strain to which they have been subjected. Extreme neurasthenics do not appear in the school population for the very good reason that they are home in bed. Their vitality is too low for any exertion. Their friends and family may regard their exhausted condition as mere imagination, but this attitude is quite wrong. The exhaustion is real; however, the causes of exhaustion are emotional, not physical. Because a person lies or sits still and does nothing but worry over some insoluble difficulty, the casual onlooker often supposes the accompanying fatigue to be imagined. He argues that since the individual has done nothing, he cannot be tried. Actually, an inactive day spent in worrying is far more fatiguing than a day spent in physical exercise without worry. The first characteristic, then, of neurasthenics is that they are tired, usually without any obvious reason for being so.

Many neurasthenics do not run away either actually or emotionally from whatever situation confronts them. They simply stay facing the situation and doing nothing whatever about it. Sometimes a neurasthenic adolescent substitutes daydreams of escape from the emotional problem in the place of actual escape or adjustment, but in other cases the daydreaming is a relatively unimportant characteristic. The neurasthenic has, however, a preoccupation with his emotional problems and therefore may give an impression of daydreaming when he is really thinking around and around his difficulties and not escaping from them by the use of fantasy. On the intellectual side neurasthenics show a frequent failure to attend to objective stimuli—such as the directions given by the teacher in class. The second outstanding characteristic is, then, a mental preoccupation, which may or may not result in daydreaming but which certainly does make the pupil oblivious to what is going on about him.

The neurasthenic is usually a person of social isolation. If he were not, he would be more likely to find a solution to his emotional difficulties by talking them over with friends. Thus, a girl with a domineering mother who never allows the girl to do anything she wants to do, may develop into a neurasthenic because she has stopped making any effort to be herself. She still wants the same things she has always desired, but she has worn herself out trying to get them and has finally stopped asserting herself against her mother's domination. If, however, such a girl had had a number of intimate friends she might have escaped such a development, because her friends would have helped her in her efforts at self-assertion. Part of her collapse is doubtless due to social isolation and the failure of her social contacts to support her in moments of acute distress. A third symptom shown by the neurasthenic adolescent is a failure to make friends and a preference for staying alone.

The neurasthenic is then a person who is tired, preoccupied, and isolated. Obviously, such a condition soon gives rise to new problems, to which the same type of response is made, and the vicious circle continues until the individual is completely exhausted. In the early stages an outsider may be able to arrest further unfortunate developments. At all events, the teacher can be trained to recognize, first, those individuals who are socially isolated and of negative personality. These are the pupils who will, under strain, develop into neurasthenics. The teacher can learn also to recognize emotional preoccupation when she sees it and to observe a discrepancy between work done and fatigue shown. Those pupils who are developing a neurasthenic condition rarely make any trouble in the classroom; in fact they are in the process of losing their own personalities to such an extent that the teacher hardly notices their existence. A really neurasthenic adolescent can sit in almost any classroom in the country and worry himself into a state of exhaustion without anyone more than barely noticing his condition, because he never becomes a disciplinary problem. His trouble is that he has too little overt behavior rather than too much.

Illustrative case studies.—The case studies shown below should be read with an eye to noticing the following points: What was the central situation to which adjustment could not be made? What were the early symptoms of maladjustment? What were the final symptoms of neurasthenia? How were the reactions supported by environmental influences? What behavior was clearly outside the range of normal responses and should have been recognized by the individual's teacher?

Mary S was a girl of nineteen.[10] She lived with her father and stepmother. Following her own mother's death, she had lived with grandparents, since her father drank and gambled and his home was not regarded as a suitable place for a child. After ten years he married again and has apparently reformed. The family is, however, practically an armed camp in which the father and daughter are constantly opposing the stepmother and her daughter by a former marriage.

Mary finished the second year in high school, took a short term in a normal school, and then taught in the country school for a year. She resigned from this position because of ill-health, although she seems to have had no definite illness or disease. Since then she has intermittently helped her father as an extra clerk in his store.

After her father's remarriage she began to complain of backaches and stomach trouble. These difficulties have steadily increased until now she is unable to do any work and has become confined to her room. She receives, however, scant attention from her stepmother, and it is sometimes necessary for her to go down to the kitchen to get food. She is, however, able to make any exertion she really wants to make, so to some extent the stepmother's attitude is probably justified. Mary has practically no friends. She never had very many and during the last few months that she has remained in her room, none of them have been to see her. While she was teaching she became acquainted with a young man in the country who sometimes came to see her on week ends; but she was always so tired she did not want to go out anywhere, and her stepmother made it impossible for them to have any privacy in the house. As a result of this situation, he soon ceased coming. At present, Mary does nothing except read a few magazine stories, manicure her nails, occasionally do a little embroidering, and write voluminously in her diary. This she keeps locked in her desk and allows no one to read.

Toward her stepsister she shows a deep and bitter hatred. She will not even allow the girl in her room. The stepsister is an alert and capable senior in high school who has no particular objections to Mary but regards her with considerable scorn as a weak and inefficient person. The stepsister is not particularly brilliant, but she has a somewhat dominating personality which draws the average person's attention to her.

Mary is evidently in a state of exhaustion. She has chronic indigestion, constipation, and absence of appetite. Some days she is too weak to get out of bed at all. She is evidently much preoccupied with her own emotional life and physical symptoms. The only time she shows any real pleasure is on Sundays when she usually lies in bed, dressed in expensive robes her father has bought for her, and allows her father to wait on her. At other times she is childish, fretful, unstable, and irritable.

There is every evidence of conflict in this home situation. Mary is evidently unable to compete with her stepsister who is more capable than herself. Mary seems, therefore, to have resolved the conflict by competing for attention along an entirely different line, mainly by appeal to sympathy through illness. She has withdrawn almost completely from reality, after finding herself incapable of adaptation.

It has been recommended that Mary be sent away for a month into the country, where effort should be made to rehabilitate her health, and should then attend some private school away from home. In her present condition she is totally unable to face her home situation. She must, therefore, be removed from competition with her stepsister until she has built up some other interest than herself and has been successful in some other environment. In the meantime, she should receive help in understanding her own condition. Mary is by no means stupid, so there is hope of a final adjustment, although it is improbable she will ever be able to live at home for any length of time without relapsing into her present neurasthenic state.*

Paul was a foreign boy of seventeen who had been in this country two years. At home his people talked Czech exclusively. His own English was hesitant and broken. Because of this handicap he was only a freshman in high school. He was referred for study because he seemed to be deaf. His ears tested normal, however; but his diffident and harassed manner suggested some other type of difficulty.

Paul had always been studious. He was the oldest boy in the family and had been destined from infancy to become a priest. As he grew older he had developed severe religious doubts, which he kept to himself. His sexual desires had become strong, and he had formed the habit of daily masturbation. What with his difficulties of adjustment to a new country, his language handicap, and his personal problems, he had been doing barely passing work in school. His family still wanted him to be a priest and were making real sacrifices to keep him in school. But he knew he would never succeed in being "good enough." Once when he had tried to intimate his lack of interest his father had simply beaten him—and considered the matter settled.

Even in his own country Paul had been allowed few friends because of his need to study. In America he had none. It happened that the family lived in a neighborhood populated by Hungarians. Paul was repeatedly warned by his parents to keep away from these "foreign" boys who might contaminate him. He met no Czech friends, and he was too shy to talk with Americans.

Day by day Paul became increasingly aware of his family's sacrifices and of his own unfitness. He dared not tell anyone of his situation, yet he could not conquer his doubts. Slowly the day of reckoning was creeping upon him—for his schoolwork became steadily worse. In an agony of fear he sat and awaited the storm.

In the meantime his active mind furnished him with daydreams. He could escape from his dilemma if he thought about his boyhood days or made fanciful plans for a future in which family pressure had no part. Sometimes he spent hours puzzling about the Virgin Birth, the Trinity, or the miracle of the Sacrament.

* This material is used by permission of The Macmillan Company.

He often became so lost in such thoughts that he failed to hear what the teacher said.

Paul's condition was serious. He was underweight, exhausted, fearful, completely without friends, torn by inner conflicts. One can understand his absorption in pleasant fantasies when reality was so cruel.

Mary Louise, a freshman in a city high school, was recommended for examination by the school psychologist. This recommendation was interesting because it was made by a student, not a teacher. One of the senior girls had noticed Mary Louise sitting, day after day, in the corner of the girls' rest room, looking tired and woebegone. This senior had tried to make friends but without success, so she asked the school psychologist to talk with the girl.

Mary Louise had just come to the city from a small town where her mother had recently died. She was, at the time of the investigation, living in the home of relatives where her father paid for her room and board; she had no brothers or sisters. The people with whom she lived were elderly and were definitely pleased that Mary Louise was so quiet and well behaved.

The girl's earlier childhood presented an interesting history. In the first grade she had formed an intense emotional attachment to another girl of her own age. The two became practically inseparable chums for several years. The other girl was considerably more capable than Mary Louise but was quite devoted to her. The relationship between the two was more that of a messiah and a disciple than that of equals. The mother apparently had been more than willing for Mary Louise to be continually with this friend because the other girl came from a family whose social standing and economic level were conspicuously high. This friendship had continued until Mary Louise was twelve when her friend's family moved to another state. This event was apparently a real crisis. From the first grade on, Mary Louise had developed no other friendships, and after her chum departed she made no effort to replace her. Soon Mary Louise began to daydream, inventing scenes in which she and her chum participated. She continued to do reasonably good work in school. While other children had no objection to her, they never made friends with her.

When Mary Louise was ready for high school her father thought she should receive a better education than she could get in her small home town, so he sent her to the city and enrolled her in the Central High School. Here she became completely lost. She knew no one and she had never learned how to strike up an acquaintance with strangers. The elderly people with whom she lived were too old to furnish much companionship or to have friends who were Mary Louise's age. From being lonely and moody, Mary Louise became completely isolated and profoundly depressed.

At the time of investigation, Mary Louise made no real complaints in regard to her life, except that she was always tired. She had given up trying to understand people or to get along with them. She was resigned to being an unobtrusive shadow in the schoolroom and she definitely did not want to take part in any extracurricular activities. She was utterly out of touch with human relationships. She admitted constant daydreaming, mostly of a harmless character. She showed a consistent mood of depression and a fatigue to which she could assign no cause. The most serious item in this girl's condition was her resignation to things as they were and her total lack of ambition. The readjustment of such a completely isolated and shut-in personality is extremely difficult.

HYSTERIA

The second type of abnormal adolescent is the hysteric. Hysteria is another kind of response made to an insoluble emotional difficulty. The difference between the neurasthenic and the hysteric lies in the individual, not in the external conditions. The neurasthenic is a person of relatively low vitality and negative personality who will sacrifice himself rather than get into a fight. The hysteric is a person of high vitality and extroverted personality who will not sacrifice himself no matter what happens.

When such an individual gets into an emotional crisis, there are fireworks. There is shouting, screaming, crying, swearing, and general excitement. Since there is no obvious escape from the situation causing the difficulty, the hysterical attacks come on whenever the fundamental problem arises. Thus, as in the example given above, the domineering mother's attempts at controlling her daughter are met, not with hopeless acquiescence on the part of the daughter, but by violent emotional scenes. The domination may, of course, be equally successful in any particular instance; that is, the mother succeeds in controlling her daughter, but the spirit of resignation is never present. The hysteric may acquiesce, but she puts up a fight first.

It may be that the fundamental difference between a potential neurasthenic and a potential hysteric is merely one of vitality. However, certain outside influences doubtless enter into the production of one type of person rather than another. The potential neurasthenic is socially isolated, while the potential hysteric usually has both many enemies and many friends. Some of the behavior may then be due to the absence or presence at critical times of the moral support furnished by one's own group. Another evidence of environmental influence is to be found in the relative frequency of these two types of behavior in the sexes. There are few adolescent or adult male hysterics. Masculine tradition is emphatically opposed to such emotional outbursts, but feminine tradition permits them. In a nursery school one finds plenty of little boys with a temperament inclined to hysteria, but such behavior is totally inexcusable to other boys and by the years of adolescence the hysteric male has very nearly disappeared. There is, then, some evidence that hysteria can be both produced and controlled by circumstances.

The hysteric adolescent simply cannot be overlooked by any teacher; the emotional outbursts are all too obvious. What is not so obvious is the discrepancy between the apparent stimulus that causes an outburst and the intensity of the emotional fireworks. For example, a teacher gives an hysterical girl a slight reprimand and the girl responds with an outburst of violent weeping. The uninitiated observer naturally supposes the scene to be a response to the reprimand. It usually is not. The reactions are violent, but they are being made to the pupil's central, unsolved emotional problem; they have merely been kept in check for a little while and are released by the teacher's remarks. Hysterical behavior always lies in wait just below the surface, ready to be unleashed by any accidental stimulus. Whenever incidental comments bring about totally unwarranted emotional reactions, the teacher should suspect the existence of hysteria. In the early stages the reactions consist chiefly in crying or screaming. If the fundamental problem remains unsolved, the attacks increase in severity. The girl may throw herself upon the floor and become perfectly rigid; she may act as if she were choking to death; her attacks may assume the symptoms of almost any physical disease. The two chief clues to the hysterical nature of such attacks are, first, the discrepancy between the apparent stimulus and the response, and, second, the relative lack of consistency. When a girl has an apparent epileptic seizure one week and the next week seems ill with a sudden infectious delirium, one can make a fair guess that she is neither epileptic nor delirious. A teacher or anybody else can easily be fooled once by such violent seizures as sometimes appear, but one ought not to be fooled twice, especially since the hysteric usually recovers from her attack in record time and, while tired, is by no means exhausted.

In between attacks, the hysteric is an excitable person. She is voluble, irritable, overactive, interested in almost everything and everyone. More often than not, she is lavish in her demonstrations of affection, but at the same time she is fundamentally selfish and egotistical. She is moody—laughing happily one moment and overcome by despair the next. She is an emotional chameleon. No one—not even the hysteric herself—knows what she will do or say next or how she will react to any given stimulus. She can, however, be trusted to take everything personally. The atmosphere around a hysteric is always crackling from its charge of emotional intensity. A teacher who has one really hysterical adolescent girl in her room will find herself in a continual state of exasperation—but life will never become dull. The hysteric is quite as recognizable between outbursts as during them.

If the hysteric personality is allowed to continue unchecked, a number of phobias and obsessions are likely to develop. The relationship between any given fear or compulsion and the central, unsolved problem is sometimes logical and sometimes purely fortuitous. The mental mechanisms by means of which such emotional attitudes are developed need not be understood by a teacher, but she should realize the hysteric nature of obsessions and phobias of all types. These manifestations are among the commonest symptoms of hysteria.

EMOTIONAL DEVIATE

As in the case of the neurasthenic the only cure consists in a careful analysis of each individual case and a determination of what emotional problem is unsolved. This work, however, is not the teacher's business. Her task is to recognize the behavior as abnormal and send the pupil to someone else for expert diagnosis and remedial treatment.

Illustrative case studies.—In reading over the case studies below the following points should be observed: What was the central emotional problem? What were the early reactions to the difficulty? How were these reactions supported by environmental influence? What were the most obvious symptoms? What symptoms should a teacher be able to recognize?

Dorothy R [10] is a young woman of twenty-one who has recently moved from the country into a large city. She comes of a family in which there is considerable dissension and criticism. No two members of the family live together or seem to have a good word for each other. Dorothy has always been hard to discipline. She has had a bad temper with terrific outbursts when she would scream and throw herself about. Usually, these tantrums were precipitated by the merest trifles. She has never been popular with boys because of her overemotionalism, although she has been seriously boy-crazy for several years. Since moving to the city she has been living alone until recently and reports several undesirable relationships with men. A few weeks ago, she attended a revival, became tremendously excited, was converted, and determined to reform. She obtained a room at the Y.W.C.A. where she has been conspicuous by having attacks of weeping over her former transgressions. The matron reports that Dorothy is not content unless she is the center of attention.

In appearance Dorothy seems quite distraught, but she talks almost constantly in an irrelevant manner. She frequently has outbursts of laughing or crying. Under stress of a little excitement she becomes noisy and offensive. She seems to have no intellectual interests, although she is of average intelligence. Her attention is somewhat erratic. She talks about her troubles readily but soon becomes flighty and digresses.

For the past month or so Dorothy has insisted there is a man annoying her. She showed letters from him, written in the most passionate language. She showed also other letters from a girl friend asking her to return to her "old life" and receive the man as her lover. Since the arrival of these letters she has refused to leave the Y.W.C.A. unless accompanied by someone. One evening she received from the man another threatening letter which apparently terrified her. She immediately had an attack of screaming, during which she appeared to lose consciousness. The matron's patience finally gave out and she asked that Dorothy be examined by a psychologist. After a few interviews, Dorothy's confidence was won and she admitted writing the letters to herself, using a disguised handwriting. After making this confession, the fundamental conflict which was suspected earlier became evident. Actually, she had never been immoral at all. She had always wanted lovers but had never been sufficiently attractive. Her supposed immorality was wholly of an autoerotic nature, the result of daydreaming and imagination. She felt keenly her lack of attraction to men and had invented a situation in which she appeared as the center of intense masculine attention. The letters were part of her dramatizing to give it the appearance of truth. She was trying to effect a compromise between her desires and environment, but the compromise was not adequate, as is made clear by her emotional upsets.*

Pauline B was a junior in high school. She had always done good work in all subjects. She was a careful student who prepared her assignments well and often handed in extra assignments because she was really interested in her classwork. On three different tests of intelligence she earned I.Q.'s of 114, 107, and 109. During the first three years of elementary school she had been regarded as an unusually promising pupil. In the fourth grade she had her first experience with examinations. Her teacher was considerably surprised when Pauline's examinations were well below the average of the class. She did not, however, take the matter seriously, since Pauline was so young. The girl's fear of examinations grew during succeeding years in school. Every teacher had the same experience. Pauline did excellent classwork, showed through her recitations that she had mastered the subject matter, but always turned in atrociously bad examinations. She was always passed because her teachers felt so sure she really knew the material, even though her examinations were unsatisfactory. One teacher became interested in the situation and, during the month before the end of school, asked Pauline in class every one of the question that would appear on the final examination. All questions were answered reasonably well, some of them brilliantly. Yet, on Pauline's examination paper not a single question was passing.

* This material is used by permission of The Macmillan Company.

Pauline was always in a pitiable state when she entered the examination room. She was pale, her hands trembled, she perspired, her voice shook, and she was likely to cry on the slightest provocation. Sometimes she seemed unable to write at all and would spend half the period staring in front of her or else crying. During her junior year, things became even worse and Pauline became so sick she had to be excused from three or four examinations. The first time this occurred, she was allowed to make up the test by means of an oral quiz given after school hours by the teacher. This test was passed easily and well. Since that time Pauline has never taken a written examination because she is always too sick.

Pauline comes from a good home where she is the youngest of four children. Both parents are college graduates, the oldest brother is a young doctor, the next oldest child is in graduate school, while Pauline's sister, a year older, is a junior in college. All three of the older children have made superior records in school and are regarded at home as being distinctly brighter than Pauline. Pauline has always been treated as a child by her family; in fact, she is still called "Baby." Special concessions are usually made whenever she thinks she needs them. The mother reports that in her preschool years Pauline had marked temper tantrums whenever she was crossed. Later on, she became nauseated whenever she was supposed to do something she disliked. Since she has been in high school Pauline has complained of numbness in her right hand and arm whenever she had a composition or report to write and found difficulty in doing it. Between her temper outburst and her illnesses she had managed almost always to have her own way.

Pauline has a dislike of examinations because she is in a panic of fear about failing them and being regarded at home as stupid. Whenever she finds herself in the situation she fears, she simply becomes sick. By this technique she dodges altogether the need of facing the dreaded situation at all, and, in addition, receives sympathetic attention during her illness—and what is for her a much easier type of examination later on. There will obviously be no improvement in the situation as long as Pauline is allowed to run away from her problems and as long as her family continues to put so much emphasis on high marks in school.

Miss L [12] seemed to be the victim of a most unusual chain of misfortunes. For years she had been caring for an invalid mother who had only recently died. Now she found herself going blind for hours at a time when she could see nothing. She consulted oculists in vain. Finally a friend persuaded her to go to a psychiatrist. He refused to pay any attention to her symptoms and insisted that she talk about her family and her plans in life. After considerable hesitation, she admitted the rebellion which she had felt during the many years when she had been confined to her home while her relatives, who were just as responsible as she for the invalid, were allowed to enjoy themselves. It appeared further that an aunt had recently become paralyzed and had no one to care for her. Other relatives had family responsibilities and were quick in agreeing that the responsibility should really fall upon Miss L. The psychiatrist constructed for himself a picture of emotional craving for release from this nursing responsibility, complete unwillingness to abandon duty, and so this unconscious development of a situation which would make it impossible for her to accept the responsibility. She would never consciously refuse to do her duty, but if she were blind, she obviously couldn't do it. When it became clearer that this might be the operating motive in producing hysterical blindness, the analyst tried the effect of direct attack. He painted the situation in plain, brutal words. He attacked with bitter sarcasm and eventually with angry curses a person who would do such a trick. The storm apparently brought the desired result. The blindness disappeared, succumbing to the pressure of the new emotional situation. Other relatives were invited in for conference and the problem adjusted on the basis of divided responsibility.*

THE FANATIC ADOLESCENT

For the third kind of emotional deviate there is no technical name. However, the type may be recognized rather easily. It is, in adult life, seen less often than the neurasthenic or hysteric, but it occurs with some frequency among adolescents, many of whom are at times dogmatic, opinionated, unreasonable, prejudiced, and generally fanatic about almost anything. The average adolescent, however, outgrows these characteristics, he never shows them in as violent a form as the true fanatic, and he practically never systematizes his erroneous ideas. With a little practice a teacher can see the difference between the temporary, unreasoning prejudice of a normal adolescent and the permanent mental rigidity of the true fanatic.

The outstanding symptoms of a fanatic personality are

* This case study is used by permission of the authors.

three in number. In the first place, adolescents of this type have a chronic attitude of suspicion and mistrust. They expect unfair treatment and they read into other people's behavior the worst possible interpretation. They feel the world is distinctly against them and they will trust no one. In the total experience of such individuals the attitude observed was probably at one time a reasonable reaction to particular circumstances; but the attitude has persisted in the face of all kinds of situations, until it has become a settled frame of mind.

The second symptom is a marked fixity of ideas. Fanatics will not change their minds, once they have decided upon something, no matter how many or how cogent reasons may be advanced. Their acquaintances regard them as obstinate and opinionated; it is not possible to reason with them successfully. Whatever ideas they develop they hold to through thick and thin. Unlike the hysteric, who has a different idea every day, the fanatic has the same idea every day. They are the material from which dangerous lunatics are made.

The third characteristic is a tendency to build up a whole system of interrelated ideas, many of which are demonstrably untrue. They complain, for instance, that a teacher is unfair to them, although the other students insist she is perfectly fair, and they support this contention with a systematically organized series of ideas, in which the true and the false are inextricably interwoven. Their essentially untrue beliefs usually hang together so perfectly and are backed up by so much circumstantial evidence that it is very hard to make any impression upon the situation. Once such a system of erroneous convictions has developed, practically nothing can be done to save the adolescent's personality from becoming permanently twisted and warped.

The original situations that brought about the responses just described are, of course, emotional in character and are usually the same situations that cause other adolescents to become neurasthenic or hysteric. Fanaticism is a mode of response to life. It is an unsatisfactory mode because it is too one-sided and because it rests on beliefs, some of which are undoubtedly false. It is an abnormal response, made to situations that are either not understood or not acceptable or not endurable. Thus, a fanatic evangelist may be driven into his uncompromising and one-sided attitude by his fear of death and his inability to tolerate the idea of a personal annihilation. Whatever the fundamental cause in any particular case may be, the building up of a system of more or less fanatical beliefs is one means of escape from the chronic burden of emotional maladjustment.

Illustrative case studies.—In the case studies appearing below attention should be centered upon the following points: What was the central emotional problem? What were the early reactions to the difficulty? What were the final symptoms? What environmental influences aided in the development of the situation? What symptoms should a teacher be able to recognize?

Gertrude K [9] was already a woman of about thirty when she first came to the writer's attention. To understand Gertrude's difficulties, a brief consideration of her childhood and youth is necessary. She was one of a family of three daughters. Her father had died when the girls were still little children, and they had been brought up by their mother, their grandmother (on the mother's side) and an aunt (the mother's sister). The mother's father (Gertrude's grandfather) had been a minister of narrow and bigoted beliefs and dominating personality. He had completely ruled his wife and had succeeded in bringing up his two daughters —the student's mother and aunt—according to his strict notions. The three little granddaughters therefore fell heir to a heritage of religious and moral ideas and attitudes passed on to them from their grandfather through their mother and aunt; they were dominated by the convictions of a grandparent who had been dead for nearly forty years! Moreover, the family was altogether feminine, and had been so ever since the student could remember.

This woman had grown up in an atmosphere of inhibitions, suppressions, anxieties, misconceptions, intellectual and social isolation. The girls were all earnestly, almost fanatically, religious, and their religion was of the extreme fundamentalist type. Their religious and intellectual attitudes were those of a narrow sectarianism of fifty years ago. Socially they were almost completely cut off from healthy companionship with others of their own age. They were taught both to idealize men and to fear them. They were allowed no boy friends, and friendships with girls who went around with boys were discouraged. They were sheltered from what the older women of the family mysteriously referred to as "life." Modern amusements were almost without exception regarded as inventions of the devil. As might be expected, the three had to act as companions for each other; the amusements, interests, topics of conversation of the average modern girl were all largely taboo to them. What social life they had centered around the church, but even there they mixed little with others of their own age. However, while they were all at home they were reasonably happy together, and were so apart from the world that they did not know how "different" they were.

When Gertrude went away to college it was inevitable that a multitude of adjustment problems should at once arise. She was shocked by the lack of interest in formal religious observances among both students and faculty. The after-lunch rubber of bridge, the dances, the corner moving-picture show, all outraged her moral sensibilities. And she was convinced that the free and easy companionships of the college boys and girls were fundamentally licentious. After two years the intellectual conflict became so intense, and the social isolation so painful, that she dropped out of college and for five years taught in a country school.

She then returned to college to finish the work for her degree —and of course all the old difficulties came up again; but since she was now older and surer of herself than before, her reactions were somewhat different. Thus, instead of submitting to what she considered irreligious teaching, she tried to refute the statements of her instructors. She also became embarrassingly active in the campus Y.W.C.A. and in the local church of her denomination. She became a militant crusader against the wickedness of modern life as she saw it. As a result of her incessant controversialism, she was receiving poor marks, and came to the writer for consultation concerning her study methods. There was little wrong with her methods of work; she simply insisted upon taking everything she read as a personal affront to her beliefs, and kept herself in a continual emotional ferment which made consistent study impossible.

Various means of dealing with this woman were tried. Two or three "coeds" of the best type were asked to cultivate her acquaintance, with the hope that she might come to realize that not all bridge players and movie addicts were utterly depraved. There was an effort to broaden her interests by reading on social and economic problems and by work at a local social settlement, in the hope that her crusading energies might be turned in more profitable directions. It was pointed out that at least as a matter of courtesy to her instructors, who were doubtless quite as sincere in their beliefs as she was in hers, she should refrain from constant criticism of them; and in consideration of the other students she should not take an undue amount of class time in discussion of her own special point of view. As tactfully as possible it was suggested that she might be a case of "everyone out of step but our Johnny"; that she was decidedly in the minority as regarded her religious and moral convictions; and was destined, if she persisted in her attitude, to spend her life in useless though well-meaning efforts to turn back a tide that had already carried the great majority of people along with it.

As may be imagined, with a person of her age and history, not much was accomplished. In some degree she was able, intellectually, to see her position. But emotionally she still rebelled against giving up any of her pet convictions. She will probably go on through life—with a religious and moral earnestness in itself admirable—antagonizing or cramping and repressing all with whom she comes in contact. And she will probably become more and more discouraged, embittered, uncomprehending.

Edward is a sixteen-year-old boy with a chronic grouch. He believes himself to be a promising young inventor, but somehow things go wrong with each of his inventions. He has already had correspondence half a dozen times with the Patent Office because his applications had been turned down. Actually, his inventions, while often excellent, are nothing new. On one occasion, for instance, he invented an egg-beater with a double set of bearings so that one rotation of the wheel would produce two rotations in the lower part of the instrument. The only difficulty with this invention is that it has already been invented. As an original effort of a sixteen-year-old boy it shows real promise, but what Edward cannot seem to understand is that sixteen-year-old boys are too uninformed to know what has been invented and what has not.

Edward's schoolwork has been good along lines dealing with mechanics and average along other lines. Two years ago he had a series of infections in his ears, developed a mastoid, and was in bed for six months. Upon advice of his doctor, he remained out of school during the second semester, although by then he was able to be up and working at a bench he had built in the back of the garage. This year of illness had a most unfortunate effect, aside from its undermining of his vitality. He lost his former contacts with school friends, he had a disproportionate amount of time during which to work on his inventions, and when he returned to school he was a year behind pupils with whom he had been since his kindergarten days. He now feels annoyed with the school because he is in classes with pupils he looks down upon as being too young for him, he is chronically annoyed with the Patent Office for refusing his applications, and he is constantly in hot water at home because of his increasing indifference towards school.

About a month ago Edward left school and went to work in a garage. He held his job only two weeks and was fired because he insisted upon trying to sell the customers various little gadgets he had invented. He was surly when reprimanded and on several occasions refused to carry out orders. The boss mechanic reported him as having excellent mechanical ability and even admitted the value of some of Edward's inventions but stated that the boy could not tell a good gadget from a poor one. Criticism, however, was taken in such bad humor that Edward rarely received any assistance from anyone else in estimating the value of his ideas. Within a few days Edward got another job which he held less than a week, and from which he was discharged for very similar reasons. He is now at home spending practically his full time puttering around and trying to work out an invention for which he has neither the equipment nor the scientific preparation; moreover, it has already been invented.

Edward is definitely the fanatic type. Everyone else is always wrong, everyone is jealous of him, everyone treats him unfairly. He is always able to defend his side of a discussion with a mixture of arguments half true and half false. He still does not see why the Patent Office refuses to give him patents and ascribes their behavior primarily to jealousy of his youth. Nobody can tell Edward anything, and he is so completely isolated from his friends that there is no one in whom he has any real confidence.

Herbert came to a state university from a denominational private school in the South. This latter school is maintained by one of the fundamentalist denominations, and most of its students are recruited from the backwoods by means of scholarship contests. Until his eighteenth year Herbert had lived at home on the farm, attending country school about six months a year. In this school he had been an industrious student of rather more than average capacity. He had added to his scant training by reading such books as he could get hold of—mostly English classics and books on religious topics. When he was eighteen he won a scholarship and spent two years in a small denominational college enrolling two hundred pupils and situated in a small town. At the age of twenty he entered the state university in the freshman class with the intention of becoming a minister.

The university was situated in a modern city of about 500,000. It took Herbert several days to find his way around, and he never became accustomed to the noise and bustle. He had never seen traffic lights; he had never ridden in an electric car; he had never bought a meal in a public restaurant. For the first month Herbert was in a daze because of the complete change in environment. At the university he enrolled in the classes in English literature, zoology, and psychology. In the English literature course he read samples from both classics and modern writings. It seemed to him the actions of many characters were not condemned nearly enough. The modern novels struck him as immoral and indecent. In the psychology class he was at first simply bewildered but later became profoundly distressed because the instructor paid no attention to the soul. He frequently interrupted the lectures to ask questions in regard to free will, the power of God, the existence of a conscience, or some other religious matter. But it was the zoology class that really angered him. The stress was naturally upon the doctrine of evolution, which outraged every belief Herbert had previously been taught. After about a month he stayed after class one day and read the instructor quite a riot act, accusing him of contaminating youth, of teaching false doctrines, and of being an atheist. The instructor, sensing the young man's sincerity, tried to present arguments on his own behalf, but Herbert only threw his textbook on the table and stalked out of the room; he never attended that class again.

At the end of his first semester he failed his work in zoology from nonattendance and his work in English because in his examinations he insisted upon debating points of morality instead of answering the questions. These failures put him on probation. He was sent to the Dean of his college by one of his second-semester teachers who felt herself unable to cope with the boy's problems. The Dean and two members of the psychology department all took turns in trying to argue Herbert out of his fanatic viewpoints, but to no avail. In the middle of the second semester, Herbert wrote a scathing denunciation of the university, sent it to all administrative officers and such members of the faculty as he knew, as well as to several newspapers who, however, knew too much about libel laws to print it. Having delivered this blast, Herbert packed his trunk and went back to his home with the determination later on to attend some theological school where he would find the teaching less irritating to his convictions.

THE ADOLESCENT WITH FEELINGS OF INFERIORITY

The term "inferiority complex" is often applied to individuals for whom it is anything but appropriate. There is, however, such a thing as a true feeling of inferiority which appears among persons who for some reason, real or imagined, do not feel sure of themselves. Its basis may be anything at all. It arises in adolescence from any situation in which the boy or girl feels at a disadvantage. The pupil need not be really inferior, although he often is in some particular respect. Thus the crippled or the defective adolescent may feel himself inadequate and actually is; however, a considerable number of these really inferior individuals make a satisfactory adjustment to society and completely escape any complex in the matter. The worst cases are those in which the inferiority is either imaginary or entirely avoidable.

Feelings of inferiority manifest themselves at all ages but are perhaps more common in adolescence than at any other time. It is during these years that the boy or girl first begins seriously to evaluate himself. The adolescent studies himself in the mirror and often gets upset because his face is out of proportion. He examines his clothes and is distressed if they are not up to the standard he observes around him. He evaluates his friends and often makes efforts to get into social groups that he feels to be more successful than his own. He begins to consider his ability and his personality. He wants to understand his place in the world and he all too often fixes upon some vocational or social ideal that is almost impossible of attainment by a person of his personality and intelligence. Social relationships between boys and girls precipitate adolescents into situations in which they feel awkward and incapable. For the first time differences in wealth and material possessions become important. Most of these considerations do not affect children at all. It is not surprising then to find feelings of inferiority especially common in early adolescence, at a time when boys and girls are facing so many new situations and have not yet had time to evaluate themselves correctly.

The bright student is especially likely to become aware of some social handicap, because he is usually younger than the boys and girls with whom he associates. Obviously it is to everyone's advantage to adjust these superior adolescents so that they may escape from the feelings of inferiority engendered by their emotional and social childishness. Altogether too many of them come to the conclusion they will never be socially competent; therefore they specialize on purely intellectual pursuits and avoid any efforts at the leadership which might be theirs when they are more mature.

The results of one definite investigation may prove of interest here. In one high school thirty-one students were selected as being of high intelligence but still failures in school and equally conspicuous failures in their social life.[7] These students were studied and the causes of this discrepancy between ability and achievement determined. All of them felt inferior for one reason or another, many of which were quite imaginary. Most of the pupils had no idea they possessed superior ability of any kind. After the period of analysis and treatment twenty-eight of these thirty-one students carried two semesters' work in one, made up their failures, and proceeded from then on to make school records and extracurricular successes consistent with their intelligence.

In high school there are a considerable number of perfectly normal children who feel themselves inferior because they do not have the right clothes, because they have less spending money than someone else, because they are unwilling to invite others to their homes, or for other such reasons. Often such situations are quite temporary, but their influence upon adolescent conduct is all out of proportion to their seriousness. Many of these situations are, of course, unavoidable accompaniments of growing up. The small child and the adult are both relatively indifferent to externals—the child because he does not notice them and the adult either because he does not care or because he has learned to evaluate them at their true significance. In between the child and the adult, however, is the adolescent who is tremendously concerned about externals. Feelings of inferiority which grow out of such situations are practically unavoidable. Indeed, one sign that a child is becoming an adolescent is the emergence of a slavish devotion to clothes, appearance, and possessions of all kinds; a sure sign that an adolescent is becoming an adult is his recovery from this overemphasis upon externals. All that either school or parents can do is to ameliorate the effects of these unavoidable conditions.

There are two quite different forms of behavior that may be shown by adolescents who are suffering from serious and chronic feelings of inferiority. The first type is simple and obvious. The pupil is unwilling to attempt any activity in which his real or imagined inability might become evident. He shows, indeed, a tendency to withdraw from any competitive activity, even along lines in which he could succeed. He is generally diffident, self-conscious, and unsure of himself. This type of behavior is shown by a pupil of relatively low vitality and high sensitiveness who had rather forfeit his opportunities than become conspicuous. If the situation continues long enough, the galling sense of inferiority spreads to all fields and the boy or girl is characterized by a total lack of self-confidence.

Some pupils, however, are not content to stay in the background. They are aware of their deficiencies, but they make every effort to cover these up, so that others will not suspect the existence of any inferiority. Usually, an adolescent tries so hard to conceal his handicaps that he overdoes the matter; his resulting exaggerated form of "overcompensation" displays his true feelings obviously and blatantly. Thus, the pupil who is afraid of physical combat and ashamed of his fear boasts loudly of his prowess, secretly hoping no one will call his bluff. The pupil who knows he is stupid persists in volunteering several times a day. The pupil who has no social graces makes repeated attempts to be the life of the party. The student who has had an uneventful life invents thrilling experiences. All such behavior, directed toward the covering up of inferiority, even from the pupil himself, is of a compensatory nature; the individual hopes, by overemphasis, to conceal his defects. The teacher should learn to see through ordinary forms of overcompensation and to recognize them for what they are.

Illustrative case studies.—In the case studies below special attention should be paid to the following points: What was the fundamental cause of the feelings of inferiority? Was the inferiority real or imagined? What adjustment was made? Did the adjustment automatically remove the conviction of inferiority, or was re-education necessary?

Pauline B [9] was a colored girl who showed a marked "inferiority complex." Her manner was cringing and apologetic. She cried at any provocation. She was deeply grateful for the slightest favor. She worshiped more successful people from afar. She usually spoke in a whisper and almost never recited in class. She was very shabbily dressed, almost in rags. All told, Pauline presented an appearance forlorn, discouraged, bewildered.

Possible causes of her inferiority feelings were not far to seek. Physically she was small and insignificant-looking, and she was much embarrassed in conversation by the fact that she had a slight speech defect. She had been brought up in the South and had had the superiority of the white race drilled into her, was in a white school for the first time, and found this situation quite overwhelming. She was terribly poor; in fact, so without funds that she had to pass in her work on wrapping paper saved from market packages and carefully pressed. She worked in a home where she was given a cold attic room (in which she had to do her studying), was made to use different china from the rest of the family, and had to live on what food happened to be left after the others had finished. In return for this "board and room" she prepared three meals a day for a family of four and did all the housework. When brought to the attention of the writer Pauline had failed every course she had taken her first term in college, and was progressing no better in her second term. In short, she was colored, was physically unprepossessing, poorly dressed, poverty-stricken, overworked, and an educational failure. It is hardly to be wondered at that she felt herself unable to cope with the world.

At first thought it might seem that Pauline was so hopelessly inadequate that it was useless to spend effort upon her. But there was something about the girl which compelled admiration, once the total situation was understood. Her difficulties were overwhelming her, and the sense of her inferiority was undermining her strength and courage. Nevertheless, she continued to struggle against the impossible odds. The writer decided to see how much she could do for the girl.

The first step was evidently to improve the gross circumstances. The people she worked for were interviewed and finally agreed to give Pauline the munificent sum of a dollar a week in addition to the room and board. With this money she was able to buy paper, pencils, and one essential book. She was given a couple of dresses in which she looked neat and attractive. She was told to take a limited schedule of studies so that she would not be quite so constantly overworked. Further she was told to drop the course which was giving her the most acute distress—a course in college algebra (elected because it sounded "elegant") in which she was the only girl in the class, the only colored person, and the others were all prospective engineers. These changes resulted in an improved physical condition and were the basis for certain more specifically educational adjustments. Thus, since Pauline was a very poor reader, she was given special help in methods of reading. She developed better procedures in note-taking. She was encouraged to recite in classes, was aided in the correction of her speech defect, and gradually developed more classroom confidence.

In spite of all these changes Pauline will not, however, remain long in college. She will soon find other courses that she cannot pass. It will not be long until someone again imposes on her. She will soon run out of money. She should preferably go back to her own people, and was so advised. She has not, in short, been brought to the point at which she is a success as a college student. She has, nevertheless, been to no small degree rehabilitated physically and emotionally. She is a good example of the fact that a college may do much even for those students that it does not graduate.

Carl is a graduate student in his middle thirties,[12] with an excellent background of experience. He gives an impression of considerable ability. His more intimate friends notice his constant craving for assurance from friends that his public performances are well done, his extreme anxiety when preparing an essay or appearing in public, his tendency to escape from such appearances when possible, and his need for someone upon whom he can rely to help him with whatever he is doing. His interests are likely to run into unusual channels where he can succeed with less competition.

Careful study of the case seems to indicate that some of the following facts may be relevant. Apparently up to the age of seven, he was a normal, healthy boy, keen on books, excelling in school. He was brought up as an only child in a small New England town, and perhaps given too much shelter. At seven he had a serious accident to his left hand, requiring an operation which left it awkward and numb for several years. A cousin a year older, more efficient and daring, less safely brought up, left Carl feeling ashamed and incumbent. Carl was taught not to fight, and when the other boys teased him, he ran home in fear. His injured hand made it possible for him to avoid developing manual skills. He let his father take care of any practical repairs around the house. When ten years old, he moved to a larger town. The child's family found themselves in financial difficulty. He felt that this meant social inferiority also. In the new school there was an element of tougher boys who regarded him as a "pet" of the teacher, who was much disliked. Carl did find certain satisfaction in the boy choir. One of his happiest experiences was five months on a Vermont farm. He returned there often, rather enjoying its relative independence. During his childhood there came a baby sister, several other experiences of moving, a need for glasses which handicapped him in games, and a chance, which he very much enjoyed, to take piano lessons.

In high school Carl excelled in school studies and graduated first in his class, but missed all extracurricular activities. He looked up very much to one older student, who tried to interest Carl in tennis and billiards with little success. Carl did not dance and felt that he was uninteresting to most young people of his own age. He developed an enjoyment of classic literature and music. He kept up nominal relationship with the church young people's society, but found most satisfaction in lonely practice on the pipe organ.

In college he felt again his inferiority in athletics and, added to that, a strong feeling that he could not speak and write as ably as could other students. Financial circumstances were improved, but he practiced more economy than was necessary and did very little remunerative work. It would be a mistake to think of him as a "grind." He studied with enthusiasm, read widely, argued and discussed with the like-minded, did social service teaching, cultivated foreign students, and others providing they were not too far from his economic level, and worked for religious causes, such as conferences, temperance, and foreign missions, with nearly as much tact as inventiveness. In the fall rush he worked as a salesman in the college store, but in the main he met college expenses by winning fairly large scholarships. Self-doubt kept him back from tutoring work for which he was well equipped, until he was sought out. Similarly the distrust of his ability to write was not shaken by high grades in composition, nor by the immediate acceptance of the first essay he sent to the college literary magazine. The social side of college he touched only by extending hospitality at home to his circle of friends. One of these became the most intimate friend he has, and to him he transferred the attitude of dependence built up previously.

Nevertheless there was progress in adjustment. Volunteering for foreign missions became a unifying ideal, and led to facing these inferiority nightmares with courage, and to venturing experiments to annul them. The award of Phi Beta Kappa in the junior year gave standing and more confidence. It was seen to be an obligation, not an extravagance, to buy an athletic outfit, so he joined the cross-country squad. Humor and sociability were essential, so he ventured out on his father's jokes, and discovered social enjoyment. A friend taught him some dances in his senior year, and he suddenly discovered girls. Formerly his friendships with womankind had all been ultra-Platonic, and with people much older than himself. The acquisition of these new social tools brought new behavior patterns in the emotional life, and at the end of the college epoch the sense of social inferiority had greatly lessened in many directions. He realized that he could be interesting and could be interested, and that he did not need to seek compensation in some unrelated world of his own. Lack on the athletic side was not so keenly felt, the financial side had been improved, and, moreover, did not seem so important. Fears of responsibility in leadership were keen, mechanical awkwardness was felt even more by the family's purchase of an automobile which might need repair, experience gained in teaching classes and speaking to small young people's groups had not removed the panic reaction at the thought of wider public speaking; in fact, in the next years this stage was maintained for fear of the next step.

In graduate school he turned to one of his college friends and later to two successive roommates as persons who must help him make all his decisions. He dropped his interest in dancing and in girls, although he felt that the fact that he had so little interest in the opposite sex was a symptom of his lack of normality. He developed during these years a great interest in private mystical prayer. Each small success in his work he seized upon and asked all his friends whether that indicated that he had sufficient ability to amount to something in the world. He never was quite convinced. When a good idea came to him, he elaborated upon it in conversation. He pictured himself making great achievements with it, but he substituted this sort of daydream for the actual intermediate steps. In the end he was likely to give up the project with a feeling that his education had been too mismanaged for him to become a success.*

Caroline was a senior in college, and a good student.[15] She had made herself very conspicuous by adopting noticeable mannerisms, posing, and availing herself of every opportunity to attract attention, and had lost the respect and good will of many of her fellow students. Her efforts to attract attention had begun with such dramatic attempts as keeping strange pet animals in her room, to the consternation of the other residents of the dormitory. The next year

* This case study is used by permission of the authors.

she had attempted something slightly more sophisticated, namely, announcing her engagement to a young newspaper man who was well known on the campus. During her junior year she became much interested in telling people all about herself and her fancied problems, trying to gain their sympathy, and apparently seeking their advice; but it had soon become clear that again she was merely working for attention, for she gave little heed to the advice she received, and would take advantage of each new person available to her, to repeat the same performance. Her roommate of that year was said to have "slumped noticeably," both students and members of the faculty having observed that Caroline's influence on the girl was debilitating, enervating, and generally poor. During Caroline's senior year she used such simple devices as appearing late at meals, and making extraordinary remarks at table in order to attract attention.

This young woman was referred to the psychiatrist for help in overcoming her unpleasant desire for attention. The first thing that was learned about her was that she had had an unusually close relation with her mother, a widow with sufficient means to enable her to indulge the girl in most of the luxuries of life and keep her closely by her side both at home and while traveling.

Caroline experienced a feeling of insufficiency and inadequacy when she was put on her own in college and no longer found herself the most important individual in her immediate environment. Although she realized the desirability of becoming independent of her mother, and frankly tried to free herself, she tried at the same time to satisfy her craving for attention in some other way. There was also the factor that she had come from a dull, small town and was in some respects trying to compensate for the experiences enjoyed by girls coming from a richer background.

Caroline had several conferences with the psychiatrist, in the course of which an effort was made to help her find the reason for her various undesirable forms of behavior, and to find a satisfactory solution. She improved noticeably during the remainder of the year, and became so interested in the field of personality adjustment that she took a postgraduate course in this work, and now has a position in which she does investigations of children with behavior problems, carrying on her work in an entirely satisfactory manner.*

* This case study is used by permission of the D. Appleton-Century Company.

THE PSYCHOPATHIC PERSONALITY

The term "psychopathic personality" has been used in psychological literature to cover a multitude of slightly abnormal but highly divergent characteristics. It seems, in fact, to be a sort of wastebasket into which one puts those cases that are not neurasthenic, not hysteric, not fanatic, not inferior, but who are still not queer enough to be insane. In spite of the lack of clearness in defining exactly what a psychopathic personality is, there seems some excuse for mentioning it in a textbook on adolescence because the condition, vague though it may be, often becomes prominent at that time.

For the purposes of this presentation the concept has been somewhat narrowed and therefore clarified. The writer's first step was to read through a large number of case studies describing psychopathic personalities and to determine what characteristics seemed fundamental. There is all too often an admixture of hysteric, neurasthenic, or fanatic characteristics in any particular case, but if one only reads enough descriptions these confusing elements disappear and the main symptoms can be seen. When one subtracts the incidental characteristics of this or that individual and the symptoms already included in some former classification, there seem to be only two outstanding traits remaining. But these two are permanent possessions of a few individuals and temporary characteristics of a considerable number of adolescents. In fact, the psychopathic personality is so closely associated with the adolescent years that theories have been advanced to relate the symptoms shown to the glandular readjustments of the period. Whether the causes be due to physical or social pressures the fact remains that numerous adolescents show a psychopathic personality for a few years and then "outgrow" their condition, to some extent at least, as soon as they reach adult age.

The first impression one gets of an adolescent with a psychopathic personality is certainly an impression of utter irresponsibility. These students can never be trusted to do anything at any particular time or in any particular way. They may do a task twice as well as expected, half as well, or not at all. These psychopaths are often genial and likable individuals. They are usually popular with other students, although they do not enjoy the confidence given to more normal persons. It is generally not difficult to convince them that a particular thing they have done is inacceptable. They will admit they have been at fault and will often take censure in perfectly good nature, but five minutes later they have forgotten all about it. They are childishly unable to control themselves; indeed, much of their behavior is the result of adolescent drives, practically adult mentality, and infantile inhibitions. They simply do not know what responsibility means.

Their second characteristic is that they do not learn by experience. Thus a boy with such a personality may lose his job as errand boy through irresponsibility; a week later he gets and loses another job for exactly the same reason. This performance may go on for months, and at the end of that time he had not yet learned the obvious lesson. In school, pupils showing this type of personality are not amenable to discipline. They may react to discipline satisfactorily enough for the moment, but whatever punishment is given leaves no permament trace. The next day they do exactly the same kind of thing for which they have been punished and seem surprised that anyone should object to their behavior. They are not different intellectually from other pupils, in so far as mastering subject matter is concerned, but they cannot seem to learn how to get along with others, even though life deals them one blow after another. They bounce back like rubber balls, apparently unmodified by experiences that would profoundly alter anyone else. The adolescent with a psychopathic personality is a thorn in everyone's side.

Some adolescents show these symptoms for a few years and then gradually settle down to a more normal personality. That is, they eventually do learn by experience, but they require longer than the average person. Even then, they show a tendency to be irresponsible whenever they are subjected to prolonged emotional strain. Others do not recover. There is no

EMOTIONAL DEVIATE

more complete nuisance in the world than the adult who retains this emotionally childish and uninhibited personality.

Illustrative case studies.—In the case studies below the following points should be kept in mind. Was there any emotional problem? What symptoms were shown? In what way did irresponsibility and failure to learn manifest themselves? What symptoms should a teacher have recognized as indicating an abnormal personality?

Dr. Franklin is a woman professor nearly forty years old. During her undergraduate days she seemed in general a normal person, although she showed even then a tendency (a) to become irresponsible if the work were uninteresting or too difficult and (b) to impose on her friends. She had two or three serious arguments with her teachers and on one occasion had to be moved from one section to another because she and the teacher had become so profoundly antagonistic. She participated freely in nonacademic activities but, while efficient, she did not command much confidence from her associates because they sensed her irresponsibility. She was a member of several class athletic teams. On some days she would play well and on other days poorly, but she always resented being taken out of a game even though she knew she was playing badly. She knew she was supposed to retire early the night before any class game but she would often stay up late, either because she became interested in something or from sheer negative suggestibility, and then would play poorly the next day. In spite of several such experiences she never learned to go to bed on time or to submit to any other training rule.

After leaving college she took graduate work and became a professor of history in a small college. This position she held for two years but was then asked to resign. Three reasons were given: First, she was irregular about meeting her classes; if she were interested in doing something else she would simply cut class. Second, her teaching was often careless; her presentation was sure to be badly prepared if she happened not to feel like teaching. Finally, she had developed several intense feuds with members of the faculty and administrative officers. Anyone who criticized her at once became her enemy. She constantly justified her absences from class and her poor teaching by complaining about the "inferior students"; actually, the students were above average in ability and preparation. At other times she would complain of overwork, absence of academic freedom, or lack of sympathetic understanding.

After losing her first job she obtained a position as assistant in a research project being carried on by a national foundation. Here she had the same difficulties. She accused her superiors of prejudice against her, of unnecessary criticism, and of overworking her. She had been so generally unsatisfactory that when she handed in a careless and inaccurate report of certain funds she had had charge of expending, this matter was made an excuse for eliminating her.

For over a year Miss Franklin had no job. Eventually, however, she was offered a chance to take over the contract of a former friend for the duration of the academic year, with the understanding her appointment would be renewed in case she was satisfactory. In spite of knowing she was on probation, Miss Franklin again neglected her classes and antagonized people. This particular position paid a much larger salary than any she had ever had, but instead of saving the money, she spent it on excursions to various large cities where she remained for several days and naturally failed to meet her classes. By the end of the year she realized she would not be reappointed, became very indignant, and left without ever turning in the grades for her courses. In spite of urgent requests she flatly refused to turn in any report. Finally, the college sent a personal messenger, who discussed the students' work with her and succeeded in getting from her some verbal statement of each student's standing. But even this information was difficult to obtain because of her constant complaints about the poorness of the material, the inadequacy of the library, and the lack of academic freedom.

There next intervened four or five years during which her only employment was writing book reviews, typing theses, tutoring, doing minor research jobs or library work for other people. During this time she became permanently embittered and turned to communism and other forms of propaganda as outlets for her emotional attitudes. One of her more objectionable traits became emphasized during this period; she "sponged" constantly on every acquaintance for meals, transportation, cigarettes, books, shows, or anything else. There were several people who would willingly have supplied her with such things if she had not tried so obviously to get them for nothing. In spite of her serious characterological defects, she was an intelligent and stimulating conversationalist. For an evening's entertainment one could hardly have a more charming guest. For short periods of time and in a congenial atmosphere none of her outstanding defects appeared at all. But she always defeated her own ends by her grasping attitude.

Through the combined efforts of several friends, Miss Franklin finally obtained a summer school position in a normal school. Here she repeated the identical tactics which had led to her dismissal from three previous positions. At the end of the appointment, she was again out of a job. During the following years she succeeded in supporting herself, rather precariously to be sure, with odd jobs, but with the beginning of the depression she became completely destitute. For the last four years she has been on the relief rolls and is regarded as a totally unemployable individual, in spite of her high level of education and very real intellectual capacity.

Joseph Brown is a man of about thirty-five. His personality is to some extent understandable in terms of his history. His father, while a successful artist, was a dissolute individual from whom his mother obtained a divorce when Joseph was about three years old. The mother herself was an irresponsible person who boarded Joseph and his sister with their grandmother out in the country while she worked rather intermittently in the city. She visited the children only two or three times a year and never contributed regularly to their support. When Joseph was about eight the grandmother died, and he and his sister (who was five years older) continued to live alone on the farm. The mother was not willing to have the children with her in the city because they would interfere too much with her good times, and there was no other relative to whom they could be sent. Joseph's sister was not old enough to control him, and for the next few years he did practically what he pleased. At that time his mother made a second marriage and arranged for the two children to live with her. The sister did not like her stepfather; after living with the family for a few months she eloped.

Joseph continued to live with his mother and stepfather, and seemed to be making a reasonably good adjustment. Although he had attended country school most irregularly, he quickly made up the work he had missed and entered high school at fifteen. A year later he was severely injured in football practice. For months he was in the hospital, and was subsequently in bed for about two years. During this time he was the center of lavish devotion from both his mother and stepfather. When he was finally well enough to return to school he felt himself too old to be a high school sophomore, so he took some tutoring and entered a trade school.

There his irresponsibility first became prominent, although it had probably always existed. His earlier environment, first on the farm with his grandmother, then with his sister, and then at home in bed had permitted irresponsibility without serious consequences. For the first time, in the trade school, he was meeting normal competition and difficulties. He remained only one semester and left without taking the final examinations. He complained that the instructors were unfair, that the work was uninteresting, and that nobody liked him. He next held half a dozen odd jobs, from none of which he was actually fired because he walked out of his own accord after giving his superior a "piece of his mind." In fact, he was always proud of having "bawled out" his superiors and of leaving his jobs voluntarily.

He next got employment as salesman for a hardware company. He had always liked to travel about and talk to people, and he usually made, at first, a rather favorable impression. For several months all went well, and Joseph's family believed he had found himself at last. During this time, he married a naïve and not very intelligent country girl from a tiny hamlet in his district. She regarded Joseph as a brilliant and rising young man, much too good for her. While she was totally unsophisticated, she was completely reliable and not afraid of hard work. The marriage started off well, and the girl's dependable nature seemed to have a stabilizing effect on Joseph's personality. Gradually, however, he became dissatisfied with his work, got into arguments with the head salesman, failed to keep appointments with customers, and became a general nuisance. As usual he sensed almost to a minute when he was going to be discharged, wrote an angry letter to the head of the concern, marched into the head salesman's office, criticized everybody, and loudly resigned his job. After this emotional flurry he again settled down for a few months as an insurance salesman. But this job also was drawing to a close when the depression threw him out of work completely.

His wife had a horror of living on charity; she therefore got a part-time job as sales girl during rush hours in a large store and spent the rest of the time raising vegetables, which she sold to neighborhood markets. Joseph sat around the house, nursed his grievances, and made no effort to get any kind of work. At about this time he met some Italian friends who were Fascist supporters and became greatly interested in Italy. While his wife worked fourteen hours a day, he read every book on modern Italy he could find, talked with his enthusiastic friends, and made plans for a visit to their relatives in Italy. All of this seemed a mere daydream, but at this moment an uncle died and left him $500. In spite of his wife's pleading, he spent this money making a visit to Italy. As he had been warned by others before he started, his friends' relatives did not like him and he did not like them. It annoyed him that they talked no English and that the Italian he had studied for three or four weeks before leaving home proved so inadequate! He remained less than a week, terminated his stay with an emotional display, and returned home. In the meantime, his wife determined to leave him, but upon his return he became repentant, promised her to be more responsible in the future, and persuaded her to take him back. One cannot blame her too much, for Joseph is the one colorful experience in an otherwise drab life.

Since that time he has alternately lived with his mother, who is now a widow, and with his wife. At present, at the age of thirty-four, he has decided to become a doctor. Joseph undoubtedly has the mental capacity to enter one of the professions, but he cannot understand that he has an inadequate preparation, that his characterological defects may prevent his success, or that he is too old now to start on such a long program of work. He is at present taking premedical courses in which he does no more than average work. He will never be allowed to enter medical school because his grades are too poor. The money for this work has been paid jointly by his mother and wife, the former out of her meager inheritance from her husband and the latter out of her daily earnings. As Joseph nears the end of his premedical work, he is realizing the impossibility of becoming a doctor. He is beginning to cut his classes and to project the blame on everyone but himself; he is gradually working himself up into a rage, at the height of which he will undoubtedly deliver an emotional blast to the college officials and then withdraw from his classes.

In 1917 Howard was a sixteen-year-old junior in high school, but in physical development he was as large as the average man. Howard's teachers complained constantly about his flightiness, childishness, irresponsibility, and desire for attention. He asked continually for special concessions. If an English teacher assigned a composition on a given topic, Howard wanted to write on something slightly different. If the chemistry teacher assigned Experiment No. 17, Howard asked permission to work on Experiment No. 22 instead. He was never content to be treated like other people. If he did not get his special dispensation he became irritable and often refused to complete the assignment; if he did get it, he was as likely as not to complete the assignment poorly. Howard tried to take part in extracurricular activities, but other students objected because they could not depend upon his co-operation and because he always wanted to be the center of attraction, although he did not have the intellectual or social capacities for leadership. Howard continued through two years of high school, constantly in trouble with his teachers, constantly projecting blame on others, constantly demanding recognition he did not deserve.

At this time, the United States declared war and Howard immediately enlisted, after lying about his age. This falsehood may have fooled the none-too-scrupulous enlistment officer, but it did not fool anyone in his company. He was assigned to an engineering outfit in which he was the youngest and dullest recruit. He could do nothing in the way of technical work satisfactorily. His company went through a short period of training, was shipped at once overseas, and remained there for the duration of the War. For a year and a half Howard worked at such uninteresting jobs as running errands, polishing metal, cleaning boots, disinfecting toilets, peeling potatoes, checking equipment, etc. Army life was never for a moment the glamourous adventure he had expected. During the first six months he had several flare-ups of emotion, but the older men and the officers in his company had no time to bother with an adolescent boy's peculiarities of temperament. Every time he "blew up" somebody cracked him down again. Army discipline was much stronger than he was.

After returning to the United States, Howard re-entered high school. By chance, he was assigned in English to the teacher whose class he had attended during his freshman year. He was a few days late in entering school, so after his first class he stopped to get the necessary assignments from the teacher. She told him the topics on which he was to write and asked him if he thought he could do it. He replied, quite simply and with no desire to be funny, "I can do *anything* I am told." The rigid discipline of the Army had had its effect in counteracting the psychopathic tendencies in this boy's personality. Since that time he has completed high school and gone to work. There has never been the slightest effort on his part to curry favor with his superiors or to dodge normal responsibility. What he needed was an environment in which his unpleasant traits met with immediate, severe, and inescapable punishment; for this purpose anything better than army life would be hard to find.

THE PREVENTION OF ABNORMAL PERSONALITIES

One point on which Freud was undoubtedly right is that most peculiarities of personality arise in the early years of childhood. Modes of response often become fixed even before a child enters school and remain relatively unmodified from that time on. It is, therefore, not surprising to discover unusual personalities and abilities making their first appearance in nursery school.

Permanence of traits.—The predelinquent child, the mentally defective child, the brilliant child, and the peculiar child are recognizable very early in their educational careers. Usually, however, little if anything is done about these unusual children, on the principle that they will outgrow their defects. The educational world has finally become convinced that the mentally defective child will never catch up with his normal schoolmates. But there is apparently no assurance in the minds of teachers that all other types of children will not become different as they grow older. Such is, however, not the case—in so far as the fundamental outlines of personality are concerned, even though minor characteristics and especially particular modes of response may vary greatly from one age level to another. The nursery school child who hides behind the piano and plays by himself grows up into the high school pupil who avoids social contacts and lives in a world of fantasy. The nursery school exhibitionist grows up to be the high school pupil who loses the ball game because he cannot submerge his exhibitionism into the required teamwork. The intractable, defiant nursery school child who resents all discipline merely gets worse and worse as he grows older and more and more capable of showing his resentment in dangerous ways. The nursery school youngster who throws herself on the floor and screams when she cannot have what she wants, grows up into the high school girl who sobs and cries because she is not taken into some club to which she wants to belong. The preschool delinquent becomes first the elementary school delinquent and then the high school delinquent, in case he stays in school that long. As more and more research is done it seems clear that not only differences in intellectual capacities remain fairly stable during the school years, but also differences in emotional and social adjustment. The overt behavior, of course, alters, but the underlying attitudes seem to become fixed very early in life. As one psychiatrist has said, unusual individuals merely get to be more and more like themselves as they grow older.

The situation as regards differences in intelligence involves considerations that will be left for discussion in a later chapter. The maximal level of ability for each individual is apparently fixed by heredity, and all education can do is to teach a person to use his ability in the best possible way. In regard to emotional attitudes, however, there is no proof of deciding heredity factors. A child's personality apparently develops in response to the stimuli he meets. Even identical twins, if separated at birth and brought up under different circumstances, show divergent personality traits, although their intellectual capacities remain closely parallel. The hopeful point in all work with personality is the conviction that emotional traits and attitudes are acquired. The main difficulty, however, in all remedial work along lines of personality comes from the failure of the specialist to get hold of children soon enough. What usually happens is that a peculiar child who is not absolutely delinquent completes his schooling, gets out into the world, and then develops difficulties which eventually land him in the office of a psychiatrist. By this time he or she is twenty-five years old or more, and the traits of personality have become so fixed that changing them is a stupendous task. Yet, the fundamental traits could undoubtedly have been recognized in the first grade. If a child's peculiarities are recognized when he is six years old there is hope of altering them by the end of his school career.

Recognition of unusual behavior.—For the first observation of character defects, the elementary school teacher is, of course, responsible. During childhood the traits shown at entrance to school develop as regards expression, but they remain relatively stable as regards fundamental attitudes. With the coming of adolescence there is likely to be a change, often for the worse. Adolescence, as already noted, imposes physical, emotional, and social strain upon the boy or girl. Both acceptable and inacceptable traits are emphasized by these new demands of existence. The child who has always gotten along reasonably well with others and has occasionally stood out a little from the group, suddenly develops into a good organizer and leader. The child who has always been shy and inclined to stay alone is suddenly found to be quite isolated from society. In neither case has adolescence changed the individual but has rather emphasized traits already in existence. Difficulties of adjustment are usually brought into high relief during adolescence. It may therefore be the high school teacher who first observes a pupil's abnormal reactions, not because they have not existed earlier but because they have been less obvious. Whenever a pupil with abnormal traits is observed, he or she should be sent at once to a competent diagnostician for observation and treatment. Altogether too much time has already been lost. The pupil has been practicing unfavorable modes of response for thirteen, fourteen, or fifteen years, and there is only a short time left for remedial treatment before he or she finishes school.

There are in every large high school a few children whose peculiarities are already serious and for whom the strain of adolescence is entirely too much. Such pupils find themselves unable for one reason or another to face the demands of ordinary living. They have already built up a habit of withdrawing from reality whenever adjustment is difficult and of substituting imaginary for real situations. Perhaps as a little girl, a certain high school pupil has imagined herself a princess, cared for by a good fairy, and has in fantasy graciously accepted gifts from her loyal subjects. Such fantasies have probably not disturbed either parents or teachers. But the situation becomes serious when the same girl, under the various strains of adolescence, imagines herself the most popular girl in the school, the daughter of the wealthiest man in the city, and the object of every boy's devotion. As far as attitude toward life is concerned, one fantasy is just as serious as another; but whereas one is treated as a mere childish whim, the other is regarded as obviously abnormal. The time to bring such a girl back to reality, however, is during the period of the socially harmless "fairy" fantasy, not when she has developed "boy-crazy" delusions.

In the case of pupils who have, through circumstances or personality, become socially isolated, the teacher should always be on the lookout for symptoms of dementia praecox. This type of insanity makes its appearance in the great majority of the cases between the ages of thirteen and twenty-one, and it incapacitates the individual for the rest of his life. It appears to have no physical basis, aside from a general rather low vitality, but it occurs only in isolated individuals. It is primarily an extreme development of the withdrawal mechanisms, seen in milder form among the daydreamers and neurasthenics. For the development of dementia praecox two elements seem necessary: a period of social isolation and a "shut-in" or "seclusive" personality on the part of the person isolated. The disease never develops in a socially and emotionally well-adjusted adolescent, nor in a physically, intellectually, and socially vigorous person. It comes to those who have been showtheir predisposition to it ever since they entered nursery school.[11]

A teacher is, of course, no technical diagnostician of personality. Some teachers, however, have a natural flair for such work and become able, after a little training, to recognize the most common types of abnormal pupil. In this chapter the outstanding behavior symptoms of certain personality types have been described. It is not necessary, however, for a teacher to go so far as to make any classification of a given pupil. She can, and inevitably does, observe items of behavior. All she really needs is (1) to recognize when a reaction is abnormal and (2) to send the pupil showing the behavior to an expert for diagnosis and treatment.

As a guide to teachers in the recognition of abnormal behavior—the first step in the prevention of abnormal personalities—the writer presents a list of those deviations which have appeared with the greatest frequency in the extensive research done in recent years, both by the case-study method with individuals and by the group-test technique * with entire school populations. Children showing such behavior traits as those given below are not absolutely normal. Single instances on the part of a child are naturally not significant, but repeated behavior of the types shown is undoubtedly symptomatic of some emotional or nervous difficulty. The extent and seriousness of the difficulties underlying these deviations from normal behavior can be estimated only after careful expert analysis.[8]

Physical symptoms of nervousness.—Habitual twitching of muscles, scowling, grimacing, twisting the hair, continuous blinking, biting or wetting the lips, biting nails, stammering, blushing and turning pale (especially when called upon to recite or spoken to unexpectedly), constant restlessness as

* For information in regard to measurement of personality the reader is referred to pages 72 and 269.

moving around the room to sharpen pencils, opening windows, and consulting the dictionary, frequent complaints of minor illnesses and indispositions.

Symptoms of emotional preoccupation.—Undue anxiety over mistakes, marked distress over failures, absent-mindedness, daydreaming, lack of voluntary participation in class, meticulous interest in detail, tendency to wander off alone at recess, refusal to take part in games, refusal of any recognition or reward, willingness to do some other student's work without getting credit, evasion of responsibility, withdrawal from anything that looks new or difficult, chronic attitude of apprehension.

Hysterical symptoms.—Uncontrolled laughing or giggling, chronic inattention, attention paid to extraneous circumstances instead of to classwork, explosive and emotional tone in argument, tendency to feel hurt when others disagree, unwillingness to give in, marked fears, anxieties, or obsessions, jumping at sudden noises, shrieking when excited.

Exhibitionism.—(Often in response to an underlying inferiority.) Bullying and teasing, striking people, pushing or shoving people (especially in corridors between classes), trying to act tough, trying to be funny, wanting to be conspicuous on public occasions, effusiveness, exaggerated courtesy, marked agreement with everything the teacher says, constant bragging about exploits or places seen or people met, frequent attempts to dominate younger or smaller children, inability to accept criticism, constant efforts to justify self, frequent blaming of failures on accidents, false causes, or other individuals, refusal to admit any personal lack of knowledge or inability, frequent bluffing.

Emotional immaturity.—No ability to work alone, desire to have someone else solve problems, continual requests for assistance after assignment is understood, frequent requests for more time on an assignment, crushes on older persons of the same sex, tendency to cling to a single intimate friend, inability to rely on judgment, fear of examinations, childish attempts to make teacher lenient.*

The paragraphs above list the danger signals shown by adolescents in distress. Teachers should memorize this list; when they

* This list is presented by permission of The Macmillan Company.

see a pupil consistently showing any of these deviations, they should send him or her at once to whatever person or agency is best equipped for complete investigation and treatment. Neurotic conditions could be considerably lessened in frequency through early recognition of symptoms by teachers. There is some evidence to show that even dementia praecox could be avoided if the children likely to develop it were found and treated soon enough; by the time most adolescents come to the attention of a specialist, the disease has already progressed too far for a cure. Other types of insanity appear mostly during middle and old age, but dementia praecox makes its attacks early and usually conquers the individual so completely that his life is worthless from almost any point of view. High school teachers can help in the prevention of this disease by reporting at once those pupils that show abnormal personalities.

BIBLIOGRAPHY *

1. Bassett, C., *Mental Hygiene in the Community,* The Macmillan Company, 1933, 394 pp.
2. Bell, H. M., *The Adjustment Inventory,* Stanford University Press, 1934, 4 pp.
3. Cavan, R. S., "The Murray Psychoneurotic Inventory and the White House Conference Inventory," *Journal of Juvenile Research,* 1934, 18: 23-27.
4. Faris, R. E. L., "Cultural Isolation and the Schizophrenic Personality," *American Journal of Sociology,* 1934, 40: 155-165.
5. Gardner, G. E., and Pierce, H. D., "Inferiority Feelings of College Students," *Journal of Abnormal and Social Psychology,* 1929, 24: 8-13.
6. Hayes, M., "A Scale for Evaluating Adolescent Personality," *Journal of Genetic Psychology,* 1934, 44: 206-222.
7. Karlan, S. C., "Failure in Secondary School as a Mental Hygiene Problem," *Mental Hygiene,* 1934, 18: 611-620.
8. Koos, L. V., and Kefauver, G. N., *Guidance in Secondary Schools,* The Macmillan Company, 1932, 640 pp.
9. Pressey, L. C., *Some College Students and Their Problems,* Ohio State University Press, 1929, 97 pp.

* See also the references in the Appendix.

10. Pressey, S. L., and Pressey, L. C., *Mental Abnormality and Deficiency,* The Macmillan Company, 1927, 356 pp.
11. Smalldon, J. L., "Pre-psychotic Personality of Manic-Depressive Patients," *Psychiatric Quarterly,* 1934, 8: 129-147.
12. Spence, R. B., and Watson, G. B., *Sketches in and out of School,* 1927, 286 pp.
13. Steinbach, A. A., "A Survey of Adjustment Difficulties in Children and Youth Drawn from the Normal Population," *Elementary School Journal,* 1933, 34: 122-130.
14. Symonds, P., "Measuring the Personality Adjustments of High-School Pupils," *Psychological Bulletin,* 1933, 30: 664-665.
15. Thom, D. A., *Normal Youth and Its Everyday Problems,* D. Appleton-Century Company, 1932, 367 pp.

CHAPTER X

THE INTELLECTUAL DEVIATE

SOME pupils have obviously more intellectual capacity than others. As already pointed out, about 64 per cent of the general population have normal or average intelligence, while another 30 per cent have mental ability that ranks them as slightly superior or slightly inferior—that is, as "bright" or "dull." The "dull" group, about 15 per cent of the school population, contains those children who learn slowly the basic facts of the elementary school curriculum, who generally lose at least one year in getting through elementary school, and who have great difficulty with high school work if they attempt it. The "bright" group, again about 15 per cent of the school population, includes those who learn a little better than the average and are a little more mentally alert. They usually complete their schoolwork in about a year less than the average pupil. While their work is uniformly good, it is only occasionally of outstanding merit. About 3 per cent of the school population is so superior in ability as to be termed "brilliant," while another 3 per cent is so inferior as to be termed "defective." With members of this latter group, the junior high school teacher has rarely to deal, and the high school teacher never, because the real mental defectives rarely get beyond the third or fourth grade. The "brilliant" pupils, however, generally continue through high school.

In the elementary grades, the "intellectual deviates" consist of all children outside the central two-thirds of the distribution, but by the time high school is reached, there has been a change. In the table on p. 329 some fundamental facts are presented in regard to the differences in the distribution of abilities between the first grade of elementary school and the first year of high school.

TABLE XVIII
Range of I.Q.'s in the First Grade of Elementary School and First Year of High School

Group	First Grade Elementary School	First Year High School
Lowest 3%	50–63	74–83
Next 15%	64–73	84–95
Middle 64%	74–106	97–120
Next 15%	107–126	121–135
Highest 3%	127–149	136–149
Median I.Q.	88	106
Number of pupils	109	61

This table is based on the intelligence scores made by 109 pupils ten years ago in the first grade of a large elementary school in a poorer section of a large city. Any children entering with these 109 but moving away during the compulsory school ages were excluded from the study. Of the 109 remaining in the city, sixty-one had entered high school by the end of the tenth year after they came into the first grade. The others had dropped out or were still in elementary school.*

The selective effect of schooling is evident. The entire group of "deviates" at the lower end of the elementary distribution has disappeared. Most of those who were "average" in the first grade are the "deviates" at the bottom of the high school group. Most of the "bright" group of the first grade are now included in the "average" group of high school freshmen. And the lower limit for "brilliancy" has gone up about ten points. The intellectual deviates at the high school level are, therefore, not the same pupils who would be so classified at any earlier level.

In the remaining sections of the chapter there will be discussion of the brilliant group and of the two lower groups. Probably some of those with I.Q.'s between 97 and 120 must also be classed for the time being with the lower end of the distribution, since the I.Q. necessary for finishing high school has been estimated to be between 105 and 115. This estimate is, of course, based upon the requirements of the usual academic sub-

---
* From unpublished material by the author.

jects; a change in curriculum would undoubtedly result in lowering the minimal intelligence necessary to success. Because of the relatively high I.Q. needed for work in high school, most of the pupils who were in the "bright" group in elementary school are too near the average of the school population—certainly after the elimination that occurs during the first year of high school—to be considered as deviates. Naturally, the line cannot be drawn hard and fast between the end of any group and the beginning of another; the limits are only relative. The main thing to remember is that even these relative limits shift from one level of education to another.

THE BRILLIANT ADOLESCENT

Characteristics.—Brilliancy is not merely a state of mind. A brilliant individual is usually superior in all respects to those of less ability. The brilliant child is tall and heavy for his age;[1] he grows faster than the average and matures earlier.[1] This physical superiority is often obscured because brilliant children are so accelerated in school that they are placed in grades with others from two to five years older than themselves. In comparison to these older pupils they almost always appear small; hence the popular idea that intellectual superiority is associated with physical inferiority.

In later years, of course, this may actually be the case, but the cause is environmental. The superior child, finding himself in a group with which he cannot possibly compete in games, often retires from competition and devotes himself to his books—a field in which he can succeed so well as to shame the older children who dominate him in play. By the time a bright child has finished high school, college, and perhaps some years of graduate work, with as complete as possible abstinence from exercise, he is frequently underweight and strained. All too often the most bookishly superior adults are lacking in qualities of physical superiority. But this result is not due to a poor start; the growth rates through childhood and adolescence are all in favor of the brilliant child. If he becomes a physical inferior the fault lies with those who have allowed him to do so.

Intellectually, the brilliant pupil stands out clearly and has done so from early childhood.[15] He learns with unusual rapidity and retains what he learns. Usually he concentrates without effort and uses economical methods of study. His chief mental characteristics are, however, the abilities to see relationships, to generalize, to distinguish the essential from the nonessential, and to see through facts to their logical conclusions. For the brilliant pupil ideas have a real fascination. He is vitally interested in both facts and theories. He wants to learn. From his earliest years he shows a liking for playing with ideas and for rearranging them in new combinations. This sort of mental exercise develops by the years of adolescence into real originality and resourcefulness. Indeed, the essence of brilliancy is probably a combination of the ability to make generalizations and this spontaneous originality in handling ideas. The merely bright child with the perfect memory has neither of these qualities in any larger measure than the average person.

Characteristically, the brilliant student is an academic success.[15] He is commonly accelerated at least two years and sometimes more. His school marks are high, especially in subjects demanding judgment, generalizing, and logical thinking. When a child of superior ability fails to do good schoolwork there is something radically wrong—with the child or with the school. A few brilliant children are erratic and unstable, from the same causes that produce these characteristics in others. More frequently, however, the fault is with the school because the work gives no opportunity for the exercise of independent thinking. Ordinary schoolwork that is more than enough to occupy the concentrated attention of the average child is so simple as to contain no challenge at all to the brilliant. More than one intellectually superior child has been "cured" of poor marks by the simple expedient of loading him down with more and harder work than two ordinary children could get done. Because of the lack of challenge in most of the elementary school subjects, some brilliant children do not show their real ability until after they get into high school and meet a type of teaching that requires them to think for themselves rather than to memorize what someone else has thought. For this reason there is occasionally the sudden emergence of a pupil with a quite ordinary record into the ranks of the brilliant. The fundamental ability has always been there—as previous teachers will testify—but nothing has ever before awakened it. Whenever a brilliant pupil does not do good work in school the cause is often not far to seek. He is an unawakened person who has never been intellectually stimulated, or else he is being forced into lines of work that are distasteful to him, or else he is trying to do so many things at once that nothing gets done well. In any case, society cannot afford to let him be a mediocrity. There are altogether too few superior individuals born; none of them can be wasted.

Socially, the brilliant adolescent is—like everyone else—what his environment has made him. If he has been treated as a prodigy and has been a center of interest, he may have an unpleasant personality. If he has been allowed to concentrate upon academic work to the exclusion of social activities he may be markedly introverted. If he has had special favors given him because of his intellectual success, he may still have childish emotional reactions. Unless environmental factors have been unfavorable, however, the brilliant adolescent is usually a cooperative and responsible person.[3] He is willing to be guided in his work and personal development. He gets along with others at least as well as the average pupil. His participation in extracurricular affairs is slightly higher than that of his classmates.[15] He has somewhat more chance than others of being a leader.[8] There is more probability that the intellectually superior child will be well adjusted than that he will be poorly adjusted.

One common situation likely to impose social and emotional strain upon the intellectually superior child is his acceleration in school, which almost always breaks up his normal social relations with others of his own age and inevitably puts him into a group of children too big for him to play with and too mature in their interests for him to fit into their social grouping. It is only because a brilliant child is actually large and mature for his age that he may be accelerated at all without doing him harm. The degree to which extra promotions are desirable depends upon the non-intellectual characteristics of each individual brilliant child. Some bright children are so babyish in their behavior that they become the butt of all the jokes if they are advanced into a grade with older and bigger children; others are so mature that they take their place more naturally with slightly older children than with those of their own age.

With the coming of puberty the differences between the young brilliant child and his older classmates are exaggerated. Even though superior children mature earlier than children of average ability their acceleration is likely to more than offset this maturity. Many of them enter high school before puberty and before their final adolescent growth has taken place. Consequently, the discrepancy in size is intensified and the differences in social interests brought into high relief. Bright, young, accelerated high school pupils want to play childish games with other children their own age and sex. They do not fit at all into the extracurricular activities at the high school level. They cannot get excited about dances and parties, they have no interest in members of the opposite sex, they are not big enough to be successful in athletic competition. They are social children lost in a world of adolescent interests and enthusiasms. The nonacademic problems of brilliant pupils are far more acute in high school than at any other stage of their development.

In one study [11] of fifty-seven students who were so far accelerated as to enter college at sixteen years of age, several important points were discovered. These fifty-seven were matched with the same number of students two years older than themselves, but having the same average high school grade, the same average on the Regent's examinations, and the same intelligence score on their college intelligence test. In academic work the averages for the two groups were practically identical; in other words, these young brilliant students did just as good academic work, but no better. The proportion of students in the two groups receiving distinction at the end of their college course was also essentially identical. The differences come in the field of personal adjustment. While less than 3 per cent of these unusually young students reported a feeling of intellectual inferiority, 32 per cent of them reported a feeling of social handicap in college, and 46 per cent a similar sense of social inferiority in high school. Many of those who did feel social handicaps have undoubtedly forgotten the matter, many others are unwilling to admit their difficulties, and still others did not sense there was any difficulty; it is therefore safe to guess that at least two-thirds of these young and brilliant college students were actually handicapped in their social relations during their high school years.

Training.—The successful handling of superior students requires an understanding both of the characteristics of brilliant children and of the school situation into which they are precipitated at their entrance to high school. A bit of historical perspective is here necessary. Originally, the high school was intended for the further education of mentally superior individuals. In fact, it enrolled primarily above-average students until the last two decades. With the recent enormous increases in the number of average and below-average pupils, high school teachers found it necessary to simplify their courses, since no teacher is likely to keep her position if she maintains a standard of work that will result in failure by any large proportion of her pupils. Mere pressure of numbers has forced down former standards. The result is satisfactory to no one. As will presently be shown, these simplified courses are not at all what the below-average students should have; for the brilliant student, the simplification has been a tragedy. The courses have been made relatively uninteresting, they are far too easy, and they do not contain the basic material needed by the pupil who will continue on to college. As a result, the brilliant student learns in high school mainly to loaf and to criticize. He does not have enough work to keep him busy and very little of his work challenges his best efforts. When he gets to college he finds he does not know many things he should know; these deficiencies dog his footsteps right through his graduate work, in case he persists that far. If many brilliant college freshmen are slipshod in their methods of study and uninterested in their work, it is not entirely their fault. Their high school course has not given them what they needed.

One investigator [10] has recently studied the academic and extracurricular load of high school juniors. The results are chiefly interesting as regards the pupils of superior ability. The normal load in this high school was four units of academic work a year. Among the pupils of average intelligence, there were 80 per cent who had at some time carried more than four units; of the superior students, 89 per cent had sometimes carried more than the minimum load. All pupils were asked to state whether they felt themselves overworked, underworked, or kept satisfactorily busy by the amount of work taken. Seventeen per cent of the brilliant pupils reported themselves as overworked, 81 per cent as kept satisfactorily busy, and only 2 per cent as being underworked. Since the load of average and superior students was so nearly the same, it would seem that the brilliant pupils could not have been even reasonably busy. Further evidence was obtained by the students' own statements of how many hours per week were spent in different activities. The superior pupils averaged fifteen hours per week in study, including work both in study halls and at home; the time spent in study by average pupils was exactly the same. The brilliant students devoted twenty-five hours per week to extracurricular and purely recreational activities, while the average students spent twenty hours. These superior adolescents were obviously underworked—and yet only 2 per cent of them realized it. They were so underworked they had time to spend ten hours more in nonacademic activities than they spent along academic lines. Such results would undoubtedly be found in any other inquiry into the activities of brilliant pupils in high school.

For the superior adolescent, certain changes in high school courses and methods of instruction are badly needed. An improved course of work for them would doubtless have the characteristics to be described.[3] It would, first of all, lead to a real mastery of the tools of learning. The brilliant adolescent should acquire at least one modern language and preferably two; he should read and read until he is conversant with his heritage of culture; he should obtain a mastery of elementary facts in biological and nonbiological science; he should reduce elementary algebra to a technique he can use; he should know the outstanding facts in the history of the world and should have some grasp of social and economic developments; he should make a start on acquiring a philosophy of life. These are the tools of the brilliant mind; without them, thinking on the higher levels cannot be done. The ordinary high school course gives the superior student too little, not too much. It fails to provide him with those essentials which must act as the basis for his future development if he is to take the place in social evolution reserved for the talented. No amount of social adjustment and agreeable personality will atone for lack of these elements of thought essential to the levels beyond high school.

A second characteristic of high school education for the brilliant pupil is that it must give him training in self-discipline and hard work. Genius may not be an infinite capacity for taking pains, but it cannot grow without an infinite capacity for concentrated work. In the commendable effort to make a high school curriculum that will not discourage and bewilder the average pupil, educators have managed to ruin the working habits of the brilliant. The really superior student learns so rapidly and forgets so little than ordinary classwork calls for barely more than a casual glancing at assignments. Most people simply do not realize how little burden is placed on the superior child.

For example, the writer remembers one brilliant girl who returned to high school on a certain Thursday evening after an illness which had kept her out of school since the beginning of the year. She found her Latin class was to be given an examination covering the first book of the Aeneid on the following Monday. Between Thursday evening and Monday morning she read the first book, took the examination—including grammar, vocabulary, and knowledge of the story—and received a grade of 99 per cent. During the remaining two-thirds of the school year she loafed through the next three books. Naturally, the first book was read under somewhat too much pressure, but the others were certainly read under far too little.

In general, the amount of work demanded from brilliant adolescents is greatly below their abilities. It is no wonder that many come to regard extracurricular activities, in which they do have to work, as more important than their courses.

Finally, the material to be learned should be presented in as stimulating a manner as possible and the student encouraged to use his initiative and originality to the greatest possible degree. It is not necessary, as some teachers seem to think, to get away from traditional materials in order to make schoolwork interesting. Practically any sort of subject matter which is at all congenial to pupils will become interesting if they are allowed to put their own initiative into it. Nothing is more fascinating to a person of alert mind than the process of thinking. The challenge lies, not in the nature of the subject matter, but in the way it is taught. Whereas the dull pupil must have a simplified presentation, the brilliant student must not have. The dull pupil must have facts organized for him, but the brilliant adolescent is better off if he makes his own organization. The dull child must have the help given by such aids as the construction of models, but the superior child does not need such assistance; his imagination is quite sufficient. Whereas the dull pupil requires work closely associated with his everyday life, the brilliant one may be encouraged to make excursions into distant places and periods of time. Finally, the brilliant should be given every chance to handle the theories, implications, and generalizations that the dull must avoid.

These general comments may be made clearer by examples taken from actual subject matter. Thus, in English literature, the objective for average pupils is the ability to read with reasonable ease such modern stories, newspapers, and magazines as they can appreciate, and to get so much enjoyment from their reading that they will continue it after leaving school. The objective for brilliant students should be the acquisition of as complete a survey as possible of the developments in English literature, with much reading from both classical and recent authors. In geometry, the average pupil needs to have most demonstrations worked out for him, but the alert adolescent is better off if he works out his own proofs. In Latin, the teacher should stress for average students the relationship of Latin to English; the objective of the course should be a better understanding of the student's own language rather than a mastery of Latin. But the brilliant can learn to read Latin, in case they are interested in languages. Along all lines, both objectives in teaching and methods should be entirely different.

In three respects, then, the treatment of brilliant children should differ from that given their classmates: in the nature of the material studied, in the amount studied, and in the manner of presentation. If such a program were adhered to, the awakening of the superior pupil would take place in high school, instead of being delayed till the last years of college and sometimes even later. The curriculum as taught in many present-day high school classes involves a tragic waste of the best intellects in each generation of students.

Personal adjustments of brilliant pupils.—The superior adolescent has problems of various kinds—intellectual, vocational, social, and emotional. His chief intellectual problem is to find something on which to sharpen his mind. A second problem in the same field is to delimit his interests sufficiently to prevent spreading his activities too thinly over too many different fields. The brilliant adolescent is typically the person who sets out to master the entire universe. His intellectual interests need to be limited, not diffused.

Vocationally superior adolescents need a certain amount of guidance. They are often not aware of their own superiority; even if they are, they sometimes want to enter fields for which they do not have the personal requirements. Unless deterred by economic conditions, most brilliant adolescents will enter the professions. What they need most is guidance into courses that will furnish a sound preparation for later work. For them, work in algebra, modern languages, history, science, literature, or written English is so much technical training. Guidance should also extend to arranging for an extra heavy load of work and enrollment in those classes most likely to supply stimulation.

The main problems of the brilliant child are undoubtedly personal. There is probably no more difficult task than the proper guidance of a prodigy. Such an individual has certain abilities developed far beyond the normal for his age; along these lines he is especially successful. Because he is successful he is likely to concentrate more and more upon his special interests. Thus the child with musical ability gets praise chiefly through exercising this ability—and the more he exercises it the more he deviates from other children. If such a child practices the violin three or four hours a day and carries on an average amount of schoolwork he obviously has no time for social contacts. He does not learn to get on with others because he has so little experience in doing so and because he has so little in common with other children. An intellectually brilliant child has the same kind of difficulty. The things he likes best to do are those that will further develop the abilities which already separate him from others in his own age group. Like any other individual, he does not like to do those things at which he is unsuccessful. By the time such a child reaches high school he may have become quite isolated and unsocial. He is, therefore, in need of help along personal lines to assist him in making social adjustments.

Brilliant students who are maladjusted show it clearly enough. Outside of class they stay by themselves; they avoid others, and others are scornful of them. They lose their self-assurance the moment class is over. They sometimes try to fight back at the discrimination they feel being exercised against them by flinging out caustic remarks about the utter futility of all nonacademic pursuits. They publicly refuse to attend football games, dances, or any other such activity, for which social rather than intellectual maturity is necessary. In short, according to their degree of vitality and combativeness, they show either a humiliating acceptance of their social ineptitude or else a derisive attitude toward others—an overcompensation for their maladjustment.

It should be unnecessary to point out the necessity for immediate attention to any poorly adjusted brilliant child. They are pre-eminently worth saving, and they can damage society to a greater extent than most people if they are allowed to grow up with twisted personalities.

Illustrative case studies.—The case studies below illustrate types of brilliant children and types of treatments. The reader should note at what age unusual ability was first noted, how it was shown, and how consistently it developed. Special adaptations by school or family should also be observed.

Donald was a talented boy of fifteen. He had shown an interest in music by the time he was two years old. When he was three he had gone with his mother to a symphony orchestra and had sat entranced through the entire performance. The next day he got two pieces of wood and held them in the position of a violinist holding his violin and bow. From this time on he began to pester his family to get him a violin. He was not yet four when he was finally given one. Within two hours he had taught himself to play a scale and within a week he was able, without any training, to play a correct scale beginning anywhere on the instrument. By that time also he had picked out two or three simple melodies. He had no lessons until he was five but by then he could play any melody he heard by ear, usually rendering it in the exact key in which it was written. His particular joy was to attend a concert and then rush home and play the tunes before he forgot them. If a concert singer had sung twelve songs, he was usually able to remember four or five perfectly, and two or three more with some slight variation. After he began to have lessons he progressed rapidly. His teacher told his mother what a genius he was, and his mother very unwisely let him know. In the pursuit of a musical education Donald is indefatigable. His mother has encouraged him to devote as much time as he will to his music. Consequently, he practically never plays with other children and has few social contacts except with his mother and teachers. His schoolteacher reports him as being disobedient, unco-operative, impudent, and aggressive. The other two children in his own family dislike him intensely because of the favoritism shown him. He never has to do anything around the house. In fact, he never even has to hang up his own clothes when he takes them off. His younger brother wipes the dishes at noon and at night, and his older sister makes his bed, dusts his room, keeps his things in order, and hangs up his clothes. He has twice as much spending money as the other children, so that he will have funds for buying music or new strings when he breaks one. Donald is scornful not only of his brother and sister but of all children who are not musical. No one except his music teacher and his mother has a good word for him. Undoubtedly Donald will some day be a famous musician, but unless he modifies his personality, he will always be a solo artist because he cannot work with others. He is a living example of how not to bring up a talented child.

Dora has an I.Q. of 168.[15] She was selected as a gifted child by her teacher when she was nine years old and in the fifth grade. She has given evidence of superior intelligence ever since her entrance into school. She skipped the first grade because she had taught herself to read when she was only five. Since then, she has been recommended for double promotion several times but has been held back by her family's disapproval. Even as early as nine years of age, Dora was described as being unusually prudent and conscientious, with an intellectual curiosity, good judgment, keen sense of humor, and an exceptional degree of artistic appreciation.

INTELLECTUAL DEVIATE

Dora is now, at the age of fourteen, in the third year of high school. She has decided to become a classical scholar and is studying both Latin and Greek, together with other classes in the academic schedule. All her work is excellent, although her linguistic work is more outstanding than her achievements in other fields.

Dora has an attractive personality. She is popular with other children and a decided leader. Recently she has grown to be very pretty, although she is still smaller than others in her class. Her play interests are normal, but she has a preference for quiet and sedentary games. She shows, however, no inclination to withdraw from competitive games on account of her size. She is a thoroughly wholesome, likable girl, from a middle-class environment to which she is well adjusted. No unusual pressure has been brought to bear upon her; she has not been pushed ahead in school nearly as rapidly as would have been possible, but has been kept with other children whose interests and nonacademic abilities parallel her own. Her high intellectual capacity has been given plenty of scope through additional assignments, through permission to take an extra heavy schedule, and through participation in extracurricular activities. As a result, she shows as good a social adjustment as any child of normal intelligence.*

At the age of sixteen Donaldine is a musician and composer.[15] The piano has always been for her a source of interest and exploration. By the time she was four years old she had shown so much spontaneous interest in music that she was given instruction. From then on music has become an increasingly important element in her existence. She has exceptional ability in sight reading and in ability to memorize a musical score. She can memorize a forty-page concerto at two or three sittings. She never brags about her musical ability, but, on the other hand, she is not embarrassed over appearing before large audiences. She began her public appearances at an early age, sometimes as a piano accompanist and sometimes as a soloist. Recently she has appeared in several important concerts. Beginning in childhood, she has steadily composed music and within the last two or three years has had several of her compositions accepted and published.

Her I.Q. on the Binet scale at the age of eleven was 138. Now, at sixteen, her Terman group scale score is slightly below the median of the entire group of sixteen-year-old gifted girls, but in the upper ten per cent of unselected girls of her age. On the

---

* These two case studies are presented by permission of the Stanford University Press.

Iowa High School Content examination she scored at the seventy-fifth percentile of unselected high school seniors. These test scores suggest that Donaldine is more talented in music than in general verbal intelligence, although she stands high in the distribution for her age even in verbal ability.

She has completed twelve grades of schoolwork in nine years and has maintained a high record of scholarship. Her extracurricular interests have included various musical productions, tennis, student government, and the German club. She is rated by her teachers as being enthusiastic, co-operative, self-reliant, and industrious. Her classmates are fond of her, although she has no special talents in leadership. She appears to be in all fields a generally superior individual who has adapted herself to the ordinary demands of society without sacrificing either her independence or her interest in music.

THE ADOLESCENT WITH INFERIOR MENTAL CAPACITY

There was a time not so long ago when a child with less than average ability was supposed to have neither vocational nor educational prospects worth considering. When the extent of individual differences was first realized it was assumed that mentally inferior individuals furnished the criminals, the paupers, the unemployed, and the unemployable. Since that time more has been learned as to the nature of mental inferiority, and of late years considerable has been done in the way of adjusting dull people to their environment. It now appears that while delinquency and other forms of asocial behavior are more frequent in a group of dull adolescents than among average or bright youngsters, they are by no means necessary accompaniments of mental inferiority.

The individuals whose mental capacity is below the average of the population may be grouped roughly into four divisions. Lowest are the idiots whose adult mental age does not exceed two years; they never go to any school. Next come the imbeciles with a mental age from three to seven or eight years; they can complete about the first two grades of school. Then come the morons with a mental age from about eight to eleven; very few of them ever finish elementary school. Finally comes the

INTELLECTUAL DEVIATE 343

dull group with adult mental ages between eleven and thirteen. These pupils form the intellectual deviates on the lower end of the high school distribution. In considering the psychology of high school pupils, the first three groups may obviously be eliminated from consideration, except as results with them illustrate what may be done even more successfully with the fourth group.

In recent years there has been considerable interest in following up the careers of defective pupils trained in the special classes of the public schools or in an institution for the feeble-minded. In one study [9] of 449 special class pupils, the social adjustment was found to be "good" for 254, "fair" for 110, and "poor" for only 85. Of this group, 230 pupils had already left school; these were further studied as to vocational adjustment. Eighty-three per cent of these graduates were adequate in their vocational adjustment; the remaining number were unemployable either because they would not work or because their earning capacities were so low as to be commercially valueless. Of the entire group, both in school and out, approximately 20 per cent were delinquent. This is a higher per cent than is usually found among well-trained children of low mentality. In another investigation only 9.2 per cent of 9,885 special class pupils were found to be delinquent.* The following study [5] shows what good results may be obtained from training children with even lower mental ability. One hundred and two feeble-minded girls, all of whom had been in an institution, were sent out into various communities, on parole. Fifty-two of these girls were living in their own homes; forty-one had made a good adjustment and were economically valuable in the home, leaving only eleven who were not getting along well. Of the other fifty girls who were living at their places of employment, only one was rated as doing poorly, twenty-five as doing well, and twenty-four as doing excellent work. In both studies, the main emphasis in the special class or institution was put upon correct behavior and vocational preparation, with an almost complete disregard for academic learning.

If morons and high-grade imbeciles can be trained so that the majority of them make good social and vocational adjust-

* Reference is made to this study in No. 9 at the end of this chapter but no exact citation was given; the study appears to have been made by the Massachusetts State Board of Education whose bulletins are not available to the writer.

ments in the community, it would seem inexcusable for the high school to fail as completely as it often does in preparing the dull and dull-normal pupil for successful work after he leaves school. To be sure this group is a relatively new component of the high school population. Below-average children did not appear in secondary school in any considerable numbers before 1910. At the present time many children with I.Q.'s as low as eighty attend high school. Because the demands made by the usual curriculum are high, these dull and low normal children occupy the same relative position to the high school population that the morons do to the elementary school group. Follow-up studies of their adjustment after leaving school, with and without previous curricular adjustments, should be made, and the education they receive in school should be modified until their success is at least as good as that shown by trained defectives.

Characteristics.—The dull and dull-normal adolescent shows his inferior ability chiefly along purely intellectual lines. He learns slowly, he has great difficulty with abstractions, he has little if any interest in books. He is typically a nonverbal, nonacademic individual. Quite often, his inferiority does not become noticeable until the years of junior high school or even later. The definite, factual material presented in elementary school he can learn—perhaps a little more slowly than other pupils. It is not until the subject matter becomes (a) too extensive and (b) too theoretical that his defects stand out clearly.

Socially and emotionally, dull adolescents are no different from anyone else, provided their environment has not made too heavy demands upon them. They can usually make and keep friends of their own or even superior ability. They can fit into the social milieu from which they come. Indeed, these dull children often get along rather better in nonacademic pursuits than brighter children; they are willing to be led, they are delighted with any attention shown them, and they are devoted to their friends. There is no reason to suppose that social incompetence is inherent in dull and low normal individuals.

Naturally, however, many dull adolescents develop undesirable personal traits because too much is asked of them. They become discouraged, disillusioned, unhappy, truculent, and sometimes delinquent. Such traits appear at any level of intelligence among those who believe themselves to be chronic failures. A good adjustment is made out of successes—not failures. If dull children show unfavorable traits more frequently than those of average ability, it is because they have more occasion for despair. In school they occupy an unenviable position at the bottom of the class. They soon learn that no matter how hard they try, their efforts will rarely be successful. As the school years roll by, they are retarded more and more until, by the time they are ready for high school, they are from one to two years behind others of their age. Such a situation arouses either a profound feeling of inferiority or a defiant attitude toward the school. Outside of school, an environment of urban civilization is too complex for them. They are called upon to render judgments involving the abstract thinking they are characteristically unable to do satisfactorily.

On the moral side, this inability to think in abstract terms is especially noticeable. The word "amoral" has been coined to describe the condition of a person who behaves contrary to accepted moral standards, not intentionally but because he is unable to grasp the underlying concepts. As explained in earlier chapters, an adolescent must achieve a mental age of at least twelve before he develops even elementary concepts; a mentality of fourteen is needed for any really adequate understanding of generalized principles of behavior. Since the dull adolescent does not have this degree of mental ability, he cannot do such thinking as is involved in a new situation. For instance, a dull adolescent boy may know that stealing is wrong and may have no intention of stealing, but he may be easily persuaded to stand guard while a friend steals. The idea that he is an accomplice in the theft or that his behavior comes under the category of dishonesty may simply never occur to him. The unscrupulous adult often gets dull adolescents into trouble by such means.

The dull adolescent is, then, a nonintellectual person who has great difficulty with any kind of abstract thinking. His school standing is usually fair to good in elementary school, but becomes steadily lower thereafter. His social adjustment depends upon his particular experiences, but is more likely to be poor than not—unless he receive special training—because both in school and out his environment makes demands that cannot be met with his intellectual equipment.

Training.—Few people seem to realize how little academic learning is necessary for the sort of work open to individuals of dull mentality. The writer once had the task of placing feeble-minded men and women in jobs. To her great surprise there was no difficulty at all in finding employment for these defectives, providing they had desirable personal traits. In fact, there were not enough defectives to satisfy the demand!

An illustration may make this point clearer. Thus, in a certain wholesale drug company twelve aspirin tablets come down a small chute when a lever is pressed. The person packing the tablets holds under the chute a box which will contain exactly twelve and arranges the pills as they come out into the box. The box is then laid on a traveling belt, which takes it to another person who puts a protective cover over the pills and closes the box. Neither of these operations requires a mental age of more than six, but, since they have to be done quickly and without spilling the pills, they require adult muscular and nervous control. Except during the depression, the employment manager has a hard time keeping such monotonous jobs filled. The trouble is that a person of average intelligence soon gets hopelessly bored and leaves his job. It takes a person of dull or defective intelligence to arrange pills in a box all day long, week after week, and still like the work. There are, undoubtedly, more "feeble-minded jobs" in any industry than there are reliable feeble-minded people to fill them.

The scholastic moral is quite clear, although it may prove distressing to certain teachers: Dull pupils need to be taught comparatively few academic skills. If a dull adolescent can read the newspaper and a few magazines, can write acceptable personal and business letters, can keep a cash account, can apply simple arithmetic to practical problems, and can make some sort of budget, he has an adequate scholastic equipment for any kind of work he is likely to do. He needs neither algebra nor Latin in order to become a good plumber. A girl needs neither chemistry nor French in order to give finger waves in a beauty parlor or to file letters correctly in a lawyer's office. There seems no good reason why the junior high or high school teachers should exhaust themselves in trying to develop in dull boys and girls skills that will never be required. The time saved from subjects that are utterly useless to inferior students can be used in training these boys and girls in good personal habits, satisfactory emotional responses, and adequate social adjustments. These matters are desirable in every individual, but to the dull they are *absolutely essential*.

A constructive program for dull adolescents in high school would, then, start with an abandoning of the traditional curriculum, which is not only overly hard but irrelevant. A program having several different elements should be substituted. First, there should be a review of the essential skills from elementary schoolwork, with direct application to various common adult problems. Second, there should be immediate preparation for earning one's living. For girls, this phase of the training would include such courses as typing, office work, sewing, cooking, domestic service, buying, child care, and so on. For boys, this vocational training would require courses in the skilled and semiskilled trades—bricklaying, carpentry, cement-mixing, tile-setting, printing, shoe-repairing, upholstering, and so on. A third element in the high school program would give direct preparation for living; this training would consist mainly of courses dealing with problems of personal hygiene, social adjustment, and homemaking. Fourth, there would be an adequate amount of training in good uses of leisure time: experience in games, in various avocational forms of handwork, in reading whatever books or magazines will be read at all, in evaluating movies, and so on. Finally there would be what, for lack of a better term, might be called "moral training." For this purpose, extracurricular activities to give experience in actual social contacts would be needed.

It should be noted that in this proposed program there is no inclusion of the subjects typically taught in high school. There would, naturally, be no objection to a given dull pupil electing, for instance, French if he felt a desire to do so. One or two such experiences will soon convince him he had better let purely academic subjects alone. The main thing to remember is that the curriculum for these pupils should in the main be different—not merely a diluted form of what already exists.

The schools that come closest to approximating a desirable schedule for dull pupils are certain of the continuation schools. These schools enroll, for the most part, children from the lower half of the distribution of intelligence. One study [7] has compared the mental growth and educational progress of pupils in regular and continuation schools. The results are summarized below for 1,197 cases.

TABLE XIX

COMPARATIVE DEVELOPMENT OF REGULAR AND CONTINUATION SCHOOL PUPILS *

	Chronological Age			
	14		15	
	Mental Age	I.Q.	Mental Age	I.Q.
Regular School	14.1	102	15.1	104
Continuation School	12.4	85	12.7	87

* This material is presented by permission of the Harvard University Press.

The pupils in continuation schools are obviously an inferior group, so far as verbal intelligence is concerned. The educational treatment of these students before leaving the regular schools deserves comment. When one compares their grade placement with their mental age one finds a curious maladjustment, as indicated below:

TABLE XX

MENTAL AGE AND GRADE PLACEMENT

	Elementary School	High School
Per Cent Accelerated	50	3
Per Cent Normal	30	8
Per Cent Retarded	20	89

Neither elementary nor high school adjusts well to these pupils; in the former they are promoted too fast for their mental ability and in the latter, too slowly. It is probable that the high school course of study was for them quite inappropriate; hence the failures which resulted in grade placements below the level of their ability. Because of the nature of its pupils the continuation school has been forced into making a more adequate adjustment to dullness than the regular schools.

It goes without saying that the dull adolescent needs vocational guidance. In the selection of a vocation, he is more likely than not to make mistakes. Many occupations are closed to him, but he is not yet old enough to know it. He may fix his imagination upon some occupation which is not at all appropriate to his abilities. If he persists, in the face of advice, in going on with his unfortunate choice he meets with years of discouragement and failure. If he listens to advice and gives up his ambition, he is at best temporarily disillusioned and may carry a feeling of discouragement for the rest of his life. Early and frequent help in selecting a vocation is needed.

However, the dull pupil has one characteristic that is of great commercial value—only he does not know it. In all probability he likes monotony. He likes it for the same reason a child does. Anything that occurs often enough to become monotonous is also very familiar. Both children and dull adults are uncomfortable if they have to change from what they are doing to something new. During the high school years inferior pupils should be so well trained for simple, monotonous jobs that they can fit easily and well after leaving school into some task already familiar to them.

Personal problems of dull adolescents.—The dull adolescent requires careful and tactful handling. His first problem is to learn how to live contentedly in a social milieu to which he can adjust. A solution to this problem requires that he achieve an unpleasant emotional tone towards those things he cannot do and a pleasant emotional tone toward the things he can do successfully. Many a dull boy who knows from working in a garage that he can repair cars becomes ashamed of such work because he thinks labor with one's hands is somehow degrading. He believes he will command greater respect if he tries to enter a "white-collar" occupation, even though he may feel a consistent dislike for the kind of thing a white-collar man does. What such a boy has gotten from his education is a discontent with the type of thing in which he is both interested and successful. Any school that tries to make scholars out of its dull adolescents will succeed only in producing academic failures instead of successful artisans.

One of the unfortunate effects of recent efforts at universal education has been this tendency to look down upon honest labor. There are many causes for this attitude. Some teachers are undoubtedly sincere in their efforts to "raise the standards" and "uplift the downtrodden" by means of education. Such enthusiasm is touching, but largely impractical. Secondly, teachers themselves belong to a white-collar occupation; they are therefore likely to convey to the pupils their own attitude toward other types of work. Practically all teachers in the elementary schools and the majority of teachers in the upper years are women; they do not know much about masculine trades and are inclined to look down upon what they do not understand. Then there is the bookish curriculum that rewards the verbally gifted and punishes by failure those not so endowed. Finally, there is the widespread opinion—which may or may not be justified by facts—that the further students go in school the higher type of job they are likely to get. (No one knows if this statement is true because investigations fail to take account of the differences in verbal competency and general mental level between those who drop out of school at any given point and those who continue with their education beyond that point.) As a result of all these tendencies there has developed a general attitude that "handwork" is degrading.

This attitude must be overcome and supplanted, in the case of the dull, with a feeling of pride in a job well done, no matter what it is. All kinds of honest labor are necessary to a community and no kind is any "better" than any other. The writer can and does repair her own car, fix electric fixtures, resole shoes, prepare meals, clean rooms, iron clothes, engrave silverware, and raise vegetables. Why any of this should be thought of as more "menial" than writing a book or teaching a class remains a mystery. If the dull adolescent can be so conditioned as to feel a warm glow of satisfaction over such work as a good job of house-painting, half his troubles are over because he has learned to be content with "that state of life into which it has pleased God to call him."

The dull adolescent's second personal problem is the acquisition of acceptable social and moral behavior. For his own safety, he must have achieved the necessary habits before he leaves school. Before him lie the usual stresses and strains incident to anyone's life. He will be called upon to make decisions, and he will not have the independent mental capacity to reason out for himself what decision he should make. Only habits so ingrained as to be an integral part of himself will bring him safely through danger. He—like everyone else—will be given opportunities to steal, drink, or gamble; he will be tempted to dodge his responsibilities; he will come in contact with many unscrupulous people. What he does in crises will depend upon how thoroughly he has been trained in acceptable modes of behavior. If he leaves high school as a thoroughly happy individual, well adjusted to his social group, equipped with what vocational and academic skills he will need to earn a living, enthusiastic about his work, and well grounded in fundamental habits of honesty, responsibility, and decency, the dull adolescent is no more likely to err than the rest of mankind.

Illustrative case studies.—In reading the case studies below one should keep in mind the following points: What were the signs of inferior mental ability and at what age did these symptoms appear? What adjustments did the school make to low capacity? Could it have made any other adjustments? What reactions made by the pupils described seem due to unnecessary demands made by the school? In those cases showing delinquency what other elements than stupidity brought about difficulty? In the studies not showing delinquency, what were the stabilizing influences that prevented such developments? What vocational ambitions did these adolescents have and to what extent did these ideas lead to disillusionment? Did the pupils have any interest or skill that might have been of commercial value?

Warren was a boy with an "average" mental equipment.[16] He went through the elementary grades without any special difficulty and was standing above the middle of his class when he finished the sixth grade at the age of eleven and a half years. He began to slump in the seventh grade and by the time he had reached the eighth grade his work had become so poor, and was so carelessly done, that his father had to begin helping him at home.

Warren's father was a clergyman. Little is known about the early relation between father and son. The mother reported that on one occasion the father had cried out impatiently something about Warren's being a "stupid" fellow who never could learn anything. She attached considerable importance to this and thought it accounted for Warren's feeling of inferiority.

It was not until Warren entered high school, however, that the trouble became acute. His father's own description of this experience is most enlightening.

"Warren's first year in high school was very bad for him. He was taking the college preparatory course. I gave him constant attention, assisting him with his Latin and algebra, and, towards the end of the year, with his ancient history. He did his English by himself but I think he would have failed in this if his teacher had set proper standards. In March he became very nervous, and it was evident that he could not carry all the work. He dropped his Latin, and, by dint of personal attention from me, succeeded in getting through the rest of his studies.

"He spent the summer at Camp B and did very well, winning the camp letter and passing the Junior Red Cross lifesaving test.

"In the fall he returned again to the local high school. It soon became evident that he could not carry the work without a great deal of help. He was *very greatly discouraged* and *nervous*. When I worked with him he would get "nerved up." It was wearing on me. At this point his mother took things practically into her own hands and made arrangements for him to go to a private school.

"He appears to have been very happy and to have behaved well, but he has failed most of his subjects."

The father's letter then continues with a revealing description of the boy's behavior.

"One of the marked features of his case is that he refers to himself as a 'dumbbell' and says that he will never amount to anything. One night this June, after he had been at home for about two weeks, he had a bitter crying spell about his failure in school and said that he would have to go off and live as a hermit for the rest of his life as he could not be of any use in the world.

"He teases his younger brothers and that has many times led to bad quarrels. At times he has exasperated me almost to distraction by his insolence. I used to give him corporal punishment, and I have at times struck him in anger. I am fully aware that I have not always dealt calmly and wisely with him.

"Since he has been back from New Hampshire, he has been working in a local store, using an adding machine and doing miscellaneous clerical work. So far he has not been discharged. He seems happy in this work and likes both his superiors and his associates.

"So far as we know, he is clean morally. He does not smoke."

INTELLECTUAL DEVIATE

This perhaps serves to suggest enough of the father's attitude. His letter continues for several more pages in the same vein. He is chagrined to the limits of his power of self-control that *he*, a man who has always set great store by intellectual accomplishments, and was always successful in his own scholastic endeavors, should have so stupid and dull a son!*

Louise F,[13] a robust, dull sixteen-year-old girl, was referred as a conduct problem, having handed in another girl's homework for her own, forged her parents' signatures on her report cards, changed F's for failures in two subjects to P's, and stolen money from a pocketbook. Her classroom record was "lazy, talkative, defiant, and disobedient." She ranked as a third-term pupil, academic course, but should have been sixth.

Louise is the oldest of three children, all girls. Both parents received considerable education in Russia, their native country. They came to America when young and speak English fluently. The father has been successful in business, has provided a comfortable home for his family in a good neighborhood, and both he and his wife desire to give their children all possible advantages, chief among which is an education. The mother is a domineering, energetic nervous woman who likes to plan ahead and who is apt to be upset if things do not turn out as she expects. She has been greatly disappointed over Louise's high school record, which for lack of a better reason she has attributed to inferior application and effort. The second daughter is delicate and neurotic, but to her mother's joy she is well advanced in her classes, and she is continually urged to fresh achievements by bribes of money and fine clothes. The youngest is healthy, but has night terrors and resorts to tantrums if foiled in her attempts to get her way.

It was easy to understand Louise's problem. She has not sufficient intelligence to enable her to master an academic high school course, but her family and most of her teachers have not realized this fundamental difficulty. Her mother openly expressed her disappointment and vexation. She attempted to goad her to do better by ridicule, sarcasm, and constant comparison with her brighter sister, of whom Louise was bitterly jealous. She was referred to as "the successful failure"; she was made to study aloud that her mother might know that she was studying; recreation was reduced to a minimum in order that she might concentrate on nothing but school. For the same reason she was compelled to give up a Sat-

*This case study is used by permission of the D. Appleton-Century Company.

urday position as sales girl. This she had greatly enjoyed, as she had the satisfaction of knowing that in this work she was acceptable and it was pleasant to earn, even though her family made sarcastic comments on her lack of ambition in being willing to be a Fourteenth Street clerk.

She dreaded the time when report cards were given out, as it meant humiliation, a fresh sense of failure, renewed bitterness of invidious comparisons between her and the "darling daughter"—as she cuttingly called her more favored sister—and often the loss of things promised her. Hence her cheating. The classwork was so far over her head that she had no real interest in it; consequently she was bored, restless, disorderly. The defiance and disobedience shown to certain teachers probably sprang from a revolt against authority and a desire to be self-assertive, which may have been a compensation for her very definite feeling of inferiority.

Naturally, she was an active, happy, rather boisterous girl, whose greatest delight was in sports. She liked, too, certain kinds of handwork where she got concrete results from her efforts, such as making bead bags and sweaters. For the same reason she was interested in cooking "fancy dishes" for the family which, because they were out of the ordinary, brought her favorable comment.

The plan for this girl involved (1) an attempt to make her family realize that she was not fitted for academic work. Great care was taken during the interviews to stress the fact that she could do something of a more practical nature, an ability as valuable in its way as the ability to deal with abstract material. Emphasis was laid on the faultiness of the mother's methods. All this paved the way for permission for (2) a change of course to include cooking and sewing. Then, (3) special efforts were made to get her teachers interested in her, and she was encouraged to believe that she could succeed in new lines of work. And (4) she was allowed to join a club of boys and girls of her own age.

Her mother proved most co-operative and asked to be told of books and lectures that would aid her in understanding and properly training her children. The school was most helpful in carrying out suggestions, and, as she became happier and more interested, Louise ceased to be a conduct problem.*

John [16] was a well-developed boy, thirteen years of age, whose family background had supplied him with sufficient cultural and social interests to assure his maximum intellectual development. He was referred to the psychiatrist because of his failure to live

* This case study is used by permission of the authors.

up to the expectations of his parents who were disappointed in the poor quality of his schoolwork and disturbed over his attitude of rebelliousness and resentfulness toward all authority at home.

John had an ordinary intellectual equipment with an I.Q. of 103. He was receiving low marks in most of his school subjects, and even those marks were questioned by his parents who thought that the masters were inclined to pass too lightly over his failures. He had been kept up with his class by much extra effort during the school year and persistent tutoring during his vacations. He had, however, reached the stage where repeating a grade seemed inevitable.

Unfortunately for John, both his father and mother had so few interests outside the home that their chief occupation was trying to stimulate their only son to do better work in school. When they were not themselves actively engaged in this occupation, a tutor and governess were doing the job for them.

This boy had already come to a realization of the fact that, compared to most of the boys attending his school, he was intellectually inferior. His self-assertive attitude at home was in part an outward expression of his resultant feeling of inadequacy and in part an effort to break away from the constant supervision which he felt he had outgrown.

Unfortunately this boy's family traditions required that he have a college education—not only that, but an education in a college where scholastic standing was the highest and athletic competition the keenest. The mere preparation for college was an intellectual task of which this boy was manifestly incapable and in which, in spite of all application and effort, failure was inevitable.

John is still grinding away, unhappy and disgruntled with life, getting nothing out of his school life but mediocre marks. He is cut off from the social contacts he should be developing, and he contributes nothing to the satisfaction of his parents except in so far as he keeps alive the flame of hope that some day he will be allowed to enter the sacred halls in the temple of learning where his father trod.*

BIBLIOGRAPHY †

1. Baldwin, B. T., and Stecher, L., "Mental Growth Curves of Normal and Superior Children," *University of Iowa Studies in Child Welfare,* Vol. II, 1922, 61 pp.

* This case study is used by permission of the D. Appleton-Century Company.
† See also the references in the Appendix.

2. Burks, B. S., Jensen, D. W., and Terman, L. M., *Genetic Studies of Genius,* Vol. III: *The Promise of Youth,* Stanford University Press, 1930, 508 pp.
3. Cohen, H. L., and Coryell, N. G., *Educating Superior Students,* American Book Company, 1935, 340 pp.
4. Eckert, R. E., "Who is the Superior Student?", *University of Buffalo Studies,* 1934, 9: 11-50.
5. Frankel, E., Heyer, H. E., *et al.,* "Institutional Education and Training for Community Release," *New Jersey State Board of Control of Institutions and Agencies,* 1933, No. 24, 28 pp.
6. Hollingworth, L. S., *Gifted Children,* The Macmillan Company, 1926, 374 pp.
7. Hopkins, L. T., *Intelligence of Continuation School Children in Massachusetts,* Harvard University Press, 1924, 132 pp.
8. Lamson, E. E., "A Study of Young Gifted Children in Senior High School," *Teachers College Contributions to Education,* No. 424, 1930, 117 pp.
9. Lord, A. B., "Survey of 445 Special Class Pupils," *Journal of Educational Research,* 1933, 27: 108-114.
10. Mills, H. C., "Subject and Activity Load of High School Juniors," *University of Buffalo Studies,* 1934, 9: 87-102.
11. Sarbaugh, M. E., "The Young College Student," *University of Buffalo Studies in Administration,* 1934, 9: 75-84.
12. Schott, E. L., "A Study of High School Seniors of Superior Merit," *University of Missouri Bulletin,* Vol. 26, No. 13, 1926, 52 pp.
13. Spence, R. B., and Watson, G. B., *Sketches in and out of School,* 1927, 286 pp.
14. Steckel, M. L., "A 'Follow-Up' of Mentally Defective Girls," *Journal of Social Psychology,* 1934, 5: 112-115.
15. Terman, L. M., *Genetic Studies of Genius,* Vol. I, Stanford University Press, 1925, 641 pp.
16. Thom, D. A., *Normal Youth and Its Everyday Problems,* D. Appleton-Century Company, 1932, 367 pp.

CHAPTER XI

THE VOCATIONAL MISFIT

An adult's chief business in life is to work, and his chief joys come from his successes in the world of practical accomplishment—whether his achievements consist in selling real estate, composing operas, laying sewers, or designing hats. Because success on the job is so important in adult life, it is a terrific blow to fail—either actually or in relation to one's expectations. Indeed, there is no emotional experience to be avoided more zealously than the realization that one is an economic failure. In addition, the individual concerned—now handicapped by an exhausting emotional experience—must start all over in some new line of work, which must obviously be no better than a second choice. Not all debacles can be either foreseen or prevented, but much agony of spirit and loss of confidence can be avoided if pupils in school are started toward vocations for which they are adequately fitted.

One main task of any school is to graduate students who are well adjusted to the demands of life. A school that lets its pupils attempt work in which failure is almost certain will inevitably graduate students who are poorly adjusted. Unfortunately for educational progress, the worst economic crises come after pupils have left school. Consequently, the school does not feel the force of many calamities for which it is at least partly to blame. Economic failure and disillusionment are particularly hard to bear because they destroy an adult's self-respect, disorganize his personality, and ruin his sense of security in his world. It is always a tragedy to let pupils embark blindly on inappropriate careers.

Vocations may be inappropriate for a given student for any of a number of reasons. In the first section of this chapter various kinds of vocational maladjustment will be briefly described. This survey is for the purpose of showing the wide range of problems involved. The second section of the chapter will present certain considerations of importance for the better guidance of adolescents into their future occupations.

EXAMPLES OF VOCATIONAL MALADJUSTMENT

To some extent, the first part of this chapter will present a cross section of previous chapters. A pupil may be maladjusted vocationally because he is neurotic, because he is too dull or too bright for his ambitions, or because he possesses unfavorable personal traits. However, the vocational misfit is so common in high school that all types must be described—even at the risk of a little repetition.

(1) Some pupils are attempting to enter lines of work for which they do not have the physical vitality or strength. For instance, a diabetic boy wants to become an aviator or a tubercular girl wants to be a nurse. Although such adolescents may recover from their ailments, they are unlikely to have the physical energy necessary for occupations that make such heavy demands upon health.

(2) Other pupils may be determined to enter occupations quite unsuitable to their type of personality. Every teacher knows the boy or girl with an unsympathetic nature but brilliant mind who wants to be a doctor; even though the unfavorable personal traits may be somewhat modified by training, the individual is unlikely to attract or keep patients. There is room at the top of a profession for all kinds of people, but beginners have to start at the bottom and compete with others; in the early stages an unfavorable personality will lead to disaster. If such an unsympathetic, unpopular adolescent can be persuaded to go into medical research instead of medical practice, he and the world may both be better off. Then, there is the girl with a flair for clothes and a complete inability to get along with people, who wants to be a wholesale buyer in a large department store. She could, very likely, hold such a job once she got it,

VOCATIONAL MISFIT

but during the intervening years she would have to begin as cash girl and rise in the ranks—a matter that calls for the personal qualities she conspicuously lacks. Or, there may be a hyperactive, athletic, extroverted girl who thinks she wants to be a reference librarian, even though it is perfectly clear to others she could never sit still long enough without imposing terrific strain upon herself. A list of such *mésalliances* between personality and ambition could be continued indefinitely. To be sure, personality can be more or less modified—and will be as time goes by. The most dangerous point in such situations is the adolescent's complete lack of realization concerning his handicap. He optimistically supposes that because he *wants* to do something he has both the ability and the personal traits needed.[10] If he is willing to set about changing himself radically, that is a different matter and he can perhaps succeed; at least he should know where he stands.

(3) Still other pupils are maladjusted vocationally because they are planning to enter work either much below or much above their intellectual level. There is the brilliant, young, athletic boy who likes games and thinks he wants to be a football coach. He probably would make an excellent coach, but when he has outgrown the first flush of youth he will wish he were trained to do something requiring less physical vitality and providing more play for his mental superiority. Or, there is the dull girl who talks about becoming a dietitian, although it is clear she could never pass the required courses in chemistry. If she has an interest in the planning and preparation of food, she might forget the theoretical considerations and become a cook! As already pointed out, it is a sad commentary on modern education that so many adolescents want to enter occupations entirely beyond their mental capacity. These overambitious pupils form the largest maladjusted group.

(4) Still other pupils are headed for distress later on because they want to enter a vocation for which some special skill is needed—and they either lack the skill altogether or have it to only a slight extent. In this group come especially the embryo artists, musicians, writers, actors, and actresses. The

boy who likes to play the tuba wants to enter the ranks of the professional musician, while the girl who can make a recognizable copy of a bunch of daisies is fired with the desire to be a portrait painter. The girl with a small, sweet voice is willing to stake her family's entire financial resources on her ability to become an opera star, and the boy who can execute a couple of clog steps thinks he can earn a living in vaudeville. A little talent is a dangerous thing. It is true that a small per cent of such adolescents will actually succeed in these occupations—at the cost of Herculean effort, much expense, and many years of apprenticeship—but the vast majority are beaten before they ever start.

(5) Somewhat similar problems are presented by those adolescents who are headed for an occupation in which they will need as daily tools certain academic skills they have never acquired. In this group comes the future newspaper reporter who can neither spell nor construct simple sentences, the embryo college professor who has an active distaste for foreign languages, and the engineer-to-be who does deplorable work in all forms of mathematics. Such deficiencies can, of course, be remedied, but only by efforts far more strenuous than most young people are willing to make.

(6) Other adolescents have made the common error of so surrounding some occupation with a halo of emotional daydreams that they cannot see its true characteristics; if they could, nothing would persuade them to enter it. There is the delicate lad who wants to be a surgeon, but cannot bear the thought of touching a dead body or of seeing a live body bleed. He idealizes the work of the surgeon and never for a moment thinks of him as other doctors describe him—the "human plumber." Or, there is the girl who regards teaching as an intellectual laying-on-of-hands and has no suspicion of the interminable chores that constitute a good share of the teacher's daily work.

(7) There is another group of adolescents who want to enter occupations that will emphasize in them the very characteristics most in need of elimination. There is the overactive,

overtalkative boy who wants to become a traveling salesman; he likes to be always on the go, but he needs mainly to relax. He will make a star salesman—while he lasts. Or, there is the girl who is already intolerably conceited and artificial, who shows some latent ability as an actress; during her training days she will have to submerge her conceit, but if she is successful, these traits will be fed until she becomes an utterly impossible person. Then, there is the repressed, sex-curious, excitable girl who wants to go into clinical work as a means of gaining vicarious experiences. She will get an enormous thrill out of her cases, and she will do them more harm than good; what clinical cases need is less emotion in the environment, not more. It is admittedly hard to steer an adolescent away from occupations in which he will develop further a trait that already gives him enjoyment at the cost of sane development. However, it often needs to be done.

(8) Another group of future malcontents includes those who have settled upon a vocation for which there is little or no demand as long as one is young. Probably the most conspicuous example of this type is the adolescent who wants to "write." Such an ambition may be excellent as an ultimate goal, but the demand for youthful writers is infinitesimal. Other adolescents want to become buyers, heads of business concerns, foremen, psychiatrists, vocational counselors, school superintendents, or deans of women. The holders of such jobs are at least nearing middle age; most of them are between forty and sixty. The boy or girl must live for several years before his advice is worth listening to. Other adolescents are interested in executive positions. These also are open only to the mature, and if chance places a young person at an executive post he is usually unsuccessful. If a boy or girl wishes to plan ahead for his or her later years, that is quite desirable. But the adolescent must find some other, though related, occupation for the long years that inevitably stretch between him and his maturity.

(9) One further, and less obvious, type of difficulty is shown by those adolescents who are preparing themselves for lines of work in which there is no present demand, owing to an

existing oversupply. There are, for instance, always more stenographers and typists than there are positions. Every year too many English teachers are graduated. The maladjustment in such cases is not necessarily apparent during the period of training, but it exists and in the course of time will appear.

(10) Only those adolescents all too well acquainted with financial limitations are likely to consider the cost of an education. As a result, there are in any school many pupils engaged in types of training they cannot afford to finish; neither can they afford not to finish the training, because half the course is of no particular value. The boy from a middle-class home who has the qualifications for becoming a lawyer, for instance, may be quite unwise in his choice because his family cannot possibly support him for the next eight or ten years. Naturally, there are exceptional students who can hope for scholarships and certain other vigorous adolescents who can work their way through college and technical school without becoming physical wrecks in the process. However, any pupil is maladjusted if he cannot expect reasonable financial aid throughout a long course of training upon which he proposes to embark. He would do well to take a shorter training for some other job, preferably related to his original ambition, go to work, and save enough money to pay his own way. The main ambition does not need to be disregarded permanently, but it will have to be shelved temporarily; indeed, the only way to save it is to obtain adequate preparation as soon as possible for a less exacting vocation that may be followed for a few years. It is no accident that most doctors were first hospital orderlies, pharmacists, or laboratory assistants.

(11) Among girls there is another common type—those who are hypnotized by the idea of a career when all they really want is a home and children. In the first rush of women into occupations formerly closed to them, altogether too many girls sacrificed their true ambitions, pursued a career, and eventually became second-rate professors, lawyers, and doctors. At the present time, of course, marriage and a career can be combined, in case girls really want both. But the majority do not. They

want romance, a home, a husband, children, and social life in a small community. Many girls, however, seem to feel that such aspirations show a lamentable lack of modernity and ambition. If they would only admit their real interests and learn all they could about homes and children they would be much happier. Being a successful wife and mother is just as much a career as being a successful office manager, and it requires just as much training.

(12) Then there are the boys and girls who are pursuing a line of work because of parental pressure. If they have no other active interest, they may be as well off in that field of endeavor as anywhere else, but if they have legitimate reasons for expecting better success along other lines, or if the work they are taking is acutely distasteful, they should be encouraged to strike out for themselves. Parental approval and the resulting assistance in getting a job are valuable assets; an adolescent who throws them overboard should be very sure he knows what he is doing. The inevitable period of readjustment to the family may be difficult; it will justify the effort only if the adolescent is really maladjusted in the first place.

(13) Finally, there is the large group of adolescents without any vocational objective at all. Their one real concern is to elect courses that will not be too hard. Whatever information one can get from them is usually negative; they are no more interested in one thing than another; there are merely certain lines in which their lack of interest is particularly abysmal. Some such adolescents are as yet unawakened and will, later on, find an ambition in themselves. Others will never really want to do anything involving hard work. If these latter can be guided into the so-called "dead-end" occupations, it would be a good idea for all concerned. Such jobs have to be filled; the holders of them might well be recruited from the ranks of those who do not particularly care what they do and have neither the ambition nor the vitality to assume greater responsibilities.

Fully a dozen reasons—in fact, a baker's dozen—for vocational maladjustment have been cited, and there are doubtless others. Moreover, all adolescents need more or less assistance in planning their life work. Some get at home all the sympathetic help, understanding, and information they need; the majority, however, require guidance that can best be furnished by trained counselors in the school.

VOCATIONAL GUIDANCE IN THE HIGH SCHOOL

The material in the foregoing section should have demonstrated the need for vocational guidance. High school pupils, even with such aid as furnished them by the advice of parents and friends, are still likely to make unwise vocational choices. It is because of this situation that in recent years there has been a development of interest in vocational counseling.

In general, vocational guidance has suffered from too much giving of advice and too little giving of information. What the high school student needs from the vocational counselor is information about possible occupations and about himself. Advice should be given sparingly, and primarily to those pupils who are unable alone to face reality. The following section will discuss what information should be provided about jobs and about people, if the facts are to help the adolescent.

Information in regard to occupations.—In a later chapter dealing with the curriculum there is a recommendation for a course on "occupations," to be required of all freshmen and sophomores in high school. During the freshman year this course should present a survey of possible lines of work. During the second year there should be actual observation for each pupil according to his interests. The material here presented indicates the nature and content of this recommended program.

A general course on occupations should describe a large assortment of jobs. Naturally, there is neither time nor justification for telling pupils about every possible job any of them may sometime hold. The person in charge of such a course should, however, be sure to select a wide variety of occupations and to present, without prejudice, *all* lines of adult economic activity. In regard to the occupations presented, a considerable amount of exact information should be given.

The first items of information deal with the length of training necessary for entrance into a line of work, the average cost of training, the school courses required, the strain involved, the degree of competition, and the probable per cent of elimination during the training period. The length of time and the cost of preparation are obviously important items. The minimum amount of training is for many occupations definitely known: a college professor must complete high school, college, and at least three years of graduate study; a locomotive engineer must graduate from a trade school, must take about a year's special training, and must usually work up through the ranks as repairman and fireman; the certified accountant must have the equivalent of a college education, while the bookkeeper can get along with a year of special work after high school; the salesman needs at least to finish high school and must usually complete a special course on salesmanship varying in length from one to three months. In fact, only such unskilled jobs as running an elevator may be obtained by the person with no more than grammar school training.

The cost of education for any particular line of work depends mainly upon the length of time involved, but to some extent upon the nature of the training and the opportunities to earn one's living during the period. The cost of textbooks and equipment must both be included in estimating the financial burden of an education.[2] The opportunity for work during the training period varies according to the location of the school and the nature of the training. Students intending to work should be told something of the burdens involved in carrying the double load of a wage earner and a student. They should plan to carry only half a normal academic load and to double the length of their training period. Such matters must be considered in the plans of American youth, because a large proportion of them will find some degree of remunerative work necessary to meet the costs of their education.

It may seem to the adult that the school program necessary

for reaching a given goal is self-evident, but it is not at all obvious to high school pupils. Most adolescents do not know that an architect must also be a mathematician, or that a college professor must be something of a linguist. In the course on occupations, description of a given job should always be accompanied by sample courses of study leading toward the job, to inform the adolescent precisely what he will have to learn in order to reach his objective. Thus, the girl who wants to graduate from college in home economics with the idea of becoming a restaurant manager will see three years of chemistry, a year of physics, and considerable training in various household arts on her prospective schedule. The boy who wants to complete the college training course for football coaches will find waiting for him heavy doses in natural and social science. The high school teacher will discover technical courses in education, including statistics, plus a heavy concentration of classes in her major subject. Such programs of work will do much toward persuading the incompetent student to avoid lines of work for which he would have to master subject matter of a type he knows he cannot learn.

The strain and competition involved in preparation for a given task must also be discussed. During the training period both these elements are mainly correlated with the length of the training, but there are still differences between courses of equal length. Some lines of work require unusual physical vitality; some involve unusual nervous strain. The degree of competition in a course of study depends largely upon the demand for graduates. When there is an oversupply of people trained for a given occupation, there results a raising of standards in the training classes and a resulting increase in competition. Strain of this type becomes greater the nearer a pupil is to the minimal ability necessary for completion of the course.

Altogether too few pupils have any comprehension of the elimination that takes place during a course of training. Facts about elimination should be assembled for a large assortment of occupations and then presented to the students. The particular example here used is based on estimates instead of actual research, but it will serve to illustrate the type of information needed.

Suppose, for instance, that in the freshman year of high school in a large city one hundred pupils have the ambition to become surgeons. If a record was kept of these freshmen, their educational and economic history would be about as follows: Of the one hundred, not more than sixty would finish high school, being either eliminated altogether or diverted into less onerous lines of work. Of the sixty high school graduates, perhaps forty-five would enter college. Here they would begin a premedical course which consists largely of science. Because of the general oversupply in the medical profession, there will be a definite attempt to eliminate as many students as justifiable during their premedical years. As a result, about eighteen of the forty-five will complete the course and apply for entrance to medical school. Of this eighteen, not more than about ten will be accepted—and of the ten, not more than six will graduate. During the years of internship at least one young M.D. will be found wanting. In all probability, one of the remaining five will have characterological difficulties which prevent him from going into any kind of work in which human contacts are essential, and he will become a laboratory worker. The remaining four will discover that very few people care to entrust their lives to a young surgeon; these doctors will therefore be forced into general practice for a few years. At least one of them will find the economic burden of setting up an office and waiting for patients more than his resources will stand and will be forced into some line of work allied to medicine—and may never return. Of the three survivors, two will remain general practitioners, partly because having built up a general practice they do not dare for financial reasons to abandon it, and partly because their skill as a surgeon did not develop as expected. Finally, there may be one of the original one hundred who succeeds in becoming a surgeon.

Naturally, no such high elimination takes place in shorter and less exacting lines of work, but the exact degree per one hundred cases should be determined for many occupations and the facts set before the high school freshmen, so that they may know what to expect if they attempt to follow out a particular ambition.

The next point to consider is the usefulness of an incomplete course. There are, for instance, extremely few lines of work into which a half-trained lawyer can enter with any better chances of success than a person without half a lawyer's training. On the other hand, a student who has completed half a mechanical course can find many uses for what he has. The necessity for completing a course before it is of vocational value has been almost entirely neglected in discussions of guidance.

There remain for consideration the opportunities for employment and the probable salary range to be expected at the close of the training and in subsequent years. Pupils have no way whatever of knowing which occupations are already overcrowded and which are understaffed, nor are they likely to obtain such information from teachers of special subjects. In the last analysis, a teacher's own job is dependent upon enrollments. It is, therefore, not likely that he will tell students too much about lack of opportunities in the field for which he is training them. If, for instance, schools of education broadcasted their inability to place all their graduates, their enrollment would go down, some of their staff would be forced to resign, and less financial backing would be received. No collection of human beings is going to talk itself out of a job! If high school pupils are to be given unprejudiced facts in regard to various occupations, this information must be furnished by some individual unconnected with any department. It goes without saying that such data will enter into the making of vocational choices.

The salary range for any given job is poorly defined in the average adolescent's mind. In the first place, any sum over $5.00 looms large in adolescent eyes, and a prospective salary of $1,000 a year may seem to him sufficient for any needs he could ever have. Except for the few wealthy pupils, there is little appreciation among boys and girls of any large sum of money. In the second place, an adolescent is likely to know only of the remarkably successful individuals in a given line. He thus hears of a lawyer who receives a $10,000 fee for every case, of a doctor who charges $5,000 per operation, of an architect who never designs a public building for less than $25,000,

VOCATIONAL MISFIT

of an engineer who is paid $100,000 for constructing a bridge, of a broker who makes a half million a year on the market, of an automobile salesman who clears $20,000 a year on commissions, or of a novelist who makes $50,000 on a single book. These examples dazzle his imagination. What the pupil does not know is the range of salaries received by all lawyers, doctors, engineers, salesmen, brokers, and novelists. They do not suspect, for instance, that some doctors do not even earn their living expenses. Such information might offset the impression made by the one doctor in a thousand who earns large fees. A simple chart showing the overlapping of salaries, ranging from those of the unskilled laborer to those of the business and professional man, would be highly illuminating. Such data would also show the financial returns of white-collar versus artisan jobs; the supposed superiority of the former disappears when entire distributions are considered. Moreover, there should be some attention given to the usual number of failures, not to discourage adolescents unduly, but to show them what actually does happen in the economic world.

The need for information, even in college, along the lines just enumerated is well shown by a recent study.[8] Out of 888 university students, 95 per cent were planning to enter teaching, medicine, law, or dentistry—the four outstandingly overcrowded vocations in the country. The students were asked to state also how much they expected to earn per annum. The average student expected a salary four times as high as that earned by the average worker in whatever field he was intending to enter. If college men can be so blind to realities, one can hardly look for much judgment among high school pupils.

It goes without saying that descriptions of work along various lines should be included in a course on occupations. Verbal descriptions are, however, not particularly convincing. They make dry reading and, even when carefully studied, give an inadequate picture of a job. For this reason it has been suggested, in a course of study later to be discussed, that the second year of vocational work be devoted to actual observation in various occupations, and to some degree of apprenticeship on the job. The arrangements for such observation will naturally vary from one community to another, depending upon a variety of factors. There is, however, no substitute for direct study. An adolescent will learn more about a job during a week's observation of some individual at work than he will learn from reading innumerable descriptions.

In this connection, the writer would like to suggest the establishment of a "Work Week" during the sophomore year of high school, preferably at the close of the first semester, after the final examinations in academic courses have been given. During this Work Week each student in the school would be assigned to some worker, through arrangements already made with various individuals and concerns. Thus, the girl who wanted to be a sales clerk would be assigned to observe, and, if possible, to assist a saleslady in some store. The girl who wanted to be a teacher would spend each school day in some teacher's room observing what is actually done. The boy who wanted to be a mechanic would see work in a garage, while the prospective lawyer would spend some days in court watching cases being tried and other days in a lawyer's office observing the preparation of cases for trial. Exploratory work of this sort already done by various vocational counselors has shown that plenty of adults can be found who will take under their chaperonage for a week an adolescent boy or girl who wishes to observe a given type of work. Naturally not all phases of a particular job could be demonstrated, but some degree of practical acquaintance with various activities could be obtained, thus substituting direct knowledge for the adolescent's own imaginative notions. Such a system of apprenticeship would do a great deal toward clarifying the problem of vocational choice.

It should be noted that all points stressed above deal with information, not advice. The main objective of vocational guidance should be to get before students an array of objective facts. With adequate information at hand, most adolescents will make a wise choice. In assembling data of this sort, especial care should be taken to include all levels of work. There is a tendency in available courses on occupations to stress the types of work requiring the greatest training and to omit descriptions of simple jobs. As a result, all too many adolescents get the idea, referred to in a previous connection, that only white-collar jobs are respectable. The high school population at any given moment must furnish the individuals who will in the next generation occupy all kinds of jobs above the level of the day laborer, who is recruited mostly from those who do not reach high school; therefore, any consideration of occupations should stress equally and without prejudice the entire range of jobs into which high school students will go. In fact, there should be, if anything, rather more emphasis upon the work of the artisan and the less exacting types of clerical work than upon occupations demanding a college education. The prospective librarian, dietitian, wholesale buyer, lawyer, high school teacher, banker, or chemist will have several years beyond the first two in high school, and in these succeeding years further guidance can be given. The object in putting the required work on vocations into the first two years of high school is to make it available to those who will go no further. For the prospective plumber, carpenter, garage mechanic, filing clerk, and sales girl, the first two years of high school often give the last opportunity for constructive guidance. It is therefore essential that work of all types should be presented and that no work at any level should be labeled, openly or by implication, as being menial or unworthy. Emphasis on the social prestige of various vocations should be largely omitted. The work of the world has to be done, and it will be much better done if every worker is proud of his work.

The writer remembers riding out to Boulder Dam with a young man who worked there. On the way she got into conversation with him about the project and asked him what he did. He replied, simply, but proudly, "I'm a carpenter." Further inquiry revealed that he spent his days making the wooden frames into which concrete is poured. He enlarged upon the accuracy demanded by this task and the need to be an expert carpenter before attempting it. Recently he had found a new and quicker way of managing some detail of construction and had since been promoted. Under encouragement he talked in glowing terms of the intricacies and difficulties one had to overcome. To be sure, his English showed lapses from grammatical perfection, but his enthusiasm was as spontaneous and real as that of any professional man. He liked carpentry, he did his work well, and he had a fundamental interest in his job. If schools would turn out more young man like him there would be less discontent in the world. Pride in a job well done should not be regarded as the private possession of the highly literate.

Information concerning personal traits.—Altogether too few pupils realize the difference between desire to do something and ability to do it. They have no suspicion of the differences in mental and emotional equipment needed for this or that type of work. In all investigations the one outstanding reason given for choice of vocation was a liking for it.[3] Other reasons often advanced are: financial returns, assurance of position, and opportunity for adventure or travel. Out of 1,201 girls and boys, only 201 mentioned personal fitness for an occupation as a motive.[13] Naturally, desire and interest are important, but an extreme dependence upon them is to be avoided. Interest should be treated as one indication of possible adjustment, never as the only indication. To determine fitness for a given vocation, intelligence, personality, preparation, and interest must all be taken into account.

Because of the need for a balanced investigation of personal fitness, the second section of any course on occupations should present opportunities for adolescents to find out about themselves. This statement does not indicate an introspective analysis or psychoanalysis. In fact, the more objective such information is, the better. Students need to know where they stand in regard to the entire distribution on each of a number of traits. Fortunately, the technique of testing has advanced to such a stage that objective self-estimation is possible. Such a plan as that suggested below might well be followed.

During the second semester of the freshman year in the course on occupations, the instructor might devote a week's work to a general discussion of the relationship between types of individuals and types of work, with illustrations of how some people fail to achieve their ambitions because of their personal characteristics. If this line of thought is well presented, the students will spontaneously want to know something about themselves, so they may select occupations as wisely as possible. This interest leads quite naturally to the administration of perhaps a half-dozen objective, standardized tests; two tests of intelligence, two or three tests of academic preparation, and two or three tests of personality traits should be included. Naturally, the clerical burden from such extensive testing of the entire freshman class is considerable, but the use to which the tests are to be put suggests a solution of the clerical problem. These tests are being given to inform students about themselves; they should therefore score their own tests. If they realize these tests are not being given as examinations, will not be used to prejudice their schoolwork, and will not be shown to other people, adolescents can be trusted to score their own tests.* From these test scores a total distribution should be made, and each pupil should see where he stands.

There are always objections raised to letting pupils know what scores they make on tests of intelligence. Two such tests have been recommended as a means of avoiding chance errors in a single score. If a pupil stands third from the bottom of a class on one test and eighth from the bottom on the second, the sooner he appreciates his comparative ability the better. In the course of time he will inevitably learn of his deficiencies. The only choice lies between informing him at the beginning of his secondary school course or allowing successive blows of fate to reveal the situation to him—probably producing a series of emotional storms in the process. If the instructor has reasonable tact, he will make clear that the possession of inferior ability is nothing to be ashamed of, but rather an unavoidable fact with which one must deal. In a similar manner the results of tests of schooling and personality should be interpreted for the pupil. Each pupil should be encouraged to make a graph showing his standing, in terms of the total distributions in the three important elements of intelligence, previous school achievement, and personality. He is then ready to make a summary of his available talents and deficiencies.

In regard to this matter of information about students, the usual work in vocational guidance is altogether too secretive. The counselor administers tests, often without much explanation of her motives, and then keeps the results in a locked file where only she and her assistants can find them. Naturally such results should not be publicly announced, but there should be some arrangement whereby the individual concerned is informed of his standing. After all, it is his business rather than the counselor's. If he wants to tell his friends how he succeeded in this or that test, that also

---

* However, if precaution against cheating is regarded as essential, all tests can be marked with indelible pencils, which are collected immediately upon finishing the tests. Alterations and additions will not then usually be made, and if made are easily detected.

is his affair. The restriction of such information to the counselor's office is due partly to sentimentalism and partly to the attitude that guidance consists of giving advice instead of information.

The second portion of the vocational guidance program should then be dedicated to providing students with information about themselves. Naturally they will need assistance in interpreting the results, and there will be some need of individual interviews in the course of this interpretation. However, the pupil who comes to an individual interview provided with information about himself and numerous occupations, and able to relate his vocational choice to his own objective records, will obtain far more assistance from the interview than the pupil equipped only with his own imagination and desires. The interview is an important technique, but it should be postponed until towards the end of the freshman year, except for such students as drop out of school before that time. And, most important, the personal interview should never be regarded as taking the place of information. As a means of imparting facts, it is utterly inefficient and time-consuming; as a means of helping students adjust themselves to facts they already know, it is highly valuable.

The vocational counselor.—It should go without saying, from the above account, that a vocational counselor must be a well-informed, intelligent, and well-balanced individual—not some person who has been turned over to the vocational department because she cannot teach and is unpopular with the students, but has a contract which prevents her from being discharged. Nor should she be a highly emotional person who will sympathize too completely with adolescents, thus preventing them from gaining emotional maturity. Naturally she cannot be harsh, but she must be able to maintain her own objectivity and good judgment at all times. Adolescents can be trusted to produce plenty of emotional stress which prevents them from thinking clearly. If the vocational counselor also becomes submerged in the emotional crisis, no clear thinking will be done by anybody.

So far as the actual course on occupations is concerned, the relationship between student and counselor is merely that between any sympathetic teacher and the pupils in her class. The counselor's relationship to the pupil during interviews must emphatically be that of an older and wiser friend, not that of an emotionally attached parent. In her relations with such individuals and agencies outside the school as must co-operate if various types of work are to be demonstrated, the counselor must appear as a scientifically trained person who knows what she is doing and has practical ideas for the training of her pupils. All too often the counselor is regarded by other members of the faculty as a rather insignificant person, by the pupils as one more adult who interferes with their affairs, and by individuals outside the school as a sentimental, flustered spinster who is trying hard to do good but does not know how. In recent years, high schools have been making serious efforts to obtain vocational counselors who are really equal to the serious burden imposed upon them. The worth-while character of the vocational program depends largely upon the ability of the counselor to command the respect of those with whom she deals, to use efficient methods of procedure, and to maintain her own emotional equilibrium at all times.

ILLUSTRATIVE CASE STUDIES

There are too many different types of vocational maladjustment for all of them to be illustrated; the writer has selected a few cases showing common difficulties. The reader should note (1) the fundamental source of the maladjustment, (2) the behavior shown, and (3) the age at which realization of difficulty dawned on the adolescent concerned. Important also is a consideration of the blame, in so far as anyone is responsible. Was the maladjustment due to poor estimation of capacity, parental pressure, failure of the school to provide adequate information, idealizing of an occupation, or to some other source? How early was the difficulty recognizable? What more could a school have done in the way of either prevention or cure?

Arthur [11] was a well-endowed boy mentally and physically, with athletic build, strong features, and a pleasant personality. His mother had died when he was three years of age, and after his father's remarriage Arthur had gone to live with an aunt who was kindly and affectionate, but probably a bit too much concerned about his health, manners, and personal appearance.

Arthur pursued his scholastic work in an uneventful manner, keeping well up with his classes without any particular evidence of brilliance. He did not find it difficult to put himself across in athletic activities because he played an excellent game of baseball and had received special distinction at several summer camps for his swimming; in addition, he had a general interest in numerous other out-of-door sports. In high school he showed special interest in his courses in literature, spent a good deal of time writing poetry, and made a hobby of studying the classical authors.

In spite of what appeared to be a good all-round development, this lad did not make friends easily. He was said to be a bit too "mushy" with boys, and, at one time, it was intimated that he was showing rather precocious homosexual tendencies. He occasionally went to a dance or to moving pictures with girls, but on the whole made no effort whatever to participate in social activities where they were involved. He was more inclined to find his emotional outlets in his poetry and literature.

Arthur's father shared the boy's interest in athletics but not his interest in literature. He was a materialistic man who had been trained in engineering and who ridiculed Arthur about his literary efforts to the point of humiliation. He had his son's future well mapped out and most of his plans involved activities which the father felt would have been a distinct asset to him had he had the opportunity of engaging in them when he was a boy. He pushed the boy into all types of athletics in an effort to gratify his own unfulfilled desires along this line. He was eager for Arthur to attend the university whose degree would most enhance the boy's reputation in the social and business world. All these interests, which might have fitted in well with the father's own life, considering his personality make-up, contributed but little to the satisfaction of the boy. When presently his father had him transferred to a school where participation in athletic activities was given greater emphasis, Arthur found various ways of avoiding these pursuits and became increasingly absorbed in his literary efforts. This immediately created friction and later real conflict between father and son; it was not long before the father was complaining that the boy was getting arrogant, argumentative, and at times defiant.

Arthur, on the other hand, began to complain that his father no longer understood him, that he was cold and calculating in every move he made, and that he thought only of his own ambitions without considering what was best for his son. In other words, by the time the boy was sixteen years of age, he had himself made a diagnosis as to the reason for the incompatibility which seemed to increase each time the boy returned from school. His father's disparaging and scornful attitude toward the boy's literary efforts gradually dulled his own enthusiasm for them, without, however, increasing his interest or ability in athletic activities, and between the ages of sixteen and seventeen, the boy, as the father stated, simply slumped. His work was less and less efficient; he became self-centered, introspective, and increasingly selfish; and, what concerned his father most, Arthur began to be resentful and rebellious toward any suggestions his father might make.

In such a state of mind the lad soon became the victim of his own egocentricity and began to seek the companionship of the younger and more inadequate group from whom he could get some recognition with a minimum of effort. Several of his associations were brought down to a level which caused him to be looked upon by the rest of the group as an undesirable citizen in the school. It was only after many weeks of intensive therapy with the boy and after educating the father as to the boy's real needs and the necessity of building the boy's life around his own personality, rather than around his father's, that anything of a constructive nature was accomplished.*

Mabel [7] was a girl of about nineteen, with a stagy and affected manner, who professed great interest in nursing. It appeared at the first interview that she had always yearned to be a nurse and had entered college with no other objective in mind. At first all had gone fairly well, as the curriculum in which she was enrolled demanded some work in such subjects as English, chemistry, history, and psychology before beginning the more technical work. But with the start of the third term the trouble began. She was enrolled in a course in anatomy, went to her first laboratory period, was told to watch the dissection of a cadaver, took one look at it, fled to her college office, and promptly withdrew from the course. Several days of thinking over the situation did not serve to help matters any. She discovered she had an unalterable aversion to work with dead bodies and felt she could never finish her course. In desperation she came for advice.

* This study is used by permission of the D. Appleton-Century Company.

Apparently, Mabel had always thought of nursing as "smoothing the fevered brow," measuring out medicine, cheering the convalescent, and doing other pleasant things. She did not know that a nurse spent much of her practical training in running errands for querulous patients, sterilizing instruments, carrying bedpans, assisting at operations, and doing many other disagreeable tasks. Nor did she have the vaguest suspicion that one had to touch dead people; in her rosy dreams the patients always got well. She did not realize what courses in anatomy and physiology would be like, and apparently had no thoughts of dissection even of lower animals. She vowed emphatically she could not possibly go on, but at the same time she insisted she could nurse if only she could be excused from the nauseating details in the laboratories. Assurance that work in the hospital would be more nauseating than in the laboratory did not shake her conviction in the matter—probably because she thought she knew all about nursing from reading stories, seeing movies, and watching nurses in clean uniforms going to and from a near-by hospital. In addition to her helplessness in the presence of a dead body, she admitted that she fainted at the sight of blood, became horror-stricken on the one occasion she had witnessed seasickness, and could not bear the thought of being given a physical examination because she thought a nude body so "terrible."

As a candidate for nursing, Mabel seemed hopeless. She was told that she must do one of three things. She might set her teeth and go through with the training. She might give up her ambition and settle upon some other objective and forget about nursing. Or she could gain admission to a city hospital where the training was of the briefest, where there would be no laboratory courses, and where a certain amount of hardihood might come to her when she actually got down to work; that is, she might try practical work and see how she reacted, as she could be assured that nothing would be worse than her probation period. It was stressed on several occasions that she must make up her mind and get away from the emotional strain of her present indecision. Mabel would not even consider going back into her curriculum; she was sure she would "go crazy" if she so much as saw another dead body. As she learned more about the practical details of nursing from the experienced individuals to whom she was sent for conferences, she became convinced she could not stand nursing anyway. Finally, she came to the conclusion she must change her objective.

It should be noted that this girl was headed toward her idealized, sentimentalized idea of nursing, that she was quite ignorant of the facts and demands of the profession, and that she had already built up a series of reactions which made the possibility of success in such work very remote. It might perhaps have been possible, by long and tactful inquiry, to locate the sources of these emotional attitudes and modify them. Something of the sort was attempted, but it soon become evident that while she could be re-educated sufficiently to avoid hysteria on such critical occasions as might be involved in the average existence, she was hardly to be so made over as to enter a profession regularly involving acts that revolted her. As a matter of fact, Mabel had no interest in nursing; what she wanted was a white uniform, a position of authority (which nurses do not usually have) and what looked like an easy existence and is not.

Mabel is now in her last year of training as a prospective teacher of English. She has almost forgotten she ever wanted to be a nurse. In this particular case no great harm was done by her initial mistake in vocational choice. Mabel was disillusioned before she had spent time and energy upon her training for nursing; in fact, all her work could be counted in another curriculum so that she did not lose any credits. She is now a fairly normal girl (although still somewhat squeamish), is satisfied, doing good work, and is looking forward with enthusiasm to a position as an English teacher—only she has her feet on the ground this time and is not expecting to find her path strewn with roses.

Dorothy [7] was in the last month of her senior year of the college of liberal arts when she came to the writer for advice. Dorothy had suddenly realized she soon must find a position; there was, however, no type of work for which she was prepared. Her college major was English, as a result of a rather sentimental interest in literature and the unwise notion on the part of her parents, that, since she wrote with a certain facility, she might sometime aspire to authorship. Now she realized there was little demand for sweet-girl-graduate authors; and, as she herself said frankly, she was still so young and inexperienced that she really had nothing to write about. Since she had had no professional training for teaching, there seemed little opportunity in that field; she had applied for a secretarial job but could neither run a typewriter nor write shorthand; she had thought of social-service work but again found to her distress that there was for this work preparation she did not have. Dorothy was in a state of desperation and indignation because her alma mater had allowed her to spend her four best years in such a futile fashion as to fit her for no work by which she could support herself. She sighed gustily and said maybe she would have to get married, since that seemed the only occupation open to a person with an A.B.

Dorothy was a member of Phi Beta Kappa; she scored in the highest percentile on the University intelligence tests. She was a persistent worker at any odd jobs she had attempted as a means of earning spending money. She was attractive, efficient, and popular in campus activities. Still, here she was without preparation for any job she might be willing to accept.

Dorothy is an illustration of the most common type of vocational maladjustment—the good student with too little cultural education for any practical use and no technical education whatever.

Peter [7] had a perfectly good objective when he entered college; he knew what he wanted to do, and he had reasonable expectations of success. It happened, however, that the department in which his major would naturally fall was a department in which one could not elect work until the sophomore year at the earliest. Moreover, Peter's college insisted that he pass off certain requirements in the way of academic subjects before he began work along the line of his interest.

He had spent one year in a small college before entering the university and had lost a little credit in transferring. Since his matriculation he had taken seventy-five hours of work, only ten of which had anything to do with his ambitions. He had elected a science in which he had no interest; he had taken two courses in history, and had failed one of them; he had taken one course in a language begun at his small college, but the work was so different that he found himself inadequately prepared and had been obliged to drop this course; he had taken three terms of another language in which he had not the slightest interest; he had taken two terms of mathematics because they met a requirement and were easy for him; he had taken two courses in English; he had elected two courses in psychology to which he had no great objection but which did not greatly further his training for his selected vocation. For four consecutive terms he had put on his schedule a course in his major subject, only to have the course crossed off and a statement sent him that he must work off his requirements first. So Peter's objective had been shelved for two years, not counting the year before he entered the university. At the time of the first interview with Peter he still had twenty hours of work to be completed before he could elect what he desired.

Peter changed to a college having less rigid requirements, took four courses directly bearing on his vocational aim, and is now doing excellent work. At last he can see his way clear toward his special interest.

What was the matter with Peter? His college was interfering with his education! Certainly not all the blame for such maladjustment can be put upon the student. Although this type of maladjustment is more common in college than high school, it can be found almost anywhere. It seems as if an educational institution ought to arrange its work so that an adolescent with a definite ambition can reach it without undue delay.

"X, a seventeen-year-old boy,[15] asked for assistance in choosing a vocation. He had already eliminated from the list of possibilities a majority of the professions and had little inclination toward business or any of the arts. His father, a successful corporation lawyer, had suggested engineering. A study of X's school grades in science and mathematics, as well as X's own lack of interest in an engineering career, indicated that engineering was not a reasonable choice. So far as X's own conscious desires were concerned, his only positive stipulation was that he have an out-of-doors job. He had considered truck-driving and forestry. For social and economic reasons, truck-driving was discarded. Forestry remained, but after he and his adviser had found out all that they could about that vocation, X was still vaguely dissatisfied. The summer vacation intervened. In September he came in to report that he had had a 'great' summer, landscaping the grounds of his mother's summer cottage on a near-by lake. He had never heard of landscape architecture as a profession; in his parents' social circle there were doctors, lawyers, builders, businessmen, etc., but no landscape architects. An opportunity was made for him to spend a week with a local landscape man and X is at present studying landscape architecture in an agricultural school, convinced that he has found a vocation in which he can be both happy and economically successful.

"It is interesting to note that the problem presented by this vocational choice was not solved by 'paper' methods. The clue to it was not to be found in a study of school grades, in the I.Q. file, in the data offered by interviews with X's father, mother, or teachers, or in the record of his extracurricular activities which had included dramatics, basketball, and work on the school paper. Each of these was contributory to the answer in that the thorough investigation blocked unwise choice and at the same time convinced X that the choice of a vocation was a serious problem not to be solved hastily in order to halt adult questioning on the subject."

[X was fortunate; by chance he "fell into" a line of work that interested him. Most boys are not so lucky. A systematic survey of possible occupations, undertaken as a serious part of the curriculum, not as an incidental matter, ought to help materially in furnishing adolescents with adequate information for an intelligent choice.] *

Dorothy was a freshman in college. She came from middle-class parents who rather wanted her to be educated above their own level. She had completed one semester of work, receiving passing grades in two courses and a failing grade in another. She came to her adviser to ask what courses would be most appropriate for her second semester's work. She and the adviser went through the catalogue from start to finish, but no course seemed to arouse any spark of interest. Finally, the adviser asked Dorothy what she would do if left to herself. The girl replied promptly that she would get a job in a beauty shop. For the first time during the interview Dorothy became animated. It then appeared that she was an expert marceller and had worked for three previous summers in a first-class beauty salon where she had been highly successful. Dorothy was pledged to a sorority whose members regularly used her services instead of employing a professional hairdresser. For twenty minutes Dorothy held forth in glowing terms about the pleasure she derived from this type of work. The adviser then asked her why she should go to college when she had such a definite vocational objective of a nature she could not expect to reach through academic work. It had apparently never occurred to Dorothy that she might stop her education just where it stood, but upon thinking the matter over for a few days, she realized there was literally nothing in college classes of the slightest interest or use to her. She therefore dropped out of school, went to work, and within five years owned an up-to-date beauty salon which the counselor always patronized because Dorothy was literally a genius at hairdressing.

This story exemplifies a common type of vocational maladjustment. Girls or boys who are intelligent enough to get through two or three years of college are often encouraged to do so, whether or not they are deriving pleasure or value from the work. Altogether too many people have the illusion that a college education will automatically lead to success in every conceivable line of work.

* This case study is used by permission of Western Reserve University.

BIBLIOGRAPHY *

1. Garretson, O. K., "Relation between Expressed Preference and Curricular Ability of Ninth Grade Boys," *Teachers College Contributions to Education,* No. 396, Bureau of Publications, Teachers College, Columbia University, 1930, 77 pp.
2. Greenleaf, W. J., "Cost of Going to College," *United States Office of Education Pamphlet,* No. 52, Government Printing Office, 1934, 34 pp.
3. Hurlock, E. B., and Jansing, C., "The Vocational Attitudes of Boys and Girls of High School Age," *Journal of Genetic Psychology,* 1934, 44: 175-191.
4. Jones, A. J., *Principles of Guidance,* McGraw-Hill Book Company, 1930, 381 pp.
5. Koos, L. V., and Kefauver, G. N., *Guidance in Secondary Schools,* The Macmillan Company, 1932, 640 pp.
6. Myers, C. S., "Recent Evidence of the Value of Vocational Guidance," *Human Factor,* 1932, 6: 438-450.
7. Pressey, L. C., *Some College Students and Their Problems,* Ohio State University Press, 1929, 97 pp.
8. Sparling, E. J., "Do College Students Choose Vocations Wisely?", *Teachers College Contributions to Education,* No. 561, Bureau of Publications, Teachers College, Columbia University, 1933, 110 pp.
9. Strang, R., *Personal Development and Guidance in College and Secondary School,* Harper & Brothers, 1934, 341 pp.
10. Strong, E. K., "Attitudes and Aptitudes in Vocational Guidance," *Journal of Applied Psychology,* 1934, 18: 501-515.
11. Thom, D. A., *Normal Youth and Its Everyday Problems,* D. Appleton-Century Company, 1932, 367 pp.
12. ———, "Guiding the Adolescent," *United States Child Bureau Publication,* No. 225, 1933, 94 pp.
13. Thorndike, E. L., Bregman, E. O., Lorge, I., Metcalfe, Z. F., Robinson, E. E., and Woodyard, E., *Prediction of Vocational Success,* Commonwealth Fund, 1934, 284 pp.
14. Valentine, C. W., "An Inquiry into Reasons for the Choice of Occupation among Technical School Pupils," *Human Factor,* 1933, 7: 347-353.
15. Van Camp, R., "Vocational Investigations in the Secondary Decade," in the *Proceedings of the Conference on Adolescence,* Western Reserve, 1930, pp. 137–40.

* See also the references in the Appendix.

16. Watson, E. B., *A Source Book for Vocational Guidance,* H. W. Wilson Company, 1930, 241 pp.
17. Wood, B. D., and Beers, F. S., "The Major Strategy of Guidance," *Occupations,* 1934, 12:8-12.

PART IV

THE ADOLESCENT'S ENVIRONMENT

CHAPTER XII

THE ADOLESCENT AND HIS HOME

THE basic requirements for a healthy home in which to bring up children have been well described in numerous places.[12] For a child a home should, first, furnish adequate shelter and nourishment. Second, it should provide security, especially against emotional disturbances. Third, it should in a consistent manner control the child's behavior. Finally, it should educate children in acceptable modes of response to social situations. Homes which lack one or more of these characteristics are likely to produce children whose behavior is abnormal. The desirable characteristics of a home for adolescents are not identical with those above enumerated, because the adolescent is no longer a child. In the discussion below, adequate provision for shelter and nourishment will be assumed; attention can then be centered upon psychological and social conditions.

Since this book is primarily for teachers, a chapter on the home need not be as detailed as that on the school. Teachers are not responsible for the homes from which their pupils come. They should, however, understand what characteristics in a home situation will lead to discontent, revolt, or delinquency. They must also realize the importance of home relationships in conditioning all phases of adolescent behavior. The teacher is frequently consulted on problems which deal essentially with home conditions; she therefore needs certain basic information in order that her advice may be as useful as possible.

DESIRABLE CHARACTERISTICS OF HOMES FOR ADOLESCENTS

Emancipation from home control.—One major objective to be reached by the end of the adolescent period is the complete emancipation of the boy or girl from home control and intense parental attachment.[13] Between the ages of twelve and twenty an individual must change from a child dependent upon his home to an adult who is sufficiently detached from his parents to establish a successful home of his own. The first need, then, in a home for those of adolescent age is a wise relinquishing of the strict control necessary for children and a wise development of adequate self-control in the adolescents themselves. This process presents a difficult task for parents. During the twelve or thirteen years of childhood successful parents have consistently controlled the behavior of their children. After the beginning of adolescence they must learn *not* to control their children. Naturally, the shift from complete supervision to complete independence cannot be made overnight, but it must be finished by the time the boy or girl is twenty-one, and preferably by the age of eighteen. Attempts to continue childish dependence result only in the production of adults who act like children.

Such people are all too common. In a certain large university there is a fifty-year-old bachelor who still lives at home with his mother. If he is asked out to dinner by a colleague he calls up his mother to ask if the arrangement is all right with her. He has never attended a national meeting of men in his specialty because he does not like to leave his mother for so long as a week! He never publishes a paper until his mother has read and approved it. He eats no meat because his mother is a vegetarian. He has never had an affair with any woman and is so afraid of women he will not talk to a female professor in his own office unless the door is left open. When he needs a new suit he gets several samples from the tailor and has his mother pick out the one she likes. He wears stiff collars because she does not approve of soft ones. The undergraduates firmly believe he owns only one tie—dark blue with small white polka-dots; the truth is that he has never bought a necktie for himself, and his mother long ago settled on the polka-dot motif as appropriate and has never bought any other kind. His present solicitude for his mother is rationalized on the grounds of her age and failing health, but his behavior was exactly the same when an aunt lived with the family and would have cared for his mother during his absence had he cared to go away from home. This man's mother thinks he is a model son; he thinks she is an ideal mother. The rest of the world looks down upon him, criticizes her for ruining his life, and wonders what will happen when his emotional props are removed by her death.

In another community there is a mother with two adult daughters.[6] The mother became an "invalid" when the girls were in the late years of adolescence. Several doctors have been discharged for telling the woman she had nothing wrong with her except weakness from staying in bed so much. The mother demands constant attention and service from both daughters. She has kept them bound hand and foot to her by her unceasing demands. Whenever they show signs of any outside interest she at once reminds them how she "sacrificed" her health for them during their childhood. Neither daughter has the strength to resist this appeal or the insight to realize its basis, although both more than suspect their mother's condition. Both daughters are now middle-aged, negative, unattractive, and worn-out; neither has had normal satisfactions from life. They are mere adjuncts to a dominating personality. For them there is no escape until the mother dies, leaving behind her two prematurely old women who have never had an independent life. For them, liberty will come too late.

Another mother, known to the writer, had nine children—five boys and four girls. The boys, now grown men, all live in foreign countries; until they left the States their homes were likely at any moment to be entered by a domineering, energetic mother who marched in, rearranged the furniture, disciplined the grandchildren, ordered the maid about, and generally disrupted family life. Two married daughters have had violent quarrels with their mother and have not spoken to her for years. The third married daughter lives in the same city and carries on what in military terms is known as a running fight. Every morning the mother calls this daughter, demands to know what has been ordered for dinner, what the daughter will be doing every minute of the day, and so on. Her son-in-law allows her in the his house only on Sunday while he plays golf! His wife has taken refuge in making a joke of the situation; she puts off her mother by jollying her along from day to day. This daughter is the only real person in the family; she developed her courage by resisting a crushing degree of parental pressure that tried to drive her into a "brilliant" marriage; for ten long years she waited defiantly until the man of her choice could support her. And all this time she was the object of ceaseless attack from her mother's vitriolic tongue. The girl finally found refuge in laughter and joking. But the strain has had its effect on her physical condition, even though her personality remained normal;

she is now, at the age of forty, dying of heart disease—the only sick person in a remarkably healthy and vital family. The fourth daughter is unmarried and lives with her mother. This daughter is a frightfully abnormal person—as dominating as her mother, utterly ruthless, bad-tempered, vicious when crossed, fanatic in her attitudes. She "manages" her mother simply by being the more disagreeable of the two. This mother has driven her children into flight, disease, rebellion, and abnormality. Every one of her married children has been forced to develop a brutal defense to protect his or her own home and family. In this group there is an immense vitality that would not be subdued—otherwise the results might have been far worse.

Mothers are not always to blame, however. A few years ago the writer discovered she had one more student in a class than there were enrollment cards. Upon inquiry, the extra student turned out to be the father of a girl in the class. This student was a junior in college. She was an only child and had always been dependent upon her parents for social contacts. In educational matters, however, the father was dominant, since the mother had had only grammar school training. The girl had always studied with her father; as far as could be ascertained she had never prepared a lesson alone. During the summer before her entrance to college her father had retired from business to devote himself to his "child's" further education. For over two years he had attended every class, read every assignment, talked over all lectures with his daughter. In fact, the only class in the entire four years from which he was excluded was the writer's. She would neither permit the father to attend class nor the daughter to drop it without penalty of failure. The girl completed the work, grudgingly and sometimes rebelliously. Eight years later this student, by then a high school teacher with a permanent position, was still annoyed over the enforced separation from her father. In the meantime, the mother had died. The girl now lives with her father, who drives her to school in the morning, calls for her after school, and is her only companion. They are both enrolled in graduate school in the same classes. If a father is released from economic burdens, he may absorb the lives of his children just as completely as any mother.

Such extreme situations as those just described are providentially infrequent, but lesser degrees of possessiveness are common. In fact, a feeling by the parents that their children "belong" to them is as old as mankind. Most children become emancipated from their homes either through a violent revolt—brought on by the intensity of adolescent emotional drives—or else by purely fortuitous circumstances, such as the death of one parent, need to earn a living, better chances of work in another community, attendance at college, or the like. It is far more rational, however, for parents to give their adolescent children deliberate education for independence.

There are numerous ways in which an adolescent may gradually achieve the necessary freedom from parental attachments. For instance, there is the matter of handling money. As children approach adolescence it is highly desirable they be given an allowance, the amount of which is gradually increased so that from year to year they buy an increasingly greater proportion of what they need. Thus, a girl may first be given enough money for carfares, incidental school supplies, stockings, and underwear. Naturally, some of her selections will be unwise, especially at first. She will buy things inappropriate for her age, she will use up her allowance before the week is over, she will buy things she does not really want. However, she will never learn to spend money wisely and appropriately by any other method than actually spending it herself. As the girl grows older, her allowance should be increased until by the time she is eighteen she has available a fixed sum with which to supply all her needs. Many parents sincerely believe they help their children by allowing them to grow up without feeling any economic pressure. Quite the reverse, however, is the case. If they do not make some such arrangement as above suggested, they encourage their adolescent sons and daughters to ask or tease for money, exactly as if these near-adults were children. Such a situation not only prolongs childishness, but eventually brings on a real revolt.

An adolescent's friends should not be chosen for him by his parents. If he allows such childish treatment of himself, he will never grow up. If he does not allow it, he is soon in open conflict with his parents and will probably be driven into many unwise friendships by his desire to show his parents they cannot dominate him. Naturally, adolescents will choose some undesirable acquaintances; no one can judge character accurately who is so inexperienced and so easily deceived by externals as the average adolescent. Instead of getting into a panic and attempting to terminate such friendships by sheer authority, the parents should use these incidents as so much education in the judgment of character. No serious harm is likely to come unless the parents, by their uncompromising attitude, drive the adolescent out of his own home and force him to meet these undesirable individuals secretly. As in the case of spending money, a shifting of control from parent to child cannot take place overnight; but take place it must, sooner or later.

A few years ago a boy of fifteen from a good home entered a central high school of a large city. Here he came in contact with several older boys of somewhat undesirable character. He had never had any reason to deceive his parents; so he told them about his new acquaintances, even bringing one of them home with him. His mother took a violent dislike to this other boy; his father, who knew something of the other's family, talked severely to his son, forbidding him ever again to see his new friend. For a few days the boy did as he was told, but soon found himself ridiculed as a sissy because he let his parents "boss" him. Resenting this attitude, he accepted an invitation to the movies with those he had been told to avoid. When he came home, he explained the situation to his parents, telling them frankly where he had been and why. At the time he had no great attachment to these friends, but he was unwilling to seem a child in their eyes. His parents punished him for disobedience by cutting off his allowance for a month. This unwise and childish punishment pushed the boy into a state of profound irritation. The next day he was again asked to the movies. When he admitted he had no money, one of the boys loaned him a dollar. He did not dare tell his parents where he had been or how he had acquired the money; so he hid the balance of his cash and said he had stayed late at school to play ball. This sort of deception went on during the month he was deprived of his usual allowance. By that time, he was several dollars in debt and had been initiated into a "club" to which his new friends belonged. His lying gradually became extensive and his absences from home numerous. Questioning revealed the real situation. Still, his parents could not realize that by ruling him with a rod of iron they were insulting his sense of independence; they accordingly insisted upon his removal from the school and his enrollment in another school where he knew no one. Within a week he began to play truant, spending his time either in the "club" room or wandering about the streets with some older boys who were already out of school. His parents tightened their supervision, his teachers scolded him, his former friends distrusted him, his new pals sneered at his lack of freedom from apron strings. No one seemed to realize the boy was asserting himself in undesirable ways chiefly because of constant opposition. Bewildered and harassed, this lad determined to prove his "manliness." One evening he climbed in the back window of a drugstore, took money from the cash register, and stole some narcotics he found in the prescription room. This loot he turned over to his clubmates, who at last began to admire him. But he was still unhappy. When another boy was arrested for the theft, his conscience troubled him unbearably and he voluntarily confessed his misdeeds to the school principal. To his surprise, his story was met with real understanding and sympathy. The principal found work for him after school hours, so that he could earn enough to repay the druggist; the drugs were returned unused; the parents were interviewed several times until they came to realize their errors in treatment. The boy himself had no inclination to run away from his problems. He returned to the central high school, told his recent acquaintances they could get along without him, and renewed his contacts with earlier friends. Within six weeks the whole episode was a thing of the past and the boy emerged, with an improved judgment of character, from a situation that might easily have led him into serious danger. The moment parental opposition was removed he broke off the undesirable friendships without any help from anyone. All he wanted was a chance to grow up. He later admitted that his recent friends had revolted him from the first day he went to the movies with them. He would never have become an intimate if he had not been pushed into further association in order to maintain a respected position in the society of his peers.

In formulating his vocational plans the adolescent needs much information and some degree of guidance, but he should not be so dominated by parental decisions that he does no thinking for himself. Naturally, adolescents make unjustifiable vocational choices, and they change their plans with considerable frequency. In the end, if they have not met with open opposition from their elders, they are likely to go into exactly the type of work for which their parents think them suited. The trouble does not usually lie with the parents' estimate of their child and his probable success, but rather with their insistence upon a single goal and their opposition to intervening interests which would be short-lived if left to die out of their own accord. Healthy adolescents will revolt against domination by adults, but they are eager to obtain both information and guidance.

The type of intercurrent ambition that arises in adolescence is well illustrated by the experience of a girl who had read too many detective stories. She became suddenly filled with the idea of becoming the first great female detective. Her family was somewhat horrified but too wise to oppose their nineteen-year-old daughter. Quite the contrary. Her father told her he knew the chief of police in their city and would try to arrange for her to go into this work, if her heart were really set on it. Accordingly, he made the necessary arrangements. On the next day the girl presented herself to the chief of police, explained she would be willing to start anywhere and do anything in order to get experience, and asked for an immediate assignment. The chief sent her out to collect evidence against a degenerate who had been reported as bothering children in a near-by park. The girl started forth on her first "case" with her head in the clouds. There followed a week of hanging around a park, playing with dirty children, shaking off the advances of loungers, talking with uneducated mothers whose ideas of evidence were most extraordinary; by the end of the week she was thoroughly bored and tired of standing up all day long. Eventually, she saw a man she suspected of being the degenerate in question and followed him across the park. What she did not notice was the plain clothes man who followed her, at the command of the chief of police; in fact, she had never noticed this persistent shadow that had been with her since her first moment on the case. As soon as she was a little distance away from the children, the degenerate turned on her and began to make advances; she tried to get away from him but he seized her; in another moment her screams had brought her guardian to her assistance. The detective promptly handcuffed her assailant, and in a half hour the trio were back in the police station. She had been successful in her very first case, but by the time she had figured as the chief witness against the degenerate in court, she was more than willing to renounce her ambition. It was years before she discovered she had been "framed"! Parental opposition would doubtless have sent her to some other city where she would not have received the protection arranged for her at home. Her father had not the slightest idea of allowing her to become a detective, but he was too wise to tell her so. Instead, he and the chief of police—a kindly man with adolescent daughters of his own—let her convince herself of her foolishness, without running into any danger. A single contact with a real criminal was more effective than any amount of argument. This girl had, however, some real understanding of herself, even if her first efforts at vocational adjustment were clumsy. She is today a court psychologist.

In so far as it is possible, parents should always allow an adolescent boy or girl to get himself out of his own difficulties. Thus, if a boy gets into a row with one of his teachers, he should not be allowed to run away from the situation while his parents see the teacher and patch up the difficulty. If a girl buys a dress and then suddenly decides it is not suitable, she should be made to return the dress to the store and do the necessary explaining herself; if the store will not take the dress back, then she should not be given money to buy another. If a girl has offended some acquaintance she may, of course, be given advice as to what to do, but she should be made to carry out the advice independently. If a boy insists upon taking an extra course in school, he should not be allowed to drop out of it as soon as he thinks himself overworked. The first impulse of any adolescent who gets into difficulty is to follow a childish pattern of behavior and run at once to a sympathetic adult who, he hopes, will straighten out matters for him. This behavior cannot, however, be allowed to continue. Everyone has to learn sooner or later to face the logical results of his own behavior. Most adolescents are not resourceful and therefore need advice, but they should never be allowed to dodge the outcomes of their own bad judgment. The sooner they learn that the tail goes with the hide, the better.

The writer recalls all too well one semester in her school career during which she elected five history courses. She was warned by both parents and teachers to diversify her work. Objection merely increased her determination. Indeed, there was such an outburst of argument and coercion that she came to identify the relinquishing of her plans with a total loss of independence. When her election card finally came back approved she felt she was at last in control of her destiny. On the card there was a penciled remark that she must finish every course; if she failed one of them she would have to repeat it until it was passed. At first she had only a few qualms, but as the semester progressed she became just as tired of an exclusively historical diet as everyone had told her she would be. By Thanksgiving time she admitted she had made a mistake and tried to drop one course. But the gate had already slammed behind her. The only way to get out of the jam she had deliberately walked into was to work her way out. By the end of the semester she had learned many historical facts, most of which have been forgotten; she had, however, learned beyond forgetting the more valuable lesson that one's own foolishness has logical consequences that must eventually be faced. Neither refusal to approve the schedule nor permission to drop a course would have led to this result.

Parents and teachers both need to learn how to stand aside and let adolescents make mistakes—and then see to it that the youngsters profit by their own errors. Protection from experience does not educate; life will pound in its own lessons if parents will only let it.

Finally, the boy or girl in the late years of adolescence must be left free to choose his or her own mate. If there has been since the age of twelve or thirteen reasonable opportunity for social relations with members of the opposite sex, the adolescent has already gone through a series of temporary attachments and has educated himself sufficiently to know what he wants. Even though the final attachment leading to marriage may not find favor with the parents, they will produce only revolt and estrangement by opposition. Parents can prevent many tragedies if, in the early years of adolescence, they arrange adequate social contacts for their children and thus influence the choice of companions. When permanent attachments are made, the time for parental control has already gone by.

There has always been unwise domination of some adolescents by their parents, but the situation has become more critical within the last two generations. A mother's job has always been to bring up her children. In previous generations the average woman bore children as long as she could; she therefore had so many small children demanding her attention that she had little time or energy for interfering with the actions of any child old enough to look out for himself. Moreover, even if a woman had servants, household tasks were sufficient to keep her more than busy. Within the last two or three generations this situation has markedly changed. Most families have only one, two, or, at most, three children. As a result, the mother is still a vigorous woman when her children reach adolescence. With all the modern conveniences at her disposal, her housework can be done in half a day. She therefore has both time and energy to devote to her adolescent children. Indeed, if a woman has no interests outside her home, she has altogether too much time for this purpose. Many women have literally nothing else to do except to interfere with the lives of grown-up sons and daughters. The typical mother who regards bringing up her children as her chief business feels she is losing her job as soon as adolescents start to assert themselves. It is admittedly difficult for a vigorous woman to relinquish control over her lifework. The father has relatively less opportunity for interfering, partly because he is away from home much of the time, partly because he has other interests, partly because he needs release from the financial burden imposed on him by his children. He therefore wants them to grow up and become independent. When a father does interfere, however, he is likely to do so with an extremely heavy hand.

The first outstanding characteristic, then, of a desirable home for adolescents is the presence of parents who will encourage their children to become adults. Parents must learn how to "let go." There is already some evidence of progress in the average understanding of the situation. Just as parents have learned how to bring up babies much better than in earlier generations, so they will learn how to improve their methods of dealing with adolescents. The modern mother loves her baby—but she refuses to pick him up every time he cries; the self-control she develops should be adequate, by the time the baby is sixteen, to let him leave the house for an evening at the movies without pestering him with questions he resents.

Parental adjustment to society.—An adolescent needs a home in which the parents do not pass on to him their own maladjustments. Antagonism between the parents is too obvious a source of difficulty to need special comment. What is not so obvious is the frequent maladjustment of parents to modern social life and ideals. Conflict may be seen in its simplest form in the immigrant home in which the parents are attempting to maintain their native customs or religion in the face of American social forces. Thus, foreign parents who believe every respectable girl must be chaperoned are horrified at American laxity in this manner. If they continue to live in America but will not accept American standards of behavior, they pass on their own maladjustment; their adolescent girl must either become isolated from the society of others her own age or else must revolt violently against her elders. Parents who insist upon a fundamentalist view of religion force their children into conflict between schoolwork and home beliefs. Parents who will not tolerate smoking, use of cosmetics, or social dancing are themselves poorly adjusted to modern social customs. If adolescents from such homes insist upon maintaining their parents' standards, they will become ostracized from their own society. If they secretly abandon parental ideas, they are forced into a chronic habit of deceit. If they show proscribed behavior openly, they are forced into revolt against their homes. Many parents who have not formulated any consistent point of view on modern life force their adolescent children to make decisions on exactly the same problems for which they themselves can find no solution. They, however, can solve their difficulties by withdrawing from the world, but their children must live in the world as it is and must somehow achieve an adjustment. The above statements do not mean that parents must approve of every passing fashion or custom. If, however, they wish to prevent serious difficulties for their children, they must find for themselves some reasonable adjustment to modern life. Otherwise they are certain to pass on their own difficulties in an intensified form. The two examples below illustrate this point.

Cecile [8] sent in a schedule for the new semester's work, asking that her classes he assigned at eight, twelve, and four o'clock. This curious request led to questioning as to why such a scattering of hours was desirable. Cecile answered that her father required she be home within an hour (the time required to get there) of the time her last class ended. If she had two hours at lunch time she had to go home for lunch. She could work in the library in the evening only if her mother could come with her. Further investigation revealed that she was not allowed out of the home for any purpose whatever after six o'clock in the evening, unless she was chaperoned by an older, married woman. This girl's family are high-class, educated Spaniards. The father has brought with him the narrow, old-world background in which he grew up and is forcing his daughter to conform to his European standards. As soon as she is in the house she must become the domestic, docile, feminine daughter of her father's ideal of womanhood. The only way she can get time enough to prepare her lessons is by having her classes so distributed as to require her presence at the university all day. She is allowed no boy friends and has been told repeatedly that her father would arrange her marriage. This girl has, in many respects, a "good" home, but it is hopelessly "bad" in its irritating restrictions upon her personal liberty. She steps through the portals of her home into late nineteenth-century Spain. Even during the hours she is away from her family she carries with her the consciousness of shame that her home is "queer," of uncertainty about the "intentions" of any boy who speaks to her, of worry about getting the time for respectable preparation of her lessons, of concern because her science courses contradict her religious training. She is trying to fit an American education to the requirements of a bygone European social background, to the extreme detriment of the education, her happiness, and her adequate emotional and social development.

Everett came from a "good, old-fashioned" home.[9] He attended church twice a week, was active in the Junior Endeavor, was vigorously opposed to smoking, dancing, cardplaying, drinking, or petting. He regarded most modern novels as filthy and suspected the morals of any woman younger than his mother. All thoughts of sex had been rigidly suppressed. He was Sir Galahad come to life—but a good deal of a nuisance around a fraternity house. He tried to maintain his standards, but the steady influence of jokes, bull sessions, tales of his friends' amorous adventures, and pornographic literature have gradually brought him to a state of complete bewilderment. The situation is intensified by his parents who talk to him frequently upon the evils of life, tell him how boys who think too much about sex go insane, insist upon his continued acceptance of religious dogma, warn him against falling in love. In his college classes he finds many things which affront his religious beliefs; in his social environment he finds many friends, whom he admires, that break every restriction he thinks essential to a decent life. Everett is the epitome of bewildered adolescence, trying to find an adjustment between the narrow, uncompromising views of his home and the more lenient standards of society. His parents have managed to ignore the realities of modern existence; by so doing they have passed on to Everett a crucial problem of learning, somehow, to get along in a society that outrages his notions of decency at every turn.

Pride in the home.—If an adolescent is not proud of his home, he will not ask his friends to it, no matter how devoted he may be to his parents. Naturally, parents cannot make fundamental alterations in either themselves or their home, merely to satisfy the whims of their children. They should, however, realize that boys and girls will not stay at home unless it is an attractive place. Since adolescents set such great store by externals, almost any home can be altered on the surface with little trouble or expense. Often nothing more is needed for keeping an adolescent girl at home evenings than to let her remove one or two shabby pieces of furniture from the living room, rearrange the remaining pieces, and buy a new set of curtains. These utterly superficial changes may suffice to make her willing to entertain her friends at home. Naturally, a family unit—composed perhaps of two parents, one sixteen-year-old, and one child—cannot reorganize itself entirely around adolescent prejudices, but it can take such points into account in its thinking, especially since the issues are relatively so insignificant. Wise parents have new wallpaper hung in the dining room and engage a maid to wait on table when the daughter of the family has guests, because they prefer to reserve their authority and influence for more important matters.

Being ashamed of one's home leads to serious maladjustment. The adolescent is upset over what he thinks is unique and unjustifiable treason to those he loves; he also feels he must not accept invitations from his friends because he is not willing to return them. Many a girl who would not ask friends to her home because her father sat around in his shirt sleeves has gradually become isolated and friendless. If she is too vigorous to be crushed she will resort to meeting her friends—especially boys—in drugstores, theaters, restaurants, amusement parks, or other public places that give her no protection. Such a girl may realize the situation perfectly but she had rather take a chance on getting into trouble than let her friends think her home unrefined. Just such trivial reasons drive many boys and girls from their homes into the unprotected streets.

Even though no serious cleavage between parent and child occurs, being ashamed of one's home is an agonizing experience. And this situation is becoming all too frequent. Education, sophisticated movies, cheap imitations of refined accessories, cheap imitations of expensive clothes, and quick ways of making money have all combined to train the laboring man's son or daughter in social ambitions completely above the parents' standard. In one generation, the change from European peasant to American sophisticate may take place, inevitably causing such a gap between parents and children that no amount of love can bridge it. The case below illustrates this situation.

Elinor came to the university straight from the farm.[8] She had never before lived in a city. She was quite unfamiliar with such refinements as salad forks, butter knives, finger bowls. She had never been outside her own state; she had rarely been in any home but her own; she had never ridden on a sleeper or eaten in a diner; she had seen only one real play in all her life. Most of her clothes were homemade; she had never experienced a marcel, facial, or manicure.

Elinor happened to be a relative of a popular and sophisticated sorority girl, who adopted her as a satellite and got her into the same sorority. Elinor's clothes, English, manners, and habits underwent a sudden and profound change.

At the present time, Elinor is harassed with a positive horror that her college friends and her family will meet. Her parents seem quite oblivious to this situation and often drive to the university to spend the day with their daughter. They want to meet all her professors, especially since Elinor's work has been poor. Elinor dreads these days as they approach, shivers with agony during them, and is overcome with remorse after them, because she really loves her parents and finds being ashamed of them painful. Her vacations at home irritate her (although she has concealed her feelings quite well) and she worries over her parents' desire to have her stay at home after graduation.

Elinor has, of course, a "good" home in practically all respects, but it is a quite uncultured home. Neither of her parents graduated from grammar school, their English is full of errors, their table manners are hopelessly bad, their interests and pleasures are permanently rural. If they were not the salt of the earth their daughter would not be so distressed over her shame concerning them and her fear of hurting them. This girl has been educated both academically and socially so far above the level of her family that her home has become a focus of chronic irritation from which she cannot escape without inflicting distress on two much-loved but uncouth elderly people, who will never understand what has happened to alienate their daughter.

Security in the home.—A final characteristic of a desirable home for adolescents is the same security so needed by children. The adolescent depends upon the harmony, affection, lack of tension, and emotional security in his home mainly to help him during periods of distress. He often goes along for weeks at a time without requiring other security than food and shelter, but when he gets into difficulties he needs a harmonious and sympathetic home quite as much as any small child. As his independence increases, he falls back upon his home less and less frequently, but until he has set up a home of his own—and sometimes even later—there are sure to be occasions when he needs security above everything else.

A few years ago the writer was asked to talk with a freshman who was accused of improper relations with a high school girl. The boy admitted the situation. The bravado with which he began the interview gradually disappeared; in place of the sophisticated man of the world there emerged a bewildered and terrified boy. He insisted he would kill himself rather than face his parents. At the same time, he blamed his difficulties upon parental neglect, as revealed in the following account of himself. He had been a prominent high school athlete and had always been too busy and too well adjusted to get into sexual difficulties. During the previous summer he had spent many afternoons with a family who had a tennis court in the neighborhood. Here he met an older, married cousin who was visiting with her relatives. He amused her, and she flattered him with her attention. The mother in the home where the cousin was visiting did not like the association of this boy with an older woman; so she tried to reach the boy's mother, only to find her away from home for a month. She therefore compromised by arranging as immediate a termination of the woman's visit as she thought polite. One evening the boy dropped in for a chat; everyone except the cousin was out at a party. She asked him to stay and keep her company. In the course of the evening she seduced him. He rushed away from the house, filled with horror at what he had done. His first objective was home, but there was no one there. His mother was still absent, his father had been staying in town at his club, his brother was away at camp, and the servant had taken this golden opportunity to neglect her job. The terrified boy paced the floor of a deserted house until daybreak; he called his father's club repeatedly but could not find him. Finally, he felt he must talk to someone, so he called the woman he had been with the evening before. She, alarmed by his panic, feared to have him come to the house where she was visiting; she therefore came to his. Perhaps she had no intention of further relations—especially since she was leaving town that evening—but the empty house offered too alluring an opportunity and the previous experience was repeated. An extraordinary number of parents cannot seem to learn how unsafe an empty house is for either children or adolescents. By the time the boy's father returned for dinner in the evening his son no longer wanted any advice. The boy continued to be distressed over his behavior; he gradually became convinced he was a worthless degenerate and a disgrace to his family. Secretly he continued his immoralities, with a minimum of prudence. Six months later he was infected, unhappy, thoroughly beaten by life. While this boy was waging a game but losing fight against his first major temptation his mother was dancing at a country club and his father was sitting in on an all-night poker game with business associates. If he could have blurted out his original offense, he might well have been saved from further tragedy, but his home failed to provide security when he needed it.

The desirable home for adolescent boys and girls has thus four characteristics: First, it allows its children to grow up; second, it does not pass on to them its own maladjustments to modern society; third, it is willing to modify externals; and fourth, it provides a haven of emotional security in times of stress.

Prevention of maladjustment.—Two recent studies have served to emphasize current, sincere interest in the improved parental treatment of children and adolescents. The first study reflects the increasing dissemination of psychological knowledge among students and their ability to see their homes impersonally. The second indicates the realization by experts of the lifelong influence exerted upon individuals by abnormal home conditions.

Recently, several hundred college students were asked to describe the characteristics of a successful home and family.[10] They believed a successful family needed the following traits:

1. Little tension between parents or between the parents and children.
2. Much entertainment of friends, relatives or chums in the home and much affection between members of the family.
3. A medium degree of counseling and supervision of adolescent activities by the parents.
4. A medium degree of discipline but a high degree of uniformity in discipline between the parents.

In describing successful homes, these college students have voluntarily voted for several of the important characteristics advocated by psychologists and social workers.

Undesirable family relationships are often at the root of mental deviation and disease. A recent investigation [14] of insane adults gives relevant data concerning the characteristics of the homes in which these individuals spent their early years. They came from families in which there was one or more of the following situations: constant friction between the parents, an oversolicitous or dominating mother, a rejection of the child by both parents, or a marked emotional dependence of the child upon father or mother. These characteristics are obviously those which have been pointed out repeatedly as favoring the development of emotional deviation on the part of children.

There is hope that in the near future the collapse of personal efficiency from such causes will diminish in frequency, just as the collapse of health from the ravages of tuberculosis has become less frequent as more has been learned about the disease. When scientific knowledge about emotional reactions within the family is adequately disseminated, the normal love between parents and children will find healthy means of expression and will avoid those forms leading to tragedy.

TYPICAL BEHAVIOR OF UNEMANCIPATED ADOLESCENTS

The adolescent who is overdependent upon his home may show his childishness in either of two ways. He may, first, constantly seek the advice and help of others because he has had no practice in meeting situations alone. In the schoolroom he is constantly in need of extra help, not because he does not understand what he is to do, but because he has no independence. He often cannot follow printed directions because he is utterly dependent upon personal relationships. If he is given a choice of several assignments, he cannot make up his mind which he prefers. If a decision must be made at once, he asks a special dispensation until the next day so he can consult his parents. He usually cannot study without supervision; at home his parents help him with his work as if he were a child, and he finds independent work too lonely. He attaches himself emotionally to any sympathetic adult. He cannot submerge himself into a group because he is utterly dependent for his emotional satisfaction upon being the center of attention. If such an adolescent is sent away from home to school, he shows intense homesickness. He constantly makes ridiculous judgments if he is forced into thinking for himself. He frequently asks privately for some special arrangement: he wants some other partner in the laboratory, he prefers some other work to that assigned, he asks permission to hand work in a day late, he wants to have his seat moved nearer the window, he keeps library books out when others need them, he wants to be excused from class early, he wants a special arrangement of classes; if he gets into trouble, he begs his teachers to excuse him from punishment. In brief, he expects exactly the indulgent treatment one can expect from older people to whom one is emotionally attached. Every high school teacher has a few such pupils in her classes. They are emotional and social children who are so dependent upon their parents that they transfer this same attitude to their teachers. This simple type of childish adolescent is not difficult to recognize.

The second type is more complicated. Although an adolescent is deeply attached to his home and dependent upon it, he may at the same time desire profoundly to be independent, but he does not know how to free himself from home domination by ordinary methods. To cover up his social and emotional attachment to his home and parents, he makes numerous and dramatic overcompensations. This type of unemancipated adolescent is seen in the boy who gets drunk, uses profanity, or has illicit sexual relations as a means of demonstrating to the world his independence from home control.[13] When an overattached adolescent sets out to break the bonds between himself and his family by unwise and violent methods, it is because all ordinary methods have failed. A boy rarely succeeds in growing up by such violent means; all he does is to build up a habit of childish resentment. The adolescent who is free to buy his own clothes (provided he keeps within his allowance), free to bring anyone he will to his own home, free—within reasonable degrees of guidance—to choose his own work, and free to plan his own time, has enough opportunity for self-assertion without going to undesirable extremes. The boy who gets into serious difficulties to prove he is grown up is no more independent of his home than the boy who cannot make up his mind which book to read until he has asked his mother for her advice. One is positively conditioned, the other negatively; neither is mature and neither can regard his home objectively.

These two types of adolescent appear frequently in any teacher's class. The condition cannot be remedied overnight. A "cure" requires both time and a reasonable degree of co-operation from the home. The chief thing a teacher can do for such an adolescent is to explain to him the nature of his difficulties. Once he understands what the matter is, he is often able to

HOME

work out his own adjustment, either by obtaining greater freedom along conventional lines from his parents or by conformity to their main demands until he is old enough to leave home. An individual teacher can do little toward modifying a home situation, but much can be done through a vigorous Parent-Teachers Association by the open discussion of adolescent problems of adjustment. Such an organization permits an impersonal approach and does not imply the criticism which is always inherent in dealing with a single family. The teacher's chief individual efforts must always be centered upon showing an adolescent how he can adjust himself to things as they are.

ILLUSTRATIVE CASE STUDIES

To illustrate further the results of a failure to become emotionally emancipated from home control, the following brief case studies are presented. The reader should consider (a) what behavior indicated an unusual degree of attachment, (b) what treatment, different from that used, might have prevented the manifestations, and (c) what remedial measures might be recommended.

Dolores [8] stopped one day after class to ask advice regarding certain misunderstandings between her mother and herself. The situation, as the writer came to know it from interviews with both Dolores and her mother, was so common that it may almost be called typical of the modern home.

Dolores was an attractive, vivacious girl who was decidedly popular with boys. She pursued the usual custom of going with first one boy and then another without concentrating her attention upon anyone, said she knew enough about sex to leave it alone, and seemed innocent of anything more than the usual good times; in short, she appeared generally to be a typical, self-sufficient, modern girl. Her objective, unsentimental, easy-going boy-and-girl friendships ought to have delighted the heart of any anxious mother. But quite the contrary was the case.

Her mother simply could not understand how Dolores could be so "promiscuous" in selecting her friends. She constantly feared the worst, and seemed quite unconscious of the fact that her daughter was well armored against sex excitement by the sophistication of the modern girl. She deplored modern dancing, would not allow cardplaying in her home, scolded constantly about filthy modern novels, and generally made herself unintelligible to her children. She said she was willing for Dolores to have her friends come to the house, but what, Dolores said frankly, could they do when they got there? By the time Dolores had finished a year of college she and her mother had succeeded in coming to a complete misunderstanding. The mother argued that Dolores should not go often with a boy unless she intended to marry him. She stated that when *she* was a girl anyone who behaved as Dolores did would be an outcast from nice society, as was probably true. She was sure it was time for her daughter to settle down and find herself a mate before she built up such a reputation for recklessness that no man would want her. The daughter's reply was, of course, that she was just an average girl, that she did nothing wrong, and that her mother was out of date.

The great difficulty about this misunderstanding was that both mother and daughter were right. The mother was talking about conditions of her own girlhood, and could not realize that times have changed. Dolores was talking about conditions as she saw them, and could not realize that her mother's youth was lived under different circumstances. The mother was trying desperately and sincerely to save her daughter from what she saw as frightful ruin, for she based her interpretation of Dolores' conduct upon the attitudes current in her own girlhood. Dolores was trying to live the active, straightforward, independent, and fundamentally more healthy life of the girl of today, a life in which many young men have a part. If either had been less sincere in her convictions there would have been less trouble.

The efforts of the writer, in dealing with this situation, were directed primarily toward bringing about some understanding between these excellent representatives of two generations. Several interviews with the mother soon made clear, however, that she had become so thoroughly conventionalized, so shut in by her prejudices, that it was impossible to bring her to any glimpse of the changes in attitudes and points of view which had taken place since her girlhood. In fact, the very possibility of such changes seemed inconceivable to her; the manners and customs of rural Indiana thirty years ago seemed to her the one inspired, eternally-right-and-never-to-be-questioned code of life.

Dolores, however, soon came to an excellent understanding of the situation. She now tries to explain things whenever possible, to make allowance for differences in points of view, and to conduct herself so as to arouse as little antagonism as possible. It is probable that through her efforts any real disruption will be avoided. But as long as Dolores lives at home she will be subject to chronic criticism and nagging because she insists upon being a normal girl of her generation. Soon she will graduate, obtain a position elsewhere and proceed to live her own life in her own way.

Dolores' difficulties are those faced by thousands of girls of today. Of late years there has been added to the ever-present distrust of one generation for another the confusion and the conflict of attitudes inevitable in a society which is rapidly changing. A priori, it would seem that the parent should be the one most likely to have perspective and broad judgment in such a situation, since the parent has seen the change come about. But very often (as is the case of Dolores) it is the child only who comes to any understanding and who must bear the burden of adjustment, if any adjustment is made.

May [12] was a tall, thin girl, a sickly orphan who had been brought up in the home of a conscientious woman, mother of a girl about May's age. May suffered jealousy. One day the clothing of the daughter of the home was found slashed and snipped into pieces. May denied doing it. She was locked in a room and fed bread and milk (which she refused) until the woman finally, to avoid scandal, took May to court. May was resolute in denial. The court explained that at present it was not necessary to discover the mystery of slashed clothes; the important thing was the shocking mental and physical state into which the child had worked herself. After examination and physical restoration, May was placed in a home where she attended a small high school; the principal was asked to co-operate in [the] reconstruction of May. Years of effort by this socially minded woman are now being rewarded. May took a purse from the school within a few weeks of admission. No attempt by the principal was made to "prove" this, or to compel a painful "confession." May was told [that] the probabilities pointed to her; if she wished she could make restitution. It was explained to her that stealing is a grave symptom of inner trouble, all her friends were now trying to help her, and pending the "cure" it would be best for her to work out of school hours to repay incidental losses. She need not "confess" in words, no force would be used to make her pay if she felt innocent. Three times in two years May yielded to impulse to steal small articles; each time she made restitution. For over a year there has been no stealing; delinquency with boys broke out recently. The court offered to remove the troublesome girl from high school. "No," said the principal. "This girl is making steady progress in school. Her attitude is not rebellious; it is that of one appealing for help. This is our job, and unless we fail, or the girl begins to injure others, we are going to keep May in school."

May is about to graduate, after four years' intelligent supervision in this high school.*

A father and mother [12] of good social position quarreled constantly. The wife worried over a supposed infidelity of the husband, and on several occasions separated from him. After reconciliation, the husband left on business. The wife employed a detective who surprised the man in a hotel room with a girl and, acting under orders from the wife, took them both to the police station. There was publicity and scandal. Nevertheless, after consulting with their many friends, both parents decided "to patch it up for the sake of the children." The home is an armed camp of a triumphant wronged woman, and a half-defiant sulky male, with the children taking sides as the needs and profit of the situation suggest.

Marian [9] is a small, nervous girl of more than average ability who has to work four hours a day in a restaurant, and live at home (at a distance requiring an hour and a half each way on the street car) because her father regards education as "foolishness" and has ruled that Marian can earn her own way if she wants to be "high-class" and go to college. He criticizes her freely almost every day in an effort to break her spirit and Marian is so tired by night that she can put up no defense. She wants to teach in elementary school, a type of work for which she has both the ability and the personality, but she is worn out by her four hours of quite unnecessary work (her father has money enough to pay her way if he would) and the continual caustic criticism. She cannot concentrate when she tries to study and she can respond to the demand for better academic work only by tears. She cannot earn money enough to live anywhere but at home and she cannot stand much more overwork and "ragging" without a serious collapse that will put her out of college, thus justifying her father's low opinion of her efforts.

Lucile [9] is a small, blond, pert young thing who seems able to get herself into an unbelievable number of difficulties. For instance, she told her English teacher that she won't read a certain author

* This and the next case study are used by permission of New Republic, Inc.

because her parents think the author unsuitable for her. When the professor tried to insist upon the required reading Lucile's parents appeared and demanded that their daughter be allowed to substitute some other reference. It requires the combined personnel of two parents, one older sister and two college officials to make out Lucile's schedule for the next term. Her father has interviewed Lucile's zoology instructor and asked him to excuse the girl from the "section on evolution" because the course was "putting ideas into Lucile's head" (a thing that in the writer's opinion can't be done). No excuse from lectures was forthcoming, so Lucile—upon home advice—proceeded to cut her zoology classes for the next two weeks. Lucile's parents selected her sorority for her; they sit with her every evening and help her with her lessons; they read every textbook before she does so as to see if it is fit for her to study; they explain all obscure passages (often incorrectly); they watch over her selection of friends; they call on her instructors; they become unpleasantly vocal whenever Lucile is asked to do something they think she should not do; they write letters to the president, the dean of women, or anyone else in authority. Never in the two years she has been at the university has Lucile made an independent decision; never has she had an interview with anyone without the presence of at least one parent; never has she been made to face the consequences of her own childish judgment, until recently when two instructors got tired of her foolishness, successfully withstood the dire threats of her parents, and gave her immature, slipshod work the mark it deserved.

Every term, Walter [9] must begin during the first week to save the money for the $21 he must have, in another twelve weeks, to pay his university fees. To get this money, he cuts the desired lunch of a sandwich, a milk shake and a piece of pie down to a sandwich and a cup of coffee. By this means he can save twenty cents a day. Leaving the dessert off his supper saves another dime. Walter has to work every night from 5:30 till 1:30 as a clerk for an express company which, however, pays him hardly a respectable wage. In addition to what he can earn he had $40 from his family at the beginning of the school year—all they could scrape together. The long hours of work on the close of a day of study soon proved too much for him and he went on probation at the end of his first term. He cannot stop his work and he dreads the six or seven years that will be needed to finish his college course if he reduces the amount of academic work. Moreover, his family tell him that he must get out of college, into a regular job, in not more than the usual four years. His people worry about his health, which is being undermined by overwork. He also worries about his health. In the meantime, his $40 is nearly gone and he has less than half the money needed for the next fees, so he goes without lunch entirely. He fails an examination because he cannot buy an extra book and cannot get to the library because he has to work evenings. It becomes a question of whether or not he can last out the year physically, educationally, or financially. On top of everything else he conceives the idea that he will be disgraced if he has to withdraw because he is poor. Walter has what in many respects is a fine home, but it is a home that, through its enthusiastic encouragement of a college career and its total inability to supply funds, is driving Walter into a state of collapse.

BIBLIOGRAPHY *

1. Anderson, A., and Dvorak, B., "Differences between College Students and Their Elders in Standards of Conduct," *Journal of Abnormal and Social Psychology,* 1928, 23: 286-289.
2. Cavan, R. S., "The Relation of Home Background to Personality Adjustments of Adolescents," *Publications of the American Sociological Society,* 1934, 28: 127-128.
3. *Concerning Parents,* New Republic, Inc., 1926, 284 pp.
4. Groves, E. R., and Ogburn, W., *American Marriage and Family Relationships,* Henry Holt and Company, 1928, 497 pp.
5. Groves, E. R., *Social Problems of the Family.* J. B. Lippincott Company, 1927, 314 pp.
6. Kovacs, I., "Das Opfer," *Internationale Zeitschrift für Individuelle Psychologie,* 1933, 11: 471-477.
7. Hollingworth, L. S., *Psychology of the Adolescent,* D. Appleton-Century Company, 1928, 227 pp.
8. Pressey, L. C., *Some College Students and Their Problems,* Ohio State University Press, 1929, 97 pp.
9. ———, "Some Serious Family Maladjustments among College Students," *Social Forces,* 1931, 10: 236-242.
10. Thurlow, M. B., "A Study of Selected Factors in Family Life as Described in Life History Material," *Social Forces,* 1934, 12: 562-569.
11. Todd, A. J., "Symposium on Home and Family Life in a Changing Civilization," *United States Department of Education Bulletin,* No. 5, Government Printing Office, 1931, 34 pp.

* See also the references in the Appendix.

12. Van Waters, M., *Youth in Conflict,* New Republic, Inc., 1925, 293 pp.
13. Williams, F. E., "Confronting the World: The Adjustments of Later Adolescence," in *Concerning Parents,* New Republic, Inc., 1926, pp. 137-159.
14. Witmer, H. L., *et al.,* "The Childhood Personality and Parent-Child Relationships of Dementia Praecox and Manic-Depressive Patients," *Smith College Studies in Social Work,* 1934, 4: 289-377.

CHAPTER XIII

THE ADOLESCENT AND HIS SCHOOL

SINCE the high school is a public institution it should serve the needs of adolescents. It must concern itself with social adjustment, vocational choice, physical development, growth, and mastery of academic subjects. Some of these points have already been discussed adequately, but there remain three topics that require further consideration.

In several previous chapters frequent reference has been made to the need for a general reorganization of the high school curriculum. The desirable curricular offerings—both required and elective—of the high school will first be discussed. A second section will take up the matter of classifying adolescents for purposes of instruction, thus making possible an adaptation of both content and methods to the wide individual differences in the pupil population. Finally, a third section will deal with desirable teaching methods. If a high school is to serve the needs of youth, it must offer an appropriate curriculum, adapt it to individual differences, and teach it by methods that stimulate mastery.

THE HIGH SCHOOL CURRICULUM

The curriculum is a form of social heritage. Like most social heritages, it shows a tendency to become crystallized. Of recent years, the change in the number and type of pupils attending high school has been remarkable. The curriculum, however, has not altered nearly enough to keep pace with the changing character of the high school group.

In 1890 the curriculum was composed chiefly of Latin, Greek, algebra, geometry, English composition, and English literature, plus a relatively small number of classes in modern languages and physical sciences. These subjects were those demanded during the nineteenth century as a basis for the education of a gentleman and a scholar. They still remain subjects necessary for the scholar, but they are not and were never intended as subjects for the average adolescent girl or boy. In 1880 about two children in each hundred of the appropriate ages were in high school. In 1930 about fifty out of every one hundred children of the appropriate ages were in either high school or college. The curriculum has in the meantime added more work in the physical and biological sciences and in modern language; it has also added various special features—notably the business, technical, household arts, and manual-training courses. In some large city high schools and in various experimental schools there has been a considerable elaboration of special fields, but these elaborations are not typical of the average high school. The difference in type of pupil has automatically forced some changes in all schools. The resulting curriculum, however, is largely the result of student pressure rather than of deliberate, scientific research and reorganization.

The elementary school curriculum, on the other hand, has changed markedly in the last twenty years as the result of educational research. Certain of the early studies showed much of the elementary curriculum to be irrelevant to the average person's daily life. Other investigations proved the standards of work per grade to be higher than could be met by the average child's ability and higher than were necessary as preparation for ordinary adult activities. With this situation in mind educationalists set out to determine scientifically what elements should go into the curriculum of the first eight grades. Their method was simple and pragmatic. They wanted first of all to find out what skills in arithmetic every adult needed, how well every adult needed to write in order to hold a job, how rapidly and with what degree of comprehension he needed to read, what words every adult needed to spell, etc. Large groups of adults were studied to discover what facts and skills they actually used. It was thus found that a writing speed of ninety letters a minute was quite sufficient for holding down a job such as a sales girl or bookkeeper, in which handwriting was an important element, although for taking notes in college a speed of about one hundred and twenty letters a minute was necessary. It was also found that a fair degree of legibility, which has been objectively determined, was good enough to hold a position in which one's handwriting must be readable. In other words the average adult needed to be able to write legibly at a rate of ninety letters a minute. In arithmetic similar pragmatic studies were made. Adults from various levels of society were asked to keep an account of every transaction involving the use of arithmetic over a given period of time. When enough such studies had been made, it became evident that the average adult needed great facility in handling amounts of money up to about $5.00, some experience with about a dozen units of measurement, training in keeping a cash account, some understanding of simple interest and per cent, and ability to handle eight or nine of the commonest fractions. On the basis of this research educators eliminated such topics as cube root, square root, mathematical progressions, partial payments, compound interest, or wholesale buying and selling, because the average adult neither used nor remembered them.

The modern elementary school curriculum is, therefore, centered around the items of information and skills that will inevitably be used by all adults. The objective in handwriting is no longer to write like an expert but to write well enough and rapidly enough for the demands of an average existence. The curriculum is no longer concerned with "mental discipline." The objective in spelling is no longer to train the mind or the memory by learning to spell long and difficult words that will never be used in such writing as the average adult does. The objective is rather to learn how to spell about two thousand words which are the simplest and most commonly used in the written productions of children or adults.

Along all lines the elementary school curriculum has obviously changed. It is easier than it was twenty-five years ago. It has eliminated so much that the remaining material can be taught in six years instead of nine, and it has introduced about two years of work not included at all in the elementary curriculum of 1890. It has adapted its materials to the abilities and interests of children of the ages being taught. Its principal object is to provide children with the minimal essentials for a civilized existence.

The high school curriculum has not undergone any such comparable alteration. It has been cut down here and expanded there as this or that group of enthusiasts demanded that a change be made. It has, however, never been overhauled as a whole and has never been checked up adequately against the life of either the average adolescent or the average adult. There is a strong supposition that if such intensive study were made, the resulting high school course of study would differ fundamentally from any now in existence.

Values in high school training.—Before presenting any curriculum in detail, there should be some consideration of the ultimate values to which the course of study should lead. The three most often proposed values are cultural, disciplinary, and practical. Each of these should be examined with reference to high school work. Cultural value lies fundamentally in the way a subject is taught; no subject has inherently any cultural value whatever. Thus, Latin is not a cultural subject for a Catholic priest because the church services are written in Latin and he needs the language as part of his vocational training. Neither are modern languages primarily cultural subjects for graduates who are going to use them for purely technical ends. On the other hand, a teacher of manual training may give a course with considerable cultural value if he emphasizes implications rather than manipulation of objects. The writer knows one professor of poultry husbandry who can start a lecture with an egg and end with a history of China. She has sat through classes in English literature in which masterpieces were torn to shreds and every classical allusion hunted relentlessly to its lair—a procedure guaranteed to rob any course of its cultural profits and reduce it to the level of a crossword puzzle. In contrast, she recalls a supposedly technical course on statistics that succeeded in giving a real understanding of economic theories. Anyone who stops to reminisce can prove from personal experiences that cultural values emerge from the handling of subject matter, not from its nature. There is, then, no reason for having one subject more than another in high school as far as the development of "culture" is concerned.

There is also no subject that is perfectly certain to train the mind. Any subject that is difficult will give more training in concentration and close thinking than a subject that is easy. Any subject demanding a great deal of rote learning will train students in economical methods of memorizing; rather, it will select those students who use sufficiently economical methods of memorizing to master the subject matter. It is no accident that pupils who have studied four years of Latin are more intelligent and have better memories than those who did not study four years of Latin. But this situation is no argument for transfer of training. The Latin students passed four years of Latin because they are intelligent and had good memories; they did not become intelligent or develop excellent memories because they studied Latin. Any other subject equally difficult and making equal demands upon rote learning—anatomy, for example—would be equally successful in selecting an intelligent and efficient group of memorizers at the end of four years.

There have been innumerable studies of the transfer of training from one subject to another and from any subject in the school to life outside. Most of the evidence is negative or very faintly positive. What transfer does take place evidently depends first on the ability of the individual student and secondly upon the extent to which the teacher has attempted to bring about transfer. It seems to make no difference what subject is being studied. If any material is taught so as to facilitate transfer, a considerable degree of the subject matter or method may be carried over into another field, but there is no subject in high school that will automatically transfer to any other subject or to life outside the school, nor is there any subject that will train the mind any better than another of equal difficulty.

In earlier generations of high school pupils, the subject matter in the traditional curriculum undoubtedly did have higher cultural or transfer values than are likely to be derived at present. As long as only bright students with academic interests went to high school, the degree of transfer from any subject taught was necessarily more than can now be obtained by the same subject matter with the present enrollment of less capable high school students. It is a question whether the average high school student of today is capable of thinking in general terms to any great extent. This lowering of the average intellectual capacity among high school pupils has operated automatically to lower possible cultural or transfer values in all subjects. The methods of teaching have been modified, the amount of material covered has been cut down, and the nature of the material has been altered. Thus, in present-day high school composition classes the teacher is busy with getting punctuation marks correctly placed in very ordinary sentences. There is nothing especially cultural about this sort of teaching. When the writer's father went to high school, he was regularly required to write, in his English composition classes, essays in imitation of the classical English authors. Such an assignment at the present time would be completely beyond the ability of more than a small handful of pupils in the high school.

Since high school subjects cannot be defended upon the basis of their cultural or transfer values, it becomes necessary to find other values in terms of which to select subject matter. The high school curriculum must obviously, for certain pupils, be a foundation on which to put either a college education or training in technical schools. For other groups of students it must obviously be a technical and vocational training. For all pupils it should offer some degree of preparation to meet such needs of the average adult as cannot be covered in the elementary school because of the pupils' immaturity. Finally, the curriculum should contain the answers to the most common and vexatious problems in the lives of the adolescents themselves.

To reach these many objectives certain subjects should be taken by all pupils. These subjects would be those dedicated to the preparation of the adolescent for a normal adult life or to the explanation of his own immediate problems. The rest of the courses on each student's schedule should be those best fitted for whatever he intends to do when, and if, he finishes high school. The college preparatory or academic course is just as technical in its preparation for college work as the commercial in its preparation for an entrance into the business world. In the effort to prepare too many pupils for college, the essential subjects in the preparatory courses have been so modified that nobody gets an adequate foundation. In the Latin classes, for instance, everyone gets a smattering of Latin roots, but no one acquires any mastery of Latin as a language. What is needed is not less Latin for everybody, but more Latin for a very few. The adolescent's schedule should then be made up of two types of subject—those that fit him for normal existence in his community and those that fit him for earning his living. Whatever cultural or transfer values are possible of achievement by each individual can be gained through proper teaching methods; many pupils will not obtain such values from anything, no matter how it is taught.

Required work.—The first thing needed is a survey of adult life and of adolescent problems, to determine what elements are needed in the essential curriculum. Perhaps the most obvious thing that every individual must learn to do is to get along with his family, friends, and neighbors. Everyone is a member of a social group, and everyone's mental health and social value depend upon his ability to get along with his group. Not every child in the world can master academic subjects, but practically everyone can learn to live a reasonably normal life, if given the training necessary for a person of his ability and temperament. For getting along peaceably in a community, one needs information along two main lines: one must understand how society is organized and controlled and how human nature reacts to social stimuli. Translated into terms of curriculum, the adolescent should study the social sciences and psychology, but neither of these subjects as it is usually taught. It is doubtful if a study of the Constitution will make one a better citizen, or if a consideration of wars and political campaigns will produce an understanding of human society. On all sides there is plenty of evidence that an understanding of economic theory does not produce a sound economic life. There are, however, certain facts in regard to history and the development of society that could form the nucleus of a course in social science at the high school level. The course would differ from the social studies of the elementary school in that its content would be more difficult, more comprehensive, and more theoretical. The course in psychology would differ in practically every respect from the usual elementary course in college. What the average adolescent or adult needs to understand is how people react to each other, what reactions are within the limits of normality, what reactions are used as expressions of different emotional attitudes, what behavior on the part of one person will elicit what reactions from another, what controls may be used for emotional drives, what elements make up personality, etc. In fact, the average modern adult feels he or she *must* know the answers to such questions. It is in response to this need that the numerologists, astrologists, fake psychologists, mental healers, spiritualistic mediums, and all other pseudo psychologists exist. They are answering, honestly or dishonestly, the questions that should be answered by a good high school course in mental health and understanding of human nature and they will continue to flourish until scientifically accurate facts are disseminated through required work somewhere in the course of compulsory education.

Everyone, either adolescent or adult, needs to maintain his or her mental and physical health. If either of these is lost, the individual becomes a burden to himself and society. Any doctor can testify that physical health is usually lost either through ignorance or carelessness, and any psychiatrist can say the same for mental health.

The average adult's complete ignorance as regards symptoms of either physical or mental difficulty is almost unbelievable. Diseases are communicated from one person to another because the average adult does not know how communicable diseases are transferred. Children in every community grow up to the age of a dozen years before anyone discovers they are so nearsighted they cannot see to read their schoolbooks. In any schoolroom one can observe children with glandular defects, partially deaf children, or children with chronic temperatures, whose difficulties have never been suspected. It is not more than twenty years ago since there were so many extreme defectives in the public schools that a trained psychologist could pick them out simply by watching the class walk around the playground; yet these children were being taught as if they were normal. In any class in high school there are pupils with intense emotional problems who are getting no help whatever from the subjects they study. For guidance they must depend upon their parents, their personal relationships to teachers, or their friends—none of whom are likely to have had training adequate for the giving of advice.

There is, then, need for two more courses of fundamental character to be required of every pupil in high school. One course would be devoted to the maintenance of physical health, the other to the maintenance of mental health. These two courses are particularly appropriate to high school because they concern matters directly related to adolescent problems and interests. Moreover, they require a higher degree of mental development and a larger experience in living than are typical of elementary school children and hence cannot be given earlier. They are concerned with facts every adult needs to know, no matter what occupation he enters.

The modern world is based upon scientific discoveries in both biological and physical science. A person with no comprehension of scientific principles and no knowledge of scientific facts is not only unable to adjust to modern life but is actually in danger from the necessary use of modern appliances. Only doctors have any realization of the number of people who every year burn or shock themselves by misuse of ordinary electrical devices. People from all levels of education are constantly plugging in electrical fixtures with wet hands, whether or not they have ever studied a high school course in physics. The writer is reminded of a good friend who was an honor student in physics and in chemistry at college; yet, when the cord of her study lamp was too long, she cut the cord in two with a pair of scissors while the light was still on! In spite of all her honors, she nearly killed herself by this procedure.

There are altogether too many people whose lives remain unaffected by any required work in science. The fault obviously lies in the nature of the subject matter presented. Here and there one finds introductory courses in physics designed for those pupils who have no intention of taking more than one year of work and want to get from it whatever items of information will be most useful to them in their daily lives. They want to understand something about electrical fixtures, automobiles and airplanes, or household mechanics. Such an introductory course would not be adequate as a basis for advanced work in physics, but it would be most appropriate for the more important task of living a sensible adult existence. There would seem no good reason why ninety-nine pupils should be given a theoretical approach to physics in order that one pupil who goes on in the subject will have an adequate foundation. Physics and chemistry both have an enormous number of facts that are of pronounced usefulness in everyday living. There is no dearth of practical subject matter; the difficulty is rather one of selection. The writer recalls an illustrative incident from her own days in a girls' boarding school. She was asked to give an example of the difference between a physical and a chemical change. She replied that when a housewife scrubbed the grease off the kitchen table with sand, the change was physical, but when the housewife removed the grease by washing the table with ammonia, the change was chemical. The teacher of the science class refused completely to accept this example, although it is hard to see how any reply in a class of prospective housewives could have been more appropriate. It is just such practical points as this which should be included in the high school science course, instead of being excluded.

In the field of biological science there have also been great developments. The average adult needs facts, but there seems no way of getting the information in school unless one takes more courses in biological science than the average pupil could possibly get into his schedule. Again the task of the curriculum builder is one of selection. He needs to study average adult life and to find out what facts taught in the biological sciences will contribute most to the commonest problems of the adolescent and adult. Matters of diet, effects of drugs, and prevention of disease come at once to the mind. It is presumably in this field that training in sex education should be given. Mental conflicts arising from sexual difficulties are the business of the psychologist, but the facts in regard to sexual life concern the biologist. A course in biological science of essential value to every pupil in high school could be devised, but it would not contain the subject matter typical of the usual introductory course in biology.

Both men and women live in some kind of home and belong to a family group. Both need to know what elements go into the maintenance of a satisfactory home.[9] Boys and girls of high school age are within a few years of the time when they will establish their own homes and families. It is therefore essential for them to learn all they can about such matters. As matters now stand, such information is available only to girls; to be sure, they have the major need for technical information in regard to housekeeping, but in the social development of a home the father is quite as important as the mother. A course designed especially to fit adolescent boys and girls for their inevitable responsibility as members of a home and as parents of children should be required of all students in high school. There is no other subject matter that could conceivably be of more practical value, nor could such a course be given anywhere except in high school. Elementary school children are too young, and in the entire population of college age many are already married.

In one more field the objectives of high school work could be determined with a fair degree of accuracy. The average adult writes both personal and business letters; he reads newspapers and magazines, and he passes judgment upon a larger or smaller number of new books. Here then is an essential core around which to build the required curriculum in English. It is much more important that an adult should be able to read a newspaper intelligently than that he should be able to read Shakespeare. It is in fact absolutely essential that he should be able to read newspapers and current periodicals with a reasonable degree of comprehension, if he is to keep in touch with the world in which he lives. A course centering around letter writing, newspaper reading, and the estimating of modern books would be of use to every pupil who took it and would serve as a basis for everyday needs in the years to come. Naturally the entire offerings of an English department would not be restricted to this single course. What is being discussed in this section is the work to be required of every pupil in high school. A later section will deal with the matter of electives.

Adolescents, like everyone else, need outlets for their emotional interests and for self-expression. Their schoolwork and the constantly shifting social adjustments inevitably put considerable strain upon them. They have a real need for such subjects as music, art, physical education, and for participation in all kinds of extracurricular activities.

A clear distinction needs to be made in these subjects between the few for whom the subject is a specialty and the many for whom it should be a means of relaxation and self-expression. There is no kind of human endeavor more exacting than the training given the grand opera singer, but there is also no form of self-expression more enjoyable to most people than singing. The object of the required work along any of these lines should be to provide for such enjoyable self-expression as can be indulged in by the untalented. The games in physical education should be those that can be played even by the clumsiest, rather than those demanding such expert co-ordination as can be achieved by only a few pupils. The technical aspects of these subjects should be included in special courses to be taken as electives by those who have special talents. They should never be included in the required work, any more than integral calculus should be required of every pupil just because a very few would find the subject interesting or profitable.

As a conclusion to this section, it would seem advisable to make a list of those courses that should be on every pupil's schedule. These courses are either immediately useful to the adolescent in his own problems or else will be useful to him in his everyday life as a normal adult.

1. Social Science
2. Psychology
3. Physical Hygiene
4. Mental Hygiene
5. Biological Science
6. Nonbiological Science
7. Homemaking and Child Care
8. English Composition and Reading
9. Music, Art, Physical Education—Extracurricular Activities

Most of the first eight courses in this list would presumably be only a semester in length. At the end of the total discussion concerning the curriculum, sample schedules will be presented to show how required courses, vocational courses, and elective courses may be fitted together to make a comprehensive schedule for the high school pupil. This matter of fitting the requirements into the four years of high school has therefore been left for later discussion.

Elective courses.—Theoretically, there is no limit to the number or nature of electives. All that is needed for establishing an elective course is a group of interested students and an adequately prepared instructor. Both the interests of students and those of teachers should be allowed full play. If there are in a high school pupils who have desire and ability to study Sanskrit, calculus, plant pathology, or pre-Shakespearean drama, and if there are teachers who have desire and ability to present such material, there should be no objection to the inclusion of relevant courses in the high school curriculum. In fact, elective courses should purposely be designed to serve and develop adolescent interests in many lines. The limits of knowledge are the only theoretical limits to elective offerings.

There are, however, many practical reasons why elective work cannot be expanded indefinitely. If a high school employs thirty-five teachers, some of whose time must be given to required courses, there can be only the number and type of electives which can be given during the remaining class periods by these teachers. Therefore, the courses offered must be those that will serve the greatest number of pupils. The pure electives within a department should rest on the mature and balanced judgment of experienced teachers in the department as to what topics can and should be covered. It is only the required work that need be concerned with the practical question of the average individual's everyday needs. Interest and ability form the basis for the elective program.

No attempt will be made to list possible elective courses. Such a list must depend, in each school, upon the local instructional resources and pupil material. Naturally, as many and as varied electives as possible should be included, since the major objectives are the awakening, furthering, and broadening of interest.

Vocational courses.—The descriptive course on occupations for freshmen and the apprenticeship course for the first semester of the sophomore year have already been described and need no further discussion here. These are the introductory courses, after which pupils would progress into increasingly technical work along one or more lines. This section will concern itself only with additional points in regard to the vocational program.

The same course may be vocational for some pupils and a free elective for others. The future carpenter may take a course in woodworking as a preparation for his job, while a future philosopher may elect it because he likes to build things in his spare time. A girl in the commercial course takes stenography as part of her vocational training; another pupil may elect shorthand merely because she wants to learn it. For students in the college preparatory course, algebra is a "tool" subject because it presents facts they will need to use in college courses; yet, elementary algebra may be an elective for students who do not plan for college. One cannot, therefore, draw any sharp line between vocational and elective courses so far as the initial work in a subject is concerned.

There should be, however, in the high school program some courses that will lead directly into occupations. For many pupils, the years of high school work mark the end of formal training. These students must not be neglected. The number and type of strictly vocational courses is naturally limited by the available equipment and instructional force. In cities it is probably better for each high school to specialize along certain lines, so that equipment need not be duplicated; this arrangement permits of a relatively large number of different vocational classes. Any required work should, of course, be identical from school to school.

Every pupil who is not reasonably certain to succeed in college should complete some type of vocational training before he leaves high school. A college-preparatory course alone prepares only for college, not for earning one's living. Completion of such a course guarantees verbal intelligence, but nothing else. An adolescent who cannot expect to add a college course to the preparatory work should not be allowed to graduate without some other form of preparation for life. He needs a second string to his bow.

It is not within the scope of this text to list possible vocational courses, any more than to list any other forms of elective work. The number and character must be determined by local need, equipment, and teaching personnel. The main objectives are that these courses should be truly vocational—not prevocational—that they should be as varied as possible, and that they should be elected by those who most need them.

Integration of required, elective, and vocational work.— Below is presented a skeletonized schedule to show how the available hours might best be apportioned.

SCHEMATIC GENERAL SCHEDULE

		First Year Semesters			Second Year Semesters	
		1	2		1	2
Prepared Work	Social Science	4	4	Physical Science	4	..
	Physical Hygiene	3	..	English	3	3
	Mental Hygiene	..	3	Occupations	3	..
	English	3	3	Homemaking	..	4
	Occupations	2	2	Elective	3	6
	Elective	3	3	Vocational Subjects	2	2
	Total	15	15	Total	15	15
Unprepared Work	Music, Art, or Dramatics	1	1	Music, Art, or Dramatics	1	..
	Games	2	2	Games	2	2
	Clubs	1	1	Clubs	1	1
	Total	4	4	Total	4	3
		Third Year			Fourth Year	
Prepared Work	Biological Science	3	..	Psychology	..	3
	Elective	6	9	Elective	9	6
	Vocational Subjects	6	6	Vocational	6	6
	Total	15	15	Total	15	15
Unprepared Work	Games	2	2	Games	1	1
	Clubs	1	1	Clubs	1	1
	Total	3	3	Total	2	2

The assignment is based on an assumption of six sixty-minute periods per day. An average pupil would have fifteen classes per week for which preparation was needed, three to four unprepared classes, and eleven hours for study during school time. The number of unprepared hours is diminished from year to year. It is assumed that pupils will, through the earlier requirements, be guided into appropriate extracurricular activities. The object of the freshmen requirements is to bring each pupil in contact with several such activities during his first year, instead of leaving the whole matter to his own initiative. Thus, if a boy elects music during one semester, dramatics during the other, soccer in the fall term, swimming during the winter, tennis in the spring, and uses his "club" hour to visit (in the course of the year) the literary, radio, carpentry, mechanical drawing, French, auto mechanics, and printing clubs, he should have made enough contacts to continue on his own interests without further requirements.

The majority of the required hours are placed in the first two years. Those who drop out after one or two years remain in high school too short a time to receive much vocational training in any case, but they can be given a maximum of preparation for normal living. Moreover, by postponing specialization, transfer from one course to another is greatly facilitated.

This generalized schedule must, of course, be adapted to each student's requirements. The "elective" and "vocational" hours are to be used for preparing a pupil specifically for what he intends to do after leaving high school. In order to demonstrate the possibility of maintaining the required work while permitting sufficient flexibility, several typical schedules will be given. In the first year, there is only one course that differentiates pupils in different lines of work. This one course has purposely been made of a definite preparatory nature for future work; a pupil should therefore find out during the first year if he really wants to continue in the line he has started. At the beginning of his sophomore year he can transfer with little, if any, loss of time and no loss of credit, since there are some purely elective hours in all courses. It may seem that the number of free electives is extremely small, but it must be remembered that each student has already selected a course of study, thus indicating the nature of the electives he desires. The few remaining electives are for his use in dipping into lines of work excluded by his original electing of his own course. The extracurricular clubs must also be kept in mind as techniques by which a pupil can come in contact with various departments outside his own selected fields.

Schedule for Student in Academic Course

First Year

		Semesters	
		1	2
Prepared Work	Social Science	4	4
	Physical Hygiene	3	..
	Mental Hygiene	..	3
	English	3	3
	Occupations	2	2
	Latin	3	3
		15	15
Unprepared Work		4	4
Total		19	19

Second Year

		Semesters	
		1	2
	Physical Science	3	..
	English	3	3
	Occupations	3	..
	Homemaking	..	4
	Latin	3	3
	Algebra	3	3
	Elective	..	3
		15	16
Unprepared Work		4	3
Total		19	19

Third Year

		Semesters	
Prepared Work	Biological Science	3	..
	Geometry	3	3
	French or German	3	3
	English	3	3
	History	3	3
	Elective	..	3
		15	15
Unprepared Work		3	3
Total		18	18

Fourth Year

		Semesters	
	Psychology	3	..
	Review Mathematics	..	3
	Chemistry or Physics	3	3
	French or German	3	3
	English	3	3
	Elective	3	3
		15	15
Unprepared Work		2	2
Total		17	17

The above schedule has been planned with due respect to the unit requirements of the North Central Association. There are twelve elective hours left for further adjustments to local needs.

Schedule for Student in Technical Course
(Not for Engineering Prospects)

First Year

		Semesters	
		1	2
Prepared Work	Social Science	4	4
	Physical Hygiene	3	..
	Mental Hygiene	..	3
	English	3	3
	Occupations	2	2
	Shopwork	3	3
		15	15

Second Year

		Semesters	
		1	2
	Physical Science	3	..
	English	3	3
	Occupations	3	..
	Homemaking	..	3
	Shopwork	3	3
	Mechanical Drawing	3	3
	Elective	..	3
		15	15

SCHOOL

	First Year	Sem. 1	Sem. 2		Second Year	Sem. 1	Sem. 2
	Unprepared Work	4	4		Unprepared Work	4	3
		19	19			19	18

	Third Year	Sem. 1	Sem. 2		Fourth Year	Sem. 1	Sem. 2
Prepared Work	Biological Science	3	..		Psychology	3	..
	Chemistry	3	3		Physics	3	3
	Shopwork	3	3		Shopwork	3	3
	Shopwork	3	3		Shopwork	3	3
	Elective	3	3		Printing	..	3
	Commercial Geography	..	3		Elective	3	3
		15	15			15	15
Unprepared Work		3	3	Unprepared Work		2	2
		18	18			17	17

No attempt has been made to specify the nature of the shopwork courses; both the pupils' objective and the local equipment must determine the actual assignments.

SCHEDULE FOR STUDENT IN BUSINESS COURSE

	First Year	Sem. 1	Sem. 2		Second Year	Sem. 1	Sem. 2
Prepared Work	Social Science	4	4		Physical Science	3	..
	Physical Hygiene	3	..		English	3	3
	Mental Hygiene	..	3		Occupations	3	..
	English	3	3		Homemaking	..	3
	Occupations	2	2		Bookkeeping	3	3
	Bookkeeping	3	3		Shorthand	3	3
					Typing	..	3
		15	15			15	15
Unprepared Work		4	4	Unprepared Work		4	3
	Total	19	19		Total	19	18

	Third Year	Sem. 1	Sem. 2		Fourth Year	Sem. 1	Sem. 2
Prepared Work	Biological Science	3	..		Psychology	3	..
	Bookkeeping	3	3		Bookkeeping	3	3
	Shorthand	3	3		Shorthand	3	3
	Typing	3	3		Typing	3	3

THE ADOLESCENT'S ENVIRONMENT

		Third Year Semesters		Fourth Year	Semesters	
		1	2		1	2
Prepared	Office Practice	3	3	Commercial		
Work	Elective	..	3	Geography	..	3
				Elective (Economics if possible)	3	3
		15	15		15	15
Unprepared Work		3	3	Unprepared Work	2	2
		18	18		17	17

If differentiation of course between prospective bookkeepers and prospective stenographers is desired, the above schedule would demand rearrangement.

SCHEDULE FOR STUDENT IN HOME ECONOMICS OR AGRICULTURE COURSE

		First Year Semesters			Second Year Semesters	
		1	2		1	2
	Social Science	4	4	Physical Science	3	..
	Physical Hygiene	3	..	English	3	3
Pre-	Mental Hygiene	..	3	Occupations	3	..
pared	English	3	3	Homemaking	..	3
Work	Occupations	2	2	Home Economics (Agriculture)	3	3
	Home Economics (Agriculture)	3	3	Home Economics (Agriculture)	3	3
				Elective	..	3
		15	15		15	15
Unprepared Work		4	4	Unprepared Work	4	3
		19	19		19	18

	Third Year			Fourth Year		
	Biological Science	3	..	Psychology	3	..
	Chemistry	3	3	Home Economics (Agriculture)	3	3
	Home Economics (Agriculture)	3	3	Home Economics (Agriculture)	3	3
	Home Economics (Agriculture)	3	3	Home Economics (Agriculture)	3	3
	Elective	3	6	Elective	3	6
		15	15		15	15
Unprepared Work		3	3	Unprepared Work	2	2
		18	18		17	17

The exact nature of the courses in Home Economics and Agriculture have not here been indicated. The object of this schedule is merely to demonstrate the integration of required, elective, and vocational courses.

The above schedules require four years. More and more schools are establishing two-year courses for those who cannot take more time or do not have enough ability to complete four years of work. The main problem is to arrange courses so they will be as useful as possible. It must be admitted at once that no two-year preparation is sufficient for any work above that of the semiskilled artisan. Such courses of study should, then, be dedicated to preparing a student for normal living and for the relatively simple lines of work open to him. Three possible schedules are presented below:

SCHEDULE FOR STUDENT IN TWO-YEAR COURSE
(Business)

	First Year				Second Year		
		Semester				Semester	
		1	2			1	2
	Social Science	4	4	Physical Science		3	..
Pre-	Physical Hygiene	3	..	Occupations		3	3
pared	Mental Hygiene	..	3	Homemaking		..	3
Work	English	3	3	Bookkeeping		3	3
	Occupations	2	2	Typing		3	3
	Office Practice	3	3	Elective		3	3
		15	15			15	15
Unprepared Work		4	4	Unprepared Work		4	3
	Total	19	19	Total		19	18

SCHEDULE FOR STUDENT IN TWO-YEAR COURSE
(Mechanics)

	First Year				Second Year		
		Semester				Semester	
		1	2			1	2
	Social Science	4	4	Physical Science		3	..
Pre-	Physical Hygiene	3	..	Occupations		3	3
pared	Mental Hygiene	..	3	Homemaking		..	3
Work	English	3	3	Shopwork		3	3
	Occupations	2	2	Shopwork		3	3
	Shopwork	3	3	Elective		3	3
		15	15			15	15
Unprepared Work		4	4	Unprepared Work		4	3
	Total	19	19	Total		19	18

SCHEDULE FOR STUDENT IN TWO-YEAR COURSE
(Home Economics or Agriculture)

	First Year	Semesters		Second Year	Semesters	
		1	2		1	2
	Social Science	4	4	Physical Science	3	..
	Physical Hygiene	3	..	Occupations	3	3
Prepared Work	Mental Hygiene	..	3	Homemaking	..	3
	English	3	3	Home Economics (Agriculture)	3	3
	Occupations	2	2			
	Home Economics (Agriculture)	3	3	Home Economics (Agriculture)	3	3
				Elective	3	3
		15	15		15	15
Unprepared Work		4	4	Unprepared Work	4	3
	Total	19	19	Total	19	18

In the above schedules, four points should be noted. First, the English requirement is omitted from the second year, to get time for concentration along vocational lines. Second, the course on occupations has been extended and altered. Only in the first semester of the first year—the period during which jobs open to these pupils are being discussed—would those in the two-year courses attend the regular occupations class. Thereafter, time would be spent in direct apprenticeship of some kind, preferably in several simple lines of work. Third, there is time left for an elective in the second year. This time could be added to the apprenticeship hours or it could be used as special preparation for a particular job a student has located and expects to enter. Finally, a pupil who changes his mind and decides to take a four-year course can do so with no loss of time or credit; moreover, transfers at the end of the first year are relatively easy.

Further courses of the usual four-year length could be worked out for the prospective social worker, minister, nurse, or engineer. Those presented above should serve, however, to illustrate the main points requiring demonstration.

ADJUSTMENTS TO INDIVIDUAL DIFFERENCES

Adjustments to individual differences in capacity, interest, and personality have taken three forms: homogeneous grouping, special classes, and complete individualization of instruction. The teacher should have an understanding of all three and an appreciation of their usefulness. All have a place in the high school.

Homogeneous grouping.—The term "homogeneous grouping" means merely the classification of children of similar abilities into classes for purposes of instruction. Many efforts to segregate bright, average, and dull pupils have been made during the last twenty-five years. In a recent survey [2] of the literature, an investigator found 136 articles dealing with attempts at homogeneous grouping; between 40 and 50 per cent of the material taught in most schools was presented to groups of children so selected as to represent different levels of ability or educational achievement. With such a considerable interest in the matter it would seem as if there should be a mass of information in regard to the relative success of homogeneous versus heterogeneous classification of pupils for purposes of instruction. Nothing, however, is further from the truth. Of the 136 articles, thirty-two were purely theoretical and ninety-eight reported uncontrolled experiments, leaving only six that were either partially or wholly controlled. Of these six, three came out definitely in favor of homogeneous classification, two were doubtful, and one was definitely against such grouping. Hence, no one knows definitely whether homogeneous grouping is or is not beneficial, because not enough thoroughgoing experiments have been completed to establish the necessary facts.

If one wishes to put together pupils of the same ability, one must first decide what bases to use for the classification. The bases most frequently reported are teachers' ratings, teachers' marks, intelligence quotient (from either group or individual tests), mental age, educational test score, chronological age, social maturity, physical development, health, score on prognosis tests, or a combination of two or more of the foregoing measures. Experiments for which selection was based on several factors appear to have been more successful than those for which only one measure was used. Obviously, the more bases used, the more adequate is the estimate of each child and the more accurate the classification.

For an adequate assignment of a pupil to one group or another, evidence along at least four lines is desirable. There should be first a measure of intelligence. The results of whatever intelligence test is used should be expressed in terms of mental age, not I.Q., for grouping purposes. The I.Q. is an expression of the relationship between mental and chronological development; mental age is a statement of mental maturity. If, for instance, all the children in a junior high school with an I.Q. of 125 were put together in a group, the mental level would vary all the way from about nine and one-half to about eighteen. Such a grouping is obviously not homogeneous. On the other hand, if all the pupils with a mental age between thirteen and fourteen are put together, these individuals will show I.Q.'s ranging all the way from high to low, with a similar diversity of chronological ages. What can be learned by a pupil at any particular time depends upon his mental maturity; the rate at which he can be expected to progress from that time on depends upon his I.Q. Hence, mental age is a more appropriate measure than I.Q. for classification at any one time.

Intelligence, however, is by no means the only factor to be considered. There should be, secondly, some measure of educational standing. This measure may take the form of teachers' marks or of educational test scores. The latter are preferable to the former in case the tests used are long enough and cover enough subjects to provide a statement of entire academic preparation to date. A child's readiness to learn any particular material depends quite as much upon what he already knows as upon his innate intelligence.

There must also be consideration of social maturity and of physical development. These last two bases for grouping are somewhat more difficult to determine. Physical development is a more important basis for classification in childhood and youth than during the adult years, because mere physical size has a good deal to do with social adaptation. In the junior high school years there are marked differences between those children who are sexually mature and those who are not. Finally, there is the matter of social maturity and adjustment. As already mentioned, there are now various scales for measuring the degree of social and emotional maturity. If scales are not

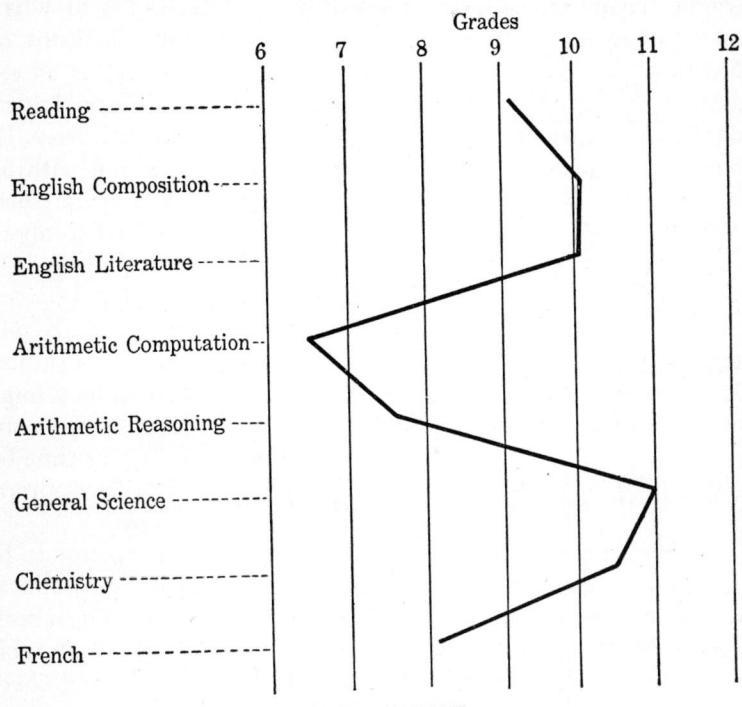

CHART XXVIII
PROFILE GRAPH OF ONE PUPIL'S STANDING

used, some kind of rating of each child should be required from teachers so that this factor will not be neglected.

Various techniques have been devised for summarizing each individual child's standing in regard to these various measures of readiness to do work of any given type or level. One simple device is presented above. The curve recording this child's development along various lines is called a profile. Such a profile is obtained in the following manner: Tests, ratings, and measurements of all kinds—whatever is in existence—are first assembled. Naturally, these are expressed in different terms and must be reduced to some common denominator if the development along one line is to be compared with that along others. There are basically three different ways of expressing the standing on a diverse series of measurements.

The first is to compare the child's score in each measurement to the total distribution of his age or grade and to determine at what percentile in the distribution he scores. A profile based on such a technique might indicate a given child to stand at the ninety-fourth percentile in intelligence for his age, the eighty-seventh percentile in reading ability, the ninetieth percentile in mathematics, the ninety-fifth percentile in social adjustment, and the ninety-seventh percentile in physical development. Such a child should obviously be in a higher school grade than most children of his chronological age, but unless a great deal is known about the overlapping of abilities from one grade to another, such a profile will never tell a teacher how far this particular pupil should be accelerated. The situation is not improved if the percentiles are in terms of a grade instead of an age distribution. A second technique consists in translating all scores on all forms of measurement into the age standard given for each test. Thus, a given child may have a mental age of fourteen, a reading age of thirteen, a mathematical age of fourteen and one-half, an English age of twelve and one-half, an emotional age of ten, a physiological age of fifteen, and a chronological age of fourteen. A profile of this type is an improvement over the percentile profile. It shows the interrelationship of growth along various lines. It still, however, requires interpretation before it can be used for placement in a particular grade or section. The third technique is to base the profile upon the grade norms for each test used instead of the age norms. By such a technique a given child makes an intelligence score in the high ninth grade, a reading score in the low eighth grade, a mathematics score in the low ninth grade, an English score in the high seventh grade, a social adjustment score in the low tenth grade, and a physical development score in the low ninth grade, while his chronological age would place him in the high ninth grade. This profile has the advantage of being directly translatable into terms of grade placement. In a high school, it is of course possible for pupils to be assigned to a different grade in the different subjects, if results indicate such an arrangement.

In the extensive investigation already referred to,[2] there emerged one fact which may account for the lack of enthusiasm shown by some teachers who have tried homogeneous grouping. Not more than one-half of the schools thus classifying pupils had made any adaptation of either the curriculum or methods of teaching to the abilities of the pupils being taught. Unless the material and methods are altered, the entire purpose of grouping is lost. The basic idea in classifying is to assemble pupils of about the same total learning capacity *in order that* modified methods and materials may be used. The nature of such modifications has already been indicated in previous sections.

Even with the most careful selection, a few pupils are incorrectly classified. The number, however, who require transfer from one group to another is surprisingly small—somewhere between 1 and 10 per cent. Moreover, the majority of these transfers are made for reasons having nothing to do with the accuracy of the original grouping. Pupils are transferred chiefly because of schedule difficulties or the necessity to get certain hours free for a part-time job. The transfers due to obvious misplacement are not more than 3 per cent of the total number classified. It may be, of course, that teachers do not sense an incorrect grouping even when it exists. However, the obvious misfit in a group is such a nuisance that teachers are usually all too willing to get rid of him. The exceptionally small number of transfers would, then, indicate that classification made upon reasonably adequate bases usually proves satisfactory.

Grouping of pupils has an influence on both academic and nonacademic development. As regards the effects of grouping upon traits of personality, relatively little is known. To be sure, a few individual cases of disadvantageous results have been presented in the literature. Obviously these children, who represent the extreme misfits, must be compared with the total number for whom the classification has been beneficial. As to this latter number, there are no figures in existence, nor has anyone attempted to determine quantitatively the nonacademic products of classification with large numbers of children. One must therefore admit complete ignorance in this matter of character development.

Along academic lines there is a little more light. Three parallel experiments have been done with groups of dull, average, and bright children.[2] Progress of these three types when grouped was carefully compared with progress when not grouped. The results—which are expressed in highly technical terms—show the advantage of homogeneous over heterogeneous grouping for each level of ability. The main summary of these experiments has been expressed in the chart shown below, from which the figures have purposely been omitted be-

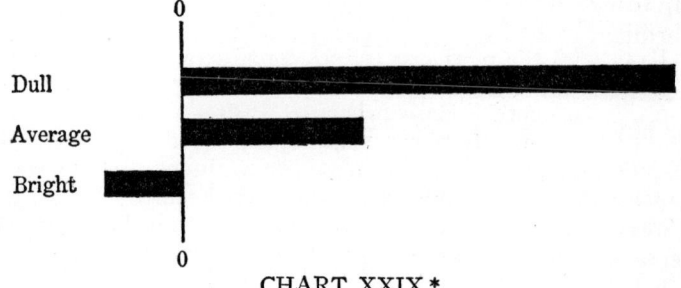

CHART XXIX*

EFFECTS OF HOMOGENEOUS GROUPING FOR DIFFERENT TYPES OF PUPILS
(Billett [2])

cause they would be unintelligible to the average reader and because they readily lend themselves to the erroneous idea that they are percentages. What is expressed in this chart is merely the relative advantage, in terms of subject matter learned, of homogeneous grouping at each intellectual level. There is no question concerning the enormous advantage of classification to slow pupils. Their academic achievements are far beyond those gained when they were left in classes with pupils brighter than themselves. For the average pupil there is some advantage in grouping; perhaps there is enough to justify the administrative difficulties involved. For the brilliant pupils, however, there appears a small but definite disadvantage. Their academic

* This material is presented by permission of the United States Bureau of Education.

achievements are lower when they are grouped together than when they are left in unselected classes. One must then conclude that the chief value of homogeneous grouping is for dull pupils, for whom ordinary classwork proceeds far too rapidly.

Special classes.—Logically, the special class is simply a homogeneous grouping of those pupils at the extreme ends of the distribution. Nine out of every ten special classes reported in a recent investigation [2] were for dull children. The remaining classes were used to accelerate brilliant pupils, to adjust emotionally unstable pupils, or to reclassify children who had been out of school for some time or had failed to get along in the group to which they had been assigned; a few were exclusively for brilliant children.

In practically all special classes there is a marked modification of both subject matter and methods. The special class has been, however, a development in the lower grades, although there were a few such groups reported from high schools. In any case, there is nothing essentially new in the special class; it is merely an extension of the homogeneous group into the extremes of the distribution.

Individualized instruction.—The last thirty years of educational research have proved the existence of individual differences among school children. The more one studies pupils, the larger and more significant do the variations become. The first adjustment historically to this realization of individual differences was the special classes for the lower extreme in intelligence. Those pupils whose deviations were both glaring and inconvenient in the classroom naturally got attention first. As the conviction of individual differences grew, the technique of homogeneous grouping was developed. At first it seemed an adequate solution of the situation, but when teachers began to work with these classified groups, they found the individual differences still too large for efficient teaching. In fact, if one compares the achievements of fast, average, and slow groups—even where the classification has been made with the utmost care—one finds a considerable range of ability still existing within each group and a marked degree of overlapping in achievement from one group to the next. Homogeneous grouping has therefore been found insufficient, although at some levels of ability it is better than no grouping. School pupils are simply not enough alike to be grouped at all; what they require is completely individualized instruction.

There have come into existence within the past fifteen years three fairly well-known and recognized plans for the complete individualizing of instruction—the Morrison plan, the Dalton plan, and the Winnetka plan. In a recent survey, the number of schools reporting the use of one or the other of these plans was not more than 1 per cent of the total number of schools considered. In spite of their restricted use, these plans are the logical development of the discoveries in regard to individual differences. Their lack of wider use is based largely upon factors having nothing to do with their intrinsic merit.

Although these plans differ from each other as regards details, they have certain elements in common. In all three, each pupil has some kind of assignment sheet for a given unit of work. This sheet tells him what goal he must achieve; it tells him where to find the practice material he will need for reaching this goal; and it states the time by which the goal should preferably be reached. Each pupil works through a series of assignments at his own rate. Even though a class of pupils starts work on the same day, some will complete their assignment in considerably less than the allotted time and will soon be ahead of others who have to be given extra time for achieving the desired goals. When a pupil thinks he has reached the goal assigned, he presents himself for examination. If he gives clear evidence of achievement, he starts with the next assignment sheet in the series. If he has not reached the goal, the teacher analyzes his mistakes and gives him suggestions for guiding his remedial work. Each pupil therefore, under these individualized plans, knows what he has to do, he knows where he is at the moment in relation to this objective, he knows what his errors are (in case he has failed in his first attempt), and he knows when he has completed what he set out to learn. The achievement demanded of pupils for a given grade of work is therefore kept constant, but the time used to effect this achievement is varied. This scheme is in direct opposition to the ordinary grade system, which keeps the time constant but allows the achievement to vary from very good to very poor. Individualized instruction has the further advantage that in a given series of exercises any number of extra assignments may be added for brilliant but socially immature children who should not be allowed to progress too fast for their personal development.

Not all subjects can be treated in this individualized manner. The technique applies primarily to mastery of subject matter. The opponents of individualization usually base their objections on its failure to teach pupils how to work with each other—that is, its failure to provide for normal social adjustments. This objection is, however, not as serious as it appears. Under the Winnetka plan, for instance, the morning session is devoted to mastery of subject matter by use of individual assignments, while the afternoon session is given over to such subjects as depend upon the co-operation of groups of children. Social adjustment need not be neglected in order to bring about an economic learning of subject matter. In fact, individualization saves so much time there is plenty left for work demanding socialization. In recent years, since the educational spotlight has been turned upon social and emotional development, mastery of subject matter has been neglected quite as much as personality was earlier. There is no reason why both lines of development cannot proceed harmoniously and efficiently.

There are relatively few high schools in which there is thorough individualization of instruction. Where it does exist it has been brought about by some one teacher who has arranged a certain part of her instruction along such lines. There are, however, many topics in high school classes which could be better mastered by individualized rather than by group teaching. The steps necessary for individualizing are three in number.

First, a teacher must break up the subject matter under consideration into units and must make quite clear to herself exactly what the objective of each unit may be. Second, she must make out assignment sheets for each unit, so that pupils may guide their own study. Finally, she must develop objective tests which will tell both her and the students when they have completed one assignment and are ready for the next. If third-grade children can direct themselves and profit in their mastery of subject matter by such individualized plans, high school pupils should be much more capable of benefiting from such an arrangement.

Many high school teachers feel that mastery of subject matter is only an incidental product of their teaching, the main result being the development of appreciations and attitudes. This point of view is entirely justifiable. However, in every course there must be *some* content; attitudes cannot be developed without subject matter. Individualized instruction applies chiefly to those facts which must form the basis for the appreciations the teacher wishes to develop. There can be no appreciation of what is unknown; that which is known fact comes under the heading of subject matter, not appreciation. Perhaps an example would make this point clearer.

The writer has a friend who teaches a year's course in Shakespearean drama in college. Like other teachers, she is anxious to develop in the students an understanding and appreciation of the plays studied. She wants them to get a feeling of Shakespeare as an individual and writer, a sense of his use of language, and some awareness of his growth and development from earlier to later writings. But, unlike many other teachers, she knows she cannot develop any of this appreciation unless her students know a given number of facts. She, therefore, proceeds in the following manner:

When it is time to start work on a new play or series of plays she hands out an assignment sheet which tells the students what to read and lists a series of questions expressing the objectives to be reached through this reading. The students are then given whatever time seems necessary for the accomplishment of the assignment. She next gives an objective test, measuring their actual knowledge of the plays. These tests cover facts about what characters are in what plays, what are the essential developments of the plot in each play, who spoke which famous quotations, what is meant by various archaic words, when the plays were written, what is meant by the more obvious of the allusions to previous literature and mythology. These items constitute so much subject matter. This professor regards her students as being responsible for learning these essential facts. Any student who does not pass the examination with a score of at least 90 per cent is excluded from the subsequent class discussions dealing with the plays about which he did not know the facts. This insistence upon the mastery of facts has come about through many years of experience in having pupils discuss plays they had not yet read. She, like anyone else who considers the matter logically, knows that appreciation can rest only upon knowledge. She therefore has adopted an individualized procedure for making sure that the necessary knowledge has been obtained before using up her time and energy in trying to develop appreciation and understanding for which the students do not have the requisite information.

Any high school teacher who wishes to do so, and can obtain support from her administrative superiors, can individualize her instruction in so far as the mastery of subject matter is concerned. The use of this material, in developing appreciation or character, necessitates group situations and interactions. There is, however, nothing incompatible with the reaching of two sets of objectives by means of two different techniques.

TEACHING METHODS

This is not a book on teaching methods but a text on the psychology of adolescence. No attempt will therefore be made to comment upon general principles of teaching or upon teaching techniques in any particular subject. There are, however, a few relevant considerations in regard to the abilities and interests of adolescents; to these, teaching methods must be adjusted, since the characteristics of the learner cannot safely be forgotten by the teacher. The following paragraphs, then, are not intended to discuss methodology in high school, but rather to focus attention upon a few outstanding characteristics of adolescents.

Boys and girls of high school age are usually impatient of drill or monotony. They want an ever-shifting variety in their lives. The teacher who day after day simply assigns the next ten pages in the textbook allows the preparation of lessons to become unbearably monotonous. These statements do not mean that no drill subjects should be taught. Since adolescents have better memories and greater concentration than children, they are able to memorize much more quickly. Work involving drill should, however, always be directed toward some purpose the adolescent wishes to achieve. Thus, the boy who has become interested in a foreign university willingly spends countless hours in mastering the necessary language. The girl with ambitions to become a private secretary will spend similar amounts of time in monotonous drill on stenography and typing. The student who wishes to enter a private college for which severe entrance examinations must be passed is no longer resistive to drill. The point to remember is the difference in motivation between children and adolescents. Children will memorize addition combinations either to please the teacher or to have a gold star placed after their name on the blackboard. During adolescence, the students must be stimulated to drill themselves because they see, through drill and monotony, the goal they are eager to reach.

The work in high school must be interesting. This statement is not made in defense of a painless education. Classroom work must compete with all the other things a boy or girl likes to do. The adolescent will spend time in studying only if the work is as interesting as the other things to which the same time might be put. If classwork is not interesting it will be neglected in favor of athletics, extracurricular activities, individual schemes of various sorts, money-making tasks, reading of light fiction, dances, or other such diversions. The adolescent can no longer be controlled, as the child can be, by mere authority, and he is not yet old enough to be controlled by economic pressure. In the intervening years he will therefore follow his interests.

Classroom work must furnish adolescents with an opportunity to exercise their minds. Naturally, the assignments appropriate for the more capable are too difficult for the dull, but for pupils of all levels of ability there must be a real opportunity for mental exercise. Boys and girls of this age spontaneously spend hours in solving all kinds of puzzles or in playing games that demand quick thinking and cleverness in outwitting one's opponent. Assignments therefore need to present puzzles that will intrigue the adolescent into thinking.

Whenever possible, subject matter should be approached through the emotions and imagination rather than through impersonal logic. Adolescents are stimulated by anything in which there is a bit of romance. They show this inclination clearly in their choice of movies or reading matter and in their hero worship of some idealized historic or fictional character. The chemistry teacher would bring about more learning of chemistry, if he would start his course with the reading of "Crucibles"; the biologist would be well advised to begin his elementary classes with the reading of "The Microbe Hunters." Such reading is stimulating to the imagination and ideals of youth and serves to maintain adolescent effort through the hours of drill necessary in the first year of any science. Naturally, a profound arousal of the emotions is undesirable, but too little stimulation is fatal to schoolwork.

One of the adolescent's favorite illusions is his conviction that he is now an adult. He therefore insists upon his ability to manage his own affairs and resents having his work arranged for him. Instead of regarding detailed directions for preparing an assignment as a help, he is likely to regard them as an unwarranted intrusion upon his sense of independence. Pupils in high school should be allowed, within reasonable limits, to plan their own work and the means of getting it done. Some guidance must of course be given—but primarily when asked for. Arranging his own work not only gives an adolescent a feeling of independence but arouses responsibility for getting the work done. If he has planned a particular task, he is working for himself, not the teacher. Decisions made in relatively unimportant matters often bring about a quite disproportionate conviction of self-direction. Thus, if an English teacher wants pupils to read part or whole of an epic, she may either assign a particular epic or she may tell the pupil to find out what epics there are and then to select for himself which one he will read. The second type of assignment is infinitely preferable.

Finally, teaching should emphasize, in so far as the particular group being taught can appreciate, the general implications, conclusions, and theories inherent in the facts under consideration. For the first time in his life, the high school pupil is able to regard a general principle as something more than a series of words to be memorized. When he discovers that theories give him an explanation of otherwise puzzling facts, he is eager to have more of them and thus achieve further enlightenment. Most adolescents want explanations of *why* things happen. In contrast, the child is content to know *what* happens. As will be pointed out in the last chapter, an adolescent has not become an adult until he has achieved some integrated attitude toward himself and the world about him. While too much theory leads to bewilderment, too little leads to failure in achieving an adult point of view.

Teaching in high school should then have the following six characteristics if it is to motivate the learner into getting his work done: It must relate drill to some desired purpose and must eliminate sheer monotony as much as possible; it must be interesting; it must give the adolescent mental exercise; it must stir his imagination; it must allow him to feel and develop his independence; and it must provide him with as many explanations as he can understand. Work that lacks these characteristics simply does not get done; no learning can be brought about without the co-operation of the learner.

ILLUSTRATIVE CASE STUDIES

Below are presented six case studies; two illustrate curricular adjustments, two show adjustment to individual differences, and two describe teaching methods. One of each pair shows a favorable and the other an unfavorable condition, of roughly parallel types. Because of the departmentalization of high school work, it is sometimes necessary to give illustrations from particular subjects. It should not, however, be inferred that adjustments in one subject are any better or worse than those in any other. The situations discussed are typical and could just as easily have occurred in any other department than the one involved. In reading the case studies one should disregard such details as apply to a single subject and should look for the general principles.

In a certain private school only one course of study is offered and only a small choice of subjects within this course. The school has a reputation for giving a good preparation for college, although not more than one girl out of four of its graduates ever attends college. A few go to a junior college or to special schools of dancing, art, or music. For more than half the graduates, however, attendance in this school is the final phase of formal education.

The catalog lists the following courses: Latin grammar, Caesar, Cicero, Virgil, elementary algebra, advanced algebra, plane geometry, two years of French, two years of German, four years of English composition, one year of American literature, two years of classical English literature, one year each of classical English and American poetry, ancient history, medieval history, one year of general science, and one course in the literature of the Bible. This school is, in its social development, a modern secondary school. Its curriculum, however, has changed little since the school was established almost fifty years ago. There is not a single laboratory within its walls. Although most of its graduates will marry and have homes of their own, there is not a course in home economics, home management, or child care. There is no course dealing with any social problem of any kind since the Middle Ages. In fact, the physical, biological, and social sciences are as completely omitted as if the scientific developments of the last hundred years had never existed. The real backbone of this curriculum is Latin and mathematics. The two modern languages are permitted but not especially encouraged. There is no subject anywhere in the course of study that would throw light upon the needs or problems of the girls attending the classes. There is not even the almost inevitable course in hygiene.

This school has a large and well-equipped gymnasium, swimming tank, basketball and hockey fields, tennis courts, recreation halls, and smaller rooms for social gatherings. It has an abundance of clubs and social affairs. It gets out an excellent yearbook and publishes a weekly paper. In general, relations between students and teachers are admirable. The school is attended by over two hundred girls from wealthy families, many of whom in later years will become social leaders in their communities. Yet, there is in their curriculum not one single course that could be of any service to them in understanding the modern world. To the girls themselves the subject matter is just so much dead weight; the courses contain little that is alive or challenging, in spite of the earnest efforts of competent teachers. Pupils in this school are often accused by students from other institutions of being completely absorbed in social life. This criticism is probably justified. Aside from spontaneous and irrepressible social activities, there is little within the school that could challenge the interest or absorb the attention of a normal, healthy, modern, adolescent girl.

In another state there is a second private school enrolling a group of students whose social and economic standing compares favorably to that of the group attending the school already described. In this second school also there is a rich and abundant social life; there are school clubs, an annual, and many social events during the year. The social life does not, however, receive the fanatic devotion accorded it in the first example.

In this second school the catalog shows the following courses: general history (a survey of outstanding developments from prehistoric times), American history since 1860, European history since the World War, social science, two years of biology, two years of physics, two years of chemistry, two years of English composition, one year of classical English and American authors, one year of English and American classical poetry, one year of modern American literature, one year of general mathematics, three years of French, three years of German, and a combined course in physical and mental hygiene. This school has a somewhat greater variety of courses than the other, but some of them run only for a semester; the number of hours taught per teacher and the size of classes are closely parallel for the two schools. This curriculum is obviously based upon the needs of modern society. The school allows any girl or group of girls who wish to study Latin, for instance, to do so under the guidance of a competent teacher and gives them academic credit for their work, but it does not offer Latin as one of its regular courses. Its general mathematics course combines such elements of algebra and geometry as could conceivably be of value in the everyday life of a modern educated woman. If the school had the funds it would prefer to give four years in each of the two modern languages. As it is, it requires its students to take three years of one language or the other before graduating, so that some facility in reading one language may be acquired rather than a little ability in each of two or three. The main emphasis in the curriculum is put upon social and natural science as being the type of subject matter most needed by the modern adolescent.

In addition to the practical and modern curriculum, the girls are required to take turns living in practice houses, each of which is an ordinary house that accommodates eight girls at a time. Each girl lives in a practice house one month during each year. While she is there she is instructed in the care of a house, cooking, caring for clothes. Most years the school "borrows" babies from a near-by orphanage; these infants live in the practice houses and are cared for by the girls. Although there is no schoolwork on home economics, the girls receive what is a great deal better—practical experience in home management. During the last year, one more feature is added; the seniors finish their examinations, both at midyears and at the end of the year, two weeks before the rest of the school. During these two weeks they work in some settlement house or help manage a public playground.

The curricular differences between the two schools are too obvious to require further comment.

Professor S, at a certain state university, is in charge of a large elementary course enrolling approximately five hundred pupils a semester. He gives the lectures and has a number of assistants who hold conferences, carry on discussion groups, and read examinations. Professor S gives a thorough and interesting course in his subject matter. His examinations are comprehensive and fair. He has carefully systematized notes from which he gives his lectures year after year. While his notes are amended from time to time, the essential facts of the course remain the same. It has been years since Professor S has talked to any student about his work. If a persistent student tries to catch him after class, Professor S immediately sends the boy or girl to an assistant without listening to whatever is to be said. Professor S is a thorough scholar, a conscientious organizer of his material, and a clear lecturer.

When it comes time to turn in his final grades, he adds up the total number of points made by each student on the monthly quizzes and the final examination, plots the distribution of these total scores, gives 3 per cent "A"s, 13 per cent "B"s, 65 per cent "C"s, 13 per cent "D"s, and 3 per cent "E"s. This distribution has remained unchanged for at least ten years. Never in all the time he has been teaching has Professor S been known to make an adjustment for individual differences among his pupils, or to take any account of changes in student population from one decade to the next. He has never given a student a second chance at an examination and he objects if students want to take his course the second time in order to improve their standing. Professor S makes the best preparation he can, sets clearly arranged facts and principles before his students, collects evidence of their mastery of these facts, applies the theory of the normal curve to this evidence, chops up the distribution, assigns his grades—and that is that.

In another university there is a large department which enrolls about six hundred freshmen a semester. Some years ago the members of this department became impressed by recent research in education and resolved to apply the main principles to their teaching. They consequently divided the material in their introductory course into ten units, each two weeks in length. They then made the following arrangement with the students: At a given hour (which was usually in the evening so that anyone who wished could attend) on the day before a new section was to be begun, there was an examination held for any students who thought they could pass the work of the forthcoming section. Naturally, only a few students ever presented themselves for examination over material not yet specifically taught, but there were always a few, most of whom passed the examinations they attempted. These students were forthwith excused from class during the next two weeks, since the work would obviously be a repetition of what they already knew. On the following day anyone not yet examined reported at the usual time, and for the next seven school days the professor in charge of the course covered in his lectures the basic facts of the subject matter included in the section. Reading assignments were made, so that the students could keep up with the lectures. At the end of this time an examination was given. Anyone who passed was excused from further work in that section of subject matter, unless he wished to improve his grade. If, however, a pupil receiving a "C" wanted to do more work and try again he was entirely at liberty to do so. The last two days of the second week were devoted to review lessons that all "D" and "E" students were required to attend; others might come if they wished. During these two hours the professor tried to isolate difficulties and review those points on which the class had been weakest. On Saturday morning a second examination was given for anyone who wished to raise his previous mark.

The class then went on to a second unit of subject matter which was treated in a similar fashion. The schedule of lectures and examinations subsequently proceeded through the ten units. Students still failing the first section or wishing to improve their standing after the second examination were allowed a couple of weeks for further study. On Saturday mornings examinations covering any desired section could be had. A student might try as many times as he liked.

The inferior students, before long, became several sections behind the rest of the class. These students were encouraged to stay away from the remaining lectures and to concentrate upon going back over the material of the earlier sections and taking further examinations until their mastery of the first part of the course was satisfactory. As a semester drew toward an end, students were allowed to choose whether they would take whatever final grade would naturally result from the work they had done or whether they wished to be given an "incomplete" and allowed to continue for another semester. All the "A" students, almost all the "B" students, and about one-half the "C" students would decide to accept whatever grade was just and to finish with the course. An occasional "B" student, half the "C" students, almost all the "D" students, and all the "E" students wanted a second chance. They therefore took the course a second time, attending only those sections on which they had done poor work during the first semester, and spending the intervening weeks on such reading as was necessary to bring all their performance up to whatever level they desired. If at the end of the second semester they were not satisfied with their mark or were still failing, they were given a second "incomplete" and again took the course during the first half of the forthcoming year.

At first this arrangement may strike the experienced teacher as an inefficient method of procedure. It was made possible only by assigning to each assistant in the course a number of students to whom he gave individual conferences and advice. When the students became accustomed to the routine there was actually little difficulty of administration. Thus a student who had received "B"s for the work of six out of ten sections, and a mixture of "D"s and "E"s in the other four, would accept an incomplete grade and simply add responsibility for these four sections to his work for the next semester, coming to class if he needed to and could, and, in any case, going over his notes and reading further references. At the end of the second semester, he would probably have raised his standing in these four sections, and would get a "B" in the course instead of the "C" that would have resulted earlier.

The distribution of grades assigned under this system was by no means a normal curve. Approximately one-third of the students got "A"s, one-third got "B"s, very nearly one-third got "C"s, and there was only the barest sprinkling of "D"s and "E"s. All those who got "A" knew enough to deserve an "A." There was decidedly no letting down of standards but merely an opportunity given to repeat work as many times as necessary in order to reach an "A" average. The professor in charge of this course had as his objective a distribution comprised exclusively of "A"s, which would be arrived at by varying the amount of time needed for mastery but keeping the level of achievement constant. He could see nothing especially sacred about achievement within a given limit of time; the essential thing was how much a student learned, not how long it took him. This type of adjustment to individual differences in ability and preparation is likely to become more popular once people get accustomed to the idea.

Miss Elliot was a high school teacher of plane geometry. She was a firm believer in the disciplinary value of mathematics and based her teaching procedure primarily upon her sincere desire to develop accurate observation, good memory, logical reasoning, and systematic habits of work in her students. She taught geometry in the manner described below:

Each theorem had to be memorized verbatim and written out from memory, not once but several times, by each pupil in the class. Each figure had to be so completely memorized that any pupil could step forward to the board and draw a diagram exactly like that in the book. If the diagram in the book showed a right triangle sitting on one side, pupils were not allowed to draw for themselves a diagram showing it lying on its hypotenuse. Miss Elliot did not insist upon exactly the same letters being used for naming the sides and angles, but she seemed to be considerably happier when there was not the slightest variation from the lettering used in the text. When the theorem was first studied there was a certain amount of inductive thinking done by the pupils as a group, but at an early point the thinking stopped and the memorizing began. The entire proof had to be given exactly as it appeared in the text. Moreover, Miss Elliot required each pupil to keep a notebook. In this notebook each theorem was written as it was being studied, the diagram placed on the board was copied—which was the same as the diagram in the textbook—and the successive steps in the proof were written down on the day the proof was worked out, these successive steps forming an exact replica of the proof already available in much more legible form in the text. Since the pupils knew by the end of the first month that a new theorem would be treated in this way, most of them simply copied the demonstration in the text verbatim and did not bother to do any inductive reasoning whatever.

This performance went on for the entire year, being varied only by work with original propositions, the demonstrations for which had to be written out and memorized as for the regular theorems. The real work of the course was the continual memorizing of figures for propositions, of the letters used in the figures, and of demonstrations leading to a proof. The class was hopelessly dull; hardly a student in it did any constructive thinking about geometry during the entire year, and disciplinary difficulties were of daily occurrence. Miss Elliot did not succeed in developing anyone's power to reason, and whatever increase in efficiency of memorizing she might have brought about was more than offset by the violent distaste for memorizing developed by all the students.

Miss Jones was a teacher of solid geometry to freshmen in a small arts college that required this course of all its students. The pupils in Miss Jones' classes varied all the way from excellent to failing in geometry. Miss Jones did not trouble with a textbook. She dictated theorems two or three at a time, each such group serving for at least a week's work. Every pupil brought to class some pieces of cardboard, some old pencils, and some pieces of string; with this equipment the students constructed figures that would serve to illustrate each theorem. Thus, for a particular theorem a piece of cardboard would serve for a plane; a pencil pushed through it and projecting several inches on either side would represent a line perpendicular to the plane; and a piece of string knotted around one end of the pencil, drawn through a hole in the cardboard and attached to the other end of the pencil, would serve to show a line dropped from the perpendicular line to the plane surface. The first step in reasoning out a proof was to construct an acceptable figure. Miss Jones encouraged the construction of many different figures, all of which would fulfill the requirements of the theorem. When everyone had an acceptable model, the students sat and turned these figures over and over, looking at them from all angles, until some facts about the interrelationships of lines and planes occurred to somebody. Anyone who thought he or she had an idea simply went to the blackboard and started writing out a proof. About two-thirds of these efforts were abortive, but at least everyone was trying to think how to get from the facts given to the one fact to be proved. This performance would sometimes go on for two or three days before the combined efforts of the class produced a correct proof. If, in the course of event, two correct but different proofs were developed, Miss Jones was delighted. In fact, the only type of assistance she regularly gave was to encourage the work of a pupil who had started off on an unusual type of proof which could still be made to work. She would not allow such a line of argument to be dropped but would encourage its use until someone in the class had seen how to reach the desired conclusion from the start already made. All correct beginnings were left on the board from day to day. By this technique, the poorer students in the class got some help in getting started on their proofs. Miss Jones did not believe in socialized work and allowed no conversation in the classroom, but she was entirely willing to have her students make use of each others' ideas as expressed on the blackboard.

Once a proof or series of proofs had been arrived at, Miss Jones gave some advice in regard to impressing these proofs upon one's mind. She frankly advised the poor students in the class to copy the shortest, easiest, and most obvious proof into a notebook and then to memorize it. She advised the most capable pupils in the class to memorize nothing at all but rather to direct their attention towards the techniques by which one got from facts given to the beginning of a proof. As the end of the semester approached she classified the pupils into groups according to the amount of original work she would expect from them on the final examination. Her final test consisted usually of seven familiar and seven unfamiliar theorems, although no student in the class was asked to solve more than six out of the fourteen. On each student's examination paper was a statement of how many theorems of each type he or she must solve. These assignments varied all the way from one or two students who were required to solve six out of the seven original problems to one or two who were required to reproduce proofs for the six already familiar. Miss Jones gauged the abilities of her students so well that little complaint against this system was ever heard.

To be sure, Miss Jones varied her standard of performance in terms of the abilities of her students. She stated frankly that there was nothing sacred about solid geometry; she regarded the subject rather as an opportunity for a pupil to learn to think as well as his ability would let him. If an individual came up to her estimate of his or her ability, that student passed the course. The total number of theorems one could demonstrate was a matter of indifference to Miss Jones. As a result of her procedure, solid geometry, which is usually a difficult and uninteresting subject, was one of the most fascinating classes on the campus; everyone in the class, even those at the tail end, had a good time—partly through the informality of the class and partly through the adjustment of the work for each pupil's ability. The obtaining of sudden insights was a frequent occurrence, although some pupils experienced this intellectual excitement more frequently than others. But everyone in the class sometimes derived pleasure from the thrill which comes from suddenly seeing through a matter which has previously been obscure. Miss Jones got plenty of work out of both the most unlikely and the most promising students because she adjusted her requirements to each student's ability, insisting only that everyone think.

BIBLIOGRAPHY *

1. American Educational Research Association, "The Curriculum," *Review of Educational Research,* 1934, 4: 123-252.
2. Billett, R. O., "Provisions for Individual Differences, Marking, and Promotion," *Bulletin of the National Survey of Secondary Education,* 1932, Monograph No. 13, Government Printing Office, 1933, 472 pp.
3. Busold, K., "Die Faktoren der beruflichen Gesamtkonstellation und ihre Wechselwirkungen unter besonderer Berücksichtigung von Eignung und Neigung," *Vierteljahresschrift für Jugendkunde,* 1933, 3: 89-106.
4. Butterweck, J. S., "The Problems of Teaching High School Pupils How to Study," *Teachers College Contributions to Education,* No. 237, Bureau of Publications, Teachers College, Columbia University, 1926, 116 pp.
5. Carroll, H. A., "Generalization in Bright and Dull Children," *Teachers College Contributions to Education,* No. 439, Bureau of Publications, Teachers College, Columbia University, 1930, 54 pp.
6. Collings, E., *Progressive Teaching in Secondary School,* Bobbs-Merrill Company, 1931, 529 pp.
7. "Curriculum Making and Current Practice," *Report of a Conference Held at Northwestern University,* Northwestern University Press, 1932, 244 pp.
8. Grizzell, E. D., *Origin and Development of the High School in New England before 1865,* The Macmillan Company, 1923, 428 pp.
9. Groves, E. R., "Courtship and Marriage," *Mental Hygiene,* 1934, 18: 26-39.
10. Harap, H., *The Technique of Curriculum Making,* The Macmillan Company, 1928, 315 pp.
11. Hart, F. W., *Teachers and Teaching: by Ten Thousand High School Seniors,* The Macmillan Company, 1934, 295 pp.
12. Hendrix, S. G., "Teaching Devices on the High School Level," *University of Illinois, Bureau of Educational Research Bulletin,* No. 56, 1931, 42 pp.
13. Keliher, A. V., "A Critical Study of Homogeneous Grouping," *Teachers College Contributions to Education,* No. 452, Bureau of Publications, Teachers College, Columbia University, 1931, 165 pp.
14. McKinney, F., "An Outline of a Series of Lectures on Mental

* See also the references in the Appendix.

Hygiene for College Freshmen," *Journal of Abnormal and Social Psychology,* 1934, 29: 276-286.
15. Mursell, J. L., *Psychology of Secondary School Teaching,* W. W. Norton & Company, Inc., 1932, 468 pp.
16. Oberteuffer, D., "Personal Hygiene for College Students," *Teachers College Contributions to Education,* No. 407, Bureau of Publications, Teachers College, Columbia University, 1930, 121 pp.
17. Piéron, H., "Quelques Données sur un Test pour l'Épreuve de hauts Niveaux d'Intelligence," *Bulletin Institutul de Nationale Orientale Professionala,* 1932, 4: 1-5.
18. Popenoe, P., *Modern Marriage,* The Macmillan Company, 1926, 259 pp.
19. Pressey, L. C., *Some College Students and Their Problems,* Ohio State University Press, 1929, 97 pp.
20. Watson, G., "What Should College Students Learn?" *Progressive Education,* 1930, 7: 320-325.
21. Webb, L. W., *et al., High School Curriculum Reorganization,* North Central Association of Colleges and Secondary Schools, 1933, 395 pp.
22. Wrenn, C. G., *Study-Habits Inventory,* Stanford University Press, 1933, 4 pp.

CHAPTER XIV

THE ADOLESCENT AND THE COMMUNITY

PEOPLE of any age above infancy are to some extent affected by the standards and customs of the community in which they live. As an individual approaches maturity, he becomes more and more aware of cultural influences. Everyone recognizes this situation, but thus far relatively little has been done to investigate the effects upon the adolescent of adult social pressure, as distinct from either home or school influence. It will therefore be necessary to consider the matter rather generally and to produce evidence only where definite measurement has been made. However, it is possible to point out certain ways in which customs and conventions influence adolescent life.

LACK OF PROTECTION

The protection of both children and adolescents is left largely to the home and the school. Children are to some extent protected by law, although not nearly as completely as they should be. Many forms of protection do not, however, extend into the adolescent years. The adolescent does not need as much protection as the child and should gradually develop self-reliance and ability to protect himself, but this adult stage is certainly not reached by anyone in the early years of adolescence and by most people not until the end of the period.

Communities can make and enforce whatever laws they wish in regard to such matters; if individuals of any age group are not protected, it is the community's own fault. One cannot, of course, eliminate the occasional person who deliberately harms either children or adolescents. Such persons who are acting on their own initiative are dealt with by the police and courts. But most dangerous situations in the community are not due to single, malicious persons, however; they arise from the general indifference of adults toward the safety of youth. It is with the opinions, attitudes, customs, and laws of the typical community that this chapter has to deal. This first section will make a brief survey of those elements in community life that, while fraught with danger, could be entirely controlled by the adult population, provided it were sufficiently interested.

In most states children of sixteen may own and drive automobiles. It is doubtful if any but the most unusual boy or girl of sixteen is sufficiently self-reliant to be permitted so much liberty. Every year much loss of life and injury result from the driving of automobiles by adolescents. In addition, there is the widespread freedom which comes from the unchaperoned use of a car. The boy who owns or borrows an automobile can, in an hour's time, get so far away from home that no one is likely to know him. He and his friends can go either to another community or out into the country. In either case the supervision which comes from the presence of those who may recognize them is completely eliminated. Most adolescents cannot safely dispense with the protection indirectly afforded them by their own community where they are known. Even the most stable and reliable of adolescents occasionally get into difficulty because of the freedom afforded them by a day's outing in the family car. A party of two boys and two girls may start out with the intention of the most innocent day's enjoyment. In their automobile they travel to places where supervision and protection do not exist; several hours of propinquity and complete freedom often lead to disastrous results. The people to blame for such tragedies are the adults who permit the issuing of driving licenses to adolescents. If adults wish to protect their boys and girls from the dangers of unsupervised adventure in an automobile, they should raise the legal age at which a license may be obtained.

In most states the legal age at which cigarettes or liquor may be bought is eighteen. It is, however, an unusual clerk in a drugstore who refuses to sell cigarettes to high school boys and girls. It is not a question here whether adolescents should or should not smoke. It is rather a matter of cigarettes and liquor being generally so available to those who are not yet old enough to exercise discretion in their use. In most high school groups there are some pupils who apparently have free access to whatever liquor they want, and not through their own families. In most cities there is an occasional outbreak of the use of drugs among high school pupils. The adolescent's ease in obtaining tobacco and alcohol is due primarily to adult indifference; the use of drugs, while due to organized vice and thoroughly condemned, is not controlled as it could be by adult society. Every year tobacco, liquor, and drugs take their toll of adolescent vitality. And the blame lies fundamentally with the indifference of the community.

A community may also regulate its places of amusement. Some effort in this direction is usually made, but the laws are by no means enforced. In fact, the owners of any place of amusement depends primarily upon young people for support. The usual amusement park is probably the least harmful type of entertainment furnished by adults and consumed mainly by adolescents and children. Naturally, the character of such places varies with the ownership, but many proprietors attempt to give reasonable protection to those who frequent their place of business. There are also some public dance halls where reasonable standards are enforced, but no owner can be too scrupulous or his income will rapidly diminish. Most dance halls offer practically no protection to the adolescents using them, and still others make a definite appeal to the baser motives of boys and girls. Dancing is a definitely exciting procedure which readily deteriorates to the primitive rituals from which it sprang and readily incites the dancer. The cheap dance hall lays traps to catch the stimulated boy or girl by serving liquor and by allowing pimps, prostitutes, drug handlers, perverts, and other undesirables to linger about. Such places can be maintained only through adult indifference. Burlesque shows and vaudeville houses are also without protection for adolescents. The programs seek definitely to arouse sex interest; the acts are designed for the lowest levels of intelligence and moral attitude in the audience; the jokes need to be laundered. Such diversions are distinctly for adults, not youngsters. The age limit below which individuals are excluded is altogether too low and is often not enforced. In any case, the matter is usually left to the judgment of the ticket-seller as to whether a given fourteen- or fifteen-year-old boy is admitted. The community that permits dance halls with low standards of morality, cheap shows, and salacious vaudeville acts will reap a harvest of adolescent moral collapse that is its own fault.

Finally, there are the various places maintained by organized vice. Public houses, gambling houses, poolrooms, and the like, damage thousands of adolescents every year. In fact, such places are dependent for support primarily upon young people whose judgment is immature. Every year adolescents lose money on gambling machines, horse racing, dog racing, roulette wheels, crapshooting, and card games. Where such losses are the result of individual enterprise it is difficult to fix the blame, but most such gambling is carried on as a more or less legalized occupation. The community in which the laws are liberal can expect some of its adolescents every year to be forced into stealing in order to meet debts incurred through gambling. Boys and girls of high school age do not have the judgment or the knowledge or the resources to gamble with any degree of safety. The lure of the house of prostitution is too obvious to need comment. There is nothing inherently wicked in shooting pool; the trouble arises from the nature of the adults who hang around the ordinary poolroom. In fact, the one harmless diversion in such places is the actual pool playing. In its indifferent attitude toward organized vice the average community sows the wind and reaps the whirlwind.

Since at the end of the adolescent period the individual has become an adult, he or she should gradually be emancipated from the shackles of childhood and should achieve freedom. At present this freedom is afforded so early that the average boy or girl cannot use it wisely. Adolescents need better protection until they are old enough to protect themselves.[1]

Thus far, this section has presented the negative side of the matter. There are certain positive steps a community can take to make itself a healthier place for adolescent growth. Primarily, these steps consist in the furnishing of a sufficient number and variety of healthy emotional outlets. A high school boy or girl can be expected to seek some form of diversion almost every day. The forms thus far discussed are entirely unsuitable, but the adolescent will resort to them unless other forms of a more desirable nature are available. School facilities, naturally, help a great deal in this matter, but are too common an experience to furnish the thrill an adolescent craves. The city that maintains a large number of playgrounds, two or three municipal swimming tanks or beaches, and a variety of clubhouses, will keep hundreds of adolescents out of poolrooms and dance halls. Any such facilities furnished by a city are certainly used. In most places it is possible to play on the municipal tennis courts only by waiting for an hour or two; adolescent ability to use baseball diamonds seems almost unlimited. Wherever settlement houses or other forms of clubs exist, the clubrooms are used almost continuously. During the late afternoon and evening hours most free meeting places are filled to overflowing with young people who have come there for social contacts or diversion. Any community house or community theater is steadily in use. If adults wish to furnish adequate protection for adolescents, it seems necessary only to supply the necessary facilities, plus a small amount of supervision, and the adolescents will amuse themselves in harmless and wholesome ways. Such a development will not, however, take place unless the facilities are provided and unless the expense of using them is appreciably less than that of attending the public dance hall or burlesque show. If a state, for instance, would spend less money in putting smooth surfaces on roads already so well paved as to invite the unwary to greater speed than is consistent with safety, it would have money to use in providing for healthy diversions for its boys and girls. There is money enough in any town, city, or state for the construction and maintenance of all the varied recreation centers its adolescents could consume, but the money is spent for adult comfort and convenience rather than for the safety of their children. Evidently adults would rather ride on smooth roads than prevent adolescent difficulties and tragedies.

In recent years proof [7] has come from work with primitive tribes to indicate the possibility of avoiding many adolescent difficulties. The period of adolescence in primitive tribes still in existence is short and does not seem to produce any considerable degree of maladjustment. Social standards are relatively simple, and approved methods of emotional expression are direct. Perhaps it is this lack of repression that leads to better and easier adjustment. If further studies of societies different from the typical bourgeois type almost universal in the United States show similar results, one may fairly conclude that, in general, society makes or avoids problems of social and emotional adjustment. From present indications it seems as if the power of society to control the environment of its own adolescents were almost unlimited. Conversely, in a community where adolescents usually encounter many difficulties in growing up, the blame is to be laid primarily upon the community. The average community could undoubtedly do much to avoid adolescent problems if it really wished to do so.

EDUCATIONAL INFLUENCES

In any community there are a certain number of educational influences. Most noticeable are the school, the family, the church, art museums, historical museums, concerts, lectures, public libraries, loan libraries, movies, and legitimate plays. One must also include the influence exerted by such people as numerologists, astrologists, mediums, and the like. The influence of school and family have already been discussed sufficiently. Nobody denies the existence of the other influences above listed, but relatively little accurate measurement has been made to determine the educational force of the elements in the environment.

As a teacher of religious beliefs the average church has undeniably lost ground within the last three generations. As an organization for the provision of social development and social contacts, the average church is still a success.

This point is made clear by a sample investigation [10] of the religious activities shown by 140 adolescent girls. These girls averaged about fifty minutes a week at church services, about thirty-five minutes a week at Sunday school, about thirty-five minutes at church clubs, and about fifteen minutes in religious activities at home. Although there were for each type of activity at least 40 per cent who spent no time at all, there were some who spent as high as 250 minutes a week at church services, in Sunday school, or on religious activities at home, while some spent as much as 440 minutes at church clubs. Only 34 per cent of these girls denied some kind of religious activity during the weeks covered by the investigation. Any institution that can stimulate interest from such a large proportion of adolescents, and such intense interest from even a few, is far from being a bygone influence in the community.

The effect of the church upon the moral attitudes of a community has never been measured well enough for one to venture an opinion.[12] One can easily find individuals on whom a particular church has had a vital and permanent effect, and one can as easily find other individuals upon whom no church has apparently left the slightest trace. Until quite recently those who were well trained in the techniques of measurement were not interested in the problems of religion. Consequently, nothing was objectively measured. Such investigations as have been made in regard to Sunday school achievement, attitudes developed in either Sunday school or church, religious beliefs, or ethical attitudes have to date produced largely negative results. This situation may be regarded as an inevitable first step. Measurement in the school subjects also began with the demonstration that schools were not teaching what they thought they were; these early negative results led, however, to constructive, remedial steps. Church influence can and probably will be so reorganized as to be a large and more vital element in community life than has been the case during the last twenty-five or thirty years.

Efforts are constantly being made to use more adequately the opportunities offered youth for instruction and development in art and music. Every year more people visit museums. Within the average museum itself, there are constant efforts to present displays which will be of such vital interest as to compete successfully with other types of diversion. Education along musical lines received its first great impetus with the invention of the phonograph; progress has since been enormously accelerated by the radio. Knowledge of music and taste in musical appreciation have both been directly affected. In spite of the many worthless musical programs heard over the radio, the average adolescent is hearing more good music and is receiving a better education in musical appreciation than any previous generation of adolescents has ever known. Moreover, the radio is the only modern invention that keeps boys and girls at home rather than sending them out of their homes.

An evaluation of the place of public and loan libraries in community life would require an entire book. The modern adolescent, from practically all groups, does do considerable reading, even if his selections are not always appropriate. As far as the public library is concerned, his selections, whatever they are, cannot do him much damage because the available books are too carefully chosen in the first place. The loan library, however, is another matter. Here the boy or girl may obtain, at a cost of somewhere between five and ten cents each, any number of salacious and deliberately stimulating books. In every generation there have been a certain number of such books, which circulated more or less secretly from one adolescent to another. But at no earlier time have so many undesirable books been so easily and cheaply accessible to so large a proportion of the adolescent population. Thus far, loan libraries are under no restrictions in regard to the type of books they put on the shelves or the age of the individual to whom the books are loaned. In many instances, the owner of an establishment refuses to buy "trash" and makes efforts to dissuade high school boys and girls from reading some book that is demanded by adults but is obviously objectionable for adolescent use. There is, however, no legal supervision.

The various pseudo scientists who flourish on all sides are equally free of restriction. If grown men or women wish to consult such individuals, that is certainly their own concern, but boys and girls are not yet old enough to exercise reasonable discretion in such matters. Every year one reads of adolescents who have gotten into difficulties either through following the advice given them by such individuals or by their reactions to fear engendered by the advice. High school teachers are keenly aware of the educative influence exerted upon certain of their pupils by such individuals. The teacher is trying to present scientifically accurate facts; she is handicapped in comparison with the "mentalist" because she cannot use the dramatic effects upon which the latter depends. If the teacher were allowed to darken the room, gaze into a lighted crystal, and go off into a trance before presenting scientific facts, this procedure might impress the pupils as effectively as they are impressed by crystal-gazers. In dramatic appeal, any "mentalist" has a distinct advantage over the classroom teacher and is consequently more likely to be believed.

Research concerning motion pictures.—The influence of the legitimate drama upon adolescents is slight because so few of them can afford the money necessary to see stage plays and relatively few of them participate even in school plays. The moving picture, however, is a different matter. In this one field there has been real measurement and research. If the material presented on this point seems to occupy a disproportionate amount of space, it is because there are many definite facts to discuss. A few of the more important studies and results are summarized below:

Investigators have measured the effect of a given moving picture upon adolescent racial prejudices.[9] The technique in all instances has been to give an objective test, designed to measure the degree of prejudice, before the picture was seen and to repeat this test on the following day. In some instances the test was again given after an interval of three months to measure the permanent effects. In most cases, the immediate effects were permanent. One picture used in these experiments presented a plot favorable to Germans as a nation. Before the picture, several nationalities had been ranked by the pupils in order of their personal preference. The Germans were fifth from the top. After the picture, however, they were next to the top, only English people being preferred to

Germans. In another instance, a picture favorable to the Chinese was shown to certain groups of children, while a picture unfavorable to the Chinese was shown to other groups. Both groups showed a similar degree of prejudice before seeing their respective pictures. The change in attitude in one direction is shown in the chart on p. 469 which shows results for the picture favorable to Chinese culture. The large number of highly prejudiced individuals has been materially reduced and the average opinion of the group raised from an attitude of prejudice to one mildly favorable. The children who saw the story unfavorable to Chinese culture varied in the opposite direction, though not to as marked a degree. The other chart shows the results obtained from showing the well-known picture, "The Birth of a Nation," which is a powerful piece of antinegro propaganda. There is no question here that the picture markedly increased prejudice. These same changes in attitude persisted for several months after the pictures were seen and became, apparently, permanent possessions.

Another investigation [3] was based on reports collected from over seven hundred juvenile delinquents and adult criminals regarding the influence of motion pictures upon their careers.

In one sample group of 252 girls in a reform school, 39 per cent give clear evidence of having been so stimulated sexually as to be led into immorality. A desire for obtaining "easy" money and for living the sophisticated, luxurious life shown in movies was a direct motive for stealing, prostitution, gambling, or other delinquency in 49 per cent of these girls. In a group of 139 delinquent boys, 45 per cent report the movies made them "want to make a lot of money easy." Among 110 male criminals, 12 admit becoming sexually aroused as the result of movies, 49 per cent say the pictures made them want to carry a gun, while 28 per cent wanted to practice stick-ups after seeing certain films.

One should not assume, however, that the effect of moving pictures upon adolescents is inevitably bad. Various effects have been observed through the analysis of 458 motion-picture "autobiographies" written by high school students.[2] These pupils obtained help from the movies in selecting clothes, acquiring acceptable manners, developing better social adjustments, learning love-making techniques, acquiring a philosophy of life, getting a better idea of modern society, developing ambition,

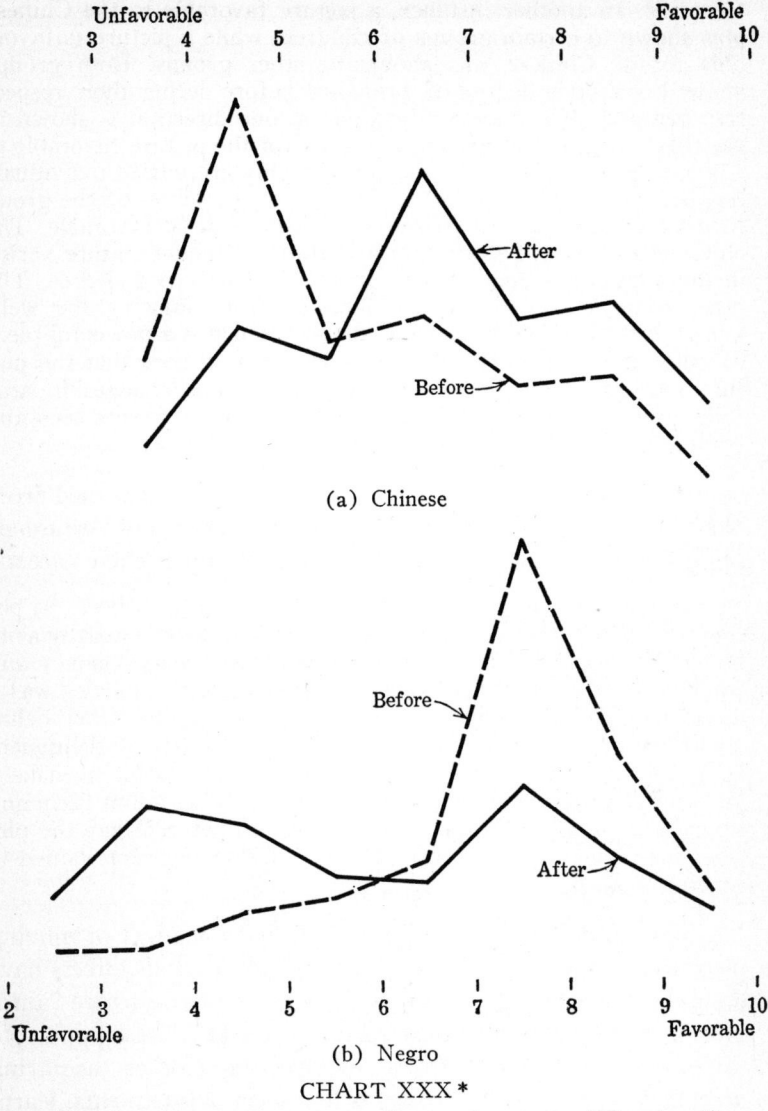

CHART XXX*

EFFECT OF MOTION PICTURES ON RACIAL ATTITUDES (Thurstone [9])

*These materials are used by permission of the University of Chicago Press.

realizing the value of family affection and loyalty, and developing religious and moral attitudes. Various results of an emotional nature were also recorded. Movies led to daydreaming, terror, sorrow, romantic love, passionate love, general tenseness and excitement, longing to be "good," and resentment at social discrimination or family interference with adolescent ambitions. As may be inferred from the large variety of effects noted, the moving picture is a significant influence in the life of the average adolescent.

It was impossible to obtain from the autobiographies a statistical count of the per cent of adolescents who had been influenced to imitate mannerisms or customs, although the number is undoubtedly large. As regards other effects, however, statistical treatment was possible. Thus, 66 per cent of the high school students gave direct evidence of daydreaming as a result of motion pictures. Only 10 per cent denied daydreaming while the remaining 24 per cent did not mention this phenomenon. Definite statements of fright and terror occurred in 61 per cent of the high school autobiographies; only 22 per cent denied this kind of experience, while the remaining 22 per cent furnished no information on this point. Sorrow and pathos felt during pictures were mentioned in 64 per cent of the life histories; only 19 per cent denied such experiences. The intensity of such feelings is indicated by the difficulty reported in controlling the tears induced by motion pictures. Of the 458 writers, 39 per cent admitted crying frequently. Reactions to romantic love was definitely mentioned in 55 per cent of the autobiographies. These adolescents spoke of having been thrilled or stirred by love stories; 30 per cent showed, either by statement or indirect evidence, that they were unusually receptive to amorous advances after watching pictures dealing with romantic love. One of the questions used in obtaining the autobiographies was the following, "Did you get any ideas of love from the movies?" Of the high school pupils, 50 per cent had evidently secured ideas in regard to techniques of love-making. Twenty per cent of these adolescents found dissatisfaction with their daily lives after observing the life of modern youth as seen amidst a film setting of luxury and freedom. Twelve per cent of the writers indicated this dissatisfaction as taking an acute expression in some form of rebellion against parental restraint. Only 30 per cent of the high school students denied the experience of such an influence. Fifty-nine per cent of these high school pupils had developed a desire for travel and 51 per cent a desire for more education, as a result of their attendance at the movies.

Motion pictures are neither exclusively bad nor exclusively good influences. It is, in fact, probable that what adolescents get from the theater is mainly a crystallization of points of view, desires, or attitudes already in existence. Thus, the predelinquent boy derives from the movies ideas about different techniques for bank robberies, holdups, or other criminal acts. The adolescent who is already sexually aroused obtains further excitement from the same pictures that furnish other boys and girls chiefly with ideas as to manners, customs, and styles of dress. Events shown in pictures are undoubtedly imitated. Thus, small boys who have seen a picture showing a bank robbery come home and, in their play, imitate the episode. This situation does not, however, call for wholesale condemnation. In previous generations boys went to the circus, saw the enactment of a stagecoach holdup, and immediately returned home to imitate the scene they had witnessed. Still earlier, boys acted out stories they heard about Indian fighting or military operations between the North and the South. Viewed genetically, there is nothing alarming in imitative play based on the movies. Small boys of any generation enact a fair number of bloodthirsty scenes, but few of them grow up to be criminals.

Imitation of love scenes among adolescents is practically inevitable—and nothing new. In generations before the motion picture, the cheap novel had a wide vogue and was read by adolescents for the purpose of stirring up their emotions. As a moral corrosive, anything worse than the salacious novel, the carnival side show, or the collections of indecent postcards—all prominent in earlier generations—would be hard to find. At the age when boys and girls are interested in romantic love, they are certain to find some means both of arousing themselves further and of learning techniques of love-making. At present, the moving picture is the medium through which such education is given. Indeed, if adolescents are to acquire anywhere a core of facts in regard to love-making, they must obtain it from the motion picture, since both the home and the school will give them little, if any, assistance. Adults who do not wish such education left to the motion-picture industry should arrange to have as efficient training given somewhere else.

Motion pictures have been credited as being causes of crime, of maladjustment to home and school, of dissatisfaction with life. If one reads a single report [3] on the effects of the movies, one may easily come to such a conclusion. But if one keeps on reading reports of research in this field, the matter seems not so simple. For instance, a girl reports that she had been puzzled about a possible vocation and was hesitating between dancing and stenography; during this period she saw a picture in which the heroine, after trials of various kinds, became a world-famous danseuse, and this picture led to her firm decision that she too would select dancing as her vocation. To say, however, that the picture "caused" her to enter this profession would be inaccurate; the movie dramatized and crystallized a problem already in her mind. If the picture were a true "cause" it would have influenced the countless other adolescents who saw it to act likewise—but in all the thousands of autobiographies collected this picture had this influence on only one girl. One cannot say, then, that motion pictures cause girls to become dancers. It is no more sensible to say that pictures cause boys to become thieves, merely because one boy in two hundred who saw a particular picture was influenced to pursue further a path on which he had already started. In both instances, the adolescent saw what he or she was previously conditioned to see. Any motion picture presents in dramatic form a large collection of ideas; each adolescent selects for himself what he wants to learn, just as he does from any other experience in life.

Because of the arousing effect and the permanence of emotional reactions instigated by moving pictures, there should undoubtedly be better supervision than there is at present. Adolescents should not be presented with undesirable ideas, even though these ideas will affect the behavior of only the small minority who have the "mental set" to accept them. If motion pictures were classified into three groups—those appropriate for children, adolescents, or adults—far less harm would be done. The horror film, the sensual love story, and tales in which open revolt against conventional morality is shown as desirable and smart, should certainly be eliminated from the lists for either child or adolescent. On the other hand, the high school boy or girl should see films dealing with romantic love, adventure, travel, boy-and-girl friendships, family relationships, or school or college life; mystery stories are also acceptable if the horror element is removed. Films involving lawbreaking, provided the scenes do not deliberately teach criminal technique and provided the wrongdoer receives adequate punishment, are acceptable. So also are sympathetic presentations of moral problems arising from modern life; adolescents are nearing adulthood and should be considering such matters. As a result of present attacks against the film industry, there is danger that stories will become too sentimental, artificial, and lacking in intellectual stimulation. Adolescents need problems to think and talk about; because of their emotional interest in movies and their identification with characters in film stories, ideas presented to them through this medium receive attention and discussion. An oversimplification would prevent the motion picture from being as useful an educational influence as it might well become.

ILLUSTRATIVE CASE STUDIES

The first rather long case study presents a picture of youthful reactions against a machine-made environment so developed as to be comfortable for adults but dangerous for children. It should be noted how the community is responsible for this boy's trouble quite as much as his family. The remaining case studies are short excerpts from some of the autobiographies written by high school pupils. Several have been presented, the samples being selected to illustrate many different effects derived from motion pictures.

Clarence, aged twelve,[11] lives in a good apartment-house neighborhood with his mother. Neither he nor his forebears on either side have been in court before. Clarence wears carefully pressed knee trousers, a white shirt, and blue tie. He has a pale face with high forehead from which rather coarse blond hair is wet-combed straight back. Physically he is sound. The physician thinks his pallor may be accounted for by the fact that he never goes to bed before eleven o'clock, eats too much sugar and starch, and drinks coffee and tea at will. He is a straight, slim, well-knit American boy, one year retarded in school, and of good average intelligence.

His misdeeds are truancy, running away, sleeping out, theft of a bicycle, burglary of a country store in the company of Mexican boys who had a revolver. Twenty-four dollars' worth of canned goods, cartridges, candy, gum, cigarettes, a bandanna handkerchief, a pair of gloves and leather belt were taken from the store which was entered at midnight by prying up a window.

The really serious part of the affair (the mother was willing to pay for the stolen articles) was the predicament of the merchant in his present state of mind. When he heard noise, he dressed and entered the store, and was confronted with Clarence's revolver pressed to the pit of his stomach, and the cry: "Hands up!" He reached for a baseball bat and Clarence retreated. Now that it was over the merchant was in panic and was sure Clarence was the boldest murderer unhung.

There was nothing remarkable in Clarence's life. He was born on a farm in the Middle West. His father was a well-to-do raiser of corn. When Clarence was four years old his parents were divorced. Two older girls went with the father, who shortly remarried and started another family. This one was not a success, either. The father lost his money and was now selling real estate and paying alimony for support of his second wife and babies. Clarence had gone with his mother. She too had remarried, a man somewhat younger; they separated at the end of three years. Clarence's mother was a brisk woman in middle age. She owned houses to rent and a small confectionery store which she managed herself. Clarence and she lived in an apartment which was neatly furnished. Clarence's days and nights went somewhat in this fashion: he slept in a bed which, during the day, folded up behind the door of the living room. He kept his clothes in his mother's closet and had a few belongings in a bureau drawer. He got up just in time for school which was six blocks away. His mother made him toast and coffee on the electric stove. Sometimes he went without his breakfast. At recess he took an ice cream soda. He was in the sixth grade. His teacher was an unmarried woman of forty. She had taught this grade was fifteen years. Her personality was patient, earnest, exacting. She believed in insistence upon detail. She never let herself go, or became angry, or enthusiastic. She lacked imagination. Clarence, because he had failed the year before, was not permitted to take any extras, such as wood carving, nature study, or civics. He pursued the basic studies: reading, endless drill in penmanship—which he had mastered in the third grade as well as he could ever hope to do—arithmetic, spelling, and geography. He was an average student, obedient, bored, tolerant, without curiosity. At recess he surreptitiously shot craps with the boys on the cement court. At noon he ate a well-cooked meal at the school cafeteria. This he detested, but the good health campaign at school made the cooking teacher inexorable; each child must eat a balanced ration. It was this meal which saved the day, physically, for Clarence. At home he was as poorly nourished as the most ignorant immigrant, although his father and grandfather had raised acres of grain and were hard-eating, husky American farmers, and his grandmother and mother were first-class cooks.

On the way home Clarence generally bought an ice-cream cone or an all-day sucker. He loitered on corners and passed knowing remarks with the "soda jerk" in the drug store. He spent half hours gazing into store windows. It being the downtown district which his mother preferred, there was not a tree or a yard for a square mile. Finally Clarence reached home. He unlocked the stale apartment and began to read the newspaper. First the comic strips, then the headlines, then every word of the "human interest" stories.

Sometimes his mother was home. Occasionally Clarence ran errands, but these never took him into the country. They ate dinners at a cafeteria, frescoed with Egyptian scenes; there was a jazz band. Clarence ate two or three desserts and the catsup of an oyster cocktail. Usually he went to a movie in the evening. The shows he passionately loved were red-blooded "he-men" scenes of adventure; great lungs heaving in open air, swift motion over vast spaces, quick decisions carried out by well-trained, swelling muscles, expansive gestures, care-free manners—sensations hot and vigorous. He would stretch his lean body forward with intolerable yearning, thrusting out his chest, breathing quickly. Why should he not thrill to these pictures of Western adventure? Had not his grandfather driven an ox team through the Missouri trails? Had not his father turned virgin soil with his plow and broken in his own horses? If the school meal saved the day physically for Clarence, the Western moving picture saved him spiritually. It was his only chance to stretch his muscles or to use his imagination, to satisfy his biological cravings. Yet the movie was his undoing also, for in it he got the idea of prying open the window to rob the store; in fact he followed the movie scenario as exactly as possible during his two weeks' delinquency, except stealing the bicycle from school—that was his own idea and he was rather ashamed of it.

Now and then in the evening Clarence would stay home and listen to his mother entertain friends; men and women from back home. They talked of real estate, illness, cures, domestic unhappiness, alimony, taxes, and movie scandals.

Clarence's relation with his mother was matter-of-fact. He liked her; he knew she was good to him. He was conscious of no yearning for affection. She was strict about his manners, school and Sunday school attendance, and very careful of his clothes. Clarence in court could give no account of the reason for his running away and robbing. He was satisfied with home. He had everything he wanted. He met the Mexican boys at the show, and asked them how far it was to Mexico, and suddenly the plan dawned on him to go. They broke into the store to get provisions and an outfit for Clarence. They had camped out two weeks, until arrested. He was willing now to go home, to take his punishment, and to be good.

As to attempting to shoot, Clarence maintained nothing was further from his thoughts. The gun, it turned out, was not loaded. But that was a mere error of sequence, for Clarence had intended to load it, if the merchant had not disturbed him. Clarence viewed this phase of the gun as a lapse from "criminalism" into heroism. His eyes took on a far-off look. They were not on the court, but on the imaginary silver-screen that he would rush off to the instant he was free. Clarence's mother maintained he was a "weak" boy, easily led, like his father. But Clarence was not "weak." It took a profound effort to hold the gun at the pit of that man's stomach. The difficulty was not "weakness of will," but conflict in goals. He did not *wish* to kill, but he deeply *wished* to feel excitement and heroism.

To the court the case was clear as to cause, but tremendously difficult as to treatment. For Clarence represents any number of American boys who run away to seek adventure, who start by committing petty offenses and end by living the parasitic life, auto-thieving, bootlegging, pimping, and robbery. Clarence is "normal" and his mother is "good," but his life is all wrong. He is encased in brick and stone, steeped in a bath of dull adult influence. There is nothing unusual about his cravings; he is the offspring of vigorous parents; he cannot find life in the downtown district or petty details of home and school. Within three generations of American life, the emphasis has changed from vigorous rearing of healthy children in enough space to grow and play—the first thought of the family—to the getting and spending of money and living with modern conveniences. This may suit the needs of individual grown-ups. To the child it is slow starvation of body and spirit. This mother values modern conveniences and hardwood floors more than she values her son's growth in muscles and imagination. All-pervasive is that atmosphere of the apartment, the downtown district, the adult, modern world without warmth, without affection for boys, without space, or intensity, or thrill.*

The appearance of such handsome [3] men as John Gilbert, Ben Lyon, Gilbert Roland, and the host of others, dressed in sport clothes, evening attire, formals, etc., has encouraged me to dress as well as possible in order to make a similar appearance. One acquires positions such as standing, sitting, tipping one's hat, holding one's hat, offering one's arm to a lady, etc., from watching these men who do so upon the screen, and especially if they do it in a manner pleasing to your tastes.

As I got into high school and into my sixteenth and seventeenth year I began to use the movies as a school of etiquette. I began to observe the table manners of the actors in the eating scenes. I watched for the proper way in which to conduct oneself at a night club, because I began to have ideas that way. The fact that the leading man's coat was single breasted or double breasted, the number of buttons on it, and the cut of its lapel all influenced me in the choice of my own suits.†

I remember once I had had trouble with my mother.[3] I said that everything that was done in the house I had to do. I was very downhearted and thought how cruel they were to me. That night I went to the movies. I do not remember the name of the picture but it hit the nail on the head. It concerned one girl who did not get along with her family and one who did. The one girl was so good that everyone loved her and her life was very happy. The other girl was not happy and people did not like her because she was not sweet, good, and kind to her mother like the other girl. This made me think that I was just like the girl who was not good. I always wanted to be liked by everyone and to be happy, so I went home that night with the intention of being as good as possible to my mother and of trying to make family life as happy and pleasant as possible both for myself and mother and father. It has been a good many years since I saw this picture and I am still trying to be that kind of a girl. I have succeeded some, but not enough yet.

* This study is used by permission of New Republic, Inc.
† This and the remaining paragraphs are used by permission of The Macmillan Company.

Movies have definitely formed part of my daydreams.[3] Every girl, I think, must have the mental image of a man to idealize and build dreams about. Before she finds an actual person, she draws an imaginary figure. In any event that was what occurred in my case. And my imaginary man was made up mostly of movie stars. At one time it was even the height of my ambition to marry Dick Barthelmess. I spent much Latin-grammar time thinking up ways of becoming acquainted with my various heroes. Sometimes, though not often, I identified myself with the heroine of a picture I had seen. The role of the fragile, persecuted woman never appealed to me; it was always as the queen, the Joan of Arc, the woman who had power that I saw myself. These daydreams took up pretty much time, especially during my second year at high school, when I was in a strange environment; but I was always inwardly ashamed of them and I do not believe that they ever carried over into action of any sort. I have never even sent for autographed pictures.

I always wanted to be a dancer [3] and I believe the movies influenced this idea very much. Such a picture as "The Broadway Melody" helps to tempt one to be a dancer because it showed how a poor girl could become famous as a dancer if she worked hard enough. The fame and beautiful clothes and luxuries always appealed to me. I always thought that after I was a famous dancer I could travel and see the world; many pictures show how, after one is famous and has plenty of money, one could travel around the world.

During my last two years of high school,[3] I did a lot of dating. That is, I had a date about once a week. My program or plan of campaign was, first, a movie, then a dance, then a slow drive home. When I first started taking girls out to the movies, I was impressed with the enormous number of fellows that put their arms around their date in the show and I became aware that heads already close got closer when love scenes were introduced. I tried the things I saw and was pleased with the results. A good love story was more inspiring on a date than a picture in which love was not the important element, and the girls seemed to enjoy themselves more under these circumstances. I didn't get a kick out of what appeared on the screen, but I did like the effect a love scene had on my dates. In "reel life" a boy usually does not go with a girl a long time before he kisses her. The average high school girl, it seems, follows this suggestion. The love scenes produce an emotional harmony that leads in some cases to kissing and necking.

One reason I went away from school [2] was I enjoyed movies better than school. I got my money from my parents for lunch. So instead of going to school, I made some excuse and went to the movies instead. And since I was not in school I would pick up a lift and go out for a little ride until the shows opened. Then after the show I walked a little ways, then picked up a lift and went home about 3:30, just as if I had just come from school. My mother never knew it. One of the times as I was coming out of the show I met a boy friend I knew. So I took in another one with him and came out about 8:30. This was too late to go home from school. So instead of taking me home I had him take me to a girl friend's. That evening I didn't go home. The next evening I and my girl friend went out. This was the second night I was away from home. I kept on going out day after day and didn't go home for a whole month.

Sometimes movies make me think of myself as a criminal.[3] I think of all the good times I could have with the money. I think of spending my proceeds of a criminal venture in an amusement park, at parties, in night clubs. Then my thought takes a different trend and I think that free spending of money and not working during the day might make the police suspicious. I then think of saving all the stolen money and working at daytime so the police wouldn't be suspicious of me. Again I think that it wouldn't be fun robbing poor people like it sometimes shows in the movies because they work hard for their money. I then think of robbing rich people, but I think again that after all they work for their money also. The plan that springs into my mind is that of robbing a gambling establishment. If I succeeded the head of the establishment would not and could not tell the police because they would arrest him for operating a gambling den. I would then give part of the money to poor people and part of it I would keep for myself. But at the end of my thoughts I realize that no matter how skillful or how clever he may be or how much protection he has, the crook is always caught sometime or other. If he isn't caught he is killed by one of his associates. So I think that after all I might as well remain honest, try to make money in an honest way and spend it if and when I want to without the fear of being arrested or killed.

I would love to have nice clothes [2] and plenty of money and nothing to do but have a good time. When I see movies of that type, it makes me want to get out and go somewhere where things happen. Like the picture ———. The girls were nothing but adventuresses and look what great times they had. I always wanted to live with a girl chum. I saw many pictures where two or three girls roomed together. It showed all the fun they had. I decided I would, too. I ran away from home and lived with my girl friend but she was older than I and had different ideas and of course she led me and led me in the wrong way.

The sort of movie I like best is Love;[2] in other words you can say Romance. One film I liked best was Rudolph Valentino in "The Shiek." It was the most romantic and lovable picture I have ever seen. It taught me to crave a lover like Rudy; he kisses his partner wonderfully. I often say to myself I wish I was the woman in the play. Every time I heard of a play that Valentino played in I begged mother to let me go. I wasn't in my teens yet either. Ever since I was a little child I craved love movies. After I've seen a romantic love scene I feel as though I couldn't have just one fellow to love me, but I would like about five; and on the way home I have a feeling or desire to have a fellow kissing me all the time, or I mean a different fellow to kiss me every minute of the day. But when I see a romantic love scene and I am with a fellow, I like to have him put his arm around me an hold my hand and keep his head close to mine; in other words, I mean his cheek. When I'm watching the play I'm so dreamy that I could fall asleep in the fellow's arms, and another thing when I'm sitting there so interested in the movie and then when the fellow slips his arm about me, it gives me sort of a thrill just like a chill going down my back. And after we leave the theater, I mean the boy friend and I, well of course, he takes me home and, well, the part I like most is when *we* are sitting on the sofa and he makes believe that he is a lover like Rudy Valentino and of course I'm so thrilled I really don't know what to do. First, he kisses my forehead, then my cheeks, and then my lips and his lips are so feverish that they hold me spellbound. Sometimes I don't know what to think of him, he acts so restless.

At one of the comedies [2] I saw I got an idea how to remove iron bars in front of a window, quick and sure. It showed how a truck was parked and some kids came up and tied a rope onto the truck to some iron bars. The driver came out and got into the truck and down the street, taking the bars with him, and continued doing a lot of crazy stunts that these kids would pull. But I thought if someone wanted to pull a jail break or to remove these bars it would be quick and sure. Of course, not that I have tried it, but there's a possibility in doing it, if you ever wanted to.

In another picture I saw how a guy used a rag saturated with ether and he put it on the face of a sleeping man, and went ahead and "prowled" the place. This is also an idea, and I know it could be used effectively.

In another picture I saw there were some burglars and all they were interested in was collecting the silverware. I thought of the thousands of dollars' worth of stuff I had passed up in the homes I had ransacked.

Another thing I learned, and I think it was from one of the pictures, is to wear gloves. They have my fingerprints now, and if it was a "big" case they would look for prints. By wearing gloves you wouldn't leave these little telltale prints.

I saw one picture where they had a plate in front of a safe and if you stepped on this plate it would snap your picture. Well, this fellow was burning the safe and he stepped on the plate and that was the way they caught him. That was another idea I got. To be on the lookout for plates that would betray you by alarm or any other purpose of detection. And, also, that an "Arc" burner can be used to burn out the combination of a safe, without noise, and with less danger of detection and physical harm.

One can certainly get an education in a movie; that is, if his mind runs in that track.

BIBLIOGRAPHY *

1. Addams, J., *The Spirit of Youth and the City Streets*, The Macmillan Company, 1914, 162 pp.
2. Blumer, H., *Movies and Conduct*, The Macmillan Company, 1933, 257 pp.
3. ———, and Houser, P. M., *Movies, Delinquency, and Crime*, The Macmillan Company, 1933, 233 pp.
4. Bruël, O., "Film als Psycho-traumatisches Kindheitserlebnis," *Acta für Psychiatrie und Neurologie*, 1933, 8: 445-454.
5. Cressey, P. G., "The Social Role of the Motion Picture in an Interstitial Area," *Publications of the American Sociological Society*, 1934, 28: 90-94.
6. Dysinger, W. S., and Ruckmick, C. A., *The Emotional Responses of Children to the Motion Picture Situation*, The Macmillan Company, 1933, 122 pp.
7. Meade, M., *Coming of Age in Samoa*, William Morrow & Co., Inc., 1928, 297 pp.

* See also the references in the Appendix.

8. Peters, C. C., *Motion Pictures and Standards of Morality,* The Macmillan Company, 1933, 285 pp.
9. Peterson, R. C., and Thurstone, L. L., *The Effect of Motion Pictures upon the Social Attitudes of High-School Children,* University of Chicago Press, 1933, 113 pp.
10. Strang, R., "Religious Activities of Adolescent Girls," *Religious Education,* 1929, 24: 313-21.
11. Van Waters, M., *Youth in Conflict,* New Republic, Inc., 1925, 293 pp.
12. Watson, G. B., *Experimentation and Measurement in Religious Education,* Association Press, 1927, 295 pp.

PART V
CONCLUSION

CHAPTER XV

THE END OF ADOLESCENCE

THERE are definite criteria by which one may know when the period of adolescence has drawn to a close. Naturally, along some lines these criteria are more definite than along others. Most of the measures of maturity to be discussed in this chapter have been derived from the analysis of adults so unusual as to require special study. The most frequent difficulties of such adults have been due to their failure to grow out of childish or adolescent points of view; the adjustments they now show were once appropriate but are no longer adequate. From the thousands of such individual case studies now in existence, and from the numerous developmental studies that have been made, one can derive a reasonably good set of criteria by which the end of adolescence may be estimated.

ADULT DEVELOPMENT

For *physical* adolescence, the end of the period may be seen most objectively and easily. A high school pupil is physically an adult when he has reached his final height, when his body has assumed adult proportions, when his heart and other organs are adult size, when his sexual functions have become completely established, and when all secondary sexual characteristics are in evidence. Skeletal growth and establishment of primary and secondary sexual functions are usually complete by the age of eighteen, but some internal growth is still in progress.

Emotional maturity is more difficult to estimate. As long as people become angry over superficial social situations, are afraid of what other people will think, are dependent upon older people or members of their own sex for happiness, or are inclined to take everything personally, they have not yet ceased to be adolescents. It is at once clear that some people never grow up and that others do not become mature until long after they have passed beyond the age of legal responsibility. The homosexual adult and the person who falls in love with much older people are both showing behavior appropriate to an earlier period and inappropriate to adult life. Typical adolescent emotional reactions and their causes have been described in an earlier chapter; as long as these situations call forth these types of behavior the individual is not yet emotionally mature.

Complete emancipation from home must take place or adolescence is not yet over. No matter how old individuals are, they remain emotional children if they must run to their parents for understanding or assistance. Probably this type of immaturity is more common and causes more adult maladjustment than any other. One should not suppose that only adults callously indifferent to their parents are mature. Indeed such people are decidedly adolescent because they are still showing a type of behavior once perhaps necessary in order to break familial ties; revolt and indifference are normal in adolescence but are indicative of immaturity thereafter. The true adult loves his parents and is willing to take their desires into consideration in making his plans, but he makes his own decisions and lives his own life.

Social maturity is also difficult to describe, although the experienced clinician can recognize it easily. Blind loyalty to one's friends and blind prejudice against anyone who is different are adolescent characteristics; a person of adult years who shows them is still a social adolescent. The social adult is able to get along in casual business relationships with practically any other normal adult. Thus, the grown woman who will not patronize a given drugstore because she does not like the looks of the clerk is displaying an adolescent social reaction. One naturally cannot be expected to like everyone in the world, or to approve of everyone, or to have no emotional reactions toward people. But a true adult can maintain ordinary business relationships with others, even if they are not his boon companions. The grown man who can work only under a friend's direction is on a social par with the adolescent who can do laboratory work only if paired with his chum.

The adolescent is typically a person who feels insecure because he does not know what to do or how to act in various social relationships. Of course, anyone of any age who finds himself in a quite new social stiuation—in a foreign country, for instance—is as lost as the adolescent, but an adult is characteristically able to adjust himself to ordinary and recurrent social situations easily and naturally. The grown person who is still embarrassed and distressed by ordinary social contacts has not yet reached the end of his adolescence.

Maturity is reflected also in one's use of leisure time. Relatively quiet diversions, reading, theatergoing, attendance at games, small social gatherings, or family outings characterize the adult. The hectic rushing about, the sowing of wild oats, the search for a thrill belong to the years of adolescence. The adult who still shows them has not completely grown up.

The end of *moral* adolescence is even more difficult to define. It consists primarily in the development of some relatively stationary and relatively satisfying attitude toward life, religion, morals, and various social problems. The truly mature person has developed ideals by which he guides his own conduct and estimates that of others. The adult who is still perplexed and emotionally searching for an answer to the Universe is showing typical adolescent behavior. A scientific search is, of course, something different. Adolescents are characteristically in revolt against existing conditions, whether moral or social. An adult does not accept unthinkingly the existing code of morals or current social situations, but he does regard such matters as facts which exist and to which one must make some reasonable adjustment. The adult who is still in a state of flaming revolt against the world has not outgrown his moral adolescence. Deep-seated racial prejudices, bigoted religious beliefs, and uncompromising ethical standards are all typical of the adolescent period. The tendency from the days of childhood through adolescence and into the adult years is from conservatism and rigid belief towards liberalism and tolerance. The change is so gradual that the exact moment when the adolescent becomes an adult is impossible to determine. But a grown person who still carries with him the uncompromising intolerance typical of adolescence has not yet reached his moral and ethical maturity.

Intellectual maturity will eventually be measured in terms of tests. At present, intelligence tests for use with individuals in their late adolescence are not satisfactory measures. Eventually, however, it will be possible to tell with exactness when an individual has reached the adult level of mental capacity. The greatest difficulty here lies in obtaining evidence of the range and average of normal adult development. Except for the psychological examinations in the Army, no unselected groups of adults have ever been tested; the Army examination, while excellent as an early mental test, was by no means as satisfactory as tests now in existence. From present data one can reasonably assume that the adult level is reached sometime between the ages of sixteen and twenty-five by those who reach it at all. In the course of time it will also be possible, by means of objective tests, to tell when an individual has reached a mature level in judgment, reasoning, imagination, or other intellectual qualities. In the absence of definite test results, the following criteria of mental development may be used:

1. A mental age of at least fourteen.
2. Ability to hold some job that furnishes support for oneself and dependents.
3. Ability to read well enough to keep in touch with current news.
4. Ability to "manage one's affairs with reasonable prudence."

These criteria are admittedly vague, but they are pragmatic.

A true adult is, then, a person of complete physical development, controlled emotional reactions and tolerant attitudes; he has economic independence and ability to treat others objectively; he is independent of parental control, reasonably satisfied with his point of view toward life, reasonably happy in his job, and usually able to get along without attracting attention in the ordinary social life about him.

PREVENTION OF ADULT MALADJUSTMENT

Dangers of arrested development.—Obviously, from the above description, many people have not left their adolescence. Indeed, most present-day adults show an occasional childish or adolescent trait, in spite of a general maturity. This one is unable to take criticism objectively, that one cannot sometimes make up his own mind, another is inclined to expect favors from his employer, a fourth is happy only when riotously in love, while a fifth will not even sell goods wholesale to an Oriental shopkeeper. No one is 100 per cent mature, but a development sufficient for adjustment to the adult world is achieved, sooner or later, by the majority of people.

Many tragedies of adult life are due to the continuance of social and emotional childhood and adolescence into the adult years. In the clinic, the hospital, and the court, emotional immaturity can be observed daily. The chief task of the consulting psychologist is to teach people how to grow up, so that they can face the responsibilities of adult life. No one can carry around with him a load of childish reactions without getting into difficulty with a society based on the assumption that people who have adult physical development are also mentally and socially mature.

Contribution of the high school to adult happiness.—The high school teacher can do much toward helping the next generation achieve adulthood sooner and with fewer tragedies than were typical of her own. The first step in this direction is an adequate comprehension of the objectives to be reached by the end of adolescence. Both teachers and parents need to know of what a normal development consists.

The world is made primarily for adults. Recent emphasis upon childhood has made many people forget that the majority of people in the world are over twenty years of age. In this country an increasing percentage of the population is over twenty-one years of age. Some people have forgotten also that adulthood is a far longer period than childhood. The main purpose of appropriate training during the early years is the production of better-adjusted, healthier adults through the development of better-adjusted, healthier children. It is the writer's hope that, once the objectives of adolescence are known, high school teachers may become vitally significant individuals in the guidance of youth from childish performance levels to a happy and normal life.

APPENDIX

The additional bibliography in the appendix is presented for the student who wishes to study the subject in greater detail. In this list will be found other general texts on adolescence, sourcebooks of case material, volumes dealing with the adolescent period of the boy or girl, and, finally, pertinent texts on mental hygiene. This list supplements the references at the end of the chapters in the text.

The books in the second group of references have been included because, even though the stories are pure fiction, they describe phases of adolescent development. This is by no means the full range of creative literature on the subject. Each instructor will undoubtedly recall other works as illustrative of adolescent behavior.

Because they give a more lifelike interpretation to the impersonal presentation of a text, novels of this type are extremely useful in connection with the study of adolescence. The instructor is urged to assign as many novels as students can be reasonably expected to read. As an assignment students should be asked to interpret adolescent problems as these are unfolded in the pages of the novels they have read. Many students who have little interest in an abstract presentation learn easily when the same principles are illustrated, vitalized, and simplified in an interesting narrative. Improperly used, novels may be misleading, but with reasonable safeguards, they are a valuable adjunct to a course in adolescent psychology.

The list here presented is a catholic one. No effort has been made to classify it, since the material is so diverse. A few of the books deal directly and almost exclusively with the adolescent period. Others trace the growth of a personality from childhood into the adult years. A few of these books were written by adolescents, and their particular value, of course, lies in the fact that they do show certain adolescent developments that are likely to be overlooked by a more mature writer. Others show quite clearly the effect of peculiar environments upon adolescents, the subsequent developments being followed into later years. Finally, a few of these volumes are concerned with abnormal conditions or personalities. While these are exaggerated, nevertheless they serve to make clear the resultant trends.

GENERAL REFERENCES

1. Arlitt, Ada, *Adolescent Psychology*, American Book Company, 1933, 250 pp.
2. Bassett, C., *Mental Hygiene in the Community*, The Macmillan Company, 1933, 394 pp.
3. Blanchard, P., and Manasses, C., *New Girls for Old*, Macaulay Company, 1930, 281 pp.
4. Blanchard, P., *The Adolescent Girl*, Dodd, Mead & Company, 1924, 250 pp.
5. Brooks, F. D., *Psychology of Adolescence*, Houghton Mifflin Company, 1929, 652 pp.
6. Burdge, H. G., *Our Boys: A Study of 245,000 Sixteen, Seventeen, and Eighteen Year Old Employed Boys in the State of New York*, J. B. Lyon and Company, 1921, 345 pp.
7. Calverton, V. F., and Schmalhausen, S. D. (Editors), *The New Generation*, Macaulay Company, 1930, 717 pp.
8. Chadwick, M., *Adolescent Girlhood*, John Day Company, Inc., 1933, 303 pp.
9. Conklin, E. S., *Principles of Adolescent Psychology*, Henry Holt and Company, 1935, 437 pp.
10. Edwards, R. H., Artman, J. M., and Fisher, G. M., *Undergraduates*, Doubleday, Doran & Company, Inc., 1928, 366 pp.
11. Furfey, P. H., *The Growing Boy*, The Macmillan Company, 1930, 192 pp.
12. Garrison, K. C., *Psychology of Adolescence*, Prentice-Hall, Inc., 1934, 337 pp.
13. Hollingworth, L. S., *Psychology of the Adolescent*, D. Appleton-Century Company, 1928, 259 pp.
14. Lindsay, B. B., *The Revolt of Youth*, Boni & Liveright, 1925, 364 pp.
15. Lippmann, Walter, *A Preface to Morals*, The Macmillan Company, 1929, 348 pp.

APPENDIX

16. Mudge, E. L., *Varieties of Adolescent Experience,* D. Appleton-Century Company, 1926, 134 pp.
17. Pressey, L. C., *Some College Students and Their Problems,* Ohio State University Press, 1929, 97 pp.
18. Pringle, R., *Adolescence and High School Problems,* D. C. Heath and Company, 1922, 386 pp.
19. Richmond, W., *The Adolescent Boy,* Farrar & Rinehart, Inc., 1933, 233 pp.
20. ———, *The Adolescent Girl,* The Macmillan Company, 1926, 212 pp.
21. Schwab, S. I., and Veeder, B. S., *The Adolescent: His Conflicts and Escapes,* D. Appleton-Century Company, 1929, 365 pp.
22. Sherman, M., *Mental Hygiene and Education,* Longmans, Green & Co., 1934, 295 pp.
23. Smithies, E. M., *Case-Studies of Normal Adolescent Girls,* D. Appleton-Century Company, 1933, 284 pp.
24. Thom, D. A., *Normal Youth and Its Everyday Problems,* D. Appleton-Century Company, 1932, 361 pp.
25. Thomas, W. I., *The Unadjusted Girl,* Little, Brown & Company, 1923, 261 pp.
26. Tumlirz, O., *Jugendpsychologie der Gegenwart,* Junker und Dünnkopf, Berlin, 1933, 98 pp.
27. Van Waters, M., *Youth in Conflict,* New Republic, Inc., 1925, 293 pp.
28. Williams, F., *Adolescence: Studies in Mental Hygiene,* Farrar & Rinehart, Inc., 1930, 279 pp.

FICTION AND BIOGRAPHY

1. Barbellion, W. N. P., *The Journal of a Disappointed Man,* Doran, 1919, 312 pp.
2. Barnes, C., *Schoolgirl,* Liveright, 1929, 240 pp.
3. Bennett, A., *Clayhanger,* Doubleday, 1932, 708 pp.
4. ———, *Hilda Lessways,* Doran, 1924, 533 pp.
5. ———, *Milestones,* Doran, 1912, 122 pp.
6. ———, *Price of Love,* Ward Lock, 1932, 320 pp.
7. ———, *Old Wives' Tale,* Hodder and Stoughton, 1911, 612 pp.
8. Benson, A. C., *Edward Fitzgerald,* Macmillan, 1905, 207 pp.
9. Bowen, Elizabeth, *The Hotel,* Dial, 1928, 294 pp.
10. Boyle, Kay, *Year Before Last,* Greenberg, 1933, 373 pp.
11. Bromfield, L., *The Good Woman,* Cape, 1933, 384 pp.

12. Bromfield, L., *The Green Bay Tree,* Cassell, 1930, 352 pp.
13. Burnett, W. R., *The Goodhues of Sinking Creek,* Harper, 1934, 88 pp.
14. Cain, J. M., *The Postman Always Rings Twice,* Knopf, 1924, 188 pp.
15. Canfield, D., *The Bent Twig,* Grosset & Dunlap, 1934, 486 pp.
16. Carmer, C., *Stars Fell on Alabama,* Farrar & Rinehart, 1934, 294 pp.
17. Carr, W. S., *The Rampant Age,* Doubleday, 1928, 330 pp.
18. Cather, Willa, *Lucy Gayheart,* Knopf, 1935, 231 pp.
19. Celine, L. F., *Journey to the End of the Night,* McClelland, 1934, 509 pp.
20. Cooper, Elizabeth, *What Price Youth?* Stokes, 1929, 293 pp.
21. Cronin, A. T., *Hatter's Castle,* Little, Brown, 1931, 605 pp.
22. ———, *Three Loves,* Gollancz, 1933, 592 pp.
23. Dakin, E. F., *Mrs. Eddy,* Scribner, 1929, 553 pp.
24. Dane, C., *Regiment of Women,* Macmillan, 1922, 413 pp.
25. Delafield, E. M., *The Chip and the Block,* Hutchinson, 1930, 288 pp.
26. Dell, Floyd, *Love in the Machine Age,* Farrar & Rinehart, 1930, 428 pp.
27. ———, *Mooncalf,* Knopf, 1920, 394 pp.
28. ———, *Janet Marsh,* Doran, 1927, 409 pp.
29. Dineson, J., *Seven Gothic Tales,* McLeod, 1934, 420 pp.
30. Dreiser, T., *An American Tragedy,* Simon & Schuster, 1929, 431 pp.
31. Dutton, Louise, *Going Together,* Bobbs-Merrill, 1923, 311 pp.
32. Fallada, H., *Little Man, What Now?* Simon & Schuster, 1933, 399 pp.
33. ———, *The World Outside,* Simon & Schuster, 1934, 569 pp.
34. Faulkner, W., *Sanctuary,* Harrison Smith, 1931, 380 pp.
35. Ferber, Edna, *So Big,* Heinemann, 1932, 360 pp.
36. ———, *The Girls,* Grosset & Dunlap, 1924, 374 pp.
37. ———, *Mother Knows Best,* Grosset & Dunlap, 1928, 267 pp.
38. Fisher, V., *In Tragic Life,* Caxton, 1932, 464 pp.
39. ———, *Passions Spin the Plot,* Doubleday, 1934, 428 pp.
40. Forrest, Noel, *Ways of Escape,* Constable, 1929, 423 pp.
41. France, Anatole, *The Crime of Sylvestre Bonnard,* Holt, 1934, 343 pp.
42. ———, *Red Lily,* Dodd, Mead, 1930, 325 pp.
43. ———, *Revolt of the Angels,* Watts, 1933, 246 pp.
44. Frenssen, G., *Jörn Uhl,* Boni and Liveright, 1905, 416 pp.
45. Gale, Zona, *Preface to a Life,* Grosset & Dunlap, 1929, 345 pp.

APPENDIX

120. Wharton, Edith, *The Old Maid,* D. Appleton, 1921, 191 pp.
121. ———, *False Dawn,* D. Appleton, 1924, 143 pp.
122. ———, *The Children,* D. Appleton, 1928, 346 pp.
123. Wilson, Margaret, *The Kenworthys,* Grosset & Dunlap, 1930, 385 pp.
124. ———, *The Painted Room,* Harper, 1926, 271 pp.
125. Woodbury, Helen, *The Misty Flats,* Little, Brown, 1925, 342 pp.
126. Wren, P., *Mammon,* Stokes, 1930, 330 pp.
127. Zugsmith, L., *The Reckoning,* McLeod, 1934, 365 pp.
128. Zweig, Stefan, *Amok,* Viking, 1931, 121 pp.

INDEX

Academic course, 430
Acceleration, 332, 333, 348
Acceptance, of religious belief, 173
Adaptation. *See* Curriculum and Individual differences
Adolescence, girls', 3, 10
Adolescent, intelligence, 191, 195, 246
  labor, 4, 9
Adolescents, in population, 10, 485, 489, 490
Adrenalin, 54, 55
Adult population. *See* Adolescent population
Agriculture schedules, 432, 434
Allowance, 391
Allport, 162, 170
Altruism, 177
Amoral, 242, 345
Amusement parks, 461
Anger, 58 ff.
  causes of, 58, 59, 60
  duration of, 61
  reactions to, 61, 84
Appetite, 31
Army intelligence tests, 191, 194, 488
Art, 218, 425, 465
Arteries, 28
Athletics, 29, 45, 49, 126 ff., 137, 155, 246, 248
Atkinson, 36
Autobiographies, movie, 468, 470, 477 ff. *See also* Diaries
Automobiles, 460

Baldwin, 19, 23, 30, 36
Bases, for homogeneous grouping, 435 ff.
Bean, 27
Bickersteth, 207
Billett, 440
Binet, 191, 192, 205, 212, 230, 340, 341
Biological science, 423, 425
Birth control, 149, 268
Blind loyalty, 86, 107, 109, 110, 117, 246, 486
Blood pressure, 28

Boas, 36
Bones. *See* Skeleton
Brain, 33, 186
Brilliant children, 306, 328, 330 ff., 332, 334, 339, 440, 443
Burlesque shows, 265, 461
Business, course, 431, 432, 433
  schools, 5, 6

Calories, 44
Cartoons, 215, 217
Catholic, 168, 170
Cheating. *See* Cribbing
Chinese, 74, 151, 153, 468, 469
Choosing friends. *See* Selection of friends
Chums, 114
Church, 167 ff., 464 ff.
Cliques, 113, 114
Clothes. *See* Conformity and Externals
Clubs, 122 ff., 131, 246
Communism, 148
Community influences, 264 ff., 459 ff., 473 ff.
  theater, 463
Compensation, 88. *See* Overcompensation
Competition, 126, 127, 159, 365
Compositions, 208 ff., 220, 221, 248
Comprehension, 212, 214 ff.
Concentration, 205 ff.
Concepts, 140, 143 ff. *See also* Ideals
Conformity, 76, 86, 101, 138, 246, 306
Continuation school, 348
Conventions, 398, 407
Conversion. *See* Crises
Cost of education, 362, 365, 411
Courtship. *See* lovemaking
Crampton, 36
Cribbing, 159 ff., 175, 176, 179, 354
Crime, 163 ff., 258, 472
Crises, emotional or religious, 167, 171, 173 ff., 178, 247, 293, 295
"Crowd," 106 ff., 113, 246
  example of, 108 ff.
Crushes, 79, 80, 94

499

INDEX

Cultural values, 417
Curriculum, elementary school, 11, 415, 417
  high school, 8, 11, 37, 82, 124, 126, 156, 203, 225, 261, 266, 272, 275, 334 ff., 347, 364, 380, 414 ff., 439, 449 ff.

Dalton plan, 442
Dance halls, 461
Daydreaming, 88, 97, 245, 287, 290, 323, 360, 470, 478
Defectives, 242, 328, 343
Defiant attitude, 91
Delinquency, 258 ff., 343, 468, 471 ff., 479, 480, 481
Delusions, 299, 300 ff.
Demand. *See* Supply
Dementia praecox, 323
Depression, 9
Diaries, 10, 167, 168, 249
Diet, 31, 32, 41, 50
Digestive disturbances, 32, 44, 47
Discipline, 18, 35, 76 ff., 245, 264
Distribution. *See* Intelligence and Extracurricular activities
Drugs, 461
Drunkenness, 180
Dull children, 144, 199, 200, 328, 344 ff., 440
  preparation of, 200, 201

Educational, objectives, 337, 346, 416, 419, 424
  tests, 435
  values, 417 ff.
Elective work, 425 ff., 429
Elimination from school, 192, 193, 194, 199, 201 ff., 328, 367
Emancipation, 387 ff., 407, 447, 462, 486
Emotional, age, 71, 72, 272
  instability, 157, 262
  maturity. *See* Emotional immaturity
Emotions, 53 ff.
  physical changes, 54 ff.
  list of, 57
  effect of movies on, 470
English, in high school, 424, 425, 434
Enrollments, high school, 5, 6, 198, 199, 344
  college, 6
Exhibitionism, 87, 90, 307, 311, 325

Externals, emphasis on, 76, 306, 460
Extracurricular activities, 119 ff., 121, 425, 429
  types of, 121 ff.
  distribution of, 128 ff.
Extroversion, 97

Failure, 201 ff., 225, 226, 307, 345, 347, 355
Fake psychologists, 420, 466, 467
Family. *See* Home
Family dissension, 264, 285, 410
Fanatic personality, 86, 87, 298 ff.
Father and child relationship, 67, 390
Fatigue, abnormal, 286, 288
Fear, 62 ff., 78, 80, 85, 95, 296
  causes of, 62 ff.
  reactions to, 65
Feeble-minded. *See* Defective
Fixation, on parents, 68, 81
Fixity, of ideas, 298
Franklin, 216
Fraternity, 124, 128, 153 ff., 160
Freud, 320
Friction, in home. *See* Family dissension
Friendships, 102 ff., 113, 138, 255. *See* Selection of friends
Furfey, 72

Games. *See* Intramural games and Athletics
Gang, 266, 268
Generalizing, 144, 175, 212 ff., 330, 337, 344, 447
Girl and boy friendships, 104, 105, 252 ff.
Glands, endocrine, 34 ff.
  sweat, 34
Goals, 442
God, 168 ff., 247
Graph, to show standing, 373
Growing pains, 26
Growth, of various organs, 24, 28, 31, 33, 41 ff.
Growth rates, 19, 24 ff., 30, 31, 33, 41 ff.
  of face, 24, 25

Habit, 144, 187, 351
Hartshorne, 158
Hayes, 130
Heart strain, 28, 29, 49, 54
Height, 19
Heredity, 263, 322

INDEX

Hero-worship, 139, 446
High school population, 5 ff., 344, 415, 418
Hips, growth of, 26, 41
Homes, 263 ff., 387 ff.
Home economics, 432, 434
Homemaking, 423, 425, 450
Homogeneous grouping, 73, 435 ff.
Homosexual, 69, 70, 71, 94, 486
Honesty, 156 ff.
Honor system, 161
Household mechanics, 422, 423
Hygiene, 44 ff., 421, 422, 425
Hysteria, 292 ff.
Hysterical blindness, 297

Idealizing occupations, 360, 374, 377
Ideals, 140 ff., 144 ff., 162, 165, 246, 446, 487
Idiots, 342
Imagination, 208 ff., 231 ff., 446
Imbecile, 342
Imitative play, 471
Immaturity, emotional, 93, 94, 154, 155, 309, 314, 315, 325, 374, 388, 405 ff., 410, 411, 485, 486
Immorality, 181, 279, 402, 403
Immortality, 172
Indians, 192
Individual differences, in college, 452, 456
Individualized instruction, 441 ff.
Inferiority, feelings of, 305 ff., 333
Insight, 164, 165, 213, 215 ff., 247, 456
Intellectual development, 186 ff., 488
Intelligence, distribution of, 195, 196, 225, 230
Interests, 188, 220 ff., 226, 248, 372
Interviews, 374, 375
Intolerance, 151 ff. *See also* Racial discrimination
Intramural games, 45, 127, 132 ff., 137
Introversion, 87, 90
I.Q., of delinquents, 259
 for grouping, 435, 436
 for high school, 11, 196, 247, 329
Isolation. *See* Social isolation

Judge Baker Foundation, 277
Juvenile court, 181 ff., 277, 473

Katz, 162, 170
Knowledge, of Bible, 172

Labor. *See* Adolescent labor
Leadership, 114 ff., 117 ff., 128, 133, 332
Life history, of emotions, 57 ff.
Liquor, 460
Loafing, 336
Loan libraries, 466
Love, 66 ff.
Lovemaking, 105, 468, 470, 471, 478
Love-object, 67, 68, 70, 71, 79, 388, 486
Loyalty. *See* Blind loyalty
Low I.Q., in high school, 196, 198, 199, 344
Lung capacity, 30

Machine civilization, 4, 9, 225
Marriage, 9, 424
Maladjustments. *See* Dull, Normal, and Brilliant
Masturbation, 38, 48
Mate, choice of, 396
Maturity, 36, 72, 437. *See also* Social maturity
 criteria of, 485 ff.
May, 158
Measurement, of attitudes, 146, 269
 of emotional development, 71, 72
 of intelligence, 187 ff., 224
 of personality, 272
 of religious interests, 465
Mechanical ability, 218, 219, 225
Memory and memorizing, 204 ff., 225, 418, 446, 454, 456
Menstruation, 35, 39, 40
Mental age, for grouping, 435, 436
Mental, discipline, 417, 418, 454
 faculties, 204
 hygiene, course in, 421, 422, 425
Minard, 152
Mixed districts, 265
Monotony, 205, 349, 446
Moral, development, 176
 training, for dull children, 347, 350
Moreno, 113, 116, 117
Moron, 342
Morrison plan, 442
Mother and child relationships, 81, 249, 388, 389, 396, 397, 404, 407
Motion pictures, 467 ff.
Motivation, in school, 445 ff.
Movies. *See* Motion pictures
Muscular growth, 21, 54

Museum, 465
Music, 218, 425, 465, 466

Negro, 74, 151 ff., 173, 468, 469
Neighborhood, delinquent, 264 ff.
Nervousness, 86, 91, 324
Neural growth, 33, 44, 53, 186
Neurasthenia, 286 ff.
Neurotics, 284 ff.
Nicknames, 21
Nonbiological science, 422, 423, 425
Normal individuals, 241 ff.
Normalcy, 241
Normal curve, 451
Norms, 189, 192, 193, 212, 438
North Central Association, 430

O'Brien, 201, 202
Observation of occupations, 369, 370
Obsessions, 294
Occupations, course, 364 ff., 426 ff.
Organized vice, 462
Organizing ability, 211 ff.
Otis, 189
Outlets, 13, 45, 83 ff., 125, 262, 266, 425, 463
Overcompensation, 88, 260, 280, 307, 311
Oversupply. *See* Supply
Overweight, 50

Parables, 215
Parent-Teachers Association, 407
Parental, maladjustment, 398 ff.
  pressure, 351 ff., 363, 376, 394, 397, 411
Partial concepts, 140
Participation, social, 261, 332, 333
Percentiles, 438
Permanence of emotional reaction to movies, 468
  of traits, 321
Personality, 173, 198, 287, 294, 298, 299, 320, 321, 358, 360, 372, 439
Perspiration, 34
Philosophy, of life, 126, 335, 468, 487
Phobia, 95, 294
Phrenology, 204
Physical development, 17, 18, 20, 24 ff., 34, 38, 39, 305, 435, 436
  education, 45, 425
  handicaps, 259, 260, 358
Pimples, 34
Pituitary gland, 32
Play interests, 222

Playgrounds, 463
Point system, 129
Polynesian children, 191
Poor whites, 230
Portenier, 196, 198, 199
Practice materials, 442
Predelinquent, 269, 272, 274
Pressey, 72, 189, 212, 243
Prevention, of abnormal personalities, 320 ff.
  of adult maladjustment, 489 ff.
  of delinquency, 267 ff.
Pride, in home, 460 ff.
  in work, 371
Primitive adolescence, 3, 464
Problem tests, in arithmetic, 214
Prodigy, 338, 339
Profile graphs, 437, 438
Prohibition, 147
Projection, 88, 98, 316
Proportions of body, 26 ff.
Prose appreciation, 218
Protection, 273, 459 ff.
Pseudo scientist. *See* Fake
Psychology course, 420
Psychopathic personality, 313 ff.
Pupil material, 195, 203
Puppy love, 105
Pyle, 206

Questionnaire, 269, 271
Quetelet, 23

Racial discrimination, 74, 75, 76, 136, 151 ff., 467, 468, 469, 487
Radio, 466
Range, of abilities, 200, 328, 373
Rating scale, 269, 270, 435
  for teachers, 77
Rationalization, 88
Reading, 223
Reasoning, 213, 214, 455, 456
Rebellion, against parental restraint, 406, 477, 479, 486
Recognition, of types, 239 ff., 284, 322 ff.
  of emotional disturbance, 86 ff.
Religion, 126, 150, 166 ff., 175, 177, 487
Religious, conflicts, 167 ff., 171, 174. *See* Crises
  fanatic. *See* Fanatic personality
Required work, 420 ff., 429
Responsibility, lack of, 313
Retardation, educational, 260, 345, 348

INDEX

Reverence, 174
Revolt. *See* Rebellion
Romantic love. *See* Lovemaking

Salary range, 368, 369
Sarcasm, 76, 77, 78, 96 ff.
Schedules, in high school, 428 ff.
School record of delinquents, 260
Secondary sex changes, 38, 44, 244, 285
Security in the home, 402 ff.
Selection, of friends, 102, 103, 104, 391, 491 ff.
  in school. *See* Elimination
  of test items, 189, 190, 227 ff.
Self-discipline, 336
Sex, development, 35 ff.
  differences, 20, 27, 30, 37, 197, 221, 222, 223, 224, 293
  education, 37, 423
  glands, 35
Shaffer, 217
Shame, concerning home, 401
Shut-in personality, 324
Sims score card, 158
Skeletal growth, 18 ff., 27, 28
Skin infections, 32
Sleep, 44
Snobbishness, 86, 109, 110, 153 ff., 176
Social, ability, 261, 344
  adjustment, 85, 226, 243
  heritage, 267, 414
  isolation, 90, 94, 113, 116, 128, 130, 135, 287, 288 ff., 307, 323, 324
  maturity, 435, 436, 486, 487
  objectives, 11, 349, 387, 486 ff.
  sciences, 420, 425
Sour grapes, 88
Special abilities, 218 ff., 359
Special classes, 343, 441
Sportsmanship, 128, 138
Stealing, 275, 276, 277, 278
Strength, 22, 23, 55
Student government, 121, 122
Student strike, 97
Study, 208
Successful homes, 404
Suggestibility, 158
Superstitions, 155, 156, 175
Supervision of play, 273, 275
Supply and demand, 361, 368, 369

Symptoms of maladjustment, 324 ff.
Systematized delusions, 299, 303

Teaching methods, 336 ff., 346 ff., 445 ff.
  for dull children, 337
  for brilliant children, 335 ff.
Technical course, 430, 431, 433
Terman, 189, 212
Test construction, 189, 190, 227 ff.
Tests of intelligence. *See* Measurement
Thorndike, 194
Thyroid, 34, 35, 39, 47
Tobacco, 460
Tools, of learning, 335, 360
Traditional attitudes, on religion, 166
Transfer of training, 417, 418
Transfers, 429, 439
Treatment of predelinquents, 272 ff.
Truancy, 260, 263, 266
Two-year course, 433

Unemancipated adolescents, 405, 406, 410, 411
Unpopularity, 116
Unwise friendships, 103 ff., 391 ff.

Van Waters, 177
Vaudeville, 462
Verbal intelligence, 218, 344
Vierordt, 42
Vocabulary, 187, 218
Vocational, counselor, 365, 374
  courses, 364 ff., 426, 427, 434
  guidance, 9, 338, 347, 348, 350, 364 ff., 393
  maladjustment, 357 ff.
  objectives, 363, 379
  placement of defectives, 343, 346
  training, 347, 417, 420

Weight, 19, 20
White-collar jobs, 349, 369
Winnetka plan, 442, 443
Withdrawal behavior, 87, 90, 307, 308, 323
Work week, 370
Worry, 286

Zoning, 273